# Casebook for *DSM-5*®

**Jayna E. Bonfini, PhD, LPC, NCC, MAC,** has significant research, teaching, and clinical experience with adolescents and young adults struggling with various mental health issues, trauma histories, and substance abuse problems. A Licensed Professional Counselor, Master Addiction Counselor, and a Nationally Certified Counselor, she has specific training in Motivational Interviewing, Dialectical Behavioral Therapy, and Eye Movement Desensitization and Reprocessing (EMDR) to offer an integrated approach that meets the needs of her clients.

Dr. Bonfini was trained clinically at Western Psychiatric Institute and Clinic and has experience working with justice-involved adolescents and adults, and with adolescents and adults struggling with transitional issues. Dr. Bonfini has presented at numerous local, state, and national conferences on counseling related topics from trauma therapy to ethical decision-making to self-esteem to diversity in graduate school programs. She earned degrees from Georgetown University, Carnegie Mellon University, Waynesburg University, and Duquesne University, where she earned her doctorate. Prior to her clinical work, she worked as a health-care policy analyst and advocate for access to care in Washington, DC.

**Elizabeth M. Ventura, PhD, LPC, NCC** is a qualitative researcher, trauma specialist, and counselor educator. She serves on local panels in her area and is a consultant for school districts regarding the implementation of care for traumatized children and adolescents. Dr. Ventura is a Senior Core faculty member in the Clinical Mental Health Counseling Department at Walden University and primarily specializes in teaching counseling techniques. For over 11 years, Dr. Ventura has educated counselors in training, teaching a variety of courses across the graduate curriculum, and encouraging graduate students to present professionally at local and national conferences. Dr. Ventura has a research agenda that focuses on counselor preparedness regarding trauma and crisis. Her professional counseling presentations have focused on educating professionals on pedagogical approaches to using clinical cases to increase the self-efficacy of counselors in training. In addition to the first edition of the *DSM 5 Casebook*, she has coauthored trauma textbooks and authored other trauma-related chapters in professional counseling textbooks. Dr. Ventura has established crisis protocols for implementing school-based therapy programs for children with emotional support needs related to self-injury and trauma.

Dr. Ventura has been practicing clinically for over 16 years in a variety of treatment centers. Her training includes the Cleveland Clinic and Western Psychiatric Institute and Clinic in Pittsburgh, Pennsylvania, where she gained expertise in dual diagnosis, trauma theory, and mood disorders. Dr. Ventura is the President of her own private therapy practice and contracts over nine providers that offer trauma-based services to children, adolescents, and adults at her office. Given her research and clinical work, Dr. Ventura is a sought out expert in the area of child trauma and, as a qualified expert witness, she has testified in numerous trauma related cases and as a result, provides expert opinions regarding the impact of trauma related to children.

Dr. Ventura regularly offers her time to students who are interested in similar areas of research and encourages them to attend and participate in conference presentations. She believes that these real world experiences offer the best preparedness for professional practice.

# Casebook for *DSM-5*®
## Diagnosis and Treatment Planning

**SECOND EDITION**

Jayna E. Bonfini, PhD, LPC, NCC, MAC
Elizabeth M. Ventura, PhD, LPC, NCC

**Editors**

 SPRINGER PUBLISHING

Springer Publishing Company, LLC
11 West 42nd Street, New York, NY 10036
www.springerpub.com
connect.springerpub.com/

*Acquisitions Editor*: Rhonda Dearborn
*Compositor*: diacriTech

*ISBN*: 978-0-8261-8633-1
*ebook ISBN*: 978-0-8261-8634-8
*DOI*: 10.1891/9780826186348

21 22 23 24 / 5 4 3 2 1

The author and the publisher of this Work have made every effort to use sources believed to be reliable to provide information that is accurate and compatible with the standards generally accepted at
the time of publication. The author and publisher shall not be liable for any special, consequential,
or exemplary damages resulting, in whole or in part, from the readers' use of, or reliance on, the
information contained in this book. The publisher has no responsibility for the persistence or accuracy of URLs for external or third-party Internet websites referred to in this publication and does not
guarantee that any content on such websites is, or will remain, accurate or appropriate.

**Library of Congress Control Number: 2021904036**

Contact sales@springerpub.com to receive discount rates on bulk purchases.

*Publisher's Note*: **New and used products purchased from third-party sellers are not guaranteed
for quality, authenticity, or access to any included digital components.**

Printed in the United States of America.

# CONTENTS

Additional bonus cases for Chapters 5 and 6 can be accessed by visiting the following url: http://connect.springerpub.com/content/book/978-0-8261-8634-8

# CONTRIBUTORS

**Heather Ambrose, PhD, LCMHC, LMFT**
Core Faculty, School of Counseling, Walden University, Layton, Utah

**Renee Anderson, PhD, LPCC-S**
Core Faculty, School of Counseling, Walden University, Butler, Pennsylvania

**Sue Banks, PhD, LPC, NCC**
Core Faculty, School of Counseling, Walden University, Minneapolis, Minnesota

**Brooks Bastian Hanks, PhD, LCPC**
Core Faculty, School of Counseling, Walden University, Southeast Idaho

**Jayna E. Bonfini, PhD, LPC, NCC, MAC**
Department of Student Services, California University of Pennsylvania, California, Pennsylvania

**Matthew Buckley, EdD, LPC, LCMHC, NCC, ACS, BC-TMH**
Senior Core Faculty, School of Counseling and Human Services, Biloxi, Mississippi

**Kathy Carmichal, MEd, LPC**
Private Practice, Dermott, Arkansas

**Susan Carmichael, PhD, LPC, ACS**
Academic Coordinator, School of Counseling, Walden University, Minneapolis, Minnesota

**Christian J. Dean, PhD, LPC, LMFT, NCC**
Core Faculty, School of Counseling, Walden University, Baton Rouge, Louisiana

**Jeannie Falkner, PhD, LCSW**
Core Faculty, Walden University, Oxford, Mississippi

**Stephanie J. W. Ford, PhD, LPC, NCC**
Core Faculty, School of Behavioral Sciences, Liberty University, Lynchburg, Virginia

**Ramone Ford, PhD**
Licensed Psychologist, Psychology Consultants, Medina, Ohio

**Jennifer M. Gess, PhD, LMHC, LCPC, NCC**
Core Faculty, School of Counseling, Walden University, Minneapolis, Minnesota

**Brandy L. Gilea, PhD, LPCC-S, NCC**
Core Faculty, Walden University, Canfield, Ohio

**Maranda A. Griffin, PhD, LPC**
Core Faculty, Walden University, Orange Park, Florida

**Aaron H. Jackson, PhD, LCMHC, LPC, NCC, BC-TMH**
Core Faculty, School of Counseling, Walden University, Minneapolis, Minnesota

**Christie Jenkins, PhD, LPCC-S**
Core Faculty, School of Counseling, Walden University, Perrysburg, Ohio

**Mita M. Johnson, EdD, NCC, LPC, LMFT, LAC, MAC, SAP, CTHP-II, ACS, AAMFT-CS**
Core Faculty, School of Counseling, Walden University, Littleton, Colorado

**Jason H. King, PhD, NCC, CCMHC, LCMHC-S, ACS**
Core Faculty, School of Counseling, Walden University, Dallas, Texas

**Sola Kippers, PhD, LPC-S, LMFT**
Clinical Counseling, Capella University, Baton Rouge, Louisiana

**Joelle P. F. Lewis, EdD, MBA, MSW, LCSW**
Core Faculty, School of Counseling, Walden University, Buffalo, Wyoming

**Leann M. Morgan, PhD, LPC, CCCE**
Core Faculty, School of Counseling, Walden University, Minneapolis, Minnesota

**Rhonda Neswald-Potter, PhD, LPCC, ACS**
Clinical Director, Manzanita Counseling Center, University of New Mexico; Contributing Faculty Member, Walden University, Albuquerque, New Mexico

**Rachel M. O'Neill, PhD, LPCC-S**
Core Faculty, MS in Clinical Mental Health Counseling Program, Walden University, Poland, Ohio

**Stacy Overton, PhD, LPC, LAC**
Core Faculty, Walden University, Fort Collins, Colorado

**Rhemma Payne, MA, LMHC, NCC**
Doctoral Student, Counselor Education and Supervision, Walden University, Minneapolis, Minnesota

**Torey Portrie-Bethke, PhD, NCC**
Core Faculty, School of Counseling, Walden University, Northwood, New Hampshire

**Amanda Rovnak, PhD, PCC-S, LICDC-CS, LISW-S**
Core Faculty Member, School of Counseling, Walden University, Copley, Ohio

**Jessica Russo, PhD, LPCC-S, NCC**
Core Faculty, School of Counseling, Walden University, Portage Lakes, Ohio

**Stephanie K. Scott, PhD, LMHC, CCTP, CCISM**
Core Faculty, School of Counseling, Walden University, Minneapolis, Minnesota

**Marian Sebe, PhD, PCC-S, NCC**
Core Faculty, School of Counseling, Walden University, Minneapolis, Minnesota

**Mariangelly Sierra, MS, LPCA, NCC**
Doctoral Student, Counselor Education and Supervision, Walden University, Minneapolis, Minnesota

**Stephanie L. Stern, MA, LPC, LBS, NCC**
Private Practice, McMurray, Pennsylvania

**Rives Whittle Thornton, MS, LMHC, NCC, ACS, BC-TMH**
Doctoral Student, Counselor Education and Supervision, Walden University, Bellingham, Washington

**Elizabeth M. Ventura, PhD, LPC, NCC**
Core Faculty, School of Counseling, Walden University, McMurray, Pennsylvania

**Cynthia Williams, MS, LMFT, LCDC**
Clinical Therapist, Walden University, Houston, Texas

**Margaret Clark Zappitello, EdD, LPC, LMFT, LAC, MAC, NCC**
Core Faculty, School of Counseling, Walden University, Brighton, Colorado

# PREFACE

The *Diagnostic and Statistical Manual of Mental Disorders, Fifth Edition* (*DSM-5*) is the result of the first significant revision of the publication *DSM-IV* in 1994. With advances in research and clinical applications, modifications were needed to accurately frame client symptom presentation and reflect the changes and advances in science and technology, as well as cultural and societal factors. With these changes, come a set of standards that practitioners-in-training should familiarize themselves with and learn to accurately apply diagnostic criteria to real world examples.

As counselor educators, we have found that the use of understanding diagnostic criteria in the absence of practical case applications is limiting for students. The power of using real world case presentations to help students conceptualize symptomology helps trainees to integrate knowledge in a way that surpasses traditional rote memory learning strategies.

The collection of cases presented in this text has been compiled from seasoned clinicians that have experienced complex client symptomology. These cases illustrate real world examples of actual clients seen in practice. The details of the cases are organized to provide readers with examples of case conceptualization examples, as well as, diagnostic impressions, conclusions, and treatment recommendations. Remembering that each client is different, and the training and skill level of the treating therapist is equally unique, the recommendations provided in the cases serve as examples for students to critically analyze and adapt their own theoretical approach when conceptualizing the cases.

This second edition features additional cases in each category with an expanded range of development and service settings (e.g., school, outpatient, residential, home-based) to meet the educational needs of a diverse mental health workforce. Additional questions for discussion and notes about each case have been included in this revision, as well as a final review chapter, making this text a helpful supplement to a variety of undergraduate and graduate courses.

Counselor educators have an ethical responsibility to act as gatekeepers in training programs. While professionalism and comportment issues are foundational elements in our profession, competence in the areas of diagnosis and theory-driven interventions have risen to the surface with managed care. Often, in short periods of time, change is expected. Counselors in training are charged with implementing theory and technique with intentionality to arrive at the correct diagnosis and treatment plan in order to effectively deliver care. This is certainly a task that requires confidence, competence, and creativity. Research has shown that trainees gain a sense of efficacy from practicing in supervisory settings with realistic examples and from a constructivist paradigm. The hope is that this text can begin the process for trainees to understand the client complexities that present daily in the counseling office and can meet those challenges with a sense of self-assurance that can, in fact, help promote change.

It is certainly the case that the clients we have encountered have changed our lives. The gratefulness and gratitude we feel for having the opportunity to walk with each of them throughout their personal journeys is inexplicable. Through our work with clients we have learned that authenticity cannot be attempted, it must to be interwoven into the fabric of the self. For 50 minutes, we are given the gift to sit across from another human being struggling deeply with aspects of his or her life. You are entrusted to help them navigate this pain. You are entrusted to know the way, sometimes as a guide, other times as a follower. Regardless of the role you play, you are entrusted to be among the few that see this level of human vulnerability and shame in its most exposed state. You are expected to be prepared for this, and to meet it with passion, integrity, and competence. Practice now for those moments on the horizon.

---

Additional bonus cases for Chapters 5 and 6 can be accessed by visiting the following url:

http://connect.springerpub.com/content/book/978-0-8261-8634-8

---

# RECOMMENDATIONS FOR USE

This casebook provides a practical and realistic way for students in such mental health professions as clinical psychology, counseling psychology, counseling, and social work to put the new *Diagnostic and Statistical Manual of Mental Disorders, Fifth Edition* (*DSM-5*) into practice by presenting actual clinical experiences from practitioners. By exploring detailed clinical vignettes, this text offers trainees the opportunity to explore their own ideas on symptom presentation, diagnosis, and treatment planning with a full range of disorders and conditions covered in the *DSM-5*. Unlike other casebooks, this text not only provides vignettes, but also explores the rationale behind diagnostic criteria and connects diagnostic criteria in the *DSM-5* with symptomology in the case. In addition, each case includes a discussion of treatment interventions that is crucial for students in helping professions. These treatment considerations are inclusive of a wide range of evidence-based approaches as appropriate for each case. Cases are presented across major categories of disorders to help students understand the nature of differential diagnosis. Cases also reflect cultural and social considerations in making diagnostic decisions. An ideal text to enhance courses in psychopathology and diagnosis, as well as practicum and internship, this casebook will diversify and broaden the classroom experience by enlightening students with compelling clinical cases that have been experienced by practicing professionals.

The new enhancements in the second edition continue to build upon the teaching tool that allows the reader to formulate his or her own reactions and diagnostic impressions to the case before the commentary section reveals the correct (or most correct) conclusion. Lastly, a techniques/treatment recommendation section will allow the reader to understand how colleagues have conceptualized the case and how specific interventions have been effective in treatment. The goal is for students to enhance their case conceptualization skills and sharpen their ability to understand symptom presentation in light of diagnosing.

# A FOCUS ON ASSESSMENT
*By Jason H. King*

# Case of Alison

## ▓ INTRODUCTION

"Treatment begins with assessment" is a sound clinical mantra that has guided my 20 years of counseling practice. Comprehensive and ongoing clinical assessment that is developmentally appropriate and culturally sensitive is essential for accurate diagnosis and ethical treatment planning. Compared to previous editions of the American Psychiatric Association's *Diagnostic and Statistical Manual of Mental Disorders*, the Fifth Edition (*DSM-5*) represents a significant shift from treating disorders globally to treating symptoms individually. Historically, assessment and diagnosis focused on a categorical diagnostic classification system and process that resulted in the excessive designation of co-occurring disorders, disputes about the clear boundaries between disorders, and disproportionate use of the diagnostic classification *not otherwise specified* (Jones, 2012). These structural problems did not capture clinical reality and put mental health professionals, of all disciplines, at significant risk for developing rigid clinical formulations, dichotomous conceptualizations, fragmented treatment planning, and poor client outcomes.

To minimize these structural problems, the *DSM-5* introduced a dimensional approach to diagnosis that broadens clinical assessment to capture developmental life span considerations, cultural issues, gender differences, and the overall heterogeneity of mental health presentations (APA, 2013). Section III of the *DSM-5* contains tools and techniques to enhance the clinical decision-making process and to understand the cultural context of mental disorders. These tools include over 60 cross-cutting symptom measures that are publicly available at www.dsm5.org. These assessment measures were developed to be administered at the initial interview and to monitor treatment progress. They are also intended to help identify additional areas of inquiry that may guide treatment and prognosis (APA, 2013). Most important, the *DSM-5* significantly expanded the use of *course* specifiers (communicate life span age-range of onset and remission status), *descriptive* specifiers (convey unique symptom profile information that can inform treatment planning), and *severity* specifiers (rate the intensity, frequency, duration, symptom count, or other severity indicators of a disorder).

In consideration of these critical changes, the following real-life case study of a female client, Alison, in her mid-30s, that previously received private practice outpatient treatment (weekly individual counseling sessions) but was referred for inpatient psychiatric hospitalization because she manifested serious and foreseeable harm. In alignment with ethical standards, actual client and family-related information have been sufficiently modified to obscure identity (ACA, 2014, F.7.f. Use of Case Examples). The content presented in the next section is from an actual referral letter written to the director of behavioral health for the inpatient psychiatric unit at a local hospital. Family history, current functioning, diagnostic impressions, diagnostic conclusions, and suggested therapeutic interventions are embedded within the letter—especially within the context of course, descriptive, and severity specifiers. The referral content and the sequencing (descending order of extreme, severe, moderate, mild, equivocal) of disorders with associated specifiers are in alignment with the *DSM-5* chapter titled "Use of the Manual" (pp. 19–24).

## INPATIENT PSYCHIATRIC HOSPITALIZATION REFERRAL LETTER

Per a clinical interview and testing using the following assessment measures: *DSM-5* Self-Rated Level 1 Cross-Cutting Symptom Measure, Adult; Level 2, Depression, Adult (PROMIS Emotional Distress, Depression, Short Form); Level 2, Anger, Adult (PROMIS Emotional Distress, Anger, Short Form); Level 2, Anxiety, Adult (PROMIS Emotional Distress, Anxiety, Short Form); Level 2, Somatic Symptom, Adult (Patient Health Questionnaire 15 Somatic Symptom Severity Scale [PHQ-15]); Level 2 Sleep Disturbance, Adult (PROMIS, Sleep Disturbance, Short Form); Level 2, Repetitive Thoughts and Behaviors, Adult; Severity Measure for Depression, Adult (Patient Health Questionnaire [PHQ-9]); Severity Measure for Separation Anxiety Disorder, Adult; Severity Measure for Social Anxiety Disorder (Social Phobia), Adult; Severity Measure for Panic Disorder, Adult; Severity of Posttraumatic Stress Symptoms, Adult (National Stressful Events Survey PTSD Short Scale [NSESS]); Severity of Dissociative Symptoms, Adult (Brief Dissociative Experiences Scale [DES-B]), I have diagnosed Alison with the following *DSM-5* disorders:

**F33.3 *Severe* Major Depressive Disorder, Recurrent (reason for visit)** (recurrent *ego-dystonic* thoughts of death and transient/stress-induced suicidal ideation and infanticide with increased intensity and frequency past 2 weeks).

With *severe* **mood-congruent psychotic features** (diminished emotional expression, avolition, alogia, anhedonia, and asociality with increased intensity and frequency past 2 weeks; non-bizarre *nihilistic* [e.g., natural disaster, bridge collapsing while driving, death of husband] and *somatic* [e.g., menstrual cycle dysregulation and excessive bleeding and remains from spontaneous fetus termination at 14 weeks' gestation] delusions with increased intensity and frequency past 4 weeks)

With **peripartum onset** (emergency cesarean section surgery in 2015 to deliver monochorionic-diamniotic female twins). Additional historical peripartum onset in 2003 resulting in psychosis (without suicidal ideation) and 2012 resulting in suicidal ideation (without psychosis).

With **atypical features** (significant weight gain or increase in appetite, hypersomnia, leaden paralysis, interpersonal rejection sensitivity, and subtle relational self-sabotage)

**F43.10** *Severe* **Posttraumatic Stress Disorder** (resulting from both *direct* and *indirect* exposure through ongoing multiple and compounded traumatic events, including threatened homicide [i.e., assault rifle placed in her mouth and bullet with her name written on it] and threatened suicide by a cop from ex-husband, motor vehicle accident, *witnessed* almost catastrophic death of current husband to cancer, almost catastrophic personal death per Preeclampsia developing into eclampsia, almost catastrophic death of identical twins born at 27 weeks' gestation per emergency cesarian section)

With *extreme* **panic attacks** (all 13 cognitive, affective, physiological, and behavioral symptoms manifest all the time during attacks)

With *moderate* **anger** (irritated, annoyed, grouchy, ready to explode, or damage property)

With **moderate sleep disturbance** (restless, unsatisfied, unrefreshed, not enough, poor quality)

**F44.7** *Severe* **and Persistent Conversion Disorder (Functional Neurological Symptom Disorder)**

With **mixed symptoms** (weakness, tingling, myoclonus [throat], syncope "psychogenic" non-epileptic attack [2015], numbness)

With **psychological stressor** (trauma triggers, loud noises/sounds, high expressed emotion, and constant verbal demands from children)

**F93.0** *Severe* **Separation Anxiety Disorder** (major attachment figures include husband and newborn twins)

**F40.10 Moderate Social Anxiety Disorder (Social Phobia)**

**F42.9 Unspecified Obsessive-Compulsive and Related Disorder** (reports unpleasant thoughts, urges, or images that repeatedly enter the mind and feeling driven to perform certain mental acts repeatedly; manifests an inflated sense of responsibility and the tendency to overestimate threat, intolerance of uncertainty, and over-importance of thought) **With good or fair insight**

**Z62.820 Parent–Child Relational Problem** (with 15-year-old daughter, avoidance without resolution of problems, negative attributions of the other's intentions, hostility toward or scapegoating of the other, and unwarranted feelings of estrangement)

Alison's medical history includes ocular (aura) migraines, gastric bypass surgery (per failed lap band), and a body mass index (BMI) = 37.4 which is considered medically obese. Alison does not manifest hypomanic or manic episodes, traumatic brain injury, substance use, or epilepsy.

## ▨ SUGGESTED THERAPEUTIC INTERVENTION

Alison should be admitted to inpatient psychiatric care for immediate self-harm resolution and overall psychological stabilization.

## ▨ FOR YOUR CONSIDERATION

1. How does the use of course, descriptive, and severity specifiers assist with an approach to clinical case formulation that is clinically sound and sensitive to Alison's developmental and cultural needs?
2. How might your clinical case formulation change if the descriptive specifiers *With moderate anger* and *With moderate sleep disturbance* were conceptualized as clinical syndromes of Alison's major depressive disorder instead of her posttraumatic stress disorder?
3. What is the clinical utility of indicating key aspects of Alison's medical history and communicating the absence of prominent psychiatric and medical conditions?
4. Considering the complexity of Alison's clinical profile, how would an additional recommendation of pharmacogenomic testing minimize unintentional client harm and promote client welfare?
5. After discharge from the inpatient psychiatric hospital, what trauma-informed treatment interventions and modalities would you recommend for Alison, and why?

## ■ REFERENCES

American Counseling Association [ACA] (2014). *2014 ACA Code of Ethics*. Located at https://www.counseling.org/resources/aca-code-of-ethics.pdf

American Psychiatric Association. (2013). *Diagnostic and statistical manual of mental disorders* (5th ed.). https://doi.org/10.1176/appi.books.9780890425596

Jones, K. D. (2012). Dimensional and cross-cutting assessment in the DSM-5. *Journal of Counseling & Development, 90*(4), 481–487. https://doi.org/10.1002/j.1556-6676.2012.00059.x

# CHAPTER ONE

# NEURODEVELOPMENTAL DISORDERS

*Neurodevelopmental disorders are conditions that affect the functionality of the brain. With many neurodevelopmental disorders, the signs and symptoms most often begin to show when a child is young, usually around preschool years. This chapter follows this pattern and includes three cases of neurodevelopmental disorders in children, including attention deficit hyperactivity disorder and autism spectrum disorder. Family dynamics and school considerations are also included with these cases given the ages of the clients. Questions for consideration are included.*

## 1.1    Case of Annalisse

### ■ INTRODUCTION

Annalisse is a 6-year-old Caucasian female who lives with her foster parents and foster brother in a single-family home in a small town. Annalisse is related to her foster mother and her father is her foster mother's nephew. Annalisse is in kindergarten and is in a regular education classroom but has an Individualized Educational Plan (IEP) due to issues with attention. Her foster mother reports that "Annalisse does well at school when she is paying attention." She attends school regularly and reports that she likes people. However, her foster mother reports that Annalisse is "so high energy that friends eventually ask her to leave."

Annalisse was removed from the care of her biological parents due to neglect. During an incident between her parents, the police were called to her residence. On arrival, the police found Annalisse strapped naked in her car seat in the corner. The police reported to children's services that they had found a neglected 6-month-old child. In actuality, Annalisse was 2 years old at that time. Annalisse was so malnourished that she gave the perception of being only 6 months old. When the police tried to remove her from the car seat, they found that she was congealed in her seat. She had not been removed from the seat for some time and had been urinating and defecating on herself. When Annalisse was examined at the hospital, they found that her vaginal walls were sealed together. They had to separate her vagina during her hospitalization.

## ■ FAMILY HISTORY

Annalisse's parents struggle with mental health and drug and alcohol issues. Her father is reported by her foster mother to have a severe temper. Annalisse's foster mother believes that her nephew is a batterer and that is why none of his relationships work out. Annalisse has many half-siblings, although she has not seen any of them. They are all in the care of children's services or live with their individual biological mothers.

Annalisse's father may have some cognitive delays or disabilities. After Annalisse was born, he read on the internet that cherry juice works just as well as formula for an infant. Her father began giving Annalisse cherry juice instead of formula. He also had given her a taste of strawberry frosting and Annalisse appeared to really like it. From then on, he fed her strawberry frosting only. This is thought to be the reason that she was so malnourished when she was found. This also caused all of her teeth to rot out. When her foster mother received custody of Annalisse, one of the first procedures Annalisse had to endure was to have every tooth in her mouth removed.

Annalisse's foster brother Keith has suffered some of the same neglect that Annalisse did as a child. Keith is 23 years old now and he and Annalisse do not get along well due to Keith being very "hard" on her. Keith talks about how he does not want her to make the same mistakes that he made. He was also raised by parents who have mental health, alcohol and drug, and battering issues. Keith calls Annalisse names and constantly yells at her when she makes mistakes. He does not admit to hitting Annalisse, but she is often left in his care and Keith reports punishing her "when she is bad." Annalisse appears to be afraid of Keith and sad in his presence.

Annalisse's foster parents have been married for 30 years. They were never able to have children of their own. They adopted Keith and his brother Kevin when they were 8 and 9 years old. They are now 23 and 22. Kevin is away in the Navy. Annalisse's foster parents also have had numerous foreign exchange students every year for at least 20 years. Currently, there is a student from Paris named Pierre living with them during his school year.

## ■ CURRENT FUNCTIONING

Annalisse is overly friendly and has no fear of strangers. She is very anxious every day and fears that her foster parents will die. Annalisse has asthma and allergies and takes medication for both. Annalisse does not listen. She does not follow through on directions and does not pay attention or sustain attention. She consistently overlooks important details. Annalisse is impulsive all of the time. She is easily distracted and forgetful. Annalisse has mood swings, which are mostly happy to sad. She is hyper every day, squirms, runs, and uses things without permission. Annalisse does not like to be quiet, seated, or noninteractive. She has a hard time getting to sleep every night, so she takes melatonin.

Annalisse cannot handle being away from her foster parents. When her foster father told her that he was going to go out to the waiting room, Annalisse began decompensating and held onto to him. She began hyperventilating and crying excessively. These behaviors are increased when Annalisse is forced to have visitation with her biological parents. The visits are supervised by her foster parents, but each visit leaves her more and more concerned that she would have to go back to living with her biological parents. Annalisse's biological mother tells Annalisse that her foster mother is not her real mother.

Annalisse is a very sweet and kind child. Her foster father tends to favor her due to what she has experienced in her life. He admits that he has a soft spot in his heart for her. Annalisse's foster parents have always wanted a girl, but it was never meant to be, until now. Annalisse's foster mother tends to be more of the disciplinarian in an appropriate and authoritative manner.

## ■ DIAGNOSTIC IMPRESSIONS

Annalisse continues to feel the effects of her early childhood trauma. She is a sweet and kind child, however, she suffers from severe anxiety due to fear that she will be sent back in her biological family's care or lack thereof. Annalisse's foster family has no intention of allowing this to happen and they have filed for her permanent custody.

Annalisse has a lot of energy and is "busy" all the time. She makes friends easily but can be "too much" for most friends. Annalisse has a hard time listening, following directions, paying attention, being impulsive and forgetful, and does things without permission. Annalisse has a hard time sleeping at night and needs melatonin to get to sleep and stay asleep.

Annalisse lacks insight into her issues. She needs to have individual treatment, community psychiatric supports and treatment, and a referral for medication. She will need to process her trauma and be taught coping skills to deal effectively with her past and future self. She has an IEP to manage her many symptoms that appear to be attention deficit hyperactivity disorder (ADHD) and that should be assessed, especially if she begins medication.

## ▧ DIAGNOSTIC CONCLUSIONS

- ADHD combined presentation
- Abuse and neglect during early childhood
- High expressed emotions in the family of origin
- Asthma and allergies

## ▧ SUGGESTED THERAPEUTIC INTERVENTIONS

Annalisse could benefit from Trauma Focused Cognitive Behavioral Therapy (TF-CBT). TF-CBT could be utilized to process the trauma that Annalisse has endured. This treatment modality can also provide coping skills such as relaxation and breathing techniques. At the end of the treatment process, a trauma narrative is facilitated with the client. The client is able to pick a piece of the trauma to analyze. This could be the first time, the worst time, or the last time that the trauma occurred. With Annalisse being so young, she may be processing trauma that is not as viable as someone older. A clinician can process her feelings and the trauma associated with the visitation.

Annalisse also needs skills to manage her ADHD. Aside from medication, a clinician can help Annalisse and her family to provide pieces to give Annalisse the best environment for growth. (a) Structure and routine need to be maintained at all times. (b) The rules and expectations need to be clear. (c) Children with ADHD need to be moving and exerting physical energy. They can be involved in play, sports, dance, and so on. (d) Nutrition can be a great adjunct to treatment. Some children can have allergies that increase their symptomatology. (e) Self-care for the entire family is paramount. Mental health concerns can be taxing and overwhelming. Family members can manage stress by doing things that they enjoy together and apart.

## ▧ FOR YOUR CONSIDERATION

1. Annalisse was very young when she was found by the police, how much do you think will affect her future life?
2. How can you be sure that Annalisse has ADHD and is not simply reacting to her neglect and past with her parents? What differential diagnosis would you consider?
3. Considering that Annalisse and Keith have been through very similar circumstances, why do you think that Keith is so "hard"

on her? There are some concerning factors in their relationship, at what point do you believe this could be an issue and you should call children's services?

4. How could you help not only Annalisse, but also her entire foster family deal with visitation issues regarding her biological family?

5. Annalisse has an IEP at school. How involved should you be with her school counselor?

# 1.2    *Case of Jacob*

## ■ INTRODUCTION

Jacob is a 9-year-old male who lives with his mother, father, and two sisters aged 15 and 17 years. Jacob's mother presented for the initial intake session without Jacob to discuss concerns she had regarding Jacob and to determine whether counseling would be beneficial. Jacob is in the third grade at a public elementary school in a suburban setting. Jacob's mother, Patricia, reported that Jacob struggles in the home setting as well as in school—both academically and with peers.

Patricia reported that from the time he was a toddler, Jacob has been "different from the other kids." Although Jacob started speaking around the age of 2 years, Patricia also reported that he used his words mainly to get what he wanted, and he did not seem to be interested in talking for any other reason. He did not use his words to express thoughts or feelings like her other children. He would often get upset (tantruming) over minor things—not having a particular cup or changing brands of common items. Jacob never asked "why" questions or appeared interested in engaging with others unless he needed or wanted something. Patricia noted that Jacob was often the child who played alone at birthday parties or family get-togethers. Jacob often resisted interacting with the other kids or failed to notice their attempts at engagement. As he got older, Jacob appeared to become more interested in peers; however, peer interactions rarely ended well. Jacob had difficulty initiating interactions with others, often "bossing the other kids around." Jacob was intolerant with games that the other kids "made up" and imaginary play, frequently getting into arguments with peers and insisting that they were not playing "the right way." From an early age, Jacob had a fascination with trains, and he would talk about trains incessantly. Trains have become a topic of irritation for Jacob's family because he does not seem to recognize that others are not following or interested in the topic. Jacob will have one-sided conversations about trains and does not seem to understand that others have different interests. Jacob has not expanded his interests and seemingly resists all attempts to engage him in other topics.

Jacob's mom reports that at home, the family feels as though they are walking on eggshells all the time. Jacob is demanding and bossy, frequently throwing "fits" when things do not go the way he wants. His mom reports that Jacob will scream, cry, and throw objects at the slightest provocation. She also reports that Jacob's need for consistency and routine has caused significant turmoil within the family. Problematic situations can include things like moving the furniture to accommodate the Christmas tree; changing brands of food, laundry detergent, or personal products; or even the changes in the route taken to school. Patricia admits that she frequently gets frustrated with his sister's refusal to adhere to some of Jacob's specifications, which has caused animosity and discord within the family unit.

Recently, Jacob has been having difficulty in school, particularly with his peers. Jacob has begun expressing dissatisfaction with his peers' behavior during class as well as a lack of friends. Patricia reports that Jacob seems to be unhappy and is concerned that his "selfishness" has affected his ability to make and keep friends. Per teacher report, Jacob has difficulty with peers who do not adhere to the rules of the classroom. Jacob will tell on his peers, even his "friends," if they talk when they are not supposed to be talking or for any other slight infractions. His teacher refers to him as a "rule follower." Jacob's teacher reports that he is often alone during recess despite his awkward attempts to initiate interactions with others. His attempts to engage with his peers are often disruptive and off-putting to others. When she approached the topic with Jacob, he did not seem to understand why his peers may be upset with him for telling on them when he was "just telling the truth." Jacob struggles with group work because he is inflexible with ideas and often tries to dictate how and what the group will do. Jacob's teacher reports spending inordinate amounts of time helping his groups resolve conflicts for which he is responsible. When the students are given the opportunity to choose their own groups, Jacob is frequently left out. Jacob blames the children for being "mean" and purposefully excluding him. He frequently yells at his peers, accusing them of "bullying," and demanding to be in their group and threatening to report them to the antibullying task force.

In addition to difficulties with peers in the school setting, Jacob's teacher reports that his grades are suffering. Jacob frequently argues with his teacher about the accuracy of tests, papers, and work materials. Jacob struggles to complete creative writing assignments, refusing to "make things up," and insisting on providing "real" and "right" information. For example, Jacob's teacher reported that when given the writing prompt: "If you could have a superpower what would it be and why?" Jacob argued the plausibility of such a thing and refused to complete the assignment. Jacob also argued with peers about their assignments, telling them that it is not real and that it could not happen. Despite his difficulties in the academic realm, both his teacher and his mother report that Jacob's ability far exceeds his current level of functioning.

Jacob presented with his mom for the second session. Jacob greeted the counselor by stating that he did not know why he had to come and that he is not the one with the "problems." When asked why he thought that his mom brought him, he stated that he "didn't know." Jacob did not make eye contact and moved about the room picking up and touching objects. When asked to describe the "problems" that others have with him, he reported that the kids in his class are mean and stupid. Jacob reported that he wants to have friends but that there are not many good ones in his school. Jacob reported that they do not talk to him and that no one plays with him. During the session, Jacob was given the opportunity to play with various toys and games. Jacob took control of the play tasks, telling his mom and the counselor how to play by using statements such as "that's not right," "this is what you're supposed to do," and "stop it." When Jacob encountered something that he did not agree with or something that was not "right," he criticized the counselor by using statements such as "don't you know anything?" and "aren't you supposed to be smart?" When asked to speculate how others may feel when he uses such statements, Jacob responded that he did not know. When asked how he would feel, Jacob stated that it never happened, so he does not know. When asked to guess, Jacob became frustrated and irritated and told the counselor, "This is stupid. I'm not talking about this anymore."

## ■ DIAGNOSTIC IMPRESSIONS

Jacob demonstrates deficits in social communication and social interaction across multiple contexts including: deficits in social–emotional reciprocity by history and continuing in the present, demonstrated by abnormal, often intrusive and disruptive, social approach, failure of normal back-and-forth conversation, failure to respond to social interactions, and reduced sharing of interests and emotions; deficits in nonverbal communicative behaviors for social interaction—abnormalities in eye contact; and deficits in developing, maintaining, and understanding relationships demonstrated by difficulties with adjusting behaviors to suit various social contexts, difficulties with imaginative play, and difficulties making friends. Jacob also demonstrates restrictive, repetitive patterns of behavior, interests, and activities demonstrated by insistence on sameness and inflexible adherence to routine reflected in his "rule-following" and bossy behavior with peers and his history of strong preference for specific objects (cup) or brands. In addition,

Jacob's intense interest in trains is a highly restricted, fixated interest that is abnormal in intensity and focus. Jacob's symptoms presented in the early developmental period and have created a clinically significant impairment in social and academic functioning in multiple settings.

## ▨ DIAGNOSTIC CONCLUSION

- Autism spectrum disorder (ASD) requiring support for deficits in both social communication and restricted repetitive behaviors, without accompanying intellectual impairment and without accompanying language impairment.

## ▨ SUGGESTED THERAPEUTIC INTERVENTIONS

Family/Individual Therapy—Individual sessions with parents to educate the parent's about the symptoms, causes, and treatments of ASD. Assist the family in developing realistic expectations based on Jacob's abilities. Individual sessions with parents will also be used to teach behavior management skills to increase prosocial behaviors and decrease disruptive behaviors. Family sessions should be utilized, with all members present, to share and work through their feelings related to the impact that ASD has on the family.

Individual Therapy—Research demonstrates that the use of cognitive behavioral therapy (CBT) for children with ASDs is effective in reducing the symptoms of anxiety and also has an impact on issues with social cognition (Kincade & McBride, 2009). Individual therapy with Jacob should focus on emotion identification and expression, perspective taking, and to develop prosocial coping skills.

School Collaboration—Therapist should assist the parents in collaborating with the school to develop a behavioral management system in the classroom to reinforce appropriate behavior and to improve school performance. In order to increase communication between the school and home, a communication system should be established (i.e., daily behavior reports). In addition, Jacob should participate in a school-based social group (e.g., a lunch bunch) to facilitate appropriate peer interaction.

Social/Peer Relationship Building—Involvement in a child-based social skills group program that focuses on peer relationships will assist Jacob in developing and maintaining appropriate friendships. The program should not occur without simultaneous parent behavior management training and ongoing collaboration with the program instructors.

## ▓ FOR YOUR CONSIDERATION

1. What other information would you like to know in determining the best course of treatment for Jacob?
2. How do the family dynamics presented contribute to Jacob's difficulties?
3. What other courses of treatment may you suggest?

## ▓ REFERENCE

Kincade, S. R., & McBride, D. L. (2009). *CBT and autism spectrum disorders: A comprehensive literature review.* http://files.eric.ed.gov/fulltext/ED506298.pdf

# 1.3    *Case of Julia*

## ▓ INTRODUCTION

Julia is an 8-year-old female who lives with her mother, father, and a 5-year-old brother. Julia presented with her mother and brother for her initial visit due to concerns that had become more pronounced as her school career progressed. Julia's father travels frequently for work and was not able to attend counseling sessions. Julia is in the second grade at a public elementary school in a suburban neighborhood.

Julia presented in a pleasant and talkative mood. Julia was very animated, exploring the room, touching, picking up objects, and often interrupting her mom by putting the objects in her face. Julia did not sit down for the duration of the initial session and moved from task to task without engaging in any one activity for more than a few minutes. Julia had to be reminded multiple times not to climb on the couch. She frequently intruded on her brother's play by grabbing objects from him and whined to her mom when he did not cooperate with her intrusion by saying that he would not "share." At times, Julia would intrude on her brother's play by giving him directions on what to do and how to play.

During the initial session, her mom reported that Julia has always demonstrated difficulty following directions and completing various tasks at home. Her mom specifically reported that cleaning her room has become a constant battle because Julia will remain in her room for hours, often "playing" when she should be cleaning. Her mom reports that she is often frustrated because Julia does not listen to her even when she is speaking directly to her. Her mom admits that Julia knows how to clean her room and can do so with constant supervision and specific instructions—what to do when—but states that they (parents) refuse to "overfunction" for their daughter who is "old enough" to complete independent chores. Her mom states that if Julia was more organized, she would not have such a big mess to tackle in her room. Her mom also states that Julia often becomes overly emotional with "things that really aren't a big deal." For example, she can become tearful when she is not going to a place she likes to eat or when her brother plays with something that is hers and she is afraid that he will break it. Her mom described a situation in which Julia was upset because she could not wear a shirt that she had outgrown, and it took her 20 minutes to calm down and stop crying.

Her mom reports that Julia has been constantly "on the go" since she could walk. Julia rarely sits still and constantly has something to say. Her mom explained that they stopped going out to restaurants when Julia was a toddler because she could not sit still and would disrupt the entire restaurant. Her mom reports constantly having to tell Julia to "sit like a lady" and that she gave up on dresses long ago because Julia is constantly climbing on objects or sprawling around on the floor. Julia's mom explains having difficulty getting anything done when Julia was little because her daughter would not remain engaged in any activity long enough.

Her mom reports that there have been additional problems as Julia has gotten older and the demands of school have increased. Based on teacher reports, Julia has difficulty remaining in her seat and following the directions of the classroom as well as specific directions from her teachers. Julia has difficulty completing her seatwork, often playing with items in her desk and attempting to engage other students or simply staring off into space. Her mom reports that getting Julia to complete her homework is a nightly struggle that takes hours to finish. Despite finishing her homework, Julia often loses homework points because she frequently fails to follow her morning routine at school and forgets to turn it in. Julia's teacher reports that she has to constantly remind Julia to raise her hand if she wants to answer a question or needs to get the teacher's attention. Another area of concern for the school is Julia's difficulty with walking and/or waiting in line—she often gets out of line to talk to peers and has difficulty keeping her hands to herself. Julia also displays some intrusive behaviors with peers, often interrupting games and taking others' belongings without asking. Her mom believes that these intrusive and impulsive behaviors have made it difficult for Julia to make and maintain friendships. Her mom reports that Julia has the habit of being too honest by saying whatever comes to her mind without considering others' feelings. Despite the various concerns in the school setting, Julia's teachers report that when she pays attention, she avoids careless mistakes and generally knows the material. All parties involved agree that Julia is a bright girl.

Julia reports that her parents are always yelling at her and that she is always getting in trouble. Julia maintains that she wants to do well in school but reports that the teachers hate her and make her work more difficult on purpose. Julia expressed sadness and frustration at not having any close friends and reported that she tries to play with the girls at recess but that they always run away from her.

## ▦ DIAGNOSTIC IMPRESSIONS

According to her mother's report, Julia has demonstrated a persistent pattern of inattention, hyperactivity, and impulsivity since she was a toddler. Julia's symptoms include making careless mistakes in schoolwork, difficulty sustaining attention/focus during tasks, does not seem to listen when spoken to directly, often does not follow through on instructions, fails to finish schoolwork and chores, demonstrates difficulty organizing tasks and activities, is easily distracted by extraneous stimuli, is often forgetful in daily activities, often squirms in her seat, leaves her seat when expected to remain, runs and climbs in situations where it is inappropriate, is unable to play or engage in leisure activities quietly, is often "on the go," talks excessively, blurts out answers, has difficulty awaiting her turn, and often interrupts or intrudes on others. The difficulties that Julia is experiencing have demonstrated a greater impact as academic expectations and the expectation of independence have increased. Julia's symptoms have persisted for at least 6 months, have had a direct negative impact on social and academic functioning, and are present in two or more settings (home and school).

## ▦ DIAGNOSTIC CONCLUSION

- ADHD, combined presentation, moderate

## ▦ SUGGESTED THERAPEUTIC INTERVENTIONS

Pharmacotherapy—Julia's mother should schedule an evaluation with a psychiatrist to assess the appropriateness of ADHD medication to reduce her symptoms.

Family/Individual Therapy—Individual sessions with parents to educate them about the symptoms, causes, and treatments of ADHD. Individual sessions will also be used to teach behavior management skills to increase prosocial behaviors and decrease disruptive behaviors coupled with family sessions (with Julia) to model and reinforce positive parent–child interactions.

School Collaboration—Therapist should assist the parents in collaboration with the school to develop a behavioral management system in the classroom to reinforce appropriate behavior and to improve school performance. In order to increase communication between the school and home, a communication system should be established (i.e., daily behavior reports).

Social/Peer Relationship Building—Involvement in a child-based group program that focuses on peer relationships will assist Julia in developing and maintaining appropriate friendships. The program should not occur without simultaneous parent behavior management training and ongoing collaboration with the program instructors.

## ■ FOR YOUR CONSIDERATION

1. What other information would you like to know in determining the best course of treatment for Julia?
2. How do the family dynamics presented contribute to Julia's difficulties?

# CHAPTER TWO

# SCHIZOPHRENIA SPECTRUM AND OTHER PSYCHOTIC DISORDERS

*Schizophrenia is a chronic, severe mental disorder that affects the way a person thinks, acts, expresses emotions, perceives reality, and relates to others. While uncommon as compared to other mental disorders, it is often the most chronic and disabling. This chapter contains three cases of schizophrenia spectrum disorder and other psychotic disorders, including delusional disorder of two types. These cases highlight disorders that cause various degrees of distress and dysfunction in three adult males. Questions for consideration are included.*

## 2.1    *Case of Tim*

### ▓ INTRODUCTION

Tim is a 32-year-old, married male, father of two children, aged 8 and 5 years. Tim is a software program developer who works freelance for large institutions. He owns and operates his own software development company and is a subcontractor who basically works alone. Tim married his high school sweetheart after he finished college; they bought a home and started their family. Currently, he is estranged from his wife, and she has filed for divorce. Prior to this, from the outside, his life looked like the "typical American dream."

About a year ago, Tim had developed a software program for universities and met with the leadership of a university that was interested in buying his program. The deal would have been a breakthrough for Tim because the university had several branches and affiliates that would also use the software and it would have opened up the possibility of other deals with other universities. However, the university was not interested after his presentation at the meeting, and the deal fell through. After this incident, Tim's symptoms surfaced.

### ▓ CURRENT FUNCTIONING

Tim began demonstrating paranoid symptomatology. He became and continues to be suspicious of others and believes people are "out to get him." He believes the university is trying to steal his ideas and his software. He states that the university has bugged his home, his phone, and his computer. He believes that the university is trying to destroy his business and his credibility and has bribed his family members and friends into trying to make him "look crazy." He reports that the university is sending him encrypted messages through the closed captioning on the TV and is trying to take pictures and video of him through his phone and computer. He refuses to share what the messages were, stating, "I will be killed if I tell you." Tim denies hearing voices or seeing things that other people do not see. His affect is appropriate. He reports that he enjoys playing with his children and that he coaches his 8-year-old son's little league team.

After Tim signed an authorization for release of information, Tim's mother reported that he had difficulty interacting with others for most of his life. His career choice was a good one for him because he could work independently. After Tim became suspicious, he refused to work on a computer and closed down his business. He is now having difficulty securing gainful employment and has not worked in several months. His home is in foreclosure.

Although he reports that his wife, friends, and family have repeatedly assured him they are not trying to sabotage his business, Tim states that because of his suspiciousness, his wife eventually became exasperated and moved out, taking the children with her. At that point in time, Tim's symptoms became worse. He states that he began stalking her because he wanted to see her and his children and that he misses being with his children. After one incident when Tim unexpectedly showed up at her house to see the children, his estranged wife became fearful and demanded that he should either immediately seek treatment, or she would contact the police. Arrangements were made for him to be admitted to an inpatient psychiatric hospital.

Upon release from the hospital, he moved in with his mother. He still holds onto the delusion but is able to manage his symptoms and function better, although not at his previous baseline. He reports feeling sad because he lost his business, his wife and children, and his friends. Although he holds firm to his delusions, he states he is hopeful that he can rebuild his relationship with his children and secure employment.

## ▨ DIAGNOSTIC IMPRESSIONS

Many times, functioning in daily life and at work is disrupted by persistent delusions and paranoia. Tim's diagnosis is a delusional disorder, persecutory type. He demonstrates symptoms that warrant the delusional disorder diagnosis, such as believing the university was sending encrypted messages through the closed captioning on the TV and trying to take pictures and video of him through his computer and phone. In Tim's diagnosis of delusional disorder, the delusions are mostly nonbizarre—meaning these are things that could happen in real life (e.g., being deceived or conspired against, having ideas and software stolen). However, what makes them delusions is the lack of evidence to support the validity of the beliefs (e.g., family members and friends are caring and supportive and would not sabotage Tim's business or intentionally hurt his well-being).

There is a fine line between schizophrenia and Tim's diagnosis. He does not meet the criteria for schizophrenia because he denies experiencing hallucinations. In addition, his affect is appropriate, speech is coherent and logical, and thought processes are organized; apart from the behavior associated directly with the delusions, his behavior is unremarkable. And although decoding messages through closed captioning can be considered symptomatic of schizophrenia, his symptoms match more closely to a delusional disorder.

## ▓ DIAGNOSTIC CONCLUSIONS

- Delusional disorder, persecutory type
- Disruption of family by separation or divorce
- Other problems related to employment

## ▓ SUGGESTED THERAPEUTIC INTERVENTIONS

Most times, delusions are fixed, and clients are quite resistant to letting them go. Challenging the delusions or trying to disprove them might make the client distrustful of the counselor and may instigate a power struggle; this inevitably damages the therapeutic relationship and clients might not return, which means they will not get the treatment they need. Although mental health professionals do not need to validate the delusions, they do need to validate the client's experience and feelings. Clients need to be able to function around the delusions.

Helpful treatment includes assisting clients in developing coping skills, decision-making skills, and problem-solving strategies; in addition, behavior modification is beneficial. For example, Tim will use William Glasser's Wise Choice process model when he is thinking about deciding, such as going to see his children unannounced for an unscheduled visit. In addition, Tim will call his estranged wife each time before he goes to her house to pick up his children for his scheduled visits. He is focusing on his strengths and is streamlining his résumé.

## ■ FOR YOUR CONSIDERATION

1. Could Tim have had a predisposition that was exacerbated by the rejection from the university (e.g., diathesis-stress model)? How could mental health professionals determine this?
2. Medication is regularly prescribed for people diagnosed with mental health disorders. What would the advantages and disadvantages be for prescribing medications for people diagnosed with a delusional disorder?
3. What advantages and disadvantages would group therapy have for people diagnosed with delusional disorder, persecutory type?

# 2.2    *Case of Jeremy*

## ■ INTRODUCTION

Jeremy, is a 26-year-old single male, currently living with his mother and his younger sister. At 19 years old, he initially presented for outpatient mental health counseling services requested by his mother, who accompanied him to his first appointment. He agreed to attending counseling if his mother, remained in the room throughout the first interview. During that session, both of them described Jeremy as becoming increasingly depressed over the past 2 years, sleeping 12 to 14 hours a day, and isolating from the rest of the family. Jeremy reported lack of motivation and problems interacting with his peers socially. He had no close friends and reported most of his energy was invested in writing science fiction and fantasy short stories. From time to time during the interview, Jeremy would connect content being discussed about his own history to details about the lives of fictional characters he developed during episodes of creative writing.

## ■ FAMILY HISTORY

The client and his mother disclosed Jeremy's history with mental health concerns beginning as early as age 3. His mother described him as "a ball of energy" and that he seemed to "have no fear" even when experiencing falls as a toddler. Jeremy's parents were divorced when he was 2 years old, and his problems seem to have been exacerbated when at age three-and-a-half he went on an extended visit to his father's home. During that time, Jeremy became violent, yelling, and biting his stepsiblings. His mother reported he was "out of control" for 3 years following unless she was present. Finally, at age 5, Jeremy was admitted to a children's psychiatric facility for several weeks. At that time, Jeremy was diagnosed with attention deficit hyperactivity disorder (ADHD), separation anxiety, and oppositional defiant disorder (ODD). He was prescribed Ritalin, which helped reduce some of his symptoms, and he was then released.

Jeremy continued to experience behavioral problems throughout grade school, including difficulties in getting along with other children, following rules, exhibiting hostility toward children and adults. Because of his behavioral concerns, Jeremy was assigned a behavior management (BM) specialist and worked with several different in-school behavioral support staff members throughout grade school. Jeremy's behavior problems caused him having to change schools in seventh grade, after he was expelled for throwing a desk across the room during class. The change in schools appeared to exacerbate his problems, and shortly afterward, Jeremy developed symptoms of obsessive-compulsive disorder (OCD). He would become distressed or act out violently if his daily routine was disturbed. Jeremy also began maintaining lists of injustices he perceived himself experiencing, and he kept a journal of his daily activities that he carried with him everywhere. Jeremy was able to maintain a close relationship with his mother, however, she was often able to communicate with him when his behavior escalated, to soothe and calm him down. He also reported good relationship with his maternal grandparents, whom he often stayed with for extended periods during his childhood.

At the age of 15, while living with his mother and his two sisters, Jeremy was admitted to a local university psychiatric facility for 3 months after having what he called "flashes" of hitting his mother over the head with a hammer and crushing her skull. During this hospital stay, Jeremy was prescribed Abilify, which helped alleviate some of his symptoms. Since his hospitalization at age 15, every 3 to 4 years the same flashes return, and Jeremy seeks inpatient psychiatric care out of fear that he may kill his mother.

## ■ CURRENT FUNCTIONING

Jeremy currently lives with his mother. A younger sister also lives with them and has limited contact with Jeremy; she does not engage him in social activities. Jeremy has one older sister who is married and has a young child. Jeremy expresses affection for his older sister and her family. For the past several years, he has held several different low-paying positions, either in fast food or in retail and has a hard time finding employment. Jeremy usually stays at a single position for about a year before having conflict with management or other employees and being asked to leave or leaving of his own accord. These conflicts usually involve perceived injustices and paranoia centered on supervisors and/or work colleagues.

He tends to seek outpatient counseling services for 6 to 18 months at a time when he is between work positions, because this is when his symptoms exacerbate as he experiences increased paranoia, isolation, and apathy and copes by becoming excessively engrossed in developing characters for his science fiction stories. When his symptoms intensify, Jeremy has trouble separating his own inner thoughts and motivations from his fictional characters and will shift midsentence from discussing himself to discussing a character from his writing. He is open to working with his outpatient counselor whom he has known for many years but does not usually follow through on plans made in the session. He responds well to structure and short-term therapeutic goals. However, if Jeremy becomes uncomfortable with content being discussed in therapy, he will excuse himself to use the restroom, returning after several minutes, and then begin discussing his fictional characters and their problems rather than focusing on his own mental health concerns. Jeremy presents with restricted affect and lethargy. He is slightly overweight and has poor judgment. For example, he has made friends in the past with those who were involved in illegal activity or have taken advantage of him financially. When his symptoms become severe, and he is fearful of harming his mother, Jeremy complies with recommendations for inpatient psychiatric care.

## ■ DIAGNOSTIC IMPRESSIONS

Jeremy presents for counseling services when he finds himself unemployed or when he recognizes his symptoms are intensifying and he fears that he may harm his mother. He has a limited support system and relies on his mother almost exclusively for emotional support. Jeremy has been diagnosed with schizoaffective disorder, depressive type and continuous. Jeremy does not meet criteria for major depressive disorder with psychotic features because he experiences periods of time, up to a month, when he reports an absence of pervasive depressive symptoms. However, during these times, thoughts related to persecution or delusions associated with his fictional characters remain present. He is slightly overweight due to inactivity and frequent lack of motivation, although when his depression lifts, he does attempt to exercise and take better care of himself physically.

Although some of Jeremy's symptoms might be explained by schizophrenia, a diagnosis of schizophrenia does not address the severity of his major depressive episodes, and while his previous diagnoses of ADHD, OCD, and ODD include some of the symptoms Jeremy experiences as an adult, they do not include his delusions or pervasive depressive symptoms. Even though Jeremy demonstrated some of the symptoms of an autism disorder during childhood, autism spectrum disorder does not account for his delusions. Jeremy's limited social support and his difficulties maintaining employment are of additional concern.

## ▦ DIAGNOSTIC CONCLUSIONS

- Schizoaffective disorder, depressive, concurrent
- Limited social support, frequent unemployment

## ▦ SUGGESTED THERAPEUTIC INTERVENTIONS

Pharmacotherapy—Jeremy evidences improvement in his social and occupational functioning when he complies with medication therapy to help reduce his symptoms. He should schedule a new medication evaluation so that a psychiatrist can determine the effectiveness of his current medication regimen and to make adjustments as needed. Jeremy is usually compliant with taking medications as prescribed, unless his depression and delusions intensify.

Family therapy—Collaboration with Jeremy's mother will help him follow through on short-term therapeutic goals related to functioning within the home and contributing to the family unit. Involving family will also help Jeremy monitor the severity of his symptoms, should hospitalization be required, and help him stay on track with his medication.

Bimonthly support group through the local chapter of NAMI—Jeremy experiences loneliness and has little social support aside from his mother. Engaging with other individuals who are managing similar symptoms will help Jeremy establish a support network and hopefully reduce his isolation.

Weekly outpatient mental health counseling—Regular counseling sessions help Jeremy monitor his symptoms and encourage him to develop and achieve short-term goals related to helping his mother with household tasks and obtaining employment.

Modalities that would be ineffective with Jeremy are those that include abstract or subconscious content such as sand tray therapy or expressive arts counseling. These modalities have been attempted in the past with Jeremy and exacerbated his delusions of persecution, preempting hospitalization for severe paranoia.

## ▦ FOR YOUR CONSIDERATION

1. Consider the many diagnoses that Jeremy had been given since he was 5 years old. What might be the reasons he was assigned these diagnoses? How do you think his developmental stage contributed to his earlier diagnoses?
2. Jeremy struggles with developing long-term goals. If you were to consider one or two long-term goals for Jeremy, what would they be and how would you introduce these potential options to Jeremy?

3.  How do you believe family have contributed to Jeremy's problems? If you were working with Jeremy and his mother in the session, what do you envision yourself accomplishing?

# 2.3   *Case of Dan*

## ■ INTRODUCTION

Dan is a 44-year-old, married male, father of two children, aged 15 and 17 years. He has been married for 19 years and has been employed at his current company for 12 years. He states that his family, friends, and coworkers describe him as a good husband and father: intelligent, thoughtful, dependable, and a good worker. He regularly arrives for sessions at the appointed time and is always appropriately dressed. Although he is articulate and polite, he often seems somewhat irritable. In addition, he seems guarded. Dan stated that he did not want to attend counseling but was compelled to come at his wife's insistence.

## ■ CURRENT FUNCTIONING

He states that his wife has been concerned about the amount of time that Dan spends on the computer and his increasing irritability when he is called away from the computer at home. Although he reports that he loves his wife and children, Dan states that he believes that he and a particular famous singer should get married. Dan believes that if the singer met him, she would instantly fall in love with him and would want to be together with him. He states that his wife and children would "be just fine" when he left her for the singer. He further reports that his wife "doesn't understand the chemistry of the love" between him and the singer.

He spends exorbitant amounts of time on the computer looking at the singer's pictures and researching everything about her. The amount of time spent on the computer has prompted his family and friends to begin to worry, especially his wife, from whom he keeps this secret. His wife only knows that Dan spends most of his time on the computer at home and that he is starting to get into trouble at his place of employment for not getting his work done in a timely manner. He reports that he is worried about getting reprimanded again at work.

Dan sent the singer several letters through her fan club and went to see her perform on a few occasions. He reports that he received a letter back from her through the fan club a few years ago; although it was a form letter with a stamped signature, he believes that she sent it directly to him in response to his attempt at contact. A few years ago, he took a flight to where the singer lived and went to her house hoping to see her. He did not knock on the door, but instead just watched the house for a couple of days and then flew back home; he denies doing this again after that one incident and denies intending on doing it again. From that one trip, Dan has pictures of the singer's children that he took from afar with a special camera lens. Although Dan acknowledges that the singer is happily married with children, he states that she would leave her family once she met Dan. He states that his "obsession" has been going on for a few years and that they are "meant to be together."

## ▦ DIAGNOSTIC IMPRESSIONS

The client's primary diagnosis would be delusional disorder, erotomanic type, because the central theme in Dan's presenting problem involves delusions of being in a relationship (mutually in love) with a famous singer. He denies feeling depressed, sad, or euphoric, but rather states he is waiting patiently for when he and the singer can be together. Apart from the delusions and recently getting reprimanded at work, Dan's functioning is unremarkable. Dan engages in typical activities and behaviors, such as attending school functions for his children; in addition, he reports enjoying household duties and responsibilities, such as cutting the grass and helping clean up after dinner.

Another possible diagnosis might be narcissistic personality disorder, given Dan's idea of "ideal love" and his feelings of being misunderstood; I think this diagnosis is plausible because the client does not appear to consider others' feelings (i.e., his wife's feelings); however, unspecified personality disorder is a more accurate fit as he does not meet the full criteria.

Also, if it is determined that a client has narcissistic personality disorder, counselors would certainly want to address any possible anxiety, depression, low self-esteem, and so forth. Because social relationships with individuals diagnosed with delusional disorder and narcissistic personality disorder often suffer in one way or another, therapy for both the client and any associated parties might be beneficial. With that in mind, the final diagnoses would guide therapeutic approaches and goals.

There is a difference between bizarre delusions that cannot occur (e.g., "the trees are walking into my bedroom every night and watch over me while I sleep") and nonbizarre delusions (e.g., "A famous singer will marry me."). While it is highly unlikely that the famous singer will marry Dan, there is the possibility—a one in a million chance, but possible.

## ◼ DIAGNOSTIC CONCLUSIONS

- Delusional disorder, erotomanic type
- Unspecified personality disorder
- Other problems related to employment

## ◼ SUGGESTED THERAPEUTIC INTERVENTIONS

In working with Dan, cognitive behavioral therapy (CBT) is useful to help him refocus and redirect his thinking and behavior (e.g., concerning the object of his affection). Assisting Dan in developing a plan to work around the delusions rather than challenging the delusions is the key. Remembering that delusions that are typically fixed helps clients function around the delusions. This is critical to helping them live as independently as possible. Mental health professionals do not need to agree with or validate the delusion but rather help the client develop coping skills. With the client's consent, encouraging family therapy (e.g., Dan's wife was affected by the delusions and self-centered, self-involved behavior) will provide more support for the client as they are progressing through the illness. Unfortunately, he refused the idea of family therapy. In addition to family therapy, psychiatric referrals for medication management are essential considering the severity of symptoms.

## ◼ FOR YOUR CONSIDERATION

1. How will you determine whether delusions are bizarre or nonbizarre? Why does this make a difference in diagnosing?
2. Similarities can be found between delusional disorders and OCDs. What are the similarities and differences? How will you differentiate between the two?
3. What would the advantages and disadvantages be of using a reality therapy approach (e.g., Wubbolding's WDEP [wants, direction, evaluation, plan]) with clients who present with symptoms of a delusional disorder?
4. In today's computer-savvy world, do you think that Dan's children might be aware of Dan's behavior on the computer but are not saying anything? How might you broach this delicate topic with Dan?

## ◼ REFERENCE

Wubbolding, R. E. (2011). *Theories of psychotherapy: Reality therapy*. American Psychological Association.

# CHAPTER THREE

# BIPOLAR AND RELATED DISORDERS

*Bipolar disorder is a mental disorder that causes unusual shifts in mood, energy, concentration, and the ability to perform daily tasks. This chapter contains three cases of bipolar disorder in adults. These cases illuminate how the same disorder manifests in different people with different backgrounds, including an African American woman, a Caucasian man, and a young Caucasian woman. Discussions of intersectionality, substance use/abuse, and questions for consideration are also included.*

# 3.1    *Case of Crystal*

## ▓ INTRODUCTION

Crystal, a 48-year-old African American female presented for an appointment following a hospital discharge. When Crystal was asked what brought her in, she stated, "I just need to get my medication." Her aunt Linda reported changes in her personality that dated back to 2007, that recently became more severe. Two months before the visit, Crystal confronted her neighbor about throwing beer cans in her yard. She became loud and threatened to kill the neighbor with garden shears when he denied discarding the cans. The police arrived and transported her to the Crisis Center, where they hospitalized her for a week. A restraining order was also issued against her to stay away from the neighbor's home, and she agreed in court to resume counseling to stabilize her symptoms. She presented her discharge papers and stated, "I wasn't going to hurt nobody." Linda also reported that about 2 weeks before the argument with her neighbor, Crystal caught her boyfriend cheating in her home. For about a week following the infidelity, Crystal was sad, crying a lot, and slept only a few hours a day. She carried on long rambling conversations and got easily irritated and angry, which took the form of yelling and throwing objects when trying to express herself. Her nights were occupied with cooking marathons consisting of seven and eight-course meals, baking several cakes and pastries which lasted until she got tired enough to sleep. Crystal shared a story about her boyfriend dominating her will by witchcraft and putting imperative thoughts in her mind, making her retaliate against the neighbor for the infidelity that occurred. She said someone told her that the neighbor contributed to the infidelity, and "I just went off on him" when she saw the beer cans in her yard. Crystal also stated that her boyfriend probably cheated because he could not handle her fits of rage. She denied ever attempting to end her life but snapped; she would stop anybody who tried to harm her. She indicated she does not need the medication, but she is "tired of getting in trouble all the time."

Crystal reported a premorbid history of unhappiness dating back to childhood. She recalled trouble functioning in the morning as early as high school, "I hated mornings because I always felt so sad and sluggish." During those times, Linda described Crystal being "sunk in gloom" in the morning, but by evening she would work, laugh, and be animated—entertaining friends with jokes. Crystal reported at least three hospitalizations for psychiatric episodes beginning in her 30s. Her first hospitalization followed the death of her mother from an aneurysm in 2007. "I haven't been right since then." After Linda became concerned about her going 8 days without eating or sleeping, Crystal agreed to go to the hospital. That marked the beginning of depression and anhedonia for Crystal. "They said I had a nervous break-down." More hospitalizations and a diagnosis of bipolar disorder followed about 2 or 3 years later. Crystal described manic episodes in 2010 that lasted about 6 or 7 months. She would work 18 hours for 7 to 10 days straight and reached a point when she threatened to "burn her sister's eyes out with a pair of hot curlers" because she was plotting to lock her up and steal her salon. Crystal landed in the hospital for a second time in 2010. Since then, she has had multiple episodes of severe anxiety, depression, insomnia, violently cursing and yelling at family and neighbors, and breaking objects (around seven episodes, each lasted about 2 to 5 months). Each episode ended with a trip to the Crisis Center for 24-hour de-escalation and discharge to family members. Crystal has been in and out of counseling over the last 10 years. She would attend for about 6 months when she "got in trouble" or needed medication. She has not been attending her counseling appointments in recent months and rarely takes her medication. She admitted that she does not like to take her medication because it makes her fat and feel wired but stated things usually go wrong when she does not take them. She also admitted to smoking a blunt or two every day for relaxation especially during her manic episodes. The discharge summary indicated a positive drug screen for marijuana at the time of her admission for aggressive behavior. She has never received treatment for substance use problems and does not believe she has a problem at this time.

## ▓ FAMILY HISTORY

Family history revealed depression in her maternal grandmother. At times, the grandmother would disappear for days and get hospitalized for mysterious reasons, and the family refused to talk about it. Crystal believes her mother suffered from depression even though she never received counseling or hospitalization. She recalled that her mother's primary care physician would prescribe her "sleeping pills." She also noted that her mother went out drinking every weekend. She denied a history of mental illness or substance use for her father. However, she indicated that her father has a brother diagnosed with schizophrenia.

Some background information, Crystal is the oldest of three children. She described a good childhood. Growing up, her father was a member of a motorcycle club and was away from home, working most of the time. He compensated them with vacations and road trips with the motorcycle club during summer months. She stated her father always made sure they had whatever they wanted. Her mother was a stay-at-home-mom and she developed a good relationship with her mother and siblings. At 18, Crystal discovered that her father "sold drugs" and decided to work for him after graduation until she was arrested during a drug raid 1 year later. Afterward, she became a licensed cosmetologist and worked at JC Penny's for 10 years before opening her salon when she was 30. She also leased two chairs to other cosmetologists. Crystal's father, sister, and brother live close by, "but I don't see them much." Her family described her as extremely tidy and organized and detect relapse whenever she gets violent and her home is found in disarray with holes in the walls and furniture caused by her fits of rage. Linda checks on her periodically to ensure she is okay. Crystal reported that her boyfriend "stays" with her, which is a frequently conflictual arrangement because he disappears for weeks when she becomes abusive. She also stated she has threatened to leave him on several occasions, but she has not been able to dissociate from the relationship. She has few recreational interests, and she has personal religious beliefs but does not participate in any religious activities. She spends her days working in her yard, watching television, or "Sometimes, I visit friends." She still does hair in her basement when she feels good even though she no longer has a license.

Crystal also has some health challenges. She reported issues with obesity and hypertension. She takes 12.5 mg of *Hydrochlorothiazide* for hypertension daily. There are some problems with carpal tunnel in both hands, and she reported a hysterectomy when she was 34 due to endometriosis and takes hormone medication. Crystal left the hospital with 1,000 mg of Depakote ER for bipolar. Despite being on this dose for at least 2 years, there were no blood level measurements of this medication. Also, 30 mg of paroxetine was prescribed for her moods.

## ■ DIAGNOSTIC IMPRESSIONS

Crystal is displaying symptoms of bipolar I disorder. Review of symptoms shows multiple episodes of depression beginning in her late 30s and clear manic episodes to date. Her recurring interpersonal conflicts, marijuana use, and paranoid delusions point to a paranoid diagnosis. For 2 months leading up to her most recent hospitalization, Crystal reported sadness moving from frequently crying to talking excessively, and violent outburst of cursing and throwing objects at family and friends. On discharge from the hospital, she was no longer hostile or aggressive but still showed some impulsivity and moodiness. During the interview, Crystal had a loud pressured voice that was sometimes difficult to understand, and she required frequent redirection. The aggression against her neighbor that lead to her most recent hospitalization was delusional, which is a symptom only present in the bipolar I category. For example, she believed her boyfriend was using witchcraft to dominate her mind and said something told her the neighbor was involved in her boyfriend's infidelity. Mood cycles and heightened states of activity; cooking and baking buffet size meals until she fell asleep days later also confirm mania. Interruptions in her normal behavior continued to be displayed with decreased sleep, violent outbursts, disorganization, and impulsivity. This is not Crystal's first episode of mania leading to hospitalization, and her mania continues to be followed by violent outbursts with homicidal tendencies.

Crystal demonstrates limited insight into the changes in her personality and behavior. She only complies with medication and treatment recommendations to avoid legal penalties and hospitalization. Crystal self-medicates with marijuana to cope with various negative moods. While schizophrenia and schizoaffective disorders are unlikely because of the absence of the flattening of affect and thought abnormality, the paranoid themed delusions she experiences during manic episodes and her genetic link to schizophrenia point to paranoid personality disorder. Also, hypertension and obesity are prevalent medical conditions among bipolar. Crystal takes 12.5 mg of Hydrochlorothiazide for hypertension, and her discharge summary includes weight management goals.

## ■ DIAGNOSTIC CONCLUSIONS

- Bipolar I disorder, with psychotic features
- Cannabis dependence
- Paranoid personality disorder

- Hypertension
- Overweight or obesity
- Nonadherence to medical treatment
- Legal circumstances
- Sibling relational problem
- Discord with neighbor

## ▓ SUGGESTED THERAPEUTIC INTERVENTIONS

An integrated treatment approach is ideal where crystal, her family members, and all care providers work together to manage her co-occurring medical, bipolar I, substance use disorder (SUD), and personality disorders simultaneously rather than treating them in isolation (Substance Abuse and Mental Health Services Administration [SAMHSA], 2016). Integrating medication, intensive psychotherapy, and case management services can help Crystal recover faster and longer. Intensive psychotherapy may include therapies such as cognitive behavioral therapy (CBT) and psychoeducation. CBT can help Crystal identify triggers to bipolar episodes and substance use and develop effective strategies to manage stress and cope with offensive situations. Psychoeducation groups can teach Crystal and her family about her treatment options, illness-management techniques, and lifestyle changes, including nutrition and exercise, to reduce weight.

Also choosing evidenced-based therapies explicitly designed for the treatment of co-occurring bipolar and SUDs can provide support and education Crystal needs to get her substance use and mood symptoms under control. Integrated Group Therapy (IGT), has helped individuals with bipolar manage substance use and mood symptoms (Weiss, 2000). IGT applies CBT methods to manage bipolar symptoms without using substances. Relapse prevention techniques focus on monitoring the previous week's substance use, mood swings, medication adherence, and high-risk situations and draw connections between bipolar disorders and substance use.

Bipolar disorder requires lifelong compliance with medication, healthcare, psychotherapy, and psychosocial interventions to reach stability and maintenance (Zik, 2019). Comorbid substance use, personality, and medical disorders frequently co-occur with bipolar disorder and may complicate the course of bipolar treatment. Given the comorbid nature of bipolar disorder, including various treatment challenges and poor medication and psychosocial treatment compliance, finding therapies that clients trust to provide the care and support they need is exigent.

## ■ FOR YOUR CONSIDERATION

1. Bipolar I disorder is a most common diagnosis in public mental health settings. What assessment instruments would you select to accurately screen, diagnose, and measure treatment outcomes for Crystal?
2. Comorbid medical, mental health, and substance use have greatly affected Crystal's life. What other treatment recommendations would you make for Crystal?
3. Personality disorders are among the commonly missed comorbid diagnoses. How is paranoid personality disorder related to bipolar I disorder?
4. If you concluded that the Crystal was in imminent danger or harming herself or others, what steps would you take next?
5. Research indicates that the best course of treatment for bipolar disorder includes medication, psychosocial treatment, and psychotherapy. Differentiate between psychosocial treatment and psychotherapy for treating bipolar disorder.
6. What transference and countertransference issues might present with Crystal?

## ■ REFERENCES

Substance Abuse and Mental Health Services Administration. (2016). An introduction to bipolar disorder and co-occurring substance use disorders. *Advisory, 15*(2). Substance Abuse and Mental Health Services Administration.

Weiss, R. D., Griffin, M. L., Greenfield, S. F., Najavits, L. M., Wyner, D., Soto, J. A., & Hennen, J. A. (2000). Group therapy for patients with bipolar disorder and substance dependence: Results of a pilot study. *Journal of Clinical Psychiatry, 61*(5), 361–367. https://doi.org/10.4088/jcp.v61n0507

Zik, J. (2019). Updated review on the integrated treatment of co-occurring disorders. *Addiction and Clinical Research, 3*(1), 1–9.

# 3.2    *Case of Andrew*

## ■ INTRODUCTION

Andrew presented as a 46-year-old Caucasian, self-identified gay male who was referred to counseling by his psychiatrist as an augment to medication treatment for bipolar disorder. Andrew reported having chronic relationship difficulties with his spouse of 25 years which were now culminating in divorce. Generally, when working with clients, there are two predominant questions I "wonder out loud" with them regarding their initiation of therapy: "Why counseling?" and "Why now?"

*Why now.* During the initial intake interview, Andrew reported that he had engaged in a short-lived sexual relationship with a man in his church congregation which led to church discipline (he identified his religious and spiritual tradition as Latter-Day Saint [LDS]) and for him, a significant deep and persistent self-loathing manifesting in periods of intense anger and resentment toward his extended family (including his in-laws) along with bouts of depression and suicidal ideation. The week prior to Andrew's contact with me for therapy, a church disciplinary committee (i.e., "church court") was convened which resulted in his excommunication from the church. He noted that his wife, to that point, had "put up with me for years but I really see that our marriage is over and honestly, it feels like a relief." He described his wife as compassionate, "longsuffering, patient to a fault," and devoutly Mormon, but she was now "at a point where she doesn't want to deal with me anymore." Regarding his motivation for therapy, he reported that his psychiatrist had urged him for years to talk to someone about his problems, but it wasn't until the excommunication that he determined to seek help from a therapist.

Andrew reported that he met Barry, a man who, a few years earlier, had moved with his family into the ward (a congregation of church members that is based on geographical boundaries). Andrew reported feeling of an immediate and intense attraction to Barry that resulted in a series of clandestine sexual encounters and what he saw as a deep mutual connection. "We really fell in love with each other which I know sounds crazy, but I've never felt anything this strong towards anyone in my life … I really miss him!" The affair was eventually discovered and apparently Barry was also subjected to church discipline which involved the church leadership requiring him to renounce his relationship with Andrew or risk losing his church membership, which resulted in Barry's refusal to have any further contact with Andrew. "I know that somehow he still loves me, but he had to choose his family over me …," and tearfully, "I don't think I can live without him." Andrew identified a history of a number of sexual encounters with men he met at nightclubs that were brief and which resulted in a predictable pattern of swearing off his "perverted" ways, seeking absolution from his wife and confessing his "sins" to the bishop (his direct church leader who oversees the ward) who tried working with him to blunt the effects of his "homosexual tendencies." Andrew reported also discussing with his wife the possibility of engaging in treatment for his same-sex attraction as a condition that she not leave him and end the marriage, but that his commitment to follow through "felt empty because I guess I always knew who and what I was deep down."

*Why counseling.* Andrew reported his recognition that he needed to "stop running" and finally "deal with my life" but also expressed hopelessness about his ability to change. He intended to utilize his Employee Assistance Program (EAP) benefits from his employer for his treatment. At the time of his first intake, he currently worked as a lead groundskeeper for a country club where he had been employed the past 7 years. Prior to that, he worked as a home health administrator but was eventually terminated for allegations of sexual harassment by two female subordinates; he reported that there was no evidence to support their claims, but he was terminated, nonetheless. His brother-in-law who was a land developer used his connections with the country club to get Andrew the job, and "he has held this over my head ever since." He described never feeling supported by his extended family and his in-laws. Andrew reported that 2 weeks prior he was manic which was characterized by restlessness, going for 3 days without sleep, increased anxiety, and anger which culminated in his creating a scene at work where he sandblasted three of the five maintenance carts in order to paint them deep purple because of his need to "refresh the image" of the maintenance staff and groundskeepers. This random activity extended to his calling each of his five staff members at 3:00 a.m. and demanding that they come into work in order to get the carts repainted by the next morning. Two of the staff members called Andrew's supervisor which led to an internal investigation of the matter resulting in Andrew being suspended for a week without pay. Andrew shared his fear of potentially losing his job and not having the support of his brother-in-law in maintaining employment.

During this point in the session, Andrew was tearful, agitated, and clearly in distress. He confessed feeling suicidal and even though he felt his wife was justified in filing for divorce, he knew that his life was "going down the toilet, and it's all my fault." He identified his sister who lived close by who he knew was ultimately supportive of him even though he believed that he had burned some bridges because she had loaned him a sum of money a few years earlier that he had not paid back. I carefully assessed the threat of suicide using the *Columbia-Suicide Severity Rating Scale (C-SSRS)* protocol (see: cssrs.columbia.edu/the-columbia-scale-c-ssrs/about-the-scale/) and determined with Andrew that he was intact enough not to be admitted to an inpatient setting in order to keep him safe with himself. He shared that during his last manic episode, he had taken his wife's Xanax and used cannabis for several days but with no intent on killing or hurting himself. He denied having or using any other available means with which to commit suicide (e.g., a gun, bullets, other drugs in which to overdose, the intent to use his car for asphyxiation or to run into oncoming traffic, etc.) and noted that though he felt hopeless, he knew that for the sake of his children, he needed to get help. I also assessed for any homicidal ideation which Andrew denied. I provided a few useful concepts related to his present experience of his distress and my experience of working with individuals with bipolar disorder as follows:

- "Andrew, you are enduring multiple losses (including anticipated losses in the form of a divorce and possible estrangement of your children) in your life, so framing your situation as grieving these losses is important and potentially helpful";
- "You understand and have been living with this condition of bipolar depression for the better part of your life and the manifestation of your symptoms may have similarities with others' symptoms, but this is also unique to you in your lived experience, including who you are as a sexual, religious, and spiritual being and how you manifest the love and passion that is inherent in who you are. An important part of treatment is getting honest about your mental and emotional condition and recognizing not only the symptoms of mania and depression, but also the risk factors that make you most vulnerable to your depression and the signs leading up to manic or depressive episodes in your life. I am here to help you manage your condition perhaps in ways you have not been able to before and that may be more effective for you";
- And "It is important that you continue to be honest about any suicide ideation you might experience. Your children and family need you to remain alive in order to give yourself time and space in which to address aspects of living that you have either neglected or avoided over the course of your life. I am here to assist you in facing the difficult parts of yourself including your behavior and beliefs about who you are in the world the drive what you do. I hope that you give yourself a chance to really do some important therapeutic work."

Andrew appeared to take comfort in discussing this orientation to his treatment. I reviewed my summative understanding of his manic and depressive patterns which he validated as accurate. This included a review of his history of bipolar disorder where, when manic, he experienced grandiose and expansive thinking, distractibility, lack of sleep, increased and intense goal-directed activity, and hypersexuality (American Psychiatric Association [APA], 2013, pp. 124–125). During those periods (which lasted a minimum of a week, thus pointing to a clear diagnosis of bipolar I disorder) he ignored any expressed concerns about his behavior from his wife and family and was unmotivated to change. During his depressive states, he would become hopeless, despondent, and long to die. Andrew shared that he made a suicidal gesture when he was 20 but it was mostly out of desperation and not lethal. Profound guilt and shame were predominant features of his depressive states and he believed that he had let down God and his family and was "beyond Christ's redemption."

Finally, at the end of our initial intake session, I encouraged him to remain connected to and compliant with the treatment he was receiving from his psychiatrist, especially being medication complaint. Andrew acknowledged that he had a history of being noncompliant with his medication, particularly during manic states. He confessed that one of the most frightening parts of his cycles was when he felt himself moving from mania to depression. He didn't see himself as drug addicted (Mormon doctrine includes a strict prohibition in the use of coffee, tea, alcohol, and illicit drugs; this law is called the Word of Wisdom), but would use substances during his manic phase as a way to attempt to sustain the mania. I also suggested a treatment regimen that would go well beyond his EAP approved sessions, and we discussed the frequency of our weekly work together. The ultimate goal in this initial and tentative treatment plan was to help him stabilize his manic and depressive cycles, engage in grief work regarding the losses in his life, and begin becoming much more aware of his personal risk factors. My assessment was that Andrew left the session feeling some hope in himself which was gratifying as I prepared to work with him.

## ■ FAMILY HISTORY

During subsequent sessions, Andrew shared some relevant and specific details that added rich and relevant context to his life situation. Andrew had been raised LDS in a home where his father was dominating and often violent and his mother was passive and obedient to his father's directives. Andrew was the second of four children (an older brother, a younger brother, and a youngest sister) and the family was active and engaged in church activities which included Sunday worship, religious education, youth activities and worship, and leadership responsibilities (he shared that he was the Deacon's Quorum President when he was 12 years old where he presided over a group of 12-year-old peers as part of his church youth program). These youth activities culminated in Andrew serving as a missionary for 2 years when he was 19 years old (he served his mission in Peru). Shortly after his mission, he met and married his high school sweetheart, Denise and they raised a family of six children (an oldest son Craig, then a daughter, Melanie, another daughter, Abigail, then a son, Dexter, and twin girls, Bethany and Sylvia) the span between the oldest and twins was 9 years. Both Andrew's and Denise's families were very close and attended the same ward together, so they were excited to see them united in marriage (they were married in the LDS temple in which marriage is solemnized by God; Mormons believe that through God's priesthood, marriage and families are sealed to one another for eternity and not "til death do you part").

During his mission, Andrew had his first clandestine sexual experience with one of his missionary companions (missionaries are presided over by a Mission President who assigns same-sex companions throughout their service to support and keep track of one another), which was against mission policy and church commandments. He and his companion both kept their multiple sexual encounters a secret. It was during this time that Andrew's depression began to manifest. After several months together, he and his companion were both reassigned to different companions and Andrew went into a deep depression and became unable to function. He was administered several priesthood blessings (hands are laid on a person's head and they are prayed over by male holders of the priesthood), but he was never "healed" and Andrew expressed the belief that his faith was not strong enough and that God was punishing him because of his sexual sin. This belief became entrenched and manifested through a significant manic episode where he had a vision of God directing him to pay penance for his sins. He confessed his sins to a dozen other missionaries during a missionary training meeting and later that night Andrew heated up his "CTR" ring (which stands for the Mormon mantra, "choose the right") on the stove to red hot and seared these initials on the side of his erect penis. He went outside his residence and laid face down in the grass until his companion called for assistance to rescue him and with the help of local church members, transported him to a local clinic in the village where they were serving in order to prevent him from bleeding to death. A few weeks later Andrew was flown back to his home in the United States to be treated by a plastic surgeon to reconstruct the damage to his penis. Andrew reported his perfect recollection of how he was led by God to perform this act of self-mutilation as a sign of his devotion and resolution to live strictly God's commandments. After his recovery, he was not permitted to finish his mission and was honorably released from his service because of mental health concerns. He again suffered significant depression where he experienced intrusive thoughts of suicide and attempted to take his own life through a drug overdose of his mother's prescription medication. He was placed in an inpatient psychiatric facility for observation and treatment and follow up outpatient therapy which he did not follow up. He did agree to take his medication and was prescribed Risperdal and Seroquel for his mania and Prozac for his depression. Andrew shared that he is often inconsistent with his medication compliance which results in increased vulnerability to episodes of mania and depression. He noted that a significant side effect of his medication is weight gain and that he feels dull and dead inside, so this disincentivizes him in remaining complaint with taking his medication.

Andrew reported his belief that he married Denise to do God's will even though he had little confidence that he would be sexually faithful to her. A persistent and significant theme throughout his life is feeling deep shame and a sense of being "never enough" and "a flawed human being." He had frequently visited with his Bishop for guidance and regular confessions for having fantasies of sexual encounters with men and during his marriage he has engaged in several sexual liaisons with men while experiencing mania. He described himself coming to life and feeling loved in ways that he had never before experienced. His mood lability is paralleled by feeling energized and fulfilled when connected with a man and feeling deep guilt and shame afterwards. During those incidents, Andrew seemed to default to outing himself to his Bishop who provided spiritual support and periodic financial and food support for the family when Andrew was struggling to pay his bills in the transition from work situations. Along with the feeling that he had disappointed God, he felt guilty for "not being the kind of man Denise deserves." According to his report, Denise had been a faithful and devoted wife until recently. A few months prior to Andrew's excommunication, their daughter Abigail was called to serve a mission of her own and his excommunication seemed to cast a pall on this event. Andrew expressed a deep fear of disappointing his children and losing his relationships with them despite Denise's assurance that he "will always be their father."

Andrew felt chronic estrangement from his family and faced the prospect of losing his relationships with Denise's family. "I have disappointed them so much that no one trusts me or believes I will be anything other than what I am." As previously noted, his brother-in-law had been supportive, but Andrew believed it was mostly out of obligation to help support his sister through a difficult and inconstant marriage. After the birth of the twins, Andrew and Denise ostensibly ceased their sexual relationship and Denise remained celibate while Andrew enjoyed periodic encounters with men. Andrew stated that Denise had known about these encounters but had been protective of him and her family and had not shared her knowledge of his affairs with her family or friends. Andrew reported that "I almost wish she would tell her family so that I can stop hiding who I am from the world." After Andrew's affair with Barry, Denise felt free to tell her family about Andrew's history of infidelity which created outrage with many members of the family. Andrew currently felt alienated from his family but also felt a strong connection with a few of his children.

## ▨ DIAGNOSTIC IMPRESSIONS

Andrew's symptom profile related to his manic and depressive episodes are consistent with the diagnosis of bipolar I disorder which was his diagnosis at the time of his hospitalization when he was 20 years old. Over the course of his life the symptoms have remained unchanged, but the context in which they occurred changed drastically. His family have not known what to do with and for him, so he has largely been left alone and treated with benign neglect. This response from his friends and family deepened his sense of isolation and alienation from those whom he sought connection. His hypersexuality is the most significant manifestation of his mania and it was clear that he connected with men because this was fundamentally who he was and how he was oriented, and it appeared to be the only way he could manifest his love and feel any sort of physical validation of his humanity. When I shared this diagnostic impression with Andrew, he resonated strongly with his need for connection. When sexually connected he felt alive and validated followed by deep self-loathing and guilt which appeared to precipitate his depressive episodes. There had also been periods of transient psychosis and delusional thinking that was largely associated with his mania and to which he was highly susceptible. His psychosis and delusional thinking were consistently centered around religious themes and periods of self-aggrandizement; it was clear to me that he needed to feel powerful in a life where he largely felt powerless.

His sexual orientation was complex, and he felt stymied and discouraged in fully embracing his own sexuality; he felt torn and condemned being who he was. As was noted, his affair with Barry felt like his best hope for being happy and his fantasy was centered around living with him after they both left their respective spouses. I was quickly aware that there were strong dynamics at play, largely centered around the intersectionality of the various cultural roles that Andrew occupied as a White, gay, Mormon male. His religious community expressed little tolerance for what was considered deviant behavior and against God's commandments and he was reinforced in seeing himself as sinful. Given these circumstances, Andrew never actively cut himself off from his church family, but passively defaulted to acting out in ways that eventually would result in his excommunication which he saw as both painful and liberating. He eventually began to see that he could finally be who he was and perhaps learn to live as a gay man while hoping to feel some modicum of happiness in his life.

## ▨ DIAGNOSTIC CONCLUSIONS

Based on his treatment history and my initial and follow-up assessment, Andrew's *Diagnostic and Statistical Manual of Mental Disorders, Fifth Edition* (*DSM-5*) diagnosis was assigned as follows:

- Bipolar 1 disorder, most recent episode manic with mood-congruent psychotic features, moderate

I determined to accentuate the specifier "manic with mood-congruent psychotic features" because while there was also "anxious distress" in Andrew's presentation, I thought it was important to call out the psychotic features to reinforce the need for targeted treatment both from a medication and a psychotherapeutic stand-point. Predominant symptoms also included a decreased need for sleep, racing thoughts, goal-directed activity, some measure of grandiosity, and hypersexuality. There was also a clear pattern of depression where the prominent symptoms were excessive sleep, vegetative symptoms, hopelessness, excessive guilt, and suicidal ideation. Even in the midst of his depression, Andrew seemed to demonstrate resilience in his ability to persist through the depression and to seek for help even though much of the help he was seeking was not psychotherapeutic in nature. His outreach to his family was also apparently reciprocated by a few of them which demonstrated to me that his support system had not totally abandoned him. My greatest concern was around his propensity toward suicidality and the current circumstances related to his pending divorce and being alone to fend for himself in life. We discussed strategies of connecting with others and receiving support whenever he felt overwhelmed.

## SUGGESTED THERAPEUTIC INTERVENTIONS

Andrew and I worked together for a little over 8 months. During that time, it was important to ensure that Andrew was empowered to ask for what he needed in his own treatment and not remain passive, even in times where life felt overwhelming for him. We planned his treatment together and I remained as a consultant and content expert in helping him contextualize his symptoms. It was important that I check in with him regularly to assess his perceptions about how therapy was proceeding, including how he say himself changing over the course of our work together. I was very interested in helping him identify the specific features of his manic and depressive states that were both common in many who struggle with the disorder, and those features that were unique to him. Our historical review of his symptomology was largely focused on helping him recognize his symptom patterns and being sensitive to the meaning he was making about his experience. I also wanted to strengthen his awareness regarding recognizing when symptoms would emerge and taking necessary precautions to protect himself as much as possible. In my approach, I was guided by the wise conclusions by Havens and Ghaemi (2005) who noted the corrective therapeutic effect this type of approach has on clients experiencing bipolar symptoms:

> The job of the clinician is twofold initially: first, to seek to existentially be with manic patients and then, to counterprojectively give perspective to those patients about their manic worldview, without completely denying it. This twofold approach then can lead to a healthy therapeutic alliance, which itself has a mood-stabilizing effect. Along with mood-stabilizing medications, this alliance can then lead patients toward full recovery. (p. 146)

It played out that our therapeutic encounters were indeed "mood-stabilizing" and therapy became a safe place where he was able to grieve the losses he was experiencing and had experienced.

I wanted to help Andrew get to know manifestations of his mania and depression not as states to be feared, but as teachers in helping him learn about himself and to expand and enlarge his self-compassion and thus, his compassion for others. This reframe was ultimately helpful in empowering Andrew to see himself much more in control of his condition. I saw Andrew's compassion toward others as a resilience factor; he had a heart to connect and support others in spite of everything he was dealing with, so it was important to help him move into a more intentional self-acceptance which was not easy. Conceptually, Andrew felt good about this way of looking at his disorder, but in practice it was often very difficult as he felt overwhelmed by these manic and depressive states when they would manifest (during our time together, Andrew experienced a manic episode along with a deep depression; to his credit, he persisted in keeping his appointments with me). I introduced Andrew to the practice of mindfulness and helped him learn the role of the "observer" whose job was to simply observe whatever was arising and retreating from the field of awareness without judgment or value, but simply seeing it as it was. I helped him get in touch with his reactivity and his propensity to condemn himself and helped him practice loving-kindness in moments where his judgment was automatic and harsh. We used the metaphor of being swept up in a large wave and instead of fighting for air, I encouraged him to allow himself to be tossed about by the wave (metaphorically) until the power would die down and he could float to the top for his much needed breath of air. This image was something that Andrew really took to and grasped as a way of looking at his mania and depression which helped him manage these difficult episodes. I engaged him in seeing when "the mania is talking" or "when the depression is talking" so that he could differentiate between his bipolar condition and the periods of his life where he was not manic or depressed. I was also active in helping challenge Andrew's thoughts about himself and his situation, all of which were a manifestation of my role as a reality-tester about how he was seeing himself within the frame of his illness. There was a mantra I continued to revisit with him which was, "You are not your mania … you are not your depression … you are not your bipolar disorder" and "You suffer from the effects of your depression, but you are much more than your bipolar disorder." This mantra also seemed to ground him in a productive way of seeing his condition and his responses. Regarding Andrew's suicidal ideation, it was important for me to keep connected to his intention and not become panicked when he expressed feelings of suicide. Sometimes when clients become suicidal, they are treated by others (including therapists) as things to be managed and not people to be related to and understood, so I was intentional in remaining relational with him regarding his occasional suicidality. This supportive stance was also a curative factor in helping himself see his suicidality as an expected part of his bipolar symptoms and not something to be feared. During our work together it became clear that Andrew had exceptional insight into his condition and needed the kind of support that would help stimulate his personal resilience.

Typically, when working with those suffering from bipolar disorder, I like to involve family and other social supports being guided by family-focused treatment (Miklowitz, 2007, 2008) which posits that educating family members and friends about this disease helps them become realistic about the course of the disorder, treatment, and how to best be helpful in working with their impacted loved ones. Identifying the concept of "family" is very important because often "family" includes nonbiologically related individuals that can lend support (Buckley & Scott, 2017). Often family members have unrealistic expectations about bipolar disorder, the course of treatment and ultimately how it can be cured. They feel chronically helpless in how to support the bipolar client (this was certainly the case for Andrew) which can move them into a place of frustration and criticism which often projects their own sense of helplessness in the face of what feels like an overwhelming and never-ending condition (Buckley & Scott, 2017). When these conditions occur, families and other supports can become highly emotionally reactive and critical which is a risk factor for the bipolar person to relapse into a manic or depressive episode, prolong the effects and intensity of the episode, or cause the affected person to isolate and avoid contact with others which only puts them at risk for suicidal ideation (Miklowitz, 2008). In this way and from this perspective, the treatment of bipolar disorder becomes a family intervention which can help alleviate unnecessary suffering on the part of the bipolar-affected person.

It was clear that there was little support for Andrew in his condition even though he was surrounded by numerous concerned and caring others. His family had become accustomed to allowing him to be on his own and had adopted a passive stance to his condition. During our work together, I attempted to connect with Andrew's children, his ex-wife, Denise, and members of his extended family, but at this point in his treatment, they were unwilling to be involved directly in his therapy. This was unfortunate and discouraging as it reinforced the idea for Andrew that he was on his own and had to figure out his own way to live his life with his bipolar disorder. Fortunately, Andrew was able to make inroads and ultimately have some meaningful encounters with his children and there was a modicum of acceptance of him as their father even though his "lifestyle" was incongruent with their values. I continued to encourage Andrew to not give up on his family even though he may have felt that they had given up on them.

I also encouraged Andrew to remain medication-compliant and asked him to sign a release for me to consult with his psychiatrist regularly; this was promising as it helped him know that there was a team of professionals in his corner. Finally, it was important in my work with Andrew that I was not only working with him on his "here and now" concerns, but that I was also thinking futuristically about the supports he would need in the future. I helped him understand that in our therapy together, we were doing pieces of work and that he would likely connect with future therapists who would help him continue in the next phase of treatment process. This helped contextualize his work and focus on his present functioning while being reminded that there were those who would be prepared to help him in the future. During our work together, Andrew was courageous in working toward grieving without constantly defaulting to guilt and shame. He seemed to reconcile himself to begin embracing and accepting his sexuality and life as a gay man. I put him in touch with national and local organizations focused on LGBTQ issues and advocacy and challenged him to contemplate creating for himself a circumstance that would be consistent with his desire to love freely and fully. This was difficult because his connection to the church and his history as a Mormon was always looming. There was much he was trying to say good-bye to as he was learning to embrace his new life. I was ultimately grateful to have him teach me about how to work closely and courageously with a person with his unique manifestation of bipolar disorder and help him see himself as a resilient and courageous person.

## ▨ FOR YOUR CONSIDERATION

1. In this case the counselor focuses on the religious culture of the client and makes connections to the concept of intersectionality. What other aspects of this client's culture could have been further explored? How would you approach expanding this concept of culture to aid in the client's treatment?

2. What other potential diagnoses could this client have been assigned? Where might there be limitations in assessing client symptoms and what would you specifically assess?

3. In this case the counselor is focused on helping the client see his bipolar disorder differently. What are the advantages and disadvantages to this approach? What additional treatment options might you initiate that would be more effective in supporting this client?

4. The counselor noted that he would have liked to involve the client's family in the treatment. What are the ethical implications of such an approach and how would you ensure that you are maintaining ethical standards when involving the family and other social supports?

5. What are the benefits and limitations inherent in how the counselor was assessing and treating this client's suicidal ideation? How might you approach addressing the client's suicidal ideation that may be similar or different?

## ■ REFERENCES

American Psychiatric Association. (2013). *Diagnostic and statistical manual of mental disorders* (5th ed.).

Columbia Lighthouse Project. https://cssrs.columbia.edu/

Buckley, M. R., & Scott, S. K. (2017). Relational functioning: Understanding bi-polar and related disorders. In J. Russo, K. Coker, & J. H. King (Eds.), *DSM- 5 and Family Systems: An Applied Approach* (pp. 55–83). Springer Publishing Company.

Havens, L. L., & Ghaemi, N. (2005). Existential despair and bipolar disorder: The therapeutic alliance as a mood stabilizer. *American Journal of Psychotherapy*, 59(2), 137–147.

Miklowitz, D. J. (2007). The role of the family in the course and treatment of bipolar disorder. *Current Directions in Psychological Science*, 16(4), 192–196.

Miklowitz, D. J. (2008). *Bipolar disorder: A family-focused treatment approach.* Guilford.

# 3.3   *Case of Michelle*

## ■ INTRODUCTION

Michelle is a 19-year-old Caucasian female who is currently in her sophomore year at a local college. Michelle has come to counseling because she "freaked out this weekend" during a blow-out fight with her boyfriend. Michelle caught him texting another woman and lost her temper. She reports that the ensuing argument quickly escalated into a physical altercation with Michelle as the aggressor. She reluctantly admits that she attacked her boyfriend and even threw a lamp at his head. He did not strike back, though he did hold her down in an effort to stop the attack. Michelle states that this made her even more angry, and she headbutted him, lacerating her own head, and becoming dizzy. Her boyfriend left at that point and she has not seen him since. Michelle begins to cry softly as she shares this information, adding "I don't even know what came over me … I felt like it wasn't even me." Since the altercation with her boyfriend, Michelle has barely slept and feels agitated most of the time. She cannot focus on her schoolwork, has barely slept, and feels a "jittery anxiety" most of the time. In fact, upon reflection, Michelle shares that she has not been sleeping well for several weeks, usually getting just a few hours a night. She's been very distracted as well, though she explains that away as "I've always had a little ADHD."

In talking with Michelle and reviewing her intake paperwork, the counselor notes that Michelle is very fidgety, shaking a foot, or wringing her hands almost constantly during the session. The counselor verbalizes this observation, but Michelle minimizes it by responding "I'm just a little nervous, I guess." When asked what she wants out of her counseling, Michelle responds that she wants to get control of her anger and never lash out like she did at her boyfriend, and that she wants to "get some kind of control over (her) brain." She adds that though she is a high-energy person and gets a lot done, sometimes her energy is "difficult to turn off."

## ▧ FAMILY HISTORY

Michelle's parents divorced when she was 6 years old. Michelle remembers little of the time when her family was together other than the constant fights between her parents. Michelle describes her father as a "kind, patient man" who wasn't perfect but who "put up with a lot of mom's crazy." Michelle shares that her mother has a good heart, but that she's "always been more than a little off." Michelle describes several memories of her mother seeming to fly into a blind rage with minimal provocation, often calming down quickly as if nothing had happened. Other times she would break into gut-wrenching sobs and lie on the floor for hours after an "episode" of lashing out, throwing objects, or screaming at Michelle or her brother. Despite these difficult memories, Michelle also insists that her mother is a vibrant, charismatic woman who draws people to her. Michelle insists that her mother has always taken good care of Michelle and Doug, making sure the house was always clean and the children's bellies always full. Her mother also worked full-time and volunteered at a local animal shelter. Michelle recognizes this was a lot for her mother to have on her plate while being a single parent, but explains "my mom never needed much sleep. Sometimes I'd wake up in the morning and find her working on some project she'd been up all night doing." Michelle also recalls times when her mother would spend all day lying in bed watching television or sometimes sleeping through an entire day. Her mother called those times "the dark place" and told the children that sometimes she just needed to be alone. Michelle's mother always made sure the children were OK during these times, though she interacted with them only minimally.

Michelle herself has some history of "the dark place" in her life as well, though only remembers a handful of times when she felt the need to isolate, avoided interacting with people, or slept excessively. Michelle can remember a few instances that stand out, including one earlier this school year when she just could not get out of bed. She shares that she had felt severely depressed and lethargic, and did not leave her dorm room for almost a week. She stopped eating regularly during this time as well, which prompted her roommate to intervene and "get (her) ass back into gear." She chuckles a bit at this, noting that if it were not for her roommate she might have "done something stupid." Michelle recalls feeling this way a handful of times over the past 5 years or so, but never thought much about it. She states that these periods always seemed to pass and she assumes the behavior comes from her mother.

Michelle's father is remarried and lives with his wife and two daughters from his second marriage. Michelle does not see her father as often as she used to, but states that she talks to him on the phone fairly regularly. When Michelle and her brother were younger, they spent every other weekend, many holidays, and half of their summer school breaks with their father and his wife; their father remarried soon after getting divorced from Michelle's mother. Michelle's describes her stepmother and half-siblings in a positive, warm manner; however, she notes that her love for them has been a problem for her mother over the years. Michelle states that her mother would often interrogate the children when they returned home from their father's, causing stress and arguments between them. Michelle and her brother stopped going to their father's regularly by late adolescence; currently they see him whenever they have a chance and do their best to avoid talking about their father at all when around their mother.

Michelle is the younger of two children; her brother—Doug—is 21 years old and currently living with their mother following his recent completion of an addiction recovery program. Doug had gone to college at age 18, but had dropped out before the end of his freshman year. He'd previously had some issues with drugs and alcohol; however, once he was in college, Doug's substance use blossomed into a significant abuse disorder. He was unable to maintain his grades and was on academic probation by his second semester. Midway through spring term, Doug got into a fight with his roommate and put the roommate in the hospital with several broken ribs. Doug was arrested and though charges were ultimately dropped, he was dismissed from the school. Doug moved back in with is mother and fell into a deep depression, rarely leaving the house for several months. Michelle states that her brother never really recovered from "failing" the way he did and has struggled with substance abuse ever since, which has been quite a burden on their mother.

Michelle shares that her mother was diagnosed with bipolar disorder around the time of her parents' divorce, which she only knows because her father shared this with her earlier this year when she was in "the dark place." He expressed concern that she might need some assistance, and encouraged her to see someone. Michelle assured him at the time that she would, but later decided not to as she thought she could control it. Plus, as she notes again, the "episodes" always pass and she feels great afterwards. Michelle adds that she does not want to take any medications and doesn't want to "become a zombie."

## ■ CURRENT FUNCTIONING

Michelle is in good health with no preexisting medical conditions. She maintains a 3.6 grade point average (GPA) currently and is involved in several activities on campus. She works part-time to help pay for school, with the rest of her expenses being covered by loans and help from her parents. She rarely misses a class or a shift at her job, except when she's in "the dark place." Michelle admits that she does tend to drink a lot of caffeine and will sometimes smoke cigarettes "just for a pick-me-up" when she's studying late or feeling tired. Michelle also admits to using alcohol—sometimes a few drinks at campus parties, other times a few drinks to help her sleep. Michelle notes that sometimes she "can't quiet (her) mind" enough to sleep and alcohol seems to help with that. Michelle also states that the "anxious, jittery feeling" she has sometimes also makes it difficult to sleep, though when that happens she prefers to smoke a little marijuana "just to take the edge off." When pressed, she admits that this happens at least a few times a week, though she does not believe she has a SUD.

## ■ DIAGNOSTIC IMPRESSIONS

Michelle is exhibiting several criteria that would support a diagnosis of bipolar I disorder. Currently, she is in a manic state, as evidenced by the decreased need for sleep, racing thoughts, lack of focus, and psychomotor agitation. The loss of control during the fight with her boyfriend and brief feeling of dissociation is also typical of a manic episode. While some individuals feel only happiness and experience inflated self-esteem during mania, others feel a significant intensification of *all* emotions—positive and negative. In Michelle's case, this manifested as severe affective dysregulation with mild dissociation. Her anger at her boyfriend was magnified to the point where it became so hard to control that she could no longer fully feel it—or feel herself.

Another feature Michelle is showing is a self-reported anxious or jittery feeling. While anxiety is not a criteria of bipolar disorder per se, clients will often use these words to describe the internal feelings concurrent with psychomotor agitation. Michelle's constant movements support this observation. In addition, Michelle notes that she has "always been high energy" and finds it difficult at times to slow down. Further exploration into this piece is warranted, as is a more thorough history of when these symptoms began and how frequently she has experienced them.

Also, it is important to note the family history of bipolar disorder. Michelle's mother was diagnosed with bipolar disorder in the past, though did not accept treatment. Michelle's brother has been diagnosed with at least one SUD; there may be a concurrent bipolar diagnosis there as well. Bipolar disorder has a strong genetic component and is significant in this case.

Based on Michelle's limited experiences with "the dark place"—otherwise known as the depressive episodes of bipolar disorder—it is possible that she either has atypical cycling (as evidenced by long periods between depressive episodes), or that she has less severe depressive episodes. Michelle may actually be having more frequent depressive episodes than she realizes, but because they are less severe, they are not standing out for her. One of the challenges to accurately identifying bipolar disorder in young adults is that biological development is still proceeding at a fairly rapid rate, and there are often many life changes happening at once. The client's reactions to these biological and environmental influences can muddy the diagnostic waters, making it difficult to conclusively diagnose bipolar disorder, as well as rule out other mood or anxiety disorders. With that in mind, it would be important in this case to make a provisional diagnosis, pending continued monitoring and observation.

There is also some indication that Michelle may have a SUD. While initially she minimized her use, it seemed apparent after additional questions that she may be using more regularly than she first indicated. Further, the bipolar diagnosis and family history of substance abuse puts her at a higher risk for a SUD herself; this needs further investigation. It is very possible that Michelle's regular substance use is buffering some of the lability associated with bipolar disorder, making a clear diagnosis even more challenging.

## ■ DIAGNOSTIC CONCLUSIONS

- Bipolar I disorder
- Rule-out: SUD

## ■ SUGGESTED THERAPEUTIC INTERVENTIONS

Short-term interventions: Because bipolar disorder needs to be observed over time for a conclusive diagnosis, it is recommended that Michelle keep a mood log for at least a few weeks. Not only would this help the clinician track fluctuations and dysregulation, but would also help Michelle become more consciously aware of her emotional lability. Another intervention to help Michelle's self-awareness would be a grounding exercise. The mindfulness associated with these exercises can be important steppingstones in Michelle's increased self-regulation.

CBT: CBT is a common therapy used in the individual treatment of bipolar disorder. Treatment goals in Michelle's case include improving her understanding of herself and releasing some of the negative patterns of thoughts and behaviors. CBT is well-suited for these goals. Further, CBT blends well with a variety of family systems approaches should the opportunity arise to include Michelle's family in the treatment.

Family-focused therapy (FFT): If there is an option to include the family system in treatment, FFT would be an excellent choice. FFT has the primary goal of understanding the impact of the disorder on the family system, including its dynamics and relationships. There is a strong psychoeducational piece, which would be helpful here as well. Michelle, her mother, and her brother could all benefit from better understanding themselves and how their struggles affect each other.

Medical referral: Michelle's diagnosis of bipolar disorder is provisional at this time, but it does seem very likely. As such, it is important to note that while sometimes mild bipolar disorder can be effectively treated without medication, moderate or severe bipolar cannot. Bipolar disorder is directly tied to chemical shifts in the brain, and more times than not requires mood-stabilizing medication for effective treatment. Michelle should be referred to a psychiatrist who specializes in young adults for a full evaluation and to discuss the possibility of medication. Though Michelle has expressed a desire not to go down this route, it is important for her to have a medical assessment and to make an informed decision about her mental healthcare.

## FOR YOUR CONSIDERATION

1. How can the clinician distinguish between mood swings and bipolar disorder?
2. How might Michelle's childhood experiences with her mother influence her beliefs about her diagnosis and treatment?
3. Why is Michelle at a high risk for SUDs?
4. How could a clinician address Michelle's resistance to medication in a way that does not jeopardize the therapeutic alliance?

CHAPTER FOUR

# DEPRESSIVE DISORDERS

*Depressive disorders are characterized by sadness severe enough or persistent enough to interfere with function and often by decreased interest or pleasure in activities. This chapter contains three cases of depressive disorders in adults, including major depressive disorder and dysthymia. These cases illuminate how depression manifests in different people with different backgrounds, including a young Caucasian woman, young biracial man, and a middle-aged woman. While the clients in these cases have symptoms that lead to a DSM-5* (Diagnostic and Statistical Manual of Mental Disorders, Fifth Edition) *diagnosis in the same category, the cases highlight how medical concerns may complicate symptoms, as well as family of origins issues that may exacerbate symptoms. Questions for consideration are also included.*

# 4.1    *Case of Pat*

## ▓ INTRODUCTION

Pat initially called to schedule an appointment because the counselor she had been working with had recently moved out of state and Pat wanted to continue with counseling. On her intake paperwork, Pat presented herself as a 26-year-old heterosexual married White woman with no children who lived with her husband of 4 years in a house with a mortgage. Pat included that she and her husband were both employed full-time and identified with the middle socio-economic class. Pat listed spiritual and religious influences during her childhood and adolescent years which included Protestant Christianity, Wiccan, and Buddhism although she and her husband currently identify with being agnostic and nonreligious. Pat reported that she did not have any developmental or acquired disabilities.

During the initial session, Pat presented the challenges that she has experienced throughout her life. Pat stated that she often feels sad, worried, and overwhelmed in her work and personal life, and has felt this way since she was young. Pat stated that she is overweight and that one of the things that she wanted to address in counseling was to develop a different relationship with food and exercise. In the past, Pat had attempted to get involved with exercise routines such as jogging and aerobics but the exercise routines would not last longer than several weeks and then she would experience guilt, shame, and self-loathing for not being able to stick with an exercise program. Pat also related that she has an overall poor diet and several times a month significantly overeats sugary foods which increases her weight as well as exacerbates her irritable bowel syndrome (IBS) symptoms. Pat stated that the IBS symptoms makes it more difficult for her to go to work, exercise, or do housework. Pat stated that she hates overeating but she feels powerless when she starts feeling sad and overwhelmed, and then she ends up "stuck" on her couch eating "bad" foods, suffering from IBS, watching movies and cartoons, playing video games, and sleeping. Pat reported that she typically gets 9 to 11 hours of sleep each night and hates that she sleeps so much, especially because she always feels tired and wants to go back to bed. Pat discussed that she has been to many medical professionals to determine the cause of her IBS symptoms as well as her oversleeping and not feeling fully rested, but that no one has been able to tell her how to address these issues or why they are occurring. Pat reported that she is very frustrated because all the medical tests that she has taken have come back "normal" and that she is increasingly worried that her problems are "all up in my head" as well as the increased time and financial strain of the medical appointments and tests.

When asked about her marriage, Pat explained that she loves her husband and that he serves as an anchor for her emotionally. Pat described her husband as having alexithymia, someone who does not express or understand emotions, and who has experienced a strong degree of emotional and physical abuse as a child. Pat stated that she would like to be closer to her husband but he typically spends much of his time at home playing video games or riding on his motorcycle. Pat reported that she and her husband do not often have sex, that she does not have much of a sex drive, and that she believes that her husband also does not have a strong sex drive but it is not something that they talk about. Pat related that recently her husband has expressed that he might have romantic desires for a mutual female friend of theirs and Pat is worried that he will leave her for the other woman.

Pat reported that she had experienced strong depression and suicidality several years ago in college which is when she first started counseling with her previous counselor. Pat stated that her previous counselor worked with her to primarily address adjusting her behaviors such as doing something when she felt depressed like taking a shower, going for a walk, doing a project, cleaning the house, or some other task to "get me out of my current mood." Pat stated that engaging in these tasks has taken her mind off of her sadness and worry somewhat, but that the diversions never last long so she would just try harder to do more tasks which would lead her to feel more overwhelmed and desperate, and typically resulted with her laying on her couch for extended periods of days eating sugary foods and watching TV. Pat stated that she does still has suicidal ideations but they are not currently strong enough that she thinks that she would act upon them.

Pat talked about how her friendships have been strained lately. Pat related that her friends have told her that they often feel like Pat is angry and puts a "happy mask" on top of her anger which is uncomfortable to be around because Pat's anger and sadness express themselves from time to time by either being irritable and/or crying. Pat expressed that she is worried that she is going to lose all her friends and that her current friends do not spend as much time with her anymore. Pat stated that her husband agrees with her friends that it is often uncomfortable to be around Pat because of her inauthenticity of emotions and her latent anger and sadness, and that when she is trying to be happy and smiling it looks strained, forced, and grimacing. Pat expressed that she often does not like spending time with her friends because she does not know how to behave. Pat related that her friends have said they do not like it when Pat is angry or sad, and although they all state that they want her to be happy and they do not like it when she is trying to be happy.

Although Pat holds a bachelor's degree in a scientific field which she reported to enjoy, she stated that she would rather work as an office manager because she really likes the organizational tasks and working with people. When asked about her current job, Pat reported that she enjoys her work but that she often must take days off because of her IBS symptoms and emotions, and that she is concerned that she might lose her job because of her absences at work. Pat stated that she often has difficulty concentrating at work because of her worry about her job, how people might perceive her, the guilt she feels because of the time she takes off of work, and wondering if she is doing an adequate job. Pat reported that she experiences the stress and anxiety from work even when she is at home and that it is hard for her to relax and stop worrying during the evening. Pat reported that she is currently looking for another job that would provide better pay and benefits as well as a more structured environment because her current place of employment is disorganized, and she often gets frustrated that she is expected to do so much. Pat discussed how she feels like she cannot connect with anyone at the office, that she feels guilty because sometimes she expresses frustration toward coworkers, that she often feels like she should know more about her job, and that she hates to be a "bother" and a "drain" to her coworkers and supervisors especially with her frequent absences.

Pat stated that her main goals in counseling were to (a) have a better relationship with food, (b) construct an exercise routine and stick to it, (c) address her moods of sadness, anxiety, guilt, and feeling overwhelmed, and (d) cultivate better sleep patterns.

## ■ FAMILY HISTORY

When asked about her family of origin, Pat described her family as White and middle-class. Pat stated that her parents were both from a Protestant Christian background although neither parent currently identified as Christian or attended church. Pat stated that her father would take her and her brother to a Protestant Christian church several times a year when they were growing up but it was not a regular occurrence, and as she and her brother reached adolescence they stopped going to church altogether. Pat stated that her mother practices Wiccan and taught Pat and her brother about the spirituality of Nature as well as Buddhist philosophy during their childhood and adolescence.

Pat recounted that her mother was often emotionally and physically unavailable to her for several days at a time and would sit alone in her room crying and not wanting to be around anyone. Pat discussed that her younger brother also suffered from depressive episodes and has had suicidal ideations throughout his life. Pat remembers vividly many instances where her father would look at Pat when she was sad as a child and say, "Where's my happy little girl?" Pat stated that she felt like her father needed her to be happy because of the overwhelming family sadness expressed from her mother and brother. Pat related that she would put on a "happy face" for her father and act happy so that he would not feel alone and despairing.

Pat described that she regularly travels 3 hours back to her home 1 to 3 weekends each month to be a "good daughter" and spend time with her mother and father and feels obligated to go there so that they do not feel alone. Pat also reported that she talks with her brother several times a week on the phone so that he will not feel alone and can cope better with his depression feelings and suicidal thoughts.

Pat related that she shares the hobby of doing craftwork with her mother and grandmother, and that they often spend weekends working on crafts together and going to craft fairs. Pat stated that doing crafts and organizing things are some of the most engaging and enjoyable activities that she has in her life. Pat has also expressed that she often feels overwhelmed by the time it takes to travel back and forth to her parents' house, to go to craft fairs, as well as the time it takes to talk with her brother. Pat stated that she feels like she does not have enough time for her husband and friends because of the time that she spends with her family members which causes her to feel guilty because she is not being a "good wife" or a "good friend." Pat also related that she feels overwhelmed because she never has adequate time to clean her own house and that her husband does not help with cleaning or cooking although she has never discussed being upset about this with him.

## ■ CURRENT FUNCTIONING

Pat explained during the initial interview that she currently misses 3 to 5 days of work each month due to her IBS symptoms. Pat described that two or three times a month she binges sugary foods (doughnuts, ice cream, cake, chocolates, cookies, etc.) for several days while living on her couch watching television and playing video games. Pat stated that she feels sad, anxious, and irritable most days and that she cannot think of a recent day where she has felt good physically. Pat's current sleeping patterns are typically 9 to 11 hours of sleep every day and not ever feeling rested or having energy.

Pat stated that she does not use alcohol or other drugs but that she does eat food for emotional comfort. Pat reported that she is not overly concerned financially because her husband makes enough money for them to survive in their current house and situation, but she is concerned that she will lose her job which would be a financial strain and would leave her without any extra spending money to make the trips to see her parents, attend craft fairs, or pay for the medical appointments and tests.

## ■ DIAGNOSTIC IMPRESSIONS

Internal Family Systems (IFS) posits that humans have a normal multiplicity of the mind which is experienced as having several subpersonalities, or parts, in everyone's psyche. A simplistic example would be: part of me really wants to be a healthy weight while another part of me would like to eat a diet that includes copious amounts of ice cream and pizza. IFS also posits that each person has an interconnected seat of consciousness, or Self, which can be successful leader and organizer in a person's psyche, but can also be obscured by a person's subpersonalities especially when traumatic or extreme circumstances have occurred.

Using IFS therapy consists of employing a nonpathologizing wellness model by viewing the internal system of relationships among a client's subpersonalities rather than using the pathologizing medical model of the *DSM-5* (*Diagnostic and Statistical Manual of Mental Disorders, Fifth Edition*) for a diagnosis (Anderson, n.d.; Schwartz & Sweezy, 2020). Even so, helping professionals are commonly required by third-party payers to provide a diagnosis from the *DSM-5* for reimbursement for their services. Keeping this diagnostic dichotomy in mind, we can conceptualize Pat's experience using the two facets of her internal relationships of subpersonalities to inform how the *DSM-5* would categorize her experience.

Pat has a part of her that is the "Happy Girl" of the family that has the strategy to assuage her Dad's perceived hopelessness and loneliness due to her

Mom's and brother's depression and suicidality. This Happy Girl part of Pat has taken on the managerial duties of being the savior or redeemer of the family. The Happy Girl perceives that Pat's expression of happiness needs to be maintained at all costs lest her Dad, herself, and her family be cast into total despair. This extreme position to always be happy to stave off collective hopelessness has carried forward to her current relationships with her family, husband, friends, and coworkers. Pat's "Happy Girl" part, to maintain this guise of happiness, continuously works to exile many of her other parts that contain the seemingly dangerous emotions of sadness, anger, and anxiety.

Sadness is primarily held by a young neglected part of Pat called the "Sad Child," anxiety is held by another young part called the "Anxious Child" which accompanies the Sad Child and helps keep it contained, and anger is held by an adolescent part of Pat simply called "The Adolescent." The emotional strain of the Happy Girl exerting so much energy to contain these exiled subpersonalities has created tension in Pat's physical system which results in the IBS symptoms Pat experiences. In addition, there is another part of Pat, named "The Governess," which seeks to manage Pat's emotions and behaviors in conjunction with the Happy Girl by reminding Pat of the societal and familial expectations which includes eating and exercising behaviors as well as how to look, act, and work around others.

There are also other reactive parts of Pat that mobilize when the Happy Girl and Governess are not able to adequately contain the emotions of the Sad Child and Adolescent. One of these parts, called the Sea Lion, has the strategy of keeping Pat isolated to her couch and reportedly "lays on me and weighs me down so that I cannot get up." While another part, dubbed "The Hippie," has the strategy of feeding the Sad Child sweet foods to quell the sadness and exile the Sad Child's emotions again. As a result, The Governess, the Happy Child, the Hippie, and the Sea Lion are often at odds with their strategies and cognitively argue about how to contain the exiles which causes mental stress, emotional turmoil, physical pain, and immobilization throughout Pat's entire system.

## ■ DIAGNOSTIC CONCLUSIONS

Pat has several parts that have taken on extreme roles in response to her perceived responsibilities in her family of origin. From an IFS perspective, there is a constraint between The Governess' and Happy Child's managerial strategies of coping with her exiles (Sad Child, Anxious Child, and Adolescent) by working harder, doing more, acting properly, expressing happiness, and being available to anyone who might need her, and the reactive strategies of The Hippie and The Sea Lion of isolating, immobilizing, and eating sugary foods to contain the negative emotions. This constraint leads to a cycle of high levels of stress and expectations followed by immobilization, shame, guilt, frustration, anxiety, binge eating, and depression.

Pat's *DSM-5* Diagnoses are:

- Early onset persistent depressive disorder (dysthymia) with anxious distress
- Other specified feeding or eating disorder
- High expressed emotion level within family
- Relationship distress with spouse or intimate partner

## ▓ SUGGESTED THERAPEUTIC INTERVENTIONS

## INTERNAL FAMILY SYSTEMS

IFS has empirical evidence for working with Pat's experience of depression (Haddock et al., 2016), stress (Engert et al., 2017), and eating disorder (Cantanzaro, 2016). Pat presents with several protective parts that are in constraint with each other as well as several exiles that can be healed. Using IFS would entail encouraging Pat's Self to work with her parts to release the constraints of the protectors and heal the exiles. The therapist and Pat's Self would collaborate together to initially work with Pat's main protectors of the Happy Child, The Governess, The Hippie, and The Sea Lion to validate their efforts at protecting Pat's entire system, address the protectors' concerns about relinquishing their extreme positions and strategies, and negotiating between the parts about how to best take care of the exiled parts. For example, the clinician and Pat could work with The Governess and the Hippie about the best way to collaborate toward nurturing the Sad Child. Then, once the protectors give their permission to Pat's Self and the therapist, the work of freeing the vulnerable parts from their burdens and being exiled could be conducted. When the vulnerable parts are healed in this way, the protectors can cease taking on their extreme protection roles and the vulnerable parts would also feel accepted and nurtured. All parts would be better able to focus and integrate their energies and talents on more productive and healthy activities as well as better cope with stressors in the external world because through this process each part would become healthily attached to Pat's Self.

## ▨ FOR YOUR CONSIDERATION

1. Using the IFS model, how do you think the previous counselor's behavioral techniques impacted each protective and vulnerable part in Pat's system? How might you see these behavioral techniques integrating the various parts of Pat or polarizing them further?
2. What might be different in Pat's treatment if the eating disorder was instead a substance use disorder?
3. How might Pat's husband and family of origin interfere with and/or encourage Pat's therapeutic progress? As a clinician how could you work with Pat while she interacts with and is affected by these external forces?
4. How could the relationships between Pat and her family of origin as well as her spiritual upbringing provide insights into the relationships between Pat's internal subpersonalities?

## ▨ REFERENCES

Anderson, R. (n.d.). *Internal Family Systems (IFS): A revolutionary & transformative treatment for permanent healing.* www.pesi.com

Cantanzaro, J. (2016). IFS and eating disorders: Healing the parts who hide in plain sight. In M. Sweezy & E. L. Ziskind (Eds.), *Innovations and elaborations in Internal Family Systems therapy* (pp. 49–69). Routledge.

Engert, V., Kok, B., Papassotiriou, I., Chrousos, G. P., & Singer, T. (2017). Specific reduction in cortisol stress reactivity after social but not attention-based mental training. *Science Advances*, 3(10), e1700495. doi:10.1126/sciadv.1700495

Haddock, S. A., Weiler, L. M., Trump, L. J., & Henry, K. L. (2016). The efficacy of Internal Family Systems therapy in the treatment of depression among female college students: A pilot study. *Journal of Marital and Family Therapy*, 43(1), 131–144.

Schwartz, R. C., & Sweezy, M. (2020). *Internal family systems therapy* (2nd ed.). The Guilford Press.

# 4.2    *Case of Nan*

## ▨ INTRODUCTION

Nan is a 46-year-old female. She is married since the age of 23. She and her husband have a 16-year-old daughter and a 14-year-old son. She has a master's degree in education and has been a schoolteacher for over 20 years. Her husband is an accountant and has a very successful career.

Nan presents with complaints of fatigue, listlessness, exhaustion, and feeling as though a great deal of effort is required just to get out of the bed. She reports foggy thinking, forgetfulness, and difficulty making decisions. Nan states she feels depressed most of the time and feels nothing will ever get better.

Nan frequently questions what the point is of trying to have a normal and happy life. She berates herself about all the ways she has failed as a parent. She grieves her children's early childhood and longs for them to be small again. She wishes she had done more with them, enjoyed them more, been more loving and attentive. She talks often of heirloom clothing passed down to her that she meant to have their portraits made in as babies and toddlers but never got around to. There are countless other examples of things she intended but neglected and now ruminates over.

She insists she is incapable of successfully completing the simplest of tasks such as sorting mail, folding clothes, or putting away groceries. She states her efforts to clean up or organize result in even more disorganization. She states these traits have caused issues with her employment. This year she was placed on an improvement plan and has just learned her contract will not be renewed for the new academic year. She will soon be unemployed.

Nan and her husband live in an upscale home in a nice neighborhood. Her children attend a private academy. She states her home is in such disarray that her children have not had friends over in years due to embarrassment. She shows me a picture of her dining room as an example and it is covered in items including dirty clothes, golf balls, nonperishable grocery items, and unopened mail. She states the kitchen counters are covered in dirty dishes, opened food containers, paper products, and wrappers. The other rooms in the home are equally eschew, unpresentable at best and unlivable in some cases. Her son's room is cluttered with piles of clothes, furniture, and miscellaneous items to such a degree that he has been sleeping on the couch for over a year.

Presenting symptoms are reported to be daily for as long as she can remember. Her husband endorses these symptoms in her as well. In person, Nan often comes across as angry, hostile, irritable, and agitated. She is pessimistic to such an extent as to be off-putting. She is also easily tearful, however. Her gait is not slowed, nor is her speech. Her affect is not flat but instead volatile. She sometimes sits too close, leans in too much, stares too long. In general, her nonverbals are intense, and could easily make acquaintances feel uncomfortable. She frequently drops clinical bombs at the end of session and requests for sessions to continue longer. She wants direct advice. She wants to be fixed. She can be demanding, desperate, but often unwilling to put in the work herself. She frequently misses appointments, perhaps due to forgetfulness and disorganization, perhaps due to lacking the energy required to come in, or perhaps due to some passive-aggressive tendencies. Her hygiene and self-care are lacking. Her hair appears as if it has not been washed for some time and she admits to such. It is usually pulled back in a ponytail. Her clothes are in disarray. This is her usual appearance although coming in straight from her job as a teacher.

Nan was diagnosed with type 1 diabetes at the age of 15. Soon after she spent several days in the ICU and in a coma. This disease continues to impact her life greatly. She has had at least three intensive care hospitalizations as an adult. She admits she does not take care of herself with regard to this illness. She wears an insulin pump and frequently forgets to replace parts essential for it to operate correctly. She does not make modifications to her diet or lifestyle, although being strongly advised by her doctors to do so. She does not check her blood sugar as required. Her husband expresses both concern and some frustration, reporting that the children have found her unconscious on two occasions in their lifetimes and have had to call 911. Nan shrugs this off and points blame to her husband for not acting more concerned. She ponders that perhaps he should ask if she has checked her blood sugar or remind her to replace parts in her insulin pump. Perhaps if he did these things she says, maybe she would try harder to take care of herself.

Nan states she has no friends to speak of but desperately wants a close friend. She cries when she speaks of how much she craves friendship. She uses the word mentor often. She has very specific ideas about the type of friend she would like to have. They would be older than her, someone she could look up to. They would offer guidance and help her do things like clean her house. She is sure she could do things like organize her home if only she had a mentor to be her friend and help her with the process. She states she has never really had close friends and has certainly never had a best friend. On the few occasions she has connected with someone, her husband has transferred to a new job in a new town and the move caused her to lose the connection she says.

## ■ FAMILY HISTORY

Nan has been married to her husband for 23 years. The two of them are in stark contrast in several noteworthy ways. His appearance is noticeably neat and tidy. His clothes are perfectly put together with crisp creases in his dress shirt and pants. He is extraordinarily polite and well-mannered. He has a pleasant demeanor that even when under attack, is not defensive. He talks calmly, soothingly, and genuinely. He wants to help. He wants Nan to feel better, to take care of herself, to be happy with the life she has. In return, Nan seethes in his presence.

Nan's relationship with her children is disconnected in her words. She describes her son as lazy, her daughter as emotionally checked out of the family unit. Both children do well in school, are active in extracurriculars and have a number of social activities and relationships. She feels they do not need her. She fears her daughter will soon graduate high school, move away to college, and never come back. She dreams of being best friends with her daughter, of helping her pick out clothing and decorating an apartment for college, of preparing large meals at holidays for her daughter to bring friends from college. She believes instead however that the clock is ticking before she has no more opportunities to be the mother she meant to be but has failed to accomplish. She oscillates between hoping, grieving, and dismissing what she always wanted.

Nan has one sister that she is not especially close to. Her mother is in a nursing home. Her father died when she was 22. She was raised wealthy as her father owned a number of businesses. She states she never received any attention from him as he was always working. She states her mother was always preoccupied as well. The only time she recalls them showing an interest in her was when she was hospitalized as a teenager due to complications from her diabetes. She blames them for her poor work ethic and household skills and states she was spoiled and pampered growing up and never had to do anything for herself. As a result, she states she never learned how to do things and besides, now she does not feel well enough to do them anyway.

## DIAGNOSTIC IMPRESSIONS

There are a number of contradictory pieces of information that complicate diagnosis. She is agitated, angry, and hostile, which runs counter to the image most have of depression. Her gait is not slowed, nor is her speech, which might be expected given the level of impairment she reports and exhibits. She is screened to rule out attention deficit disorder and the results are not significant. The role type 1 diabetes may play cannot be overlooked and is most certainly contributing to and complicating the clinical picture as well. Still, the overarching symptoms of rumination, helplessness, hopelessness, pessimism, fatigue, difficult making decisions, forgetfulness, lack of self-care, medical self-neglect, grief, and guilt are considered primary and in tandem.

Of significance, the only time Nan can recall being cared for and feeling cared about was when she was near death at age 15. She describes the look on her parents' faces when she awoke from her coma. She talks at length about how her mother and father took turns at her bedside, looking over her, worrying about her, and she felt loved. Her life since appears to be a series of attempts to reexperience this same level of being cared for and feeling cared about. If she repeats her role as sickly, needy, helpless, and fragile, perhaps those closest to her will worry over her, and she will feel loved and that she matters.

Nan longs for close relationships with others. However, she acts incongru-
ently and in ways that make this less likely rather than more. Her underlying
anger and hostility keep others at bay, almost in a self-protective and self-affirming
way. While she is bitterly angry at her husband, upon closer reflection she also
appears angry at herself. Stuck in past mistakes and missed opportunities, she
is incapable of forgiving herself. The disarray of herself, her health, her career,
her relationships, and her home will perhaps cause someone to demonstrate care
and concern. But if they do not, these things act as the punishment she feels both
she and those who are uncaring deserve.

## ■ DIAGNOSTIC CONCLUSIONS

- Major depressive disorder
- Relational problem related to a mental disorder or general medical
  condition

## ■ SUGGESTED THERAPEUTIC INTERVENTIONS

Treatment initially began with rational emotive behavior therapy aimed at shift-
ing beliefs that led to the cycles of rumination, pessimism, and guilt. Behavioral
strategies were also employed to address lack of routine or daily schedule,
disorganization of the home, forgetfulness, unhealthy lifestyle habits, and poor
self-care. However, the client was resistant to treatment. After approximately
eight sessions without progress even in combination with medication the treatment approach was shifted.

The new treatment approach focused on beginning again with building
the therapeutic relationship without any other directives. A pattern emerged
of relationship building, challenging incongruities, repairing the ruptures that
resulted, and building the relationship again. A heavy focus was placed on elements of person-centered therapy and as the relationship strengthened and the
resistance lessened, the approach then incorporated forgiveness therapy, and
later acceptance and commitment therapy.

## ■ FOR YOUR CONSIDERATION

1. What negative perceptions of Nan or her situation might you experience that impact your ability to develop a relationship with her, and
   how might this impact treatment approach?

2. How is Nan's poorly managed type 1 diabetes intertwined with her psychological health?
3. Would you recommend family therapy to include Nan's husband and two children as an effective approach to helping Nan?

# 4.3  *Case of Bashir*

## ■ INTRODUCTION

Bashir is a 19-year-old biracial (African American and Caucasian) male. He is currently unemployed and possesses a high school diploma. Bashir was adjudicated on charges of possession with intent to distribute, grand theft, destruction of property, and assault, after he had run away from home at the age of 17 years. He was caught by police after his parents reported Bashir as missing for several days. He was referred to treatment from a secure residential treatment facility to continue intensive outpatient treatment as he transitions from placement into a less-restrictive environment. This is Bashir's first foray into therapy.

## ■ FAMILY HISTORY

Bashir does not know his biological parents because they never had custody. (Bashir was a premature baby and tested positive for drugs; he went immediately to foster care.) His first foster mother filed papers to adopt Bashir when he was a toddler (aged 2 years), but she was shot and killed by her boyfriend. Bashir was in the room when this happened. He was then placed with another foster family and their two older male children. He was eventually adopted by the couple. He reports that the household was stable, loving, but very strict. He shared that he never felt good enough for the family even though they were very supportive and kind to him. He noted that his adoptive family is Caucasian, and he is biracial but looks more African American. He said that strangers would ask his parents, "Where did he come from?" when he was a child, and he would feel embarrassed.

Bashir was on the honor roll in high school before he joined a gang to have a sense of belonging. In the background file that accompanied the referral, an interview with Bashir's adoptive mother reported that he went from being a good kid to one who was always high or drunk, disobeyed curfew and other rules, and stopped caring about doing well in school. She noted that Bashir would give himself tattoos and piercings in visible areas (like his arms). She also reported that she once walked in on Bashir in the bathroom and he had what she thought were cuts all over his chest and abdomen. When she asked about the marks, Bashir brushed off her concerns.

## ◼ CURRENT FUNCTIONING

He earned his high school diploma in placement. This bothers Bashir because he views "placement school" as less-than given his pre-gang aspirations to attend college and become a teacher. In addition, prior to being charged, he had impregnated his girlfriend who gave birth while Bashir was in placement. The child, a son, is now 16 months old. Bashir has infrequent contact with his ex-girlfriend and has never met his son. He expresses regret that he will not be there for his son just like his biological parents were not there for him, and he wonders if that is for the best.

Per the rules around his release and his ex-girlfriend's request for child support, Bashir will have to find employment. His probation officer and staff at the residential treatment facility found him a job at a fast food restaurant. Bashir got into an argument with his manager and quit after 4 days of employment.

## ◼ DIAGNOSTIC IMPRESSIONS

Bashir presents as moderately depressed (exhibits feelings of unhappiness, frustration over even small matters, increased cravings for food and weight gain, irritability, etc.). An appointment was made with the psychiatrist so that Bashir may perhaps be placed on medication. However, when the appointment was over, Bashir threw away the script for Zoloft. When asked why he did so, he replied that he does not want to be on medication because that would make him weak. He also does not see the difference between using drugs on the street and using drugs that are prescribed by a physician.

Bashir is proud of his tattoos and when asked "if they hurt," he noted that pain is the entire point. Bashir seems proud of his ability to withstand physical pain, and he derives positive feelings from the pain. When asked about other forms of self-injury, he said that he might have cut himself in the past but no longer does so. It should be noted, however, that Bashir has tattoos covering his arms, hands, neck, and ear. He also has piercings in his lip, ear, nose, and brow. He seems to endorse self-injury as a way to cope with intense emotional distress.

Bashir has unresolved attachment issues as evidenced by his developmental and preadoption history. Even though he was adopted into a loving family, he had a sense that he did not belong, and it seems to have been an overarching theme throughout his life. It seems that he always kept his adoptive family at arm's length so as to not be hurt by them. Further, he does not know his infant son and fears that he could be recreating a destructive pattern for him.

## ▨ DIAGNOSTIC CONCLUSIONS

- Major depressive disorder, moderate
- Nonsuicidal self-injury
- Lack of coping skills, problems with the legal system, and difficulty with social supports

## ▨ SUGGESTED THERAPEUTIC INTERVENTIONS

Psychopharmacology—Encourage Bashir to reconsider using medication to help his symptoms of depression.

Intensive outpatient therapy (2 to 3 days/week)—to comply with rules and expectations in the community consistently. Bashir will need to identify situations, thoughts, and feelings that trigger feelings of anger, frustration, or sadness, problem behaviors, and the targets of those actions. Assist Bashir in making connections between his feelings and behavior. Use instruction, talk therapy, and/or role-playing to help develop Bashir's emotional regulation. Assist Bashir in reconceptualizing anger as involving different components (e.g., cognitive, physiological, affective, and behavioral).

Family therapy/reunification planning—to resolve past childhood/family issues, leading to less anger and frustration, and greater self-esteem, security, and confidence. Bashir's behaviors have developed, in part, as a means of coping with feelings of abandonment and childhood trauma.

## ▨ FOR YOUR CONSIDERATION

1. Would you consider extreme tattooing and piercing as a form of self-injury? Why or why not?
2. How do you respond when a client displays symptoms of something that may be well managed with medication and they refuse?
3. When they do speak, Bashir often argues with his child's mother about his lack of involvement in the child's life. (He is in placement and has been since before the child's birth.) How can Bashir be a part of his child's life without being present?

# CHAPTER FIVE

# ANXIETY DISORDERS

*While the occasional experience of anxiety is a typical part of life, people with anxiety disorders often have intense and persistent worry and fear about everyday situations. This chapter contains three cases of anxiety disorders in two adult males and one adolescent female. Generalized anxiety disorder is highlighted in this chapter as well as the less common, selective mutism diagnosis. While the clients in these cases have symptoms that lead to a DSM-5* (Diagnostic and Statistical Manual of Mental Disorders: Fifth Edition) *diagnosis in the same category, these cases highlight how cultural factors and family of origins issues may exacerbate anxiety-related symptoms. Questions for consideration are also included.*

# 5.1    *Case of Todd*

### INTRODUCTION

Todd is a 28-year-old male who is presenting to his general physician after being referred by a neighbor. His neighbor, who is also a close friend, is worried that Todd is isolating and not taking care of himself. Todd used to be seen frequently in his neighborhood. He always said hello to his neighbors and stopped to chat on the way to the mailbox. He was always neatly groomed, made good eye contact, and seemed cheerful. Lately, his neighbor has noticed that he has not been out of his house much, and when his neighbor went over to check on him he noticed Todd had not bathed recently, his house was in need of a good cleaning, and he had not been out to get groceries or basic needs in a while, relying instead on take-out food delivery services.

### FAMILY HISTORY

Todd grew up in the Midwest and has three older sisters. Two have struggled with anxiety and depression over the years. Todd is the youngest by 6 years and at times felt as if he was the "only child." He did well in school and excelled in sports until the sudden death of his father when Todd was 8 years old. Todd's family really struggled with this loss because they were close and his father was the primary breadwinner. After this loss, the family moved away from their middle-class neighborhood into subsidized housing. Todd's grades started to slide, and he dropped out of all sports. He spent a lot of time playing video games and reading and stopped interacting with friends on a regular basis.

Todd's mom, who most of his life was a stay-at-home mom, was forced to start working and found a low-paying retail job. She was eventually moved up to manager at the candle store where she worked, but this resulted in long hours and Todd found himself at home a lot in the evenings and on weekends. His family struggled with the loss of his father but rarely spoke about it, and when Todd brought things up, he was told to "get over it" by his older sisters. When Todd is feeling irritable and anxious, his mom sometimes makes comments such as "you are just like your father."

Todd dropped out of high school after his junior year and "hung out" at his mom's. His mom told him he had to get his general educational development (GED) diploma in order to stay, so he did complete it. He took a few credit hours at the local community college in computer programming but found the atmosphere to be too anxiety-provoking. He had difficulty interacting with other students, and in one class he was asked to do a group project that precipitated him dropping out of college. He did find a job at a small upstart computer company where he works by himself at night. The company moved to a different town with the intention of expanding, and Todd decided to relocate with his employer.

## ■ CURRENT FUNCTIONING

Currently, Todd lives by himself. He has moved to a very small community about 400 miles from his hometown. He does not have a lot of friends, other than the few neighbors that he has met. Todd continues to work at night and has found doing daily activities more and more difficult over the past 6 months. He used to be able to shop for groceries for himself but now just the thought of it sets his heart racing and he breaks out in a sweat. In the last few weeks, he has struggled with diarrhea and an overwhelming feeling of fear but is not able to pin down what he is afraid of. At odd times during the night (at work), he finds himself restless to the point of distraction and has difficulty concentrating. Todd has been experiencing difficulty sleeping during the day, despite many years of working the night shift, and he is starting to realize that he is easily fatigued. Several of his coworkers have mentioned that he seems more irritable lately, but he thinks this is probably a result of his increasing fatigue. Todd is so embarrassed about how he has been feeling lately that he is very reluctant to talk to anyone about his condition and finds that staying at home and going to work are about all he can handle right now. He has considered quitting his job so that he "doesn't have to deal with it." Currently, all of his presenting concerns include irritability, difficulty sleeping, easily fatigued, general worry about going places and interacting with others, physical symptoms of sweating and feeling like his heart is pounding when he thinks about daily activities, isolation, and poor hygiene.

## ■ DIAGNOSTIC CONCLUSIONS

- Generalized anxiety disorder
- R/O medical condition explaining symptoms
- R/O depression
- R/O other anxiety disorders
- Additional concerns: lack of social support, isolation, and decreased ability and interest in self-care

## ■ SUGGESTED THERAPEUTIC INTERVENTIONS

Cognitive behavioral therapy (CBT) could be very helpful for Todd. This would help him focus on thoughts in addition to behaviors. CBT could help him challenge his negative thinking patterns and irrational beliefs that fuel his anxiety. In addition to this treatment, he could consider exposure therapy. Exposure therapy could help him face his fears in a controlled, safe environment to help reduce his anxiety. Group therapy might also be helpful for Todd because he could interact with others and get support from people who are having similar experiences. Todd could also speak with his physician or a psychiatrist to discuss medication options in conjunction to therapy.

## ■ FOR YOUR CONSIDERATION

1. Research supports medication, and therapy can be helpful in treating generalized anxiety disorder. Would you recommend both for Todd? What if Todd felt strongly against either type of treatment?
2. What other therapeutic interventions would you consider for Todd in addition to CBT and exposure therapy?
3. Do you feel you have enough information about Todd to make a diagnosis and treatment recommendation, or is there additional information that you might find helpful?

# 5.2    *Case of Maria*

## ▓ INTRODUCTION

Maria is a 16-year-old female who was brought to counseling by her mother primarily because of concerning behaviors related to school. Since her parents' recent divorce, essentially resulting from her father's alcoholism, Maria had been ditching classes at school and consistently refusing to speak in the classes that she attended. In contrast, Maria's verbal communications at home and when visiting her father had not changed, although she was more irritable than before.

During the intake session, Maria spoke little and so quietly that it was difficult to hear her. This continued in spite of her mother's encouragement of Maria to speak for herself. Over the next few sessions, Maria gradually began to speak more and more clearly, and her mother stayed progressively less in each session. Maria completed homework in observing her self-care and completing an online personality inventory. She also participated in healthy self-calming skill development and worked toward increasing her attendance and verbal participation in class at school. Maria and her mother met with school personnel to make appropriate accommodations in her schedule based on her academic abilities, which they reported as being helpful.

## ▓ DIAGNOSTIC IMPRESSIONS

During the first few sessions, Maria disclosed important information about her fear and anger toward her father for drinking so much that he nearly died from related medical problems. It became clear that Maria's decision to speak only at home and when visiting her father was an expression of feeling powerless to help her father or keep her family together. Her sense of powerlessness also came from an underlying cultural attitude that she attributed to her father about not truly listening to female voices, which she considered to be a major factor in her parents' divorce. A significant event in Maria's treatment was when she identified these connections, and then determined that the strategy of speaking selectively was not accomplishing what she wanted it to because it was interfering with her goals related to school and friends.

## ▓ SUGGESTED THERAPEUTIC INTERVENTIONS

Person centered therapy was used primarily in order to develop an effective working relationship with Maria, particularly so that she would engage verbally in sessions. Dialectical behavior therapy (DBT)/rational emotive behavior therapy (REBT) was also used (as described earlier) to assist Jamie toward greater self-awareness and healthier self-management. Maria achieved her goals and was discharged after 10 sessions.

## DIAGNOSTIC CONCLUSIONS

- Selective mutism
- Problems with primary support group
- Lack of peer/social support

## FOR YOUR CONSIDERATION

1. How would the diagnosis be different if, in addition to speaking selectively, the client was also exhibiting nonsuicidal self-harming behaviors, such as cutting? Or, if the client expressed suicidal or homicidal ideation?
2. What symptoms might indicate that a concurrent diagnosis of adjustment disorder would be appropriate?

# 5.3    *Case of Jonathan*

## INTRODUCTION

Jonathan is a 19-year-old college freshman who currently lives with his mother and his 21-year-old sister—when she is home from college. Jonathan presented in a depressed mood with a congruent affect. He agreed to attend counseling at the suggestion of his mother. Jonathan identifies as a good student in high school who graduated with a 4.0 grade point average, the completion of four college courses before graduation, and the recipient of multiple scholarships and academic awards. Jonathan reported being very focused in high school even to the exclusion of a social life. He is in good physical condition and reportedly holds multiple high school records in track and field. Jonathan reports an ongoing focus with physical fitness and attending the gym multiple times per week. Jonathan presented because he is having difficulty after leaving college after only 3 weeks. Jonathan explains that he knew that it would be hard but that he was not prepared for how much work it would require. Jonathan described having difficulty keeping up with the readings and putting as much effort as is required to perform in the manner in which he had in high school. He expressed feeling overwhelmed with fitting everything in and simply could not handle it any longer. Jonathan reports that he feels like a failure and that he does not think that he is smart enough to attend college.

## ■ FAMILY HISTORY

Jonathan described a difficult childhood during which his mom and dad divorced. He identifies his relationship with his father as "not close" and indicated that his dad was controlling and emotionally abusive. Jonathan's father is very religious and holds very black-and-white beliefs about living a "moral" life. Jonathan reported a close relationship with his mother growing up—she had primary custody and Jonathan would visit his father every other weekend. Jonathan reports believing that it was his moral obligation to do his best in whatever he does. Jonathan described a history of worrying about school dating back to the fifth grade where he became focused on his future academic success. He reported that it became apparent to him that he spent considerably more time on his schoolwork than his academically comparable peers while still in high school. Jonathan reports that his need to work harder and longer than his peers means that he is just not as smart as them. He reports a history of becoming restless and irritable and having difficulty sleeping, especially before exams. In order to manage the worry, he would study and review material constantly, often not getting much more than 5 hours of sleep a night. Jonathan reported feeling nervous and unsettled when he did not fill his downtime with productive work, making it difficult to engage with peers in social activities.

## ■ CURRENT FUNCTIONING

Upon returning from college and per his mother's insistence, Jonathan returned to a job at a local restaurant that he had during high school. Jonathan discussed working at the restaurant and expressed his frustration with coworkers and how they do not seem to care about the vision that the CEO has for the company. He discussed having difficulty being as productive as his coworkers because it often takes him longer to perform certain tasks to the standards that he believes are required. He fears that he will be fired if he cannot perform the tasks to the standards that are dictated by the employee handbook. Jonathan appeared confused when asked if he liked his job or to identify times that he enjoyed his job. He maintains that he likes his job because he knows exactly what is expected of him but that he would not say that it is enjoyable. Jonathan reported that making friends at work is difficult because there really is no time for socializing. Although his coworkers frequently socialize, it is not really permitted and there are always other job duties that require attention. Jonathan reports that he and his mother have gotten into arguments lately because she offers "wisdom" that is not helpful. Jonathan's mother frequently tells him to relax and reminds him that he is not at school so he should be less anxious and stressed.

Jonathan had difficulty identifying times that he was able to enjoy himself without worry or fear that he would do or say something wrong. Jonathan expresses concern that others will get the wrong impression and draw conclusions about him that are not true. Throughout the initial session, Jonathan frequently apologized for "getting off topic," for believing that he did not answer questions correctly and for taking up so much time filling out paperwork. Jonathan had difficulty completing the *DSM-5* (*Diagnostic and Statistical Manual of Mental Disorders: Fifth Edition*) Cross-Cutting Symptom Measure, continually asking questions for clarification and reporting that he did not want to give the wrong impression stating that he knows how important the paperwork is to his treatment. Jonathan discussed some friendships that he had in high school but reported that they were mainly individuals with whom he had classes and their interactions almost always involved course work. Jonathan identifies with his friends through his academic success and fears that his friends will no longer like him because of his recent academic "failure." Jonathan reports that he goes from being irritable, restless, and having frequent headaches to being completely exhausted. At times, he is so tired that he does not have the energy to go to the gym. Despite feeling exhausted, he reports that he often has difficulty falling asleep at night because he is consumed by thoughts about what he has not done, what he needs to do, and what he could or should have done better. Most mornings he wakes up feeling "on edge," as if something is about to happen. Jonathan reports that he wants to go back to school next fall and that he would like to figure out how to relax and have more fun in life.

## ▨ DIAGNOSTIC IMPRESSIONS

Jonathan describes excessive anxiety and apprehensive expectation occurring more days than not for at least 6 months. Jonathan experienced some relief by over functioning throughout high school but was unable to continue with his coping mechanism when the workload increased in college. Despite over functioning, Jonathan was unable to control the worrying to any great extent, often experiencing restlessness, irritability, muscle tension (headaches), fatigue, and difficulty falling asleep. Jonathan's worry appears to be focused on his competence and the quality of his performance. Jonathan's worries are excessive and interfere significantly with academic functioning, work, and social/peer relationships that have a negative effect on his quality of life.

Jonathan demonstrates some insight regarding his anxiety—understanding that he cannot continue as he has been if he wants to not only manage but also enjoy his life. However, he adamantly argues that his success in high school can only be attributed to the excessive amount of attention he gave to his course work. Jonathan demonstrates a desire to do things the "right" way and believes that all matters in life should be given great value and addressed in the same manner.

## ▧ DIAGNOSTIC CONCLUSION

- Generalized anxiety disorder

## ▧ SUGGESTED THERAPEUTIC INTERVENTIONS

Pharmacotherapy—Jonathan should schedule an evaluation with a psychiatrist to assess the appropriateness of medication to reduce his anxious symptoms.

Individual therapy—Individual weekly sessions to work toward Jonathan's self-identified goal to return to college, be less stressed, and find more fun in life. The use of CBT has been well established as an evidence-based treatment for generalized anxiety disorder. Jonathan should develop a working knowledge of the cognitive, behavioral, and physiological elements of anxiety. He will also benefit from understanding the role that his negative automatic thoughts (overestimates probability of negative outcomes and underestimates his own ability) contribute to his anxiety.

## ▧ FOR YOUR CONSIDERATION

1. What other information would you like to know in determining the best course of treatment for Jonathan?
2. What contributing factors do you believe have influenced Jonathan's diagnosis of generalized anxiety disorder?
3. Why do you think it took Jonathan until this stage in his development to seek help?
4. Would you screen Jonathan for any other diagnoses? If so, which ones? Why?
5. What role do you believe the development of self-esteem plays in the evolution of an anxiety disorder?

# CHAPTER SIX

# OBSESSIVE-COMPULSIVE AND RELATED DISORDERS

*Obsessive-compulsive disorder is a disorder in which people have recurring, unwanted thoughts, ideas, or sensations (obsessions) that make them feel driven to do something repetitively (compulsions). This chapter contains three cases of obsessive-compulsive and related disorders in three adolescent males. While the clients in each of these cases have symptoms that lead to a DSM-5* (Diagnostic and Statistical Manual of Mental Disorders: Fifth Edition) *diagnosis in the same category, this chapter highlights how the disorder often presents in different ways and with different obsessive thoughts (e.g., sexual orientation obsession). Obsessive-compulsive disorder may co-occur with Tic disorder and a case that demonstrates this link is included. Questions for consideration are also included.*

## 6.1   *Case of Andy*

### ▨ INTRODUCTION

Andy is a 17-year-old male who lives with his mother and stepfather in a Midwest town. He has a 15-year-old sister. Andy is a senior in high school and has been an average to above average student throughout his school career. As his senior year progressed, he became less focused on school and began to have a drop in his grades as he failed to submit schoolwork. His parents dismissed it as "senioritis." When asked about his schoolwork and declining grades, Andy stated that he had already been accepted to college and that he was doing enough to get by. He noted he would rather do internet gaming with his "friends" and "surf" his social media accounts.

Andy identifies as heterosexual. He is not involved in a current romantic relationship. He did have a girlfriend (Sarah) throughout his junior year of high school, but they ended the relationship at the start of their senior year. Sarah was close with Andy's parents and reported to them that the two had grown apart and did not share common interests anymore. They were both members of the swim team, but Andy had decided not to swim during their senior year.

Andy's parents began to be concerned when Andy was fired from his job with a local landscaping company. His boss reported that he had been late to his shift on several occasions and then did not show up for a big job on the previous weekend. When this happened, Andy's parents began to get concerned about Andy's change in behavior. They were now noticing a pattern across several settings.

Andy stated that he has been having trouble sleeping which contributed to his lack of interest in swim team (early morning practices) and being late for work. When questioned further, he stated that he has been watching videos and surfing the internet on his phone after getting to bed. He said he's been staying up late gaming. He admits he has tried to stop but he just gets urges to be online because he does not want to miss out on things. He also admits that sometimes "the internet and gaming" consume my mind and time just passes by so fast. He initially started surfing the net and gaming to help him fall asleep but now realizes that this behavior is keeping him awake. In recent months he has opened several social media accounts and spends hours following them. He makes social media posts infrequently but prefers to follow the activities of others. Andy stated that he was falling asleep around 2 a.m. and waking at 6 a.m. to get ready for school. Before getting out of bed he would check into all his social media accounts and watch a few quick videos, making the morning a race to get out of the door. Andy fell asleep a few times in school and struggled to make it to lunch when he had a chance get back on the internet. By the time the school day ended, Andy reported irritability and was anxious to get home to see what he had missed online. He reports getting "annoyed" and having an attitude when someone interrupts his time gaming or surfing the internet. He admits to constantly being preoccupied with thoughts of being on the internet in some form. He stated he has tried to get these "constant" thoughts out of his head and ignore them, but "nothing works."

## ■ FAMILY HISTORY

Andy was raised by his biological parents until the age of 10 when they divorced. Andy's dad works for a technology firm and has a demanding job with many hours and travel. This put a strain on the marriage and resulted in an amicable divorce. Andy and his sister lived with their mom while

## ■ SUGGESTED THERAPEUTIC INTERVENTIONS

Cognitive behavioral therapy has been a known form of therapy for both addiction and OCDs. There is a high chance that Andy is trying to escape from his problems contributing to his compulsive use of the internet. Andy's treatment goals:

- Identifying his thoughts and his triggers that lead to constantly want to be on the internet in some form (i.e., social media, gaming, surfing);
- Focus on specific behaviors to control his impulses and compulsions to be on the internet;
- Self-monitoring exercises; keep log or journal of internet use; monitor moods and contributing factors;
- Help Andy create a personal inventory of the things he used to do that he no longer does due to his internet compulsion;
- Set goals with Andy that are achievable in reducing the amount of time he is on the internet;
- Refer Andy to an adolescent support group; and
- Family therapy to address any relational problems that have contributed to Andy's excessive internet use.

## ■ FOR YOUR CONSIDERATION

1. Andy's family relationships have impacted his life and continue to do so. What other treatment recommendations would you make for Andy?
2. Internet addiction is not currently recognized in the *DSM-5* (*Diagnostic and Statistical Manual of Mental Disorders: Fifth Edition*). Do you think this potential diagnosis warrants more consideration?
3. We are living in a digital age where children and teens are using technology more and more. How do we distinguish between "appropriate" and "problematic" internet use?
4. In thinking of his current diagnosis, would there be any co-occurring diagnosis to consider?

# 6.2    *Case of Dylan*

## ■ INTRODUCTION

Dylan attended his first session accompanied by his 42-year-old mother, Brenda, and 22-year-old sister, Carly. As a 15-year-old freshman in Cyber High School, Dylan was incredibly attached to his family and relied on his sister and mom as his primary supports.

A week prior to his initial appointment, Brenda called for a phone consultation to discuss Dylan's primary symptoms. At the time of the call, Dylan was not eating a majority of foods that were prepared at home. He was struggling to leave the house and seemed affected by preoccupation with thoughts around getting the stomach flu. Dylan was fearful that eating anything that was prepared at home would result in vomiting and prolonged illness. He would routinely inspect utensils at home to ensure cleanliness and oversee his parents and siblings as they participated in preparing meals. With the severity of symptoms increasing over the course of 60 days, Dylan had lost 17 pounds as a result of the eating restrictions. Brenda had notified me that his current psychologist attributed the symptoms to anxiety; however, he was not seeing any alleviation of symptoms despite weekly therapy.

As Dylan entered the office, he slipped his sleeve over his hand to open the door from the lobby to the main office but then quickly recovered and extended his hand to accept the clipboard of paperwork and pencil to finish the logistics of the intake appointment. He made very little eye contact throughout the session, and his responses were literal. Questions such as, "Tell me what has been going on" required extensive further clarification because the lack of clarity in the initial question caused intense anxiety. Dylan often looked to his mother and sister throughout the session to assist in answering questions or for clarification; however, he did correct any misinterpretations that they expressed. He was able to discuss his interests in video gaming and design, online role-playing games, and Lego building but expressed that all of these are better when interacting with others online. Although Dylan wants peer interaction and friendships, his past experience has been such that he now avoids the inevitable rejection that comes with attempting social interactions.

At numerous points throughout the intake, Dylan coughed repeatedly as he listened to his mother and sister describe the tumultuous relationship he has with his older brother, Corey, who recently returned home from college. Corey, 19, is described as having little empathy and time for Dylan's anxiety and, as a result, takes a very harsh approach with Dylan that creates stress and arguments. Dylan sleeps on the bottom bunk, with Corey often climbing over him at odd times of the night, disrupting his routine, as he has no schedule since being home from school. As Dylan discussed a recent argument over "rocking the bed," his cough became more pronounced and repetitive. Brenda discussed that Dylan has always "rocked" himself to sleep, and although this would not be much of an issue in and of itself, it poses quite an issue being on the bottom of a bunk bed.

The intake progressed to discuss more of the symptoms related to his weight loss. Dylan discussed feeling that the weight loss now was likely unhealthier than any stomach flu he could ever contract. He had no rational reason for fearing vomiting, nor could he describe a situation in which someone died from profuse vomiting. When asked, "What is the worst thing that could happen to you?" he was speechless and yet, strangely enough, a sense of calmness overcame him realizing he did not know the worst-case scenario.

Dylan coughed again. And again. And again.

Brenda commented that the coughing occurs daily and reported that it has been "happening forever." Carly reported that it has not always been coughing; he has had sniffling episodes during which he has sounded sick but was perfectly healthy.

More social history from Dylan's past reveals that he has struggled with appropriate communication that is relevant to his peer group. He has a difficult time dealing with rule breakers and has always been incredibly literal. When asked, "What would you say if I told you it was raining cats and dogs outside?" He responded, "I would first look outside to see what you were referring to and make sure there were not cats or dogs outside." Brenda and Carly both agreed that his inability to connect to other kids his age in socially appropriate activities has caused a tremendous amount of isolation in his life.

## ■ DIAGNOSTIC IMPRESSIONS

Dylan has accepted that his life, as it stands, is not worth living. He fears a life in which he is afraid to eat food prepared by another individual and wants to understand why he allows these "thoughts to take over my mind." His preoccupation with flu symptoms and vomiting creates a world in which he needs to compensate by attempting to create rules so that it does not happen. These rules are irrational and change according to the needs he may have at the time. For example, Dylan will not eat red meat prepared by his mother in his kitchen at home; however, if his sister agrees to make his dinner and it is red meat, he will eat it. He will eat out at certain restaurants with buffets, but not others. Having these rules in place gives Dylan a sense of control and this, in turn, creates a sense of safety for him that feels comfortable, but only for a moment.

Dylan is still in a place where he wants to appear somewhat socially acceptable. He secretly attempted to open the door with his sleeve; however, he quickly recovered to take the pencil and intake paperwork (although he was thinking of washing his hands the entire time the session was conducted).

His obsessions (thoughts of getting sick, contaminated, or infected) are consuming, and his quality of life has deteriorated. As a result of these obsessive thoughts, he engages in repetitive compulsive behaviors that include checking food temperatures, cleaning utensils, handwashing to the point of raw skin, and checking kitchen cleanliness. Despite his best efforts, he cannot control the urges he feels and rarely gets a break from the obsessive thoughts and compulsions that accompany them.

Motor tics co-occur often in individuals with OCD. These tics occur nearly every day and have occurred prior to the age of 18. Individuals experiencing these tics find that they are uncontrollable and involuntary. Co-occurrence of these two conditions has been fairly high with more than 60% of individuals with Tic disorder experiencing symptoms of OCD.

Dylan has experienced distress related to social relationships prior to the manifestation of the OCD symptoms. He makes little eye contact, struggles to understand social cues and nonverbal body language, and has difficulty relating to his peer group despite wanting to have friendships. Dylan fixates easily on issues or behaviors and has a difficult time with inferences or interpreting meaning. Given the symptoms presentation, there should be more diagnostic testing to determine if an autism spectrum disorder is warranted.

## ■ DIAGNOSTIC CONCLUSIONS

- OCD
- Tic disorder
- Social (pragmatic) communication disorder

## ■ SUGGESTED THERAPEUTIC INTERVENTIONS

OCD and Tic disorder are neuropsychiatric disorders that are often treated by behavior modification and/or medication management. In both cases, parental and/or familial support is also indicative of long-term success rates in those diagnosed. According to Lombroso and Scahill (2008), habit reversal training (HRT) "involves helping clients increase awareness of tics prior to their expression, self-monitoring, relaxation training, and competing responses." Individuals aware of an expression of a tic are encouraged to produce a voluntary competing response instead of the conditioned response. Early indications show that this is a positive behavior modification for those suffering from Tic disorders.

The treatment of OCD has been well established in the roots of behavioral therapy. Exposing clients to the feared stimuli and blocking the conditioned response ultimately reduces the symptoms and severity of OCD. In children and adolescents, it is imperative that parent training is reinforced so that the child can have continued support at home and/or school. In either case, medication management coupled with behavior modification is generally considered the most comprehensive treatment protocol.

## ▒ FOR YOUR CONSIDERATION

1. Given what you know about Dylan, what are some ways you can begin to help him understand his own diagnoses? Considering that certain concepts related to his condition may be confusing, be creative in your approach!
2. How might Dylan's family hinder his progress with his OCD in the home environment? Consider ways to help his family support him and not enable him.

## ▒ REFERENCE

Lombroso, P. J., & Scahill, L. (2008). Tourette syndrome and obsessive-compulsive disorder. *Brain Development, 4*, 231–237.

# 6.3   *Case of Nico*

## ▒ INTRODUCTION

Nico, a 17-year-old male high school student, has isolated himself from other males and spends the majority of his time socializing with female friends. Nico goes out of his way to avoid being alone with other males, including teachers and coworkers at his part-time job. He recently quit the men's basketball team because it required him to be in such close contact with other males.

Nico identifies as heterosexual, yet he constantly worries that he might be gay. He runs through scenarios that would provide him an opportunity for physical or sexual contact with other males and then checks in with himself to determine whether or not he would find that contact pleasurable, or more pleasurable than what he would have with a female. He has watched gay pornography online to determine whether or not he would be turned on or achieve orgasm. Because he does not orgasm, he views this as confirmation that he is straight.

He harbors some guilt for rejecting his male friends, and his former best friend in particular, who has asked Nico why he does not call him or want to hang out anymore. The friend wondered what he did wrong, and Nico, not knowing what to say, said nothing to him. Nico mentioned that when he sees his former teammates walking together in the hallways, he feels wistful, but then he quickly justifies why it "had to be done."

An only child of two progressive parents, Nico shared his anguish with them. They asked him if he was gay and told him that if he was gay, it would be fine with them. Nico was distressed by their reaction and took their open stance as, "My parents think I am gay."

Nico is obsessive about how he conveys himself to others at his affluent, suburban high school. He wears clothing that purposely conveys a "straight" persona and aims to speak in a manner that demonstrates a flat affect. He is a skilled writer but does not think he should participate in the student literary magazine because "that would be gay." He is constantly assessing what he does, thinks, wears, and feels against whether or not that means he is gay or straight.

Nico requested counseling services for himself to work through his concern about his sexuality. His parents, wishing for him to be healthy no matter what, complied with his request.

## ▓ DIAGNOSTIC IMPRESSIONS

Nico seems to be suffering from sexual orientation obsession, a manifestation of OCD that revolves around the fear of being or being perceived as gay. This is different from internalized homophobia, in which someone who is actually lesbian, gay, or bisexual suffers personal and social anxiety over their sexual orientation. In this case, by contrast, Nico does not take pleasure in homosexual thoughts but nonetheless has an obsessive need to reassure himself that he does not find them pleasurable.

OCD is characterized by the presence of obsessions and/or compulsions. Obsessions are recurrent and persistent thoughts (e.g., Am I gay?) that are experienced as intrusive and unwanted. Compulsions are repetitive behaviors (e.g., checking appearance for "straightness," watching gay pornography to assess reaction) that an individual feels driven to perform in response to an obsession or according to rules that must be applied rigidly.

## ▓ DIAGNOSTIC CONCLUSION

- OCD

## ▓ SUGGESTED THERAPEUTIC INTERVENTIONS

Psychopharmacology—Selective serotonin reuptake inhibitors to improve mood and assist Nico in working through issues therapeutically.

Outpatient therapy—Cognitive behavioral therapy to help Nico change faulty ideas and beliefs, including those prevalent in this form of OCD.

## ▦ FOR YOUR CONSIDERATION

1. How would you be able to tell the difference between Nico's manifestation of OCD versus internalized homophobia?
2. How would you counsel Nico's parents if they participated in a family session with Nico? Do you think their initial response was helpful or hurtful to Nico? Explain.

# 6.4    *Case of Adrienne*

## ▦ INTRODUCTION

Adrienne is a 14-year-old Caucasian female of Greek descent. She is the youngest of three children and is in the eighth grade in a large, suburban middle school. Her mother brought her into the initial session after a referral from Adrienne's dermatologist, who had been treating her cystic acne for over a year. The dermatologist was concerned that Adrienne was scratching and picking at her cysts, and thus, they were not healing properly.

Adrienne presented with pigmentation and large cysts over her face, neck, and chest. She noted that she has an intense urge to pick at and scratch her face during times of stress at school and said she was often relieved after the cyst popped and her skin bled.

## ▦ FAMILY HISTORY

When Adrienne was 5 years old, her mother and older brothers left her father and stayed with her maternal grandparents, with whom they still reside. Adrienne's father was physically and verbally abusive to her mother and brothers, although not to Adrienne, per self-report. Adrienne said that even though she knew that her father was "not always nice" to the other members of the family, he was kind to her, and she missed him when they left the home. She said that she used to have visits with him, but those tapered off after the divorce was finalized.

Approximately 2 years ago, when she was 12 years old, Adrienne learned from a family friend that her father had remarried and had two daughters with his new wife. This family friend showed Adrienne a smiling family photo from social media of her father with his wife and two small daughters. Adrienne said that she felt a lot of emotions in that moment, but the biggest one was that she was worthless.

Adrienne had "always" picked her skin, per self-report and that of her mother who said that she worried anytime Adrienne had a scratch or mosquito bite—her picking at the lesion would make it 10 times worse. However, after learning of the news about her father, the picking worsened, and Adrienne began picking at small pimples, whiteheads, and blackheads on her skin. She reportedly "pops" the hairs out of her eyebrows and in between her eyebrows too.

## ▨ CURRENT FUNCTIONING

In terms of peer relationships, Adrienne has a handful of friends and plays softball for the school team. She is the catcher for the team and said that her coach probably allowed her to be the catcher because the "catcher's mask covers" her face. She is teased by many of the kids in her school and painfully recalled how a small child once asked her how she "got marbles stuck in her face."

When asked if she wants treatment to manage the urge to pick, Adrienne was ambivalent. She does not want to look the way that she does, as evidenced by her visits to the dermatologist and using prescription acne medication. On the other hand, she reports pleasurable feelings from picking her skin and feels a release when she is able to pick successfully (e.g., pop a zit, remove a blackhead).

## ▨ DIAGNOSTIC IMPRESSIONS

Adrienne presents as moderately anxious. She admits to a low frustration tolerance and snaps at others over small matters, such as when others are 5 minutes late to a meeting. Her mother reports that she is often irritable for "no reason," but when she picks her skin, she seems to calm down. She also has difficulty sleeping even though she is easily fatigued. Thus, Adrienne seems to endorse excoriation as a way to cope with intense emotional distress.

The specific *DSM-5* criteria for Excoriation (Skin Picking) Disorder are as follows:

- Recurrent skin picking resulting in lesions
- Repeated attempts to decrease or stop skin picking

- The skin picking causes clinically significant distress or impairment in important areas of functioning
- The skin picking cannot be attributed to the physiological effects of a substance or another medical condition
- The skin picking cannot be better explained by the symptoms of another mental disorder

Adrienne seems to meet the aforementioned criteria and does not meet criteria for OCD. Thus, Excoriation Disorder is the appropriate diagnosis.

## ▓ DIAGNOSTIC CONCLUSIONS

- Excoriation (skin-picking) disorder
- Lack of coping skills, difficulty with peer relationships, and estrangement from father

## ▓ SUGGESTED THERAPEUTIC INTERVENTIONS

Behavioral techniques such as habit reversal, distraction, and mindfulness may mitigate the skin picking urge.

Psychopharmacology, such as a selective serotonin reuptake inhibitor, may aid in managing the urge to pick and feelings of inadequacy.

## ▓ FOR YOUR CONSIDERATION

1. Adrienne's skin picking worsened when she learned that her father had a new family. Why do you think, after all this time, Adrienne would be so triggered by this information?
2. In Adrienne's case, excoriation disorder was diagnosed with cystic acne and topical acne medication was prescribed over a year before the referral to a mental health professional. Why do you think it took so long to get Adrienne the treatment that she needed?

# CHAPTER SEVEN

# TRAUMA AND STRESSOR-RELATED DISORDERS

*Trauma and stressor-related disorders are a group of emotional and behavioral problems that may result from traumatic and stressful experiences such as exposure to physical or emotional violence or pain, including abuse, neglect, or intense family conflict. This chapter contains five cases related to trauma and stressor-related disorders including posttraumatic stress disorder, acute stress disorder, reactive attachment disorder, and adjustment disorder. The clients in this chapter also includes a broad range of ages and demographics, ranging in age from 8 to 68, and they are urban, rural, and suburban dwellers with a variety of family constellations, strengths, and challenges. Specific traumas related to child sexual abuse and neglect as well as questions for consideration are also included.*

## 7.1    *Case of Amonique*

### ▓ INTRODUCTION

Amonique is a 38-year-old, single, African American woman who lives in Richmond, Illinois. She arrives to an intake appointment on-time, dressed professionally, and with friendly demeanor. She scheduled the appointment during her lunch hour and shared that she was recommended to your practice by a close friend. She pronounces her name at the start of the session (Ah-mo-neek), but quickly appeals that you can call her "Mo" or "Monique." When asked what she prefers, she stated "Amonique." She presents with complaints of "need to get my life back in order." Upon further inquiry, she elaborates that 2 weeks ago, there was a fire in her building in which she and her neighbors had to evacuate. The fire was started from an electrical outlet in a neighboring apartment on her floor. She shared that though she has been relocated, she is having difficulty feeling comfortable in her new home. She looked down and shared feeling "guilty" for struggling because no one was seriously injured or harmed in the fires. She also reported having persistent difficulty falling or staying asleep, is constantly "on edge" during the day, and reported intrusive thoughts about having too many devices plugged into an outlet. Immediately after relocating, she stopped using extension cords for her electronics and she unplugs all of her kitchen appliances at night. Amonique reported that for a few nights during the past month, she smelt something burning, but she was unable to get out of bed to investigate further. During this time frame, she has also avoided cooking meals at home and now prefers eating out or ordering for delivery for most meals. Throughout the intake interview, Amonique referenced her faith, stating, "I know God is in control." When asked about the role of faith in her life, she shared attempts to find understanding in everything that happens but stated that she struggles to see this as "a part of God's plan." She is angry that her symptoms have changed her "at home routine" and have interfered with her work. Amonique started to cry as she expressed a longing "to regain control of my life!"

## ▥ FAMILY HISTORY

Amonique reported close family relationships. She is the oldest of three siblings (32; 25; and 24 years, respectively). Her father passed away last year from health complications related to ongoing heart problems. Her mother has recently "battled some medical scares" and Amonique has been "forced" to step up with coordinating care for her mother. She lives about 30 minutes away from her mother and she reported it is important to her to be near her mother, in case she needs to aid her mother in getting to medical appointments. Amonique considers family to be important and reported that she holds responsibilities "typical" of oldest child. She feels like "the responsible sibling." Amonique reported strong relationships with her siblings and after their father's passing, she has assumed the role of keeping family members in communication with one another.

## ▥ CURRENT FUNCTIONING

Amonique works as a branding executive for an advertising firm. She reported performing well at work and since learning of an upcoming promotion she began taking on extra clients and tasks. However, since the apartment fire, Amonique has experienced frequent difficulty remembering to attend important meetings. She also has felt more irritable in interactions with colleagues, explaining feeling more sensitive to criticism and alert to negative remarks that do not usually cause distress. She has had numerous encounters with coworkers that often are challenging and describes not letting it affect her (as if she can "turn off her body"). However, she is currently struggling to not take offense to perceived slights. Amonique shared about hearing from a close colleague that her boss has reached out to specific people within the firm to share his recommendation and support of their application for the promotion. Amonique felt slighted by this news as she has had numerous conversations with him about her interest in advancing. She felt he was sincere when suggesting she "keep working hard" and his comments that her ability to take on numerous new clients was "impressive." She is unsure what to make of this and when asked if she felt her race was a factor, she hesitated to answer and looked down. She stated, "I mean, I cannot say it hasn't been a thought in the back of my head." She has learned to "put on a happy face" to avoid being labeled "the angry Black woman" and expressed worry that her increasing irritability may jeopardize her chances at a promotion.

Amonique is actively involved in her community, specifically her interest in civic and local government. She explained her involvement has provided avenues for her to mentor young Black women. She is affectionately referred to as a supportive "Auntie" within the community. When asked to clarify, she stated that being called an "auntie" by nonrelatives is an honor in Black community and she tries to make herself available to her friends for support and advice, but at times she just wants to "fade away from others." She identifies as "spiritual," though has not found a church in town that she relates to.

Substance use history includes alcohol and marijuana during her college years. She reported drinking alcohol on special occasions and rarely keeps alcohol in her home. Amonique has not used marijuana since her time in college and reported this was social activity. She reports no trauma history, no significant medical history, and no legal issues.

## DIAGNOSTIC IMPRESSIONS

Amonique is exhibiting symptoms consistent with acute stress disorder. Despite her reserved and calm demeanor in session, Amonique described reactions to the apartment building fire that suggest she is overly reactivate to this threatened death event. Specifically, she mentioned several signs characteristic of intrusion symptoms and psychological distress pertaining to the fire. Her behavior at home and work has negatively changed, including active engagement in avoidance symptoms, frequent manifestation of arousal symptoms, and intermittent negative mood and dissociative symptoms.

Amonique mentioned involvement in community when asked about support system. However, her community involvement involves mentoring, social justice advocacy, and church volunteerism, which all hold their own share of stressors and responsibilities. Additionally, her family is a potential source of support, though her family is noted as a significant stressor in her life. Specifically, regarding her role in family which holds tremendous responsibility for the well-being of her mother and for her siblings. This is exemplified in her own explanation of a personal value and duty for "holding family together." As such, it seems her access to social supports in which she receives support is limited.

## ▨ DIAGNOSTIC CONCLUSIONS

- 308.3 Acute stress disorder
- Z60.5 Target of (perceived) adverse discrimination or persecution

## ▨ SUGGESTED THERAPEUTIC INTERVENTIONS

*Relational-Cultural Attunement-Based Interventions.* Interventions that focus on attunement with clients will be essential for working with Amonique. More specifically, culturally responsive theoretical orientations that emphasize the relational aspect of therapy will be essential for working with clients belonging to marginalized populations. Therapy interventions like Brainspotting, eye-movement desensitization and reprocessing (EMDR), and adjunctive approaches to therapy like trauma-informed yoga are specific interventions that recognize the importance of attunement between client and clinician (Gurda, 2015). In consideration of cultural impact of the oppressive experiences and stressors related to the fire that Amonique is experiencing, using interventions that incorporate approaches toward alleviating distressing symptoms using client attunement and cultural humility as the guiding approaches.

*Therapist-Client Attunement-Based Approaches.* African American clients benefit from therapy approaches that emphasize psychosomatic symptoms and cognitions that link the client with an intuitive, often unspoken permission to seek insights within themselves that line that up with their cognitive interpretation of events. EMDR therapy is a brain–body based approaches that focuses heavily on the subcortical processes of therapeutic healing that activates accelerated processing of traumatic events using bilateral stimulation (BLS). Similarly, Brainspotting is another therapeutic approach that centers clinician–client attunement and possesses a conceptual underpinning of cultural, which is particularly necessary for working with clients belonging to marginalized cultural groups. Brainspotting is an approach that is often integrated into other therapy approaches, which allows for adaptation to specific client needs.

*Trauma-Informed Yoga.* Trauma-informed yoga as an adjunctive intervention can promote posttraumatic growth for clients experiencing symptoms related to stressors, anxiety, and trauma. Particularly, trauma-informed yoga interventions are recommended for Amonique with the emphasis on enhancing coping regarding oppressive experiences and allowing for attunement that also relies on self-trust, self-direction, and guidance toward self-awareness and healing. Trauma-informed yoga that is integrated into therapy involves a clinician's use of somatic-psychotherapy approaches that resemble aspects of yoga (i.e., deep breathing, meditation, etc.).

## FOR YOUR CONSIDERATION

1. Consider the discomfort Amonique experienced when sharing about her suspicion of being mistreated based on race. This could be the client's own discomfort or her assumption of the clinician's discomfort with this topic. What are ways that you as the clinician can invite exploration of racially based issues as they present in therapy?
2. Considering the cultural factors relevant to Amonique and her sense of responsibility based on being the eldest sibling, what might be follow up questions you would want to explore in the next session?
3. For Amonique, adjustment disorder and posttraumatic stress disorder were ruled out based on criteria exhibited. Consider if you continued to see Amonique after a month, what criterion would you watch for in this case that will impact this diagnosis?
4. The use of Other Conditions That May Be the Focus of Treatment is rarely used in case presentations. What are the implications for or against adding Z-Codes? What contributions, if any, could be made regarding use of Z-Codes for treatment planning and intervention?

## REFERENCE

Gurda, K. (2015). Emerging trauma therapies: Critical analysis and discussion of three novel approaches. *Journal of Aggression, Maltreatment & Trauma, 24*(7), 773–793.

# 7.2    *Case of Dorothy*

## INTRODUCTION

Dorothy is a 68-year-old Caucasian female who is married and lives with her 72-year-old husband. Dorothy states that she has come to counseling at the advice of both her husband and her family physician, who are concerned about her. Dorothy is initially hesitant to share details of the precipitating events that prompted her coming to counseling, worrying that the counselor will think she's "crazy." After some reassurance, Dorothy shares that she has been communicating with her deceased son through the radio in her car.

Dorothy states that her deceased son began reaching out to her through the radio several months ago. At first, she thought she was imagining it; however, she has since come to believe that it is truly him in the radio. Dorothy shares that he sends messages coded through music or through news reports, so she has to listen very carefully in order to figure out what he is saying to her. Dorothy has been spending increasing amounts of time sitting in the car in her driveway listening to the radio and waiting for her son to reach out to her.

Dorothy states that her husband does not believe their son has been communicating with her, adding that he has been mostly patient and understanding of her desire to spend time in the car listening to the radio. Recently he has expressed concern, however, as has her family doctor. Dorothy acknowledges that her time in the car has been increasing lately, sometimes lasting for several hours. She agreed to talk with her family doctor at her husband's request; according to Dorothy, she is "the picture of health for a woman (her) age." Both the doctor and her husband have encouraged Dorothy to speak with someone about her son and the circumstances around his death.

Dorothy's son died in a car accident 18 years ago when he was 8 years old. Dorothy was driving the car and her son was in the passenger seat. A large dump truck ran the stop sign of the intersection they were crossing, striking the passenger side of the car. Just before impact, Dorothy saw the truck coming toward them and she threw herself across her son to protect him. She was gravely injured in the accident and her son died on the scene. Dorothy was in coma for over a month and did not learn about her son's death until she regained consciousness. Due to the circumstances resulting from the accident and her lengthy hospitalization, Dorothy was unable to attend her son's funeral. She blames herself for the accident and for her son's death.

## ▨ FAMILY HISTORY

Dorothy and her husband met in high school and married shortly after graduation. Dorothy worked as an office administrator for many years while her husband apprenticed with an electrician and took college courses in the evenings. They tried to start a family but learned that they would not be able to conceive through natural means. Since medical assistance was not an option for financial reasons, they decided they would one day adopt.

By the time they were in their late 20s, Dorothy's husband had started his own successful business as an electrician. Dorothy continued to work part-time as the couple explored their options for adoption. Twice they were matched with an expectant mother who later changed her mind after the baby was born. This was devastating to Dorothy and her husband; after the second time they decided not to pursue adoption again. They chose to focus their parenting desires on the foster care system, becoming foster parents to multiple children over the next decade. Dorothy recalls this time of her life as very happy and fulfilling, noting with some regret that this would have continued had her husband not become disabled.

Shortly after he turned 40, Dorothy's husband had an accident involving an extremely high voltage of electricity. He sustained extensive nerve damage and was subsequently unable to work. Though they had insurance and some income from the company, Dorothy was forced to go back to work full time. The couple also had to give up being foster parents, which was a difficult adjustment for both of them. A year later, Dorothy learned that she was pregnant. This was a shock to her and her husband, though they were overjoyed at their "miracle baby." They sold the business, downsized their home, and changed their lifestyle substantially so that Dorothy could be a full-time stay-at-home mother. Dorothy, her husband, and her son enjoyed a modest but very happy life until their son's tragic death at the age of 8.

The years immediately following their son's death were very difficult for Dorothy and her husband. They had little family support close by and struggled to find their way back from their devastating loss. Still, Dorothy reports that they "somehow made it through together." Recently they decided to sell their home and car, and to move to a retirement community. Dorothy states that it was shortly after they made this decision that her son started to contact her. She is now having second thoughts about leaving their home and selling the car, noting "how will he know where to find me?"

## ▓ CURRENT FUNCTIONING

Dorothy is in good general health with no history of psychotic disorder nor any in her family system. She does not use substances other than an "occasional glass of red wine." She is in a healthy, long-term relationship with a supportive spouse. Over the past few months, Dorothy has been having dreams about her son and the accident in which he was killed; she has also found herself avoiding socializing as much as she used to. In addition, though Dorothy *will* spend hours sitting in the car in the driveway, she avoids driving anywhere as it makes her anxious and nauseated. Dorothy denies having "flashbacks" about the accident but acknowledges that she has been thinking about it a lot lately and wishes she could stop. She also noted that she has been having difficulty sleeping and concentrating and has a reduced appetite.

Dorothy believes she is communicating with her deceased son through the radio of her car. She finds comfort in this communication but also worries that people will think she is "crazy." Other than communicating with her son, Dorothy shows no signs of dementia nor any cognitive decline. She expresses some apprehension about the impending transition to the retirement community and the selling of the family home and car.

## ■ DIAGNOSTIC IMPRESSIONS

Dorothy is exhibiting behaviors and traits that cross multiple groups of disorders, including the depressive and stress- and trauma-related disorders. Because her presenting symptoms seem to have started immediately following the decision to sell the family home and car, a diagnosis of adjustment disorder may seem indicated. However, this diagnosis would not account for the experience of communicating with her deceased son, nor the intrusive memories, problems with concentration and sleep, and decreased appetite. Dorothy also shows signs of a depressive disorder with psychotic features, although does not sufficiently meet criteria for this diagnosis. Still, this possibility warrants further exploration before it is ruled out.

Dorothy's presenting issues most closely align with posttraumatic stress disorder (PTSD) despite the length of time between the event and the presenting symptoms. Though Dorothy reports having "healed as much as can be expected" from the devastating loss she experienced, recent events have triggered unresolved trauma associated with the event. Furthermore, Dorothy shows signs of persistent complex bereavement disorder, which is not yet considered a (*Diagnostic and Statistical Manual of Mental Disorders, 5th Edition*) DSM-5 diagnosis but is a recognized condition currently under empirical evaluation.

In addressing Dorothy's presenting issues, it is essential for the counselor to recognize Dorothy's relatively stable functioning and to not negate Dorothy's beliefs. Psychoeducation would help Dorothy understand what she is going through, including how the recent life changes have triggered her PTSD symptoms and manifested her experience of communicating with her son.

## ■ DIAGNOSTIC CONCLUSIONS

- PTSD with delayed expression
- Rule-out: Major depressive disorder with psychotic features

## ■ SUGGESTED THERAPEUTIC INTERVENTIONS

Narrative therapy: Counseling goals for Dorothy include resolution of unresolved grief and trauma against the backdrop of Dorothy's self-concept and mother identity. This makes a narrative approach a good fit, as she can explore her constructs of self in context. Furthermore, such an exploration could provide opportunity for cognitive restructuring in a manner less direct (and thus less stressful) than a cognitive behavioral approach. Narrative therapy would also allow Dorothy to explore what communicating with her son means to her and how this communication affects her sense of self. Lastly, a narrative approach could allow Dorothy to understand how she has constructed her reality (e.g., believing she is talking to her son) to support her needs and unresolved issues.

## ■ FOR YOUR CONSIDERATION

1. Dorothy has a very strong maternal drive and identity. What role do these beliefs have in her blaming herself for her son's death?
2. How has the couple's recent decision to move from the family home and sell the car impacted Dorothy's PTSD?
3. How can you address Dorothy's belief that she is communicating with her deceased son without invalidating her worldview?
4. Is couple's counseling indicated in this case? Why or why not?

# 7.3   *Case of Keith*

## ■ INTRODUCTION

Keith, an 8-year-old Caucasian male, came to a community mental health facility through a referral from his adoption agency. An incredibly slender and intelligent boy, Keith appears to be suspicious and angry. He reports that he did not know why he had to go to counseling because he was not crazy. Keith reports having no friends his own age and constantly fights with his brother, who is 1 year younger than him. Keith appears emotionally withdrawn from his adoptive parents and does not go to them for comfort when he is upset. He does things intentionally to distance himself from anyone who shows any care for him. Keith has a flat affect and appears to be quick-tempered, miserable, and anxious.

## ■ FAMILY HISTORY

Keith has a history of abandonment and lack of the most basic human needs. He was taken from his biological parents due to the horrific neglect and abuse at 3 years of age that he suffered at the hands of his own parents and grandmother. He was shuffled through five foster homes in 5 years, before finding his "forever" family. Keith has never been diagnosed with a spectrum disorder.

Keith's adoptive parents attribute his symptoms to his disjointed upbringing. They report that his biological parents were on drugs and often left Keith and his brother in the care of his biological father's schizophrenic mother. It was reported that the grandmother locked the boys in a room and tied a rope from the doorknob of that room to another room across the hall so the boys could not get out. The adoptive parents stated that the grandmother would only give the boys a piece of bread and a cup of coffee for the entire day. They were not allowed to leave the room and would relieve themselves in a nearby closet or soil their pants. When this was discovered by neighbors, the boys were sent to foster care. Keith's adoptive parents report that he has little interest in food today, and they make him drink shakes with high nutritional value to sustain him.

The boys were given to a single male foster parent. At one of the foster parent meetings, Keith disclosed that the foster parent was making him take showers with him, and it made him very uncomfortable. This has led his adoptive parents to believe that Keith was sexually abused at this house because Keith refuses to speak of this foster parent or any of his time at this placement. He was swiftly removed from that house and placed with his biological aunt. He loved his aunt and finally felt at ease in this placement. His aunt found out that she was pregnant and could not afford to keep Keith and his brother. She returned them to foster care. Keith was devastated as this was not only hurtful to be returned, but also this was his only tie to his family of origin. He was then placed with a couple who owned a trailer park. The boys speak well of this placement, but they were removed when Keith had "an incident" with their dog. There is no additional information on this incident, but it was severe enough for the foster parents to give the boys back to foster care.

The boys were placed with a couple who already had four other foster children. The boys reported that they were verbally abused and neglected at this placement. The adoptive parents indicated that the foster parents would do things to "psychologically terrorize" the boys. Keith stated that this was the most horrific environment that he had lived in since his grandmother's home. Keith talked about this period of time with a great deal of hatred and fire in his eyes. Keith said that they "celebrated" his birthday, got him a cake, several presents, and everyone sang to him. After the song was over, they told him that he could not have any cake and gave his presents to the other foster children. Keith indicated that when his brother forgot his homework, he was made to sleep in the garage in 30° weather with no covers and that he could feel mice walking over him. Keith has trouble with wetting the bed (this behavior goes back to when he was first removed and placed with the single male foster parent). His foster mother would make him strip down naked in the driveway, and she would hose him down with ice-cold water. Keith still wets his pants, and his adoptive parents believe that he can control it because he will urinate a little or a lot depending on his mood. Although almost every horrific detail disclosed involves the foster mother, Keith is incredibly angry with the foster father whom he feels should have protected him.

During the 5-year period of foster care, his biological mother would call him and tell him that she was working on getting him back. She fled with his biological sister when he was originally taken. His sister was 2 years old at the time. He has spent the last 5 years wondering why he was not "good enough" to take with her.

## ▓ DIAGNOSTIC IMPRESSIONS

Keith is entering treatment at the prompting of his adoptive parents and the adoption agency from which he was placed. Keith has reactive attachment disorder (RAD), which is severe and persistent, because the disorder has been present for more than 12 months, and he exhibits all of the symptoms at very high levels. He has been re-homed often and taken from bad to worse placements. He is emotionally withdrawn with caregivers. He does not seek comfort when distressed and is only semi responsive when his adoptive family reaches out to him. He angers easily, is fearful, and often sad, even when the situation does not warrant such emotions.

Keith has a long history of abuse and neglect and reports that every person who was charged with taking care of him either failed him or abused him. This leaves him mistrustful of others, especially those who appear to care for him.

Keith has a history of enuresis. It is reported that this started with his first foster placement. However, given the denial of restroom facilities by the biological grandmother, this cannot be verified. It is believed that Keith is wetting his pants on purpose when he becomes distressed. He also wets the bed at night and wears "special underpants" at night.

Keith is incredibly thin, so much so that his medical provider has called Children's Services to ensure that he is being fed. His adoptive parents ensure that he drinks shakes high in nutrition and monitor his food and drink intake every day. It is likely that Keith has avoidant/restrictive food intake disorder fueled by his history of abuse.

## ▓ DIAGNOSTIC CONCLUSIONS

- RAD
- Child neglect
- Child psychological abuse
- R/O Child sexual abuse
- Enuresis
- Avoidant/restrictive food intake disorder

## ▓ SUGGESTED THERAPEUTIC INTERVENTIONS

Treating RAD can involve case management, individual treatment, group counseling, family therapy, parenting classes, and medication. Many foster parents and adoptive parents do not understand RAD. They believe that they are giving the child everything that they have ever dreamed of and do not understand why the child cannot connect to them. One of the worst things that a counselor can suggest is forcing affection on a child who may have an aversion to touch or physical affection. Although it can be very difficult for these parents to understand, their child is not apathetic regarding their relationship. These children simply do not know how to bond with the new parent and may even be fearful of rejection and/or abuse in the new home.

Another issue that often comes into play is boundaries. Parents often do not want to place rules and restrictions on a child who has been traumatized and/or neglected. This becomes ineffective rather quickly. Children need limits to ensure predictability and safety. This teaches a child about natural consequences and gives them a semblance of control over themselves. When the child is acting out, a counselor can put together a behavioral chart. Formulate the chart not only with the parent, but also with the child. Have the child draw and color the chart, so they feel that it is their chart. It is important to use positive reinforcement. For example, Keith is hitting his foster brother every day. The goal is to extinguish this behavior. While including Keith, make a chart for the month. Each day that Keith does not hit his brother, he gets a check mark. At the end of the week, if he has seven check marks, he gets a prize. The prize should be something small. It could be an hour of extra electronic time, a delayed bedtime, or so on. At the end of the month, if Keith has 30 check marks, he gets a bigger prize; this could be a meal at McDonalds, a trip to the zoo, or the purchase of a desired toy.

One of the most effective ways to help a child with RAD is by providing family counseling. All members of the family must have realistic expectations. The child's issues will not resolve overnight, and they should celebrate even the smallest victories in an attempt to empower the child toward bigger goals. The family should also be made aware that the child may backslide.

Due to excessive fear, it can be incredibly uncomfortable for a child with RAD to change. This is an opportunity for the family to show the child that they will be there for the child no matter what the challenge. A counselor should plan many therapeutic activities. Activities with the family should be fun because the day-to-day stress can be overwhelming. A counselor should address self-care. If the family is not getting good nutrition and plenty of rest, it can make the work that much harder. Develop a good resource list for the entire family. They may need options for everything from family fun night to respite care. The single best thing that you can do for the child and family is to instill hope. If the child and/or parent constantly focuses on what is going wrong, there will be little to no change. If the family is taught strength-based coping skills that they can use together and individually, it will likely produce a positive result. For example, teaching breathing exercises can be beneficial for the family. A breathing exercise can take place at home, work, school, and so on. It does not require money or additional resources. It is a great way to de-escalate many situations. Breathing exercises, guided imagery, and progressive muscle relaxation can be a no-cost way to vastly increase a family's coping skill set.

## ■ FOR YOUR CONSIDERATION

1. How might this case change if you receive confirmation that Keith had been sexually abused? RAD can be seen as a "strong" diagnosis. What steps can you take to ensure that you are not misdiagnosing RAD when it could, in fact, be a behavioral problem or a parenting issue?
2. When we think about nature versus nurture, Keith's problems seem to be environmentally founded. How do you see biology playing a role in this diagnosis?

# 7.4    Case of Eric

## ■ INTRODUCTION

Eric is an 11-year-old Latino male who lives with his mother, siblings, and grandparents in the inner-portion of a large city. Eric is in the sixth grade. He is in regular education classes. Eric has always done well in school until recently. His grade point average has declined from a 3.8 to a 2.0. Eric's grandparents took Eric out of the school he had been attending since kindergarten due to concerns about safety, drugs, and gang activity in the area. Eric has established long-term friendships at his school, and he had no desire to change the school. Eric's grandparents are devout Catholics and they want Eric to grow his faith while pursuing his education. They believe that their grandchild will be protected from peer pressure by attending a private Catholic school.

Eric also has a crush on a girl that he has known for the past 3 years at his school. Right before his grandparents pulled him out of school, it appeared that his crush also liked him. When Eric told this girl that he was transferring school, she stated, "I guess we don't have anything in common anymore." Eric was devastated and tried to get his grandparents to allow him to attend his regular school. His grandparents would not budge. Eric feels like his family is against him as they have allowed his two younger sisters to remain enrolled in the inner-city school system. What's worse is that Eric now feels responsible that his mother has to go back to work in order to afford his private education. He does not feel that it is fair that his grandparents are placing this additional burden on his mother.

Eric has been experiencing some mental health concerns since the transition to the new school. Eric has never been in counseling and he has never been diagnosed with any mental or emotional disorder. Eric does not take any medication. When Eric was asked about his mental health symptoms, he stated that he finds it hard to sleep at night due to increased expectations at his new school. He reports that he is tearful at night while completing homework. He states that the other kids in his grade level seem to be smarter than the kids at his old school. He is angry at his family for making him change the school and not taking his feelings into consideration. He finds it hard to concentrate on his studies as he is thinking about his old friends and wondering if they even care that he is not there. Eric is also worried that he will not be able to perform at the level of his "private education" classmates. He states that this makes him nervous and anxious most days to the point that he does not want to eat for fear that he may vomit on the way to school.

## ■ FAMILY HISTORY

Eric's mother takes care of her parents. That is the reason that she and her kids moved into her parent's home. Eric's grandfather has cancer and his grandmother has mobility issues. They are both in their late 70s. Eric's mother has a high school education and she has recently received her nursing assistant certificate. She needed a "good job" to be able to pay for Eric's new education. She also works in the cafeteria at his school during some weekdays to be able to get a partial scholarship for tuition.

Eric's father left 8 years ago. Eric's grandparents repeatedly tell Eric that they do not want him to end up like his dead-beat dad. Eric does not have visitation with his father and his mother has never received any child support. Eric only has fond memories of his father. Eric was sheltered from the abuse that his father inflicted on his mother. Eric's grandfather constantly reminds Eric's mother of her mistakes regarding her choices in relationships. Eric and his sisters all have different fathers. Eric finds it hard to believe the things that his grandparents say about his father. He is certain that something is preventing his father from coming to see him. He knows in his heart that if it was possible for his dad to make contact, then he would want a relationship with Eric.

Eric's mother watched domestic violence between her parents growing up. It was not until her father became ill that the violence ceased about 10 years ago. The reason that Eric's grandmother has mobility issues is due to Eric's grandfather breaking both of her legs with a baseball bat when Eric's mother was a teenager. Eric's grandfather served time in prison for this crime and upon completed his sentence was diagnosed with cancer in his mouth. Eric's grandfather smoked three packs of unfiltered cigarettes a day for 20 years, before going to prison for domestic violence. Eric's grandmother immediately took his grandfather back into the family home. She decided that it was God's will to direct her to nurse him back to health. Eric's grandfather beat cancer the first time. However, the cancer has returned. This time, the cancer is in his lungs and his prognosis does not look as good as it did during his first battle. He is trying very hard to ensure that the family is "set," so that if he passes from cancer this time, they will all be okay.

Eric's mother and grandparents constantly disagree on how to raise her children. Eric's mother believes that they have no right to tell her how to raise her children based on their parenting skills in raising her. Eric's mother is also very resentful of how they talk to her about her relationships with men. She believes that she ended up in horrible relationships based on the relationship that was modeled for her by them. Eric's mother also feels that neither of them would be in their current position had her father taken better care of himself and had her mother not allowed the violence within their family home.

Eric's two younger sisters appear to be quiet within the household. They tend to keep to themselves and do what they are told. They are both very passive and do not want any negative attention to come their way. This tends to make Eric frustrated as he knows that they will never stand up for him and so their relationship is strained much of the time. Eric is also resentful that the "girls" are favored and get to stay at his old school. Eric feels like he does not have a viable support system and he is surrounded by hypocrites.

## ▨ CURRENT FUNCTIONING

Eric recently tried alcohol at a sleepover with one of his friends from his old school. This is what prompted the quick and divisive change in schools. Eric's grandfather believed that this was the beginning of the path to drugs and gang activity. Eric stated that he only wanted to try beer, so that he would know how it tasted. However, his friend got so drunk that he threw up and his friend's parents were made aware of the drinking. They told Eric's grandparents.

Eric has never tried drugs and has no intention of trying drugs. Eric has heard rumbling over the years that his father was on drugs. Eric believes that his father's drug use may be what is prohibiting his father from making contact with Eric. Eric is concerned that if he tries drugs, he may become addicted like his father.

Eric has historically been a "good kid." He is helpful, kind, and smart. Before recently moving in with his grandparents, he was often left in charge of his younger sisters when his mother needed to go somewhere. Eric has been very mature and responsible his entire life. Eric has never been in any real trouble and he has never committed any criminal activity.

Eric used to be the "man of the house" when he, his mother, and his sisters lived on their own. He was used to taking care of his younger siblings and he had a large say in what transpired in the household unit. All of Eric's power was removed the minute he began living with his grandparents. The move to his grandparent's house has been an unwelcome and unwanted transition for Eric. He has tried to talk to his mother about his concerns, but she feels that she has a "duty" and an "obligation" to "honor" her parents. Because of this rationale, Eric and his mother are not close anymore. He feels that she is choosing them over him.

## ▨ DIAGNOSTIC IMPRESSIONS

Eric is struggling to cope with all the current changes in his life. Eric has always been a "good kid," but he is finding it difficult to make the transition to both living with his grandparents and transferring to a new school. Eric had become accustomed to being "the man of the house" and now he is faced with a situation where he has little to no power.

Eric is having difficulty sleeping. He is sad about leaving his friends behind, especially a girl that he was growing fond of and whom he believes liked him too. Eric becomes tearful at night regarding his homework. He believes that his family is against him. Eric feels responsible for his mother getting a job and helping out at school to offset his private school tuition. He feels that it is not fair that his grandparents put this burden on his mother, especially since she has to take care of them as well. Eric is angry about all the change and upheaval in his life right now. He finds it hard to concentrate as he is thinking about his previous life. Eric is worried about his school performance and feels like the other kids are farther ahead in their scholastic activities at the new school.

Eric lacks a social support system and coping skills. Eric is open to learning ways to handle his new life. However, Eric has never been in treatment and with his new academic responsibilities, it is unknown how he will do in therapy.

## ▓ DIAGNOSTIC CONCLUSIONS

- Adjustment disorder, unspecified
- Academic or educational problem

## ▓ SUGGESTED THERAPEUTIC INTERVENTION

In Eric's situation, his primary stressors (school and home) cannot be removed at this time. Therefore, it is imperative that adaptive strategies be put into place to mitigate the current emotional and behavioral implications.

Individual and/or Family Therapy—Eric has mild mental health symptoms brought on by acute change. Although "talk therapy" especially person-centered treatment could be very beneficial for Eric to get his feelings out in a supportive and empathic environment, it is equally important that Eric and his family do some work together. Much of Eric's issues stem from family-related issues. Eric can be the model client in individual treatment, but if his family environment is unchanging, he may not be able to sustain his growth.

Afterschool Activities/Sports/Community Programming—Eric is not currently involved with any extracurricular activities. It may be hard for him to connect and make friends at his new school. These activities intrinsically allow for organic friendships to grow. Eric may also need to engage in tutoring to catch up with his peers. Eric is the oldest child in the family and the only boy. Eric does not get along well with his grandfather. Eric's mother may want to enroll him a program like Big Brothers/Big Sisters, so that he will be able to have some mentorship and male influence.

## ▓ FOR YOUR CONSIDERATION

1. It is often hard to work with children, because they make amazing strides in counseling, but we send them back to the same environment that unravels them. How can you get buy-in from the family and keep them engaged in family therapy?

2. Adjustment disorders are short-term issues based on an acute and identifiable stressor. At what point would you expect this issue to resolve?
3. Eric's grandmother is barely mentioned throughout the narrative. When she is mentioned, she is spoken of as a victim or as part of the grandparent unit. How do you see domestic violence continuing to impact this family?

# 7.5   *Case of Tony*

## ■ INTRODUCTION

Tony is a 15-year-old boy who was born deaf. Tony is the only one in his immediate and extended family who is deaf. He currently uses American Sign Language (ASL) as his primary language. Tony's mother and younger sister (7 years old) are the only two members of Tony's immediate family who have learned ASL. Tony's dad and older brother did try to learn and know some signs but mostly communicate with Tony using homemade signs or by Tony lipreading. Tony's younger sister came to his family as a surprise. His parents did not plan to have any more children after Tony as they were concerned, they would have another deaf child.

Starting at age 4, Tony's has been attending the State School for the Deaf and Blind. His parents moved to a neighboring town in order to be closer to the school. When attending the State School for the Deaf and Blind, many children are bussed from all over the state to the school on Sunday night, stay during the school week in the school cottages, and then are bussed home on Friday afternoon. Tony's State Schools for the Deaf and Blind have a somewhat unique school setting with an elementary school for prekindergarten students to sixth grade students in one building and seventh grade students to 12th grade students in a different building. Students can remain in the school as a student until they are 21 years of age, at which point they have "aged out" whether they were able to graduate or not. This extended age range is due to the recognition that many deaf children may not be identified at an early age or have not had sufficient support in developing their language resulting in repeated grades. Not all students stay in the cottages during the week, but the school does recommend staying in the cottages to help immerse the child in ASL and Deaf culture.

Cottages are set up to provide as much of a "home" feel as possible. Cottages are assigned based on ages. Due to the limited number of students, the cottages are coed with the separation of sleeping quarters and bathrooms being biologically sex specific. There are full-time cottage staff who stay in the cottages to monitor the children and further support the children's development.

After being notified of Tony's deafness shortly after his birth, his mom dedicated her time to find resources for Tony. She discovered the State School for the Deaf and Blind in that search and Tony's parents agreed that this school was the best option for Tony. Tony's parents worked to move closer to the school but were unable to move into the same town due to his father's employment. As such, his mom will drive him to the school on Monday morning and then allow him to be bussed home on Friday afternoon. Since Tony has been engaged with the State School at such a young age and is surrounded by other d/Deaf children and Deaf adults, he now identifies himself as part of the Deaf community and culture. He is proud to be a Deaf person and does not see his inability to hear as a disability, even though his parents label his deafness as a disability when introducing him to others.

Tony is an athletic adolescent who excels at Baseball. He has been able to be integrated into the local high school for the majority of his classes which allows him to be able to play baseball for that high school. He is currently the starting pitcher for the Junior Varsity team and is occasionally brought up to the Varsity team to pitch. When attending the local high school, Tony has accommodations which include an ASL interpreter and a note taker for all his classes. He has recently been given a different ASL interpreter due to the current sexual abuse allegations. Tony has been able to maintain a 3.2 grade point average which he and his parents are proud of. Tony describes himself as a very social kid, until recently, who most people know in the school because of "I'm the funny Deaf pitcher."

It has recently been discovered that Tony has been the victim of child sexual abuse. A cottage staff member recently walked in on Tony and his ASL interpreter who interprets his public-school classes. The staff member saw the conversation from a distance, but clearly saw the interpreter talking about a pregnancy scare and telling Tony that he might be the father. The ASL interpreter is a 28-year-old married female. The staff member confronted them both on the conversation and the interpreter stated that the staff member was mistaken and that she and Tony were talking about a couple in his public high school. However, after the interpreter left, Tony was visibly upset and came to the cottage staff member and disclosed the sexual relationship and his fears regarding the potential pregnancy. The cottage staff member promptly called the local police and the alleged abuse is currently under investigation.

Tony's parents have been notified of the situation and wanted to pull him from both schools. Per Tony's request, he remains dually enrolled at the State School for the Deaf and Blind and the local high school as he wants to continue playing with his current baseball team. Tony has engaged in a forensic interview at the local Child Advocacy Center. The forensic interviewer was bilingual and fluent in ASL which Tony reports helped him be more open about his "relation-ship" with his interpreter. During his interview, Tony describes his relationship with his interpreter as "special" and consensual. He does not view the sexual relationship between him and his 28-year-old interpreter as abuse. Tony reported that before his "relationship" with the interpreter, he was a virgin and was often teased by his teammates about being a 15-year-old virgin. He stated that he confided in his interpreter about being embarrassed about being a virgin and that she was helpful and reassured him that it was okay for him to be a virgin. Tony discussed how the relationship shifted as his interpreter started flirting with him and wearing more suggestive clothing like shorter skirts and lower cut tops. He stated that they eventually made up excuses for extra time together like her "tutoring me in English." During those "tutoring sessions" they would often go out to her car where she had parked in a secluded spot or they drove to secluded areas and engaged in various sexual acts, including unprotected sexual intercourse. He stated that the interpreter had been confiding in him about how miserable she is in her marriage and that she wishes that she and Tony could be together. He states that they both (him and the interpreter) were aware of the age difference, but that "age doesn't matter when you are in love." After his interview at the Child Advocacy Center, a medical examination was conducted. Tony expressed concerns of a potential sexually transmitted disease (STD), but the results of the tests have not yet been received.

The police have scheduled an appointment to speak with the interpreter and the status or validity of the pregnancy is currently unknown. Tony has not been allowed or able to talk with the interpreter since the time the report was made. Tony's parents have both expressed their anger, disappointment, and fears regarding the situation. Tony's older brother is aware of the situation. Tony's older brother thinks that everyone is blowing it out of proportion and has told Tony "nice job landing an older woman." Tony's younger sister has not been told of the alleged abuse but is aware that something is wrong due to the increased number of conversations between her parents behind closed doors. Tony's sister has noticed that Tony is more distant from her than usual and is shorter with her than normal.

## ■ FAMILY HISTORY

Tony describes his relationship with his father as "intense." His father is a manager of a national store chain. It took some time, but his father was able to transfer to a store in a neighboring town of the State School. As a manager, he works long hours and every holiday. Tony believes their lack of fluid communication is the reason he and his father have an "intense" relationship. Tony states his father becomes very frustrated with Tony when he does not understand, or cannot accurately lip read what his father is saying. Tony's father was a college baseball player, so they do connect when playing catch or practicing pitcher although many of those bonding moments are ended abruptly when communication breaks down between them.

Tony describes his mother as a "helicopter mom." He states that he tends to be the sole focus of his mother which is not only "annoying," but it also causes some strain on his relationship with his siblings. Tony's mother was an accountant before he was born, but after discovering Tony's deafness, she did not return to work and has a been a stay-at-home parent ever since. Tony's mother works hard to be involved with the deaf community as much as possible and will often interpret the church services at the local church where many of the members are deaf. Tony's mother reports as having a lot of guilt regarding Tony's deafness as it was a "birth defect" and she "must have done something wrong during pregnancy." Tony's characterizes his parent's relationship as "good" and that he only sees them argue occasionally and Tony is usually the topic of the argument. Tony's mother reports feeling frustrated that his father does not make more of an effort with Tony and Tony's father states he does not need to because Tony's mom is over-involved.

Tony's older brother (17 years old) is a senior. He does not attend the same public school as Tony as his brother and family live in the neighboring town. Tony's brother is also a strong athlete who plays on the varsity team for both Basketball and Baseball. There have been times when Tony has pitched against his brother on Varsity and Tony likes talking about how he struck his brother out in one of those games. Tony describes his relationship with his brother and "pretty good." Tony stated that language is a barrier between them, but that all goes away when they play sports together at home. Tony stated that his brother is a good older brother who lets Tony hang out with his brother and his brother's friends. Tony's brother is graduating soon and has a full ride scholarship for basketball at a Junior College about 5 hours from their home.

Tony states he is closest to his much younger sister. Because of the age difference, Tony was able to teach his sister ASL from a young age and she is very fluent. As a result, Tony reports that he feels closest to his younger sister and will often use her to interpret conversations between him and other family members (mostly his father). Tony describes his younger sister as a typical younger sister who sometimes is a pest to have around but most of the time the two of them are found together on the weekends when he is home.

## ▪ CURRENT FUNCTIONING

It has only been 2 weeks since the original report of the alleged sexual abuse. Tony has been cooperative in the investigative process and has recently completed the forensic interview. Tony has been struggling to focus in school and his grades are starting to be impacted. Baseball season is starting next week and although Tony told his parent he wanted to stay at the school so he could play baseball, he is now second guessing his desire to play baseball this year. He has been struggling to concentrate on anything other than the past relationship with the interpreter and whether she is in fact pregnant with his child. Since the disclosure of abuse, Tony reports that his relationship with his parents is strained as they continue to ask him intrusive questions about the relationship and telling him "we raised you better." Tony also reports that he has withdrawn from many of his friends and younger sister in order to avoid talking about the abuse. Tony expressed all he wants to do is sleep to escape from the current "mess."

When asked what he does to cope with stress, he stated that he used to go play baseball or work out but that it does not help him anymore. He was able to identify his younger sister, two teammates, and his best friend as supports. However, he has been distancing himself from them all as he does not know who is aware of the abuse and who is not.

## ■ DIAGNOSTIC IMPRESSIONS

Due to the report of the alleged abuse being within the last 2 weeks and Tony's changes in behaviors and emotions, an initial diagnosis of adjustment disorder would be appropriate. Tony has started to struggle with his grades, has had difficulty concentrating, considerable worry about the unknowns, withdrawing from others, and sleeping to escape, a modifier of mixed anxiety and depressed mood is suggested. A diagnosis of child sexual abuse would be warranted as the report of child sexual abuse was initiated as a result of Tony's disclosure of the sexual relationship with his interpreter. As you discuss this diagnosis with Tony and his parents, be prepared for mixed responses from parents likely agreeing with the diagnosis and Tony disagreeing due to his view of the "relationship." Physically, there are concerns about possible STDs and Tony's deafness should be noted.

## ■ DIAGNOSTIC CONCLUSIONS

- Adjustment disorder with mixed anxiety and depressed mood
- Child sexual abuse
- STD (r/o)
- Deafness

## SUGGESTED THERAPEUTIC INTERVENTIONS

After contact from Tony's parents to start counseling, it is important to find an appropriately licensed/certified ASL interpreter as ASL is Tony's primary language. Because Tony's alleged offender was his former ASL interpreter, it would be wise to ask Tony for a list of preferred interpreters or offer to locate an interpreter who is not local to the area. This would help Tony feel like he is more in control of his sessions and confidentiality given that the deaf and interpreting worlds are small and interconnected. If Tony does not have a preferred ASL interpreter he would like to use for counseling sessions, the clinician make search for a certified counselor through the professional organization the Registry of Interpreters for the Deaf (RID) at rid.org. There is also the option of using an interpreter through Video Remote Interpreting (VRI) Services which is essentially the use of a program similar to Zoom or Skype where the interpreter is located in a different location than Tony and the counselor but is able to provide interpreting services. This may result in some significant time lags and may disrupt the development of the therapeutic relationship. However, it would allow for more privacy for Tony as the interpreters are geographically located around the United States continent. A key element to be aware of is that as a clinician, you will be responsible for paying the sign language interpreter and there is a billable code to help recoup those costs. For more information about your legal obligations to provide accommodations and any exceptions to these requirements, visit the Americans with Disabilities Act website, specifically related to auxiliary aids and services: www.ada.gov/regs2010/titleIII_2010/titleIII_2010_regulations.htm#a303

As Tony currently views the sexual interaction with his interpreter as a "consensual relationship," psychoeducation about sexual abuse and the grooming process will be important. Tony is currently concerned about the potential pregnancy and attention to his concerns and anxiety will be important in the early stages of counseling. Much of the early sessions of counseling will be focused on validating Tony and developing a therapeutic relationship with both him and the ASL interpreter who will be interpreting your sessions. Person centered techniques would be advised in these early sessions to help develop the therapeutic relationship, validate Tony's experience and concerns, and allow Tony the safe place to process what is happening.

If Tony is unable or unwilling to recognize the "relationship" as abuse, cognitive behavioral therapy (CBT) techniques would be helpful in assisting Tony with his concerns about his current unknowns (the pregnancy, his possible STDs, court proceedings, etc.). Helping him develop coping skills to manage his various feelings about these unknowns would be beneficial. It may also be helpful to challenge some of Tony's potential faulty beliefs regarding his view of his role within the abuse "relationship." Tony may not be ready to identify the "relationship" as abuse and may return to counseling at a later time to process the abuse. At a minimum, he will have developed positive coping skills to assist him as he navigates his various emotional responses.

As Tony starts to recognize the "relationship" as abuse, it will be important to be patient with Tony as he starts to redefine his "relationship" with his former interpreter. He may start to view the "relationship" as a violation and become angry or uncomfortable (or a variety of emotions) with what happened. Two common therapeutic treatments for children who have been sexually abused are Trauma Focused Cognitive Behavior Therapy (TF-CBT) or EMDR. According to a meta-analysis research study that examined the results of 30 studies focused on TF-CBT and EMDR treatment, both TF-CBT and EMDR has been shown to be effective when working with children who have experienced trauma (Lewey et al., 2018). A key element of TF-CBT is to work with caregivers as well. Given his parents' response to the abuse, TF-CBT may be a helpful way to assist the family in processing the abuse simultaneously to Tony's treatment.

## ▧ FOR YOUR CONSIDERATION

1. Given that this client is a deaf adolescent and you do not know sign language, what needs to be addressed with the interpreter you hire for your sessions with Tony?
   a. And, since the alleged offender was Tony's sign language interpreter, how might that impact your sessions as you will be using a sign language interpreter?
2. Does Tony's view of his relationship with his interpreter as consensual impact the way you view the situation or how you might diagnose Tony?
3. How might you personal opinion of the "relationship" impact your counseling sessions with Tony?
4. As Tony is exhibiting symptoms of a couple different diagnoses, would you diagnose him with adjustment disorder and child sexual abuse understanding that this mental health diagnosis will likely follow him into adulthood? If not, which diagnosis would you document and why?

## ▧ REFERENCE

Lewey, J. H., Smith, C. L., Burcham, B., Saunders, N. L., Elfallal, D., & O'Toole, S. K. (2018). Comparing the effectiveness of EMDR and TF-CBT for children and adolescents: A meta-analysis. *Journal of Child & Adolescent Trauma*, 11(4), 457–472.

# 7 . 6     *Case of Jessica*

## ▓ INTRODUCTION

Jessica is a 15-year-old female who was referred to your community mental health clinic by the local child advocacy center. A year ago, Jessica disclosed to her cousin that she had been sexually abused by their grandfather from the ages of 8 to 12. Jessica's grandfather passed away last year. While at the funeral, Jessica was asked by an older cousin if the grandfather used to touch Jessica too. After Jessica replied that he had, the older cousin told Jessica she was not the only one. The weeks following the funeral were full of family meetings and various professional appointments, including a forensic interview at the local child advocacy center, to assess the extent of the abuse and number of victims. During that time, it was discovered that the grandfather had molested all of his granddaughters, four in total, and all when they were between the ages of 8 and 12. Jessica has a younger sister, Emma, who was 9 years old at the time of the grandfather's passing. During Jessica's forensic interview, she stated that she felt guilty for "letting it happen" and that, because she had never told, it was her fault the younger granddaughters were abused.

## ▓ CURRENT FUNCTIONING

Since disclosing the abuse, Jessica has become more withdrawn from family and friends and is very irritable. Her grades have plummeted, and her parents have become more concerned about her. Recently, Emma discovered that Jessica has started to cut herself on her inner thighs and breasts after walking into their shared room while Jessica was changing. Jessica became very angry and threatened to hurt Emma if Emma told anyone about the cuts. Emma agreed not to tell anyone, but after 3 days, Emma told her mom and dad about Jessica's cuts. Jessica's parents called the child advocacy center for referrals and made an appointment with you the next day. Upon intake, you discover that Jessica has been engaging in self-harming behavior since she learned that her grandfather had molested all of the granddaughters, including Emma. Jessica stated that she does not want to die and does not think about killing herself, but that cutting herself makes her feel better. Jessica stated that cutting herself helps calm her down when she starts thinking about "things." When probed further about what "things" she thinks about, Jessica reported that she blames herself for Emma being molested. Jessica reported that she believes that if she had told someone that her grandfather was molesting her when it was happening to her, then her grandfather would have been in jail and not able to molest Emma. Jessica stated that she also cuts herself when she has flashbacks of the abuse she endured from her grandfather. Jessica reports that there are certain places that she avoids because they make her think about the abuse and her grandfather.

When asked what she thought about engaging in the counseling process, she stated, "Counseling is for crazy people, and I'm not crazy!" After some explanation of how you view counseling and what you think you could help her with, Jessica reluctantly agreed to come back next week. Before leaving your office, you were able to develop a safety plan with Jessica and her mother to help keep Jessica safe until you see her next week. Jessica signed the safety plan, but as she leaves, she makes the statement, "I can't promise anything, but I will try."

## ■ DIAGNOSTIC IMPRESSIONS

Due to the traumatic event and various symptoms, a diagnosis of PTSD should be considered. Because Jessica disclosed a history of child sexual abuse by her grandfather, there is a clear traumatic event that will be part of the focus of counseling. Some of the concerning symptoms of this case would include Jessica's engagement in self-harming behaviors as a way to cope with her flashbacks of the sexual abuse and excessive guilt she feels about her sister's victimization. Jessica also reported that she avoids various places because they trigger memories of the abuse she endured from her grandfather. These efforts to avoid triggers of the abuse and Jessica's inability to control flashbacks and thoughts of the abuse are clearly distressing to Jessica and should be an area of clinical focus during sessions. Jessica's parents sought out counseling for Jessica because they noticed a change in her behaviors wherein she was more withdrawn, angry, and, now, self-harming since she disclosed about the sexual abuse a year ago. Although the sexual abuse occurred when Jessica was aged 8 to 12, Jessica has expressed more clear symptoms of PTSD over the past year, and thus a delayed expression would be noted.

As Jessica's counseling will be focused on helping her process the traumatic event of child sexual abuse, a diagnosis of child sexual abuse would be appropriate. Not all clinicians may choose to incorporate the diagnosis of child sexual abuse when providing a diagnosis for Jessica. Although it is clearly applicable to Jessica's case, some clinicians would argue that the symptoms are best described by a diagnosis of PTSD and that the diagnosis of child sexual abuse is unnecessary. These clinicians may also argue that it is best to use the least stigmatizing diagnosis possible and to consider the potential harm that a client may come to because of the additional diagnosis (American Counseling Association, 2014). Still other clinicians would argue that including the diagnosis of child sexual abuse helps to create the clearest, most accurate description of the client's experience. Whether the clinician decides to include the diagnosis of child sexual abuse or not, it is an ethical expectation and best practice to discuss the various diagnoses with the client and her parents to review the pros and cons of these diagnoses and allow the client and her parents to be a part of that diagnostic decision-making process (American Counseling Association, 2014). Another diagnostic feature to consider in the case of Jessica is her self-harming behaviors. Jessica reports a history of self-harming and would benefit from specific clinical attention to the behaviors. Although this is a diagnostic feature that may be accounted for within the criteria for PTSD, a clinician may choose to identify this behavior as a separate behavior of clinical concern to be addressed during treatment.

Jessica endured sexual abuse from her grandfather for 4 years; the trauma she endured during this critical period of development greatly affects her sense of self and safe coping strategies. For many children and adolescents, sexual abuse can be confusing to understand and complicated to report. At the age of 8, Jessica and many other children are raised and trained for many years to comply with adult requests, not complain, and do what they are asked. Therefore, sexual abuse is any sexual act that a person may not be able to give consent to (Darkness to Light, 2013). In the case of Jessica, she is a minor and any sexual act between a child and an adult is abuse, just as any sexual act between a child and another child that is forced, bribed, or coerced or involves a developmental age difference of more than 3 years is considered sexual abuse (Darkness to Light, 2013). Sexual abuse includes but is not limited to sexual acts of penetration, force, pain, or even touching and sodomy. If an adult engages in looking at or showing sexual images, shows body parts, or touches self in front of the child, then it is sexual abuse (Darkness to Light, 2013). Jessica has been traumatized by enduring reoccurring sexual abuse and then, upon the loss of her grandfather, was further tormented by learning that her sister had also suffered sexual abuse by her grandfather. The stress, trauma, and guilt Jessica suffered greatly affected her healthy coping skills, leading her to intentionally engage in self-harming behaviors.

Jessica and her female family members are not alone in experiencing sexual abuse; one in seven girls is sexually abused by the age of 18 (Darkness to Light, 2013). Children experiencing childhood sexual abuse have been reported to have a high statistical association for deliberate self-harming behaviors (Romans et al., 1995). Deliberate self-harming behaviors are associated with significant relational problems within the family of origin, interpersonal mental health problems, and survivors of childhood sexual abuse who endured frequent and intrusive abuse (Romans et al., 1995). Self-harm that involves nonsuicidal self-injury (NSSI) includes but is not limited to a person causing intentional pain and harm to one's body by burning, squeezing, cutting, biting, scratching, or hitting one's self (Washburn et al., 2015). In the case of Jessica, she engages in NSSI through cutting. Approximately 16% to 18% of adolescents report one incident of NSSI as a non-socially acceptable form of coping. Jessica's onset of self-harming behaviors, PTSD, guilt, and the childhood sexual abuse have created demands on her coping that exceed her personal coping resources and available healthy responses (Washburn et al., 2015).

Jessica's mental health and treatment needs require a well-trained counselor in childhood sexual abuse and self-harming behaviors (Czincz & Romano, 2013). Counselors with limited knowledge in evidence-based psychological interventions for childhood sexual abuse need to seek professional training and supervision to provide counseling treatment and services to Jessica (Czincz & Romano, 2013). One evidence-based treatment for children/adolescents of childhood sexual abuse is TF-CBT (Cohen et al., 2004). TF-CBT uses visualization to address and cope with the intrusive thoughts. An example of how to use visualization while working with Jessica will be provided. The experiential activity of creating stress balls with Jessica will also be illustrated as an example of how clinicians might supplement the development of positive coping skills.

## ■ DIAGNOSTIC CONCLUSIONS

- PTSD with delayed expression
- Child sexual abuse
- Personal history of self-harm

## ■ SUGGESTED THERAPEUTIC INTERVENTIONS

TF-CBT is a components-based psychosocial treatment model that integrates empowerment, resilience, family therapy theories, cognitive behavioral, attachment, and humanistic counseling theories (Cohen et al., 2004). TF-CBT is commonly used to treat PTSD symptoms that are characterized by Jessica's intrusive memories and thoughts of the abuse, reminders of her secret and guilt for not telling when she sees her sister, physical reactions, and trauma-related shame (Cohen et al., 2004). In this treatment approach, Jessica will attend 12 to 16 treatment sessions to gradually explore her experience with the trauma and to process her trauma narrative by processing details of her traumatic experiences. The techniques guided by the counselor are to help Jessica directly attend to the traumatic events rather than demonstrating maladaptive avoidance. Counselors are required to attend to Jessica's distress by listening and offering therapeutic techniques that offer an open discussion addressing the trauma.

Stress management and relaxation skills are created to meet the child and family's needs. An example of a stress management skill Jessica's counselor might use is visualization. One helpful visualization for Jessica is to visually see the word *STOP* when negative thoughts and painful memories are experienced. The counselor will process with Jessica memories of the trauma along with her affect, reactions, fears, feelings, and thoughts. As Jessica explores the trauma and her reactions, the counselor will help her process how she has control over the fearful memories by visualizing the fears and thoughts and redirecting her visualization to the bottom of a long pole. The client will describe her fears and how the thoughts affect her as she moves up the pole. The counselor will direct her attention to where she feels the emotional and physical pain in her body. Jessica will process how the intrusive thoughts interfere with her present experiences. As she visually moves up the pole, she will identify how exploring her reactions and experiences in counseling fosters a sense of safety and an ability to stop the intrusive thoughts when they appear painful for her well-being. At this point, the counselor will direct her visualization to the top of the pole to mentally see the word STOP.

This intervention is intended to empower Jessica and help her gain personal strength over the intrusive thoughts and harmful reactions that may be leading to her self-harming behaviors. This process fosters an environment for self-reflection and insight into thoughts and reactions. Once Jessica arrives at *STOP*, she will benefit from therapeutic opportunities to transition her thoughts to effective and useful outlets of her emotions.

One activity to foster emotional responses is the creation of stress balls. This activity supports her developmental need for movement and manipulation of materials along with therapeutic discussion. Jessica will be provided with multiple colored balloons to select three colors. She will be asked to select a colored balloon that will be completely hidden and covered by the others. The second balloon will have a small visible section of it, whereas the last balloon will be fully visible. The counselor provides Jessica with options for creating her stress ball by filling a balloon with materials such as rice, beans, and/or flour. Jessica selects the balloon that will not be seen and fills the ball with the selected material to the size of her satisfaction. The filled balloon is tied off and balloon number two is cut off right above where the balloon fills out and the base of the neck. The second balloon is pulled over the filled balloon, with the tie part of the first balloon covered first. The third balloon covers the second balloon by offering a third protective layer. While the client is filling her balloon with material and layering the balloons, the counselor will process with the client her experience with creating the stress ball. The counselor and Jessica will discuss various times that Jessica may use the stress ball to help manage her stress and fears. Here is a list of variations the counselor may consider when engaging clients in this experiential activity:

1. Consider a therapeutic conversation around the color selection of the balloons and the placement (covered, partially covered, and fully visible). The counselor may point out that everyone has various layers of who they trust and process with the client who they identify to be within three layers of trust just like the three layers of balloons.
2. Discuss the challenges when filling the balloon and how filling the balloon is similar to stuffing in feelings and thoughts. Sometimes it can get messy, but the result is a stronger ball—much like exploring emotions helps people become stronger.
3. Discuss how you see the client responding to the filling of the balloon.
4. Consider how the client may find the stress ball useful when feeling _____ (insert whatever feeling you think the client might be experiencing).
5. Associate the balloon coverings of the middle contents to be protectors of the inside. Ask the client how she protects herself, that is, what her strengths are.

TF-CBT is not an appropriate treatment option for clients with other mental health needs that indicate imminent danger for the client such as recent suicide attempts, active substance and drug use, misuse of medications, and severely depressed conditions because these individuals need to receive treatment specific to these mental health concerns (Cohen et al., 2004). Additional reasons to rule out TF-CBT as a treatment option are when other issues take precedence over treatment decisions. A few problems that require treatment before TF-CBT are aggression, disruptive behaviors and defiance, law-breaking behaviors, and harm to others. These problems are best served by directly targeting the condition before treatment with TF-CBT (Cohen et al., 2004).

A strength of TF-CBT is the collaboration between the parents, client, and counselor, allowing for respectful consideration of the cultural needs and familial preferences (Cohen et al., 2004). In all counseling interactions, parents are the experts regarding their children and are encouraged to advocate for their children's treatment needs within the TF-CBT model (Cohen et al., 2004). Parents and the counselors work in collaboration to assess the child's well-being and coping skills in the home and community environments. The counselor works with the family to explore and educate on healthy sexual boundaries and sexual abuse.

## ▓ FOR YOUR CONSIDERATION

1. How might you determine if Jessica's self-harming behaviors are indicative of suicidal behavior?
2. Many clients who engage in self-harm find it difficult to replace these behaviors with healthier alternatives because the "release" is not the same. Consider ways in which you would help the client explore alternative coping strategies to self-harm.

## ▓ REFERENCES

American Counseling Association. (2014). *ACA code of ethics*. Author.

Cohen, J., Mannarino, A., & Deblinger, E. (2004). Trauma-focused cognitive behavioral therapy for sexually abused children. *Psychiatric Times, 21*, 52–53.

Czincz, J., & Romano, E. (2013). Childhood sexual abuse: Community-based treatment practices and predictors of use of evidence-based practices. *Child and Adolescent Mental Health, 18*(4), 240–246.

Darkness to Light. (2013). *20 Years of Protecting Kids*. www.d2l.org/site/c.4dICIJOkGcISE/b.6035035/k.8258/Prevent_Child_Sexual_Abuse.htm

Romans, S. E., Martin, J. L., Anderson, J. C., Herbison, G. P., & Mullen, P. E. (1995). Sexual abuse in childhood and deliberate self-harm. *American Journal of Psychiatry, 152*(9), 1336–1342. https://doi.org//10.1176/ajp.152.9.1336

Washburn, J. J., Potthoff, L. M., Juzwin, K. R., & Styer, D. M. (2015). Assessing *DSM-5* nonsuicidal self-injury disorder in a clinical sample. *Psychological Assessment, 27*(1), 31–41.

# CHAPTER EIGHT

# DISSOCIATIVE DISORDERS

*Dissociative identity disorder (DID) is usually a reaction to trauma as a way to help a person avoid bad memories and is characterized by the presence of two or more distinct personality identities. This chapter highlights the detailed case of an adult woman diagnosed with DID. The case offers an in-depth description of the client's identities and takes the reader on a journey through her treatment. Questions for consideration are also included.*

## 8.1    *Case of Sarah*

### ▩ INTRODUCTION

Sarah is a 35-year-old Caucasian female raised in the southern region of the United States, who was self-referred to counseling because of debilitating panic, unpredictable and uncontrollable anxiety, occasional fits of rage, and periods of intense crying. She initially presented herself as experiencing periods of depressive symptoms which included apathy, an absence of purpose, and suicidal thoughts. During the initial intake session, despite being motivated to get help, Sarah's affect was flat and appeared hopeless. She had never received therapeutic services before seeking help now. The precipitating event that brought Sarah into therapy was that she was raped by a male intruder who threatened to kill her and her family if she reported the rape to the police. Sarah acknowledged needing to have therapeutic support in adjusting to this traumatic event.

### ▩ FAMILY HISTORY

Sarah was married at 17 to her high school sweetheart, Stan (1 year her senior) who was a youth music minister for their local Christian congregation. She is the mother of five children; three female biological children (Caressa—14, Jessie—12, and Marie—9) and two adopted children (Eve—15 and Jeremiah—7). The family recently moved into a home after having lived in a mobile home/trailer for 12 years. Prior to living in the trailer, the family temporarily resided with

Stan's mother and father and older disabled sister until they were financially stable to move into the trailer. It was during this time that Stan decided to enroll at the university which was 100 miles away to work on his degree which was focused on agricultural science with ambitions to take over the family farm. He was drawn to the ministry because of his church activity growing up. Church was a central focal point for him and Sarah and this is how they met in high school. Stan's work and school activities demanded much of his time and energy as well as took him away from home and his family. As she noted during the initial visit, one late evening after the children were asleep, a man broke into the trailer, held Sarah at knife point and raped her repeatedly, threatening to kill the children if she did not submit. He also threatened her that if she told anyone about the incident, he would come back and kill her and her family.

Sarah went for a year before she told Stan about the incident. This disclosure was prompted by Stan finding a loaded gun under the mattress where Sarah slept. When he confronted her about it, she shared the story of the rape. In response to Stan's insistence that she go to the police, she vehemently resisted and threatened to leave the marriage if he persisted. Sarah reported her belief that Stan struggled with guilt and anger at not being there to protect her from the rape. It was during this time that Sarah turned to her religious faith which prompted her to share her desire for her and Stan to become foster parents which they did. She expressed feeling "called" to care for children who were abused and/or neglected. During the time of formal preparation for foster parenting, Sarah reported feeling the happiest in her life. Her life felt purposeful and she knew that God would place children in her path that she could love, help, and support. Their first foster children were Eve who was 11 years old and Jeremiah who was newly born. They came from a drug addicted, single mother during the raid of a home with a meth lab. Though the original idea was for Sarah and Stan to serve as foster parents, they were eventually able to adopt Eve and Jeremiah a few years later as permanent members of the family.

It was also during this time that Sarah began experiencing significant anxiety, flashbacks, and intrusive memories not only of the rape, but of instances in her childhood that were filled with sexual trauma. Sarah came from a family where she was the third of four children with two older brothers and a younger sister. Her father worked as a farm laborer and her mother stayed at home and was a functional alcoholic. Sarah recalled numerous times having to care for her younger sister and older brothers, including feeding, bathing, and dressing her sister because her mother was preoccupied and functionally absent; she was 5 years old at that time. Sarah's paternal grandparents were also involved in the life of Sarah's family. The grandfather was a prominent minister in the community and he and his wife would facilitate regular camp revival meetings at a church sponsored campground where church members would gather from the area.

It was during those events that grandfather would force Sarah to engage in sexual activity with a number of men in the church, including forcing her to participate in religious rituals that involved sexual activity; this also started when she was 5 years old. This abuse lasted for approximately 3 years before Sarah's father discovered what was happening. During this time the grandfather also repeatedly sexually abused Sarah and the grandmother was complicit by teaching Sarah how to please men sexually, rationalizing that it was important that Sarah learned what her duty was as a godly woman to please the men she would encounter in her life and that God expected this of her. One day when Sarah's father came to pick her up from the grandparent's home, he walked in on the grandfather sexually assaulting her and forcefully removed her from the home. Even though Sarah's father cut off the family's contact with his parents, there was never any report of the sexual abuse, nor any involvement of law enforcement to intervene in these events and actions. Sarah never saw her paternal grandparents again. Sarah also described her father being emotionally and physically violent with her and her mother as passive and uninvolved. She was able to keep these events secret from her friends at school, which was aided by her ability to repress these memories. She excelled in her schoolwork and was able to participate in numerous school activities, especially in high school. It was there within a school-based Christian group that she met and dated Stan and they discussed plans to be married soon after graduating from high school. Sarah also vowed during high school to divorce herself from her parents and joined the army as a way of manifesting her independence and the need to take care of herself and find her own way in the world. She and Stan were committed to keeping her away from the environments that were abusive and traumatizing to her as a young child and Sarah saw her action of cutting off from her family as a matter of pride in protecting herself from the people who abused and neglected her.

Sarah's counselor worked with her for 4 years of weekly counseling sessions where Eye Movement Desensitization and Processing (EMDR), talk therapy, and the development of effective coping skills focused on her posttraumatic stress disorder (PTSD) were the primary interventions. After these initial years of therapy, Sarah began to acknowledge that there was more to her story than the counselor supposed. She had always held back in her counseling sessions because of pride and the need to be in control of her life and her disclosures which manifested in continually testing the counselor for trustworthiness and keeping secrets regarding the extent and intensity of her trauma-based symptoms. Eventually, Sarah began describing her awareness of several identities that were present within her and that would emerge at various times in her life. She reported that although she had been aware of a few of these identities during high school, their presence had increased in an intrusive manner over the years which became disturbing to her and added to the anxiety that she actively tried to avoid. During this point in her therapy, Sarah described several distinct identities that were prominent in her awareness. Though Sarah was aware of the presence of these identities, she did not often know that they would say and do when they emerged; she had no memory of these instances and was mostly only aware of their activity when Stan or other family members reported that she wasn't acting like or talking like herself. Sarah reported feeling her most intense anxiety whenever Stan reported these instances and it was during those times, she became plagued by guilt, shame, and thoughts of suicide. She also described encountering bouts of depression where she would stay in bed, remain listless and restless, and experienced dissociative episodes (largely depersonalization and derealization). It was also at this point in her therapy that Sarah's oldest daughter became sexually active and started acting out defiantly. During this point in her therapy, Sarah reported that Eve was raped during a party where she was drinking excessively and passed out. A few classmates identified the assailant and Eve subsequently experienced being bullied at school as the rapist belonged to a prominent family in the community. The opposition at school grew as Sarah and Stan pressed criminal charges against Eve's assailant. It was during this time that the emergence of Sarah's identities became more intense which complicated her treatment significantly.

The cultural factors were significant for Sarah and her family. They lived in a small rural community with deeply entrenched southern values and norms. Sarah's socio-economic status was lower middle-class, but they were proud members of the community and both Sarah's and Stan's families were well-known in the area. Christianity was a significant influence in the community which was both supportive of the family and oppressive in that members of the community were closely watched by each other and people were not open to divergent points of view, especially those that deviated from established social norms which were prescriptive about how to behave and believe, especially across racial lines. Sarah bucked these norms regularly and served and associated with black members of her community, including worshipping with them as occasion would permit. She expressed having love for all people and was especially disposed to help and support those who struggled fitting in. Stan supported Sarah in her activities and attitudes and Sarah reported feeling that strengthening support.

## ■ SARAH'S IDENTITIES

After Sarah disclosed the extent of her trauma to her counselor, including that she had distinct identities that were intruding into her psychological and emotional space, a prominent identity that Sarah allowed to emerge at this point was "the Wall" which was aptly named because she (the identity was female) was stubborn and steadfast in her opposition to therapy and the uncovering of Sarah's past. The Wall initially manifested as self-destructive, angry, and defiant and would often emerge specifically after sessions where EMDR was employed as part of the therapeutic treatment regimen. The counselor was ignorant of the Wall's existence and often did not know what to make from the angry and defiant reactions Sarah manifested toward her and consulted a colleague about the possibility of a mood disorder. When Sarah disclosed having suicide ideation in the early phase of therapy, the counselor contemplated that Sarah's depressive symptoms were intense, but later Sarah acknowledged that the Wall was threatening to kill Sarah through suicide with her own gun. During Sarah's disclosure of her identities to her counselor, the Wall engaged the counselor directly and angrily disclosed that Sarah's rapist was one of the men that had sexually abused Sarah when she was 5 years old at the church camp. When the counselor asked Sarah to confirm this, Sarah reported that her rapist was unknown to her which indicated that the Wall could lie as a way to manipulate Sarah and others. Sarah reported feeling embarrassed that the Wall had lied to her counselor and felt shameful as a result. The Wall was also responsible for creating conflict in Sarah's marriage to Stan by provoking arguments and conflict. Sarah described that she would know that the Wall was responsible for this quality of conflict with her husband because the argument would always involve Sarah initiating the argument over an insignificant matter and aggressively verbally attacking Stan with the goal of emotionally eviscerating him. It was during these instances where Stan would say to Sarah, "I don't even know who you are when you attack me this way" which intensified Sarah's shame and depression.

"William" was a 5-year-old boy who emerged and who Sarah described as "a demon child." He would act out through childish behavior, including being defiant and vengeful whenever Stan would try and establish boundaries in the home and curb Sarah's occasional erratic behavior. As William emerged and began to take shape, Sarah's counselor was presented with a frightened, insecure, awkward boy who appeared lost and in need of support. He was self-conscious about his vulnerabilities which were triggered by the Wall's overbearing control, criticism, and condemnation of his presence as weak and whiny. William's presence also provided a stark contrast to the controlling personality of the Wall and also signaled that the Wall was a type of gatekeeper to Sarah's other identities which was also, among other things, a manifestation of the Wall's strict control over Sarah. As therapy progressed, William began emerging more often requesting to be read stories and confessing his desire not to be viewed as a "demon child" by Sarah. William apparently felt more empowered in manifesting himself even though he would often break down in tears and become vulnerable and even quivering as a frightened, lost, and wayward child. William sometimes emerged in the conflict that Sarah had with Eve which complicated Sarah's role as a parent. Sarah recounted several instances when, in arguments with Sarah, Eve would exclaim, "Mom, you are such a whiny baby; stop being that way!"

"Avi" was characterized as a 6-year-old girl who wanted to please everyone and who appeared to mirror the anxiety that Sarah manifested during periods of time where she felt vulnerable. Sarah described her awareness of Avi and her concern for Avi's welfare even though the emergence of her identities was distressing to her; it was clear that Sarah felt an urge and obligation to care for Avi. After the initial phase of therapy where the identities began to be known, the Wall emerged and threatened to kill Avi if Sarah persisted in seeing the counselor. It was shortly after this threat that Avi "disappeared" and did not manifest in Sarah and the counselor was only aware of her presence because of Sarah's description and her worry about Avi's welfare. It was only in these later phases of therapy that Avi actually emerged during a particular session to let the counselor know that she had gone into hiding to protect herself from the Wall and wanted to get the message to Sarah that she was alive and surviving although she missed Sarah terribly. Avi was apparently the female version of William except that William was unable to read very well and Avi, who was a similar age, was a strong reader and loved music and poetry. The existence of Avi not only contrasted William but served as a painful reminder to William of his ineptness which only intensified his shame.

"The baby" was an identity that emerged periodically during therapy and her presence was accompanied by distinct regressive behaviors (e.g., sucking the thumb, rocking back and forth, assuming a fetal position on the floor, child-like tantrums). The manifestation of the baby was the most distressing to Sarah's counselor because it signaled the need to care for the baby and to assure that Sarah was okay and well-supported. While William and Sarah were also young, frightened, and vulnerable, the counselor had never encountered these kinds of regressive behaviors during her professional experience which caused some anxiety within her when presented by Sarah. It was during this time that the counselor initiated weekly meetings with a clinical supervisor to ensure that any personalization she was experiencing was kept in check and that she was providing competent therapeutic services. During supervision sessions, the counselor described how she was experiencing Sarah and each identity as they emerged, the context of these manifestations, and her responses. During supervision, the supervisor encouraged the counselor in the direction of some potential treatments and together they developed a sequence of additional treatments that were integrated into therapy (these will be discussed in the section on treatment). The emergence of the baby was only manifested during therapy and was disturbing because it was so uncharacteristic of Sarah's personality and resilience in life. Whereas Sarah was typically strong and capable, the baby was weak, needy, and helpless.

There was a 16-year-old girl that was described by Sarah as a "minor" identity whose sole purpose appeared to be to protect the baby and who wanted to name the baby Sylvia because she was worried that the baby would not have much of a life without a name. This identity did not have a name and manifested only once during therapy; she also appeared to be very naive and compliant, as well as easily manipulated by others.

Finally, "Jane" was a female identity in her mid-teens and would show up randomly and could play the piano and sing. This was a unique identity in that her musicality differed from Sarah's typical talent. Sarah learned to play the piano growing up and while in high school she became talented enough to end up playing piano accompaniment for the church services each Sunday. Her piano playing was strictly regulated to playing church hymns and religious-themed music. However, when Jane would emerge, the genre of the music would change, and it appeared that her technical talent on the piano was enhanced. Sarah also did not characterize herself as talented vocally, but when Jane manifested, she would sing in a strong, clear, resonant, and confident fashion. This of course added to Sarah's unique character and would sometimes be confusing to Stan and the family, but not in any overtly disruptive way. It was clear that the family adapted to these manifestations largely because the moments where Jane would emerge were rare. Sarah was initially only aware of Jane when her husband or children would describe the difference in her musical performance and attitude.

The counselor noted that when Jane began to manifest, Sarah's left eye would enlarge a bit which was a physical sign of Jane's presence. Even though Jane was musically talented and artistic, initially in the presence of the counselor Jane too was timid and would sit with a yearning and longing in her eyes. Like William, as Jane began manifesting herself more regularly, the counselor began to see the resilience in this identity and determined that Jane most fully presented the creative and resilient side of Sarah that had been controlled and subdued by the Wall. Eventually the combination of the Wall permitting Jane and the other identities to come forward, and Jane asserting herself, also gave Sarah her own voice and her awareness that she could be both the Wall and Jane and both could be creative and resilient. The counselor also noted that while the Wall was deeply entrenched in being in control and often oppressive, the Wall took pride in being a protector, especially in relationships that proved to be risky and potentially dangerous. It was clear throughout therapy that the Wall was the primary protector of Sarah's life and her trauma.

## ▩ DIAGNOSTIC IMPRESSIONS

During the initial phase of therapy, Sarah's counselor was focused on developing a comprehensive assessment along with treating the overt symptoms of her trauma (i.e., intrusive memories, flashbacks, anxiety, and depression).

The counselor was also focused on helping Sarah adjust to her circumstances and various roles as a mother, wife, and woman. It was only later in therapy where Sarah disclosed about her identities that the counselor encouraged these complex identities to voice themselves and learn more about them. It was clear initially that Sarah was experiencing ongoing mental and emotional distress which included symptoms of anxiety and depression. She was not actively suicidal but did share a history of suicide ideation she considered to be manageable (i.e., she never evolved to an active plan or contemplating specific ways in which she would harm or kill herself). Sarah struggled in her relationship with her husband and conflict with her daughter Eve. She described her awareness that there were numerous times where, as a result of chronic stress or the intrusion of traumatic memories, she would "numb out" and not be herself, although she was unwilling to share with her counselor the specific mechanisms of her dissociative identities.

Sarah felt most distressed by periods of depression where she felt completely incapacitated and unmotivated to do anything but lie in bed, although these episodes were often short-lived. She described willing herself to function and engaging in activities that would help her maintain her momentum of living. She characterized herself as compliant with medical advice, but when her physician suggested that she engage in a regimen of antidepressant medication, Sarah was vehemently opposed to it. She did not want any drug that would alter her consciousness as she did not use alcohol, tobacco, or any illicit substances.

Sarah described having a healthy sex life with her husband, relatively good relationships with her children, and respectful relationships with personal and family friends and mostly enjoyed her association with members of her church and community. She described herself as being perceived as an upstanding member of the community and was active and engaged in her children's educational and social development and interested in their success. During the time where Eve was recovering from her rape, Sarah encountered a church member who shared her opinion that Eve, because she was adopted, was not really a part of Sarah's family and probably was promiscuous because of her previous upbringing with her parents and thus she invited the rape. Sarah reacted angrily to this speculation, denounced the church member, and remained a protective advocate for her daughter even though they experienced conflict in their own relationship. Sarah's counselor expressed amazement that Sarah was able to function in her life so well considering the numerous and complex parts of her personal history, her dissociation and other symptoms, and the manifestations of her identities. It was clear to the counselor that despite Sarah's challenges, she exhibited extraordinary resilience which became the bedrock of her therapeutic recovery.

## ▩ DIAGNOSTIC CONCLUSIONS

Based on the initial assessment (no formal assessment instruments were ever implemented during therapy), the *Diagnostic and Statistical Manual of Mental Disorders, 5th Edition (DSM-5)* diagnosis was as follows:

- Dissociative identity disorder
- PTSD with dissociative symptoms and with delayed expression
- Personal history of sexual abuse in childhood

## ▩ SUGGESTED THERAPEUTIC INTERVENTIONS

It is important to note that Sarah's treatment has been ongoing for over a decade and that her counselor has evolved in her mastery of treating and supporting Sarah in her recovery; essentially, as Sarah has grown in her awareness, her counselor has in parallel fashion, grown in her ability to treat Sarah effectively. As previously noted, initially there was little awareness of how Sarah's identities operated in Sarah's daily life and the counselor addressed her symptoms of anxiety and depression simultaneously in encouraging Sarah's story of childhood sexual abuse to unfold. Prior to counseling, Sarah had never initiated any therapeutic services and was initially skeptical about the merits of therapy and resistant to opening up and sharing her painful past. As a result, the counselor initiated a person-centered approach focusing on validation, encouragement, and affirmation. In consultation with her supervisor, the counselor maintained the orientation that when dealing with Sarah, the counselor was hearing both the "spoken" and "unspoken" stories emerge and purposefully reflected what Sarah shared to clarify and deepen the interaction and facilitate the building of trust. The counselor was also intentional in creating a permissive space in which Sarah was able to unpack and sort through her distressing and complex history which actually provided the primary mechanism that permitted Sarah to disclose about her multiple identities. As Sarah trusted her counselor, she trusted herself to share more fully her hidden and unknown life. It was to the credit of the counselor that she sought out supervision and consultation to support Sarah in the best way possible as the traumatic layers of this story emerged. In supervision, the counselor described evolving as a professional right alongside Sarah and noted that Sarah had become an influential teacher in developing the counselor's therapeutic technique, her theoretical orientation, and her professional approach. The following are components of treatment employed in Sarah's treatment:

EMDR—During the initial stages of therapy, it became apparent that the counselor needed to be trained in EMDR, which she initiated formally though

EMDRIA (EMDR International Association) and maintained supervision of her technique including engaging in continuing education. It was during this training that the counselor sought weekly formal supervision to contextualize EMDR toward Sarah's trauma. It was clear that the symptoms of Sarah's past sexual trauma (including the rape she experienced as a young wife and mother) needed to be specifically addressed in a way that focused on her symptoms. EMDR was effective in reducing Sarah's subjective distress. Later, when Sarah shared about her dissociative identities, the identity of the Wall more fully emerged. The counselor postulated that the Wall served the purpose of both creating and promoting chaos in Sarah's life and protecting Sarah from harm. In processing Sarah's experience of the Wall, both the counselor and Sarah determined that while the Wall stirred up chaos and distress, it was motivated by the fear that if Sarah became complacent, she might be caught off guard and become traumatized again. This awareness and insight had an immediate effect in helping lessen the emotional tension between Sarah and the Wall which also facilitated the manifestation of the other identities. Initial EMDR protocols were followed by periodic and focused treatment sessions which resulted in reducing the distressing symptoms to a tolerable level.

Family Systems Therapy and Trauma-Related Dissociation—It was helpful to conceptualize Sarah's identities as benign even as they were distressing to her and appeared to be self-destructive. This was initially difficult for Sarah to understand and accept because of her experience with her own chaos and identities. Sarah initially had the desire to integrate these "personalities" because she wanted to keep them under control which on some level made sense, but was contrary to both trauma-related dissociation (Boon et al., 2011) and internal family systems (Schwartz & Sweezy, 2020) which both promote a person's "parts" and identities as purposeful. The counselor also utilized Janina Fisher's important resource (Fisher, 2017) to help Sarah understand and embrace her identities gently, patiently, and with compassion as a form of self-love. As Sarah's identities emerged there was a period of recalibration and readjustment in treatment to accommodate the new emerging identity, to welcome it, get to know it, and to validate its purpose and existence. This necessitated flexibility in thought and attitude within the counselor and the counselor was validated in this approach several times by Sarah's report that even though the emergence of these identities was often distressing, she could feel her relationship to them shift in positive and constructive directions. This work was slow and tedious, but ultimately effective. It was a common occurrence that entire sessions would be hijacked by a particular identity who demanded attention from the counselor and the counselor would oblige and accept the need for the identity to be heard, validated, and respected. The Wall, for example, would emerge frequently and argue with the counselor, threaten, and become angry, but as time passed, the Wall allowed itself to become more vulnerable, including confessing the pain of feeling misunderstood by Sarah and the other identities. At one point the Wall disclosed that she desired to have a real name and not simply to be referred to as the Wall. This pattern of identity disclosure was also paralleled by William (an important fact was that the Wall and William were the only identities that overtly seemed to vie for the attention of the counselor and who would push themselves into the therapeutic sessions and demand time and attention from the counselor). As these identities were "heard" they lessened in their manifestations in therapy and per Sarah's report, they diminished their disruptive force in her life. It became clear that as therapy took hold and as Sarah developed an understanding of her internal process and ability to contextualize appropriately her past traumas, their purpose of protecting Sarah was growing obsolete as Sarah demonstrated consistency in protecting herself and becoming less reactive.

Grounding Exercises and Mindfulness—Throughout treatment the counselor quickly recognized the need to help Sarah create an alternate space where she could retreat from the subjective distress and chaos these identities stirred. It was apparent that these episodes of distress were not only rooted in Sarah's historical trauma, but were situational and related to her current functioning, including her role as a mother and a wife. After Eve's rape, Sarah worked to maintain a clear focus in trying to support her daughter through the aftermath and the complex social fallout from experiencing a sexual assault in a small, rural community and experiencing the resistance that occurred naturally with Eve's development as an adolescent. Incidentally, Sarah was deliberate in *not* sharing her own rape story with Eve; she maintained her intent to protect her family, even from herself and never disclosed what happened to her to anyone other than Stan and her counselor. There were times where Sarah was more successful at establishing a supportive stance with her daughter than at other times and she suffered guilt and shame for not being able to be consistently strong and constant for her daughter and other members of her family. This resulted in periods of depression which fortunately were short-lived. The counselor determined that Sarah's response to her depression was the most positive expression of her personal resilience. Sarah was committed to not allowing herself to collapse in on herself and abandon her role as a mother and a wife. Grounding exercises (Boon et al., 2011) were used to help reorient Sarah to her immediate circumstance during times where she was experiencing dissociative episodes in treatment sessions and to practice when not in session. The counselor was intentional in helping Sarah create the mental and emotional space and a place for her to access when she felt herself dissociate. Connecting to her awareness of her surroundings, including tapping into her senses (i.e., touch, sight, smell) helped counter the effects of derealization and helping her develop the mantra of who she was, that she was a survivor (Interestingly, Sarah did not like the term "survivor" because she saw herself as just another struggling human being and didn't like any designation that would specialize her experience. She opted for the phrase "fierce and powerful woman"), that she was a mother and that she was needed by her family which helped combat the effects of depersonalization that would emerge. Closely connected to developing this mindfulness ritual was the integration of a specific place of refuge. Though Sarah did not frequent the beach, she loved coastal scenes and imagining herself on a warm beach with the sound of the surf and gentle breeze was a consistent and comforting image that sustained her through the turbulence that often emerged through her therapy. Her mindfulness practice was a difficult one to establish and it was and is not perfect, but she has been able to develop it into an effective coping strategy.

The Grounding Effects of Touch—An apparent controversial part of Sarah's therapy was in the later stages when William and Avi began to emerge. These child identities had their own specific needs which aligned themselves with where they were at developmentally. This signals the reality that not only was Sarah in need of grounding techniques, but these younger and more vulnerable identities were also searching for grounding and nurturing within their own unique developmental context. There were several sessions where when William and Avi would manifest, the counselor would sit next to them (as manifested through Sarah), read stories to them, permit them to ask questions, cry, manifest their weakness, and even stroke Sarah's hair and rub lotion on her hands. Because the counselor was an older who herself was married and had raised children of her own, she likely felt a natural inclination to nurture, but she was careful and ethical enough to sort through the complexities inherent in physically touching her client. For example, during one session with William, the counselor read William a story, talked with him and then played a game where she put a layer of hand lotion on the top of William's (Sarah's) hand and drew letters and smiley faces with a Q-tip in the lotion and then helped him rub the lotion into his hands. This tactile experience was a warm and genuine manifestation of nurturing and grounding that went beyond talk therapy. At the initial stage of therapy, Sarah was distrustful of the counselor, let alone being reluctant to making overtures to having her hands touched or being able to rest her head on the counselor's shoulder when she read to William or Avi, but as therapy progressed in the later stages, it seemed natural and there were some important conversations the counselor had with Sarah to gain permission to touch her in this manner. Sarah noted to the counselor later that this occasional physical touch was the most important part of her therapy; it had the specific effect of helping to ground and nurture these vulnerable identities, validate her personhood and her needs for connection with trusted others, and helped Sarah reconnect and nurture these parts of herself in ways that were previously elusive to her. On the therapeutic side, this practice of touch prompted the counselor to continue seeking clinical supervision to ensure her interventions were themselves grounded in effective and ethical practice.

## ■ SUMMARY

It remains an important reminder that the duration of therapy and the nature of Sarah's condition was such that the counselor evolved in a parallel fashion to the therapeutic gains that Sarah made and continues to make in her therapy. The counselor recognized early in Sarah's treatment that part of her ethical obligation in providing the best treatment was the need to establish consistent supervision over her work. The counselor understood that even though she had been established as a licensed professional for 6 years at the time she met Sarah, she had an obligation to lifelong learning and continued development which was a manifestation of her professional humility and integrity. She initiated and completed formal training in EMDR and read extensively in the treatment of dissociative disorders and developing a trauma-informed posture in her work. She took appropriate risks in pushing into areas that were beyond the limitations of her training and sought guidance and direction from a senior member of the profession (i.e., her clinical supervisor) and discussed her approach and rationale with her client to negotiate a way of being together that ultimately worked for the client. There were certainly times where she was personally and emotionally impacted by Sarah, she developed therapeutic relationships with Sarah's identities and defaulted to not only validating Sarah, but engaging with and respecting fully the identities that had served their purpose in protecting Sarah in what was unimaginable trauma as a young person in her family of origin. The counselor recognized and encouraged aspects of Sarah's resilience even while others in Sarah's life wanted her to continual socializing and functioning "normally" as a patient and submissive woman. Helping Sarah understand herself was inherently empowering and in this way the counselor became an important advocate to Sarah and instrumental in helping normalize a new way of living. Sarah's counselor also was intentional in sharing with Sarah how she had grown personally and professionally through their work together. Sarah reported that this disclosure from her counselor was especially meaningful as her lived experience with her family was such that she sometimes questioned herself and the negative impact her condition had on her family; she did not want influence her family and affect them adversely. Finally, during therapy, Sarah was invited to participate in a weekly multifamily parenting group which was facilitated by her counselor, as an adjunct to her personal therapy to support her role as a parent and to help her in developing her children in healthy and life-affirming ways. Stan and the children also sometimes attended these group sessions and the group became a mainstay for Sarah. An important orientation for the counselor was helping Sarah not identify with her "disorder" and be defined by it, but to see herself as dealing with it like any other health condition and learning how to accommodate her newly evolving life.

## ▨ FOR YOUR CONSIDERATION

1. In this case the counselor appears to have determined to treat the dissociative identity disorder directly and the traumatic history indirectly. How does this square with how you would prioritize your approach to treatment? What are some treatments/interventions that could be used to address Sarah's trauma?
2. It is clear that the counselor has experienced some countertransference reactions in her work with the client. What are your thoughts about how the counselor addressed her own personalization emerging from therapy? Should these reactions be avoided, and if so, how? What else would you do to minimize the impact of these countertransference reactions?
3. What kinds of ongoing assessment are warranted with this case? How often would you utilize this assessment in your therapeutic work and how would you integrate an assessment-informed practice with this client?
4. In this case there were some cultural dynamics identified that impacted how the counselor approached working with the client. What other cultural factors do you wonder about and would you seek to identify as relevant? How would you strengthen your own cultural sensitivity in ways that might make therapy more effective?
5. During the advanced stages of therapy, the counselor engaged in sitting by the client as the younger identities would emerge, reading to them, permitting the client to rest her head on the counselor's shoulder, and engaging in physical touch through the use of hand lotion, Q-tips, and physically rubbing the lotion into the client's hands. What ethical issues arise when initiating physical touch in this way? How do these actions square with your own personal values and expectations of therapy?

## ▨ REFERENCES

Boon, S., Steele, K., & Van Der Hart, O. (2011). *Coping with trauma-related dissociation*. Norton.
Fisher, J. (2017). *Healing the fragmented selves of trauma survivors: Overcoming internal self-alienation*. Routledge.
Schwartz, R. C., & Sweezy, M. (2020). *Internal family systems therapy* (2nd ed.). Gilford.

# CHAPTER NINE

# SOMATIC SYMPTOM AND RELATED DISORDERS

*Somatic symptom disorder is characterized by an extreme focus on physical symptoms (e.g., pain, weakness, fatigue) that causes major emotional distress and problems functioning. This chapter features two cases of somatic symptom disorder in two adult women. While their symptoms may not be traceable to a physical cause, they do cause excessive and disproportionate levels of distress and dysfunction.*

## 9.1    *Case of Rose*

### ▓ INTRODUCTION

Rose is a 47-year-old woman. She lives by herself in a small rural community in a rented duplex. Rose has a high school diploma and went to community college for one semester to study accounting but dropped out quickly afterwards. She reports she had a hard time concentrating on schoolwork and felt that everyone else was smarter than her and talked about her behind her back. After dropping out of college, she found steady work as a receptionist at a landscaping business and has been at the same company for almost 23 years. Her primary duties are to answer phones and scheduling landscape installations. She currently is on paid leave and may be facing unemployment. Her boss told her that she has missed too much work because of her numerous doctors' appointments and time in the hospital. She states she does not particularly feel challenged by the job, but it does provide health insurance and pays the bills. She has never been married and does not have any children. She states she has never had a long-term romantic relationship and reports feeling awkward around men. She states she has one or two friends that she is in contact with from high school but does not consider them "close" friends. She mentioned that those friends get tired of hearing about how much pain she is in and have distanced from her a little over the last few years.

Rose was referred to counseling by her primary care physician and states she is uncertain as to why she was referred. She states she would not be here except her doctor refuses to see her until she meets with a mental health professional. Rose seems genuinely confused as to why she is here. She denies any mental health problems other than maybe being a little depressed at times and feeling as if she does not fit in but states she has always felt that way. Rose quickly wants to discuss her medical concerns including her ongoing stomach pain, digestive issues, and ongoing frustration with her primary doctor. She said her medical problems are coming to head and she worries daily with anxious thoughts that if someone doesn't diagnose her soon, she is just going to die.

## ■ FAMILY HISTORY

Rose is the only child of two parents who immigrated from Mexico City. They immigrated when they were in their late 20s and Rose was a baby. Her maternal grandmother also immigrated with the family and lived with them when Rose was young. She died around the time that Rose was entering junior high. She states her grandmother was the only person she has ever felt close to in her family. Her grandmother used to give her lots of healing "tonics" which she later found out was just warm tea but she states she always felt as if her grandmother loved her and took care of her when she needed it. When they first arrived in the United States, her mom worked hard to learn the English language and was able to go to school and earn an advanced nursing degree. Her father refused to learn English and consequently was never able to find work. Her mother was the sole provider and worked long hours to take care of her, her father, and her grandmother. Her mother retired from being a nurse after almost 50 years and then died a year and a half ago from breast cancer. She notes that her mother might have struggled with some depression but would never talk about it and was not diagnosed. Rose reports that she never felt close to her mom as she was always working and whenever she tried to talk to her about how she was feeling, her mom would try to minister to her physically. When Rose said she was sad, her mom would take her temperature and try to give her over the counter medication so that she might feel better.

    Her father stayed at home with her and her grandmother. Her father struggled with alcoholism, unemployment, and was just "down right mean" at times. Because her mother was not very present in the home, her father expected her to act as the "woman of the house" and provide him and her grandmother meals and would often ask her to do things that he just didn't want to do himself. She states because of her father and his demands and yelling, she has never wanted to get into a romantic relationship. She states in her culture, the man is always "boss" and the women are expected to "obey." She states she can remember one time when she was in third of fourth grade that her father had a bunch of friends over and they were drinking. She states at one point one of them men touched her inappropriately and her father just laughed and encouraged it. She remembers feeling terrified that the touching would continue and possibly progress. She also states she felt incredibly embarrassed and after that tried to "hide" when her father's friends came over to drink. She is unsure if her father had any mental health problems.

## ▓ CURRENT FUNCTIONING

Rose presents as well groomed, slightly overweight, wearing clothing that is baggy. She makes intermittent eye contact and takes several minutes to answer each question. She repeatedly states she is unsure why she is here and just wants to get this wrapped up so that she can reschedule with her primary care doctor.

Rose states the biggest concern is her health, after some probing, Rose discloses that she has struggled with pain since she has been young. She has difficulty describing where the pain is coming from and when asked about it, she often defers to talking about digestive problems. She states they are related; however, she has not been able to ever get a diagnosis for either. She does admit that having pain has prohibited her from having strong friendships and a romantic partner. She feels that people get tired of listening to her complaints and will eventually stop paying attention to her.

According to records sent by Roses' primary care doctor, she has presented at the hospital over 30 times in the last 2 months with vague pains and complaints about digestion. She is unable to pinpoint where the pain is coming from and will respond to questions with "everything hurts." She appears to exaggerate symptoms and has told the doctors that her pain is a 12 on a scale of 1 to 10, however she appears calm and her vitals are within normal range. The doctors have not come up with a specific diagnosis regardless of countless tests and physical assessment. Rose has been hospitalized for testing several times and staff describe her as being very demanding and wanting attention beyond what they normally see (adjusting her pillows, bringing warm blankets and special foods), to the point where they felt like she was taking time away from the "real" patients. Rose has also presented at multiple doctors' offices in the community. There was some concern that she was "shopping" for pain medication, but she did not seem to be bothered when she was refused any medication. She states she just wants to have answers to why she is in pain all the time. She thinks at times she is just going to "die" unless someone takes her seriously.

Rose denies any substance abuse now or historically. She was given an anxiolytic by a doctor a few years ago and does take that regularly. At times she states she might overuse it but understands that she cannot get a refill early.

She is on various other medications including a mild pain medication, medication for acid reflux, and two medications for digestive help. She admits that she thinks that speaking to a mental health provider is a waste of time and remarks that because of her culture and background she does not believe that mental health problems are real. She states she always feels unheard by medical staff and wonders what she needs to do to get them to pay attention.

## ■ DIAGNOSTIC IMPRESSIONS

Rose demonstrates someone who has experience childhood trauma and expresses very high worry about her pain and digestive problems. She likely had a difficult time getting attention for her emotional pain growing up and found that her mom would minister her if she presented with physical ailments. She perceives her physical symptoms as the worst and even though there is no physical indication, she frequently worries that if someone does not help her that she will die. She has spent an inordinate time at different doctors and presenting at the hospital where she demands attention and continues to deny having any mental health problems. In many ways she defines herself as her physical concerns and focuses on them to the point where she is having a difficult time creating and maintaining healthy relationships.

## ■ DIAGNOSTIC CONCLUSIONS

- Somatic symptom disorder
- Major depressive disorder
- R/O generalized anxiety disorder
- Other personal history of psychological trauma

## ■ SUGGESTED INTERVENTIONS

Cognitive behavioral therapies (CBTs) and mindfulness-based therapies are both indicated for somatic symptom disorder and could be helpful for Rose. Somatization is present when someone's symptoms of emotional pain or distress manifests in a physical form without any medical reason. Rose acknowledging that the pain is likely emotional and offering some psychoeducation about how closely the mind and body are related might be a good start to helping her understand. I would also want to continue to assess for depression and anxiety in addition to referring her to see a psychiatrist as pharmacology has also been shows to be helpful with this disorder.

## ▓ FOR YOUR CONSIDERATION

1. How would you first approach a client who is unsure why they have been referred to you and deny mental health symptoms?
2. Are there additional treatment options you would consider for this client?
3. What are some specific goals you would create in order for Rose to have a better quality of life and to help her minimize symptoms?

# 9.2    *Case of Carla*

## ▓ INTRODUCTION

Carla is a 48-year-old Asian American woman who presents at the ED at the local community hospital with complaints of "pain all over." This month Carla has been to the ED seven times and in the last year has averaged about 11 visits per month. Despite Carla's repeated visits with medical professionals, she has experienced no relief of her symptoms, which include generalized pain and difficulty sleeping. Carla has had extensive testing of symptoms including MRI, computerized axial tomography (CAT) scans, blood work, and other lab workups. Carla has excessively frequented numerous doctors and hospital EDs without any relief of symptoms.

## ▓ FAMILY HISTORY

Carla was born in the United States to parents who emigrated from Malaysia in the 1950s and she is an only child. Her parents were considered "older" when they had Carla, and she was unplanned. Growing up in rural Connecticut, Carla's parents ran their own grocery and its attached bowling alley. Her parents likely had some anxiety or depression. Both of them liked to keep to themselves and when Carla's mom wasn't working at the grocery store, she often would isolate and describe herself as "sad" and "unmotivated." Carla's dad also struggled with difficulty in day-to-day activities and didn't spend much time with the family or others. Probably owing to cultural values, neither parent would seek out intervention.

Carla was a quiet child who often felt isolated and lonely. She earned average grades in school. She was accepted at her local community college where she completed minimal requirements for the first year and then dropped out in order to work at her parents' business after her father passed away and her mother was left with the extremely difficult job of running this failing business by herself.

In the late 1980s, Carla's mother sold the business and retired. Carla now lives on her own in the community in which she grew up, and other than just a few "acquaintances" she continues to feel isolated and describes herself as "socially awkward." She states she has always felt anxious in new situations and is someone who is not likely to try something new because of it.

She started working as an assistant for an insurance underwriter a few years ago, and due to fatigue and frequent medical visits, she was forced to quit her job. She is currently in the process of applying for disability and is feeling hopeless and uncertain about the future.

## ■ DIAGNOSTIC IMPRESSIONS

Carla has been admitted numerous times to the hospital for extensive medical workups, to no avail. All of her medical testing has been negative, and the doctors are at a loss regarding the etiology of what Carla describes as "intense pain." Her hospital admissions seem to coincide with increased life stressors. When her father died, Carla presented to the ED with extreme joint pain and stayed in the hospital for almost a week. Without any prior mental health diagnosis, Carla does report symptoms that could be related to anxiety and depression. She does mention feeling anxious in social situations and often feels both "physically and emotionally down." She always presents with a blunted affect and seems to be at baseline a slow-moving, morose person who has little hope of improving. Carla has been referred to mental health counseling for pain management in the past and has never followed through.

Carla would likely be diagnosed with somatic symptom disorder, which is characterized by somatic symptoms that can be distressing and very disruptive to daily functioning including work, school, social, and emotional areas.

It is important to rule out any medical conditions or co-occurring conditions such as anxiety and depression that could be contributing to her discomfort. We would note Carla's lack of social support, lack of family support, and the possibility that in her family or culture, mental health problems are stigmatized to the point where she may be responding to stressors with physical complaints. Carla does not appear to be getting secondary gain from hospitalization. In fact, she becomes incredibly anxious when in hospital, and the last few times has wanted to leave against medical advice (AMA). Some of the things that contribute to the doctor's concerns include lack of social support, motivation, and some generalized anxiety symptoms when exposed to new things.

## ⬛ DIAGNOSTIC CONCLUSIONS

- Somatic symptom disorder
- R/O any medical conditions
- R/O anxiety
- R/O unspecified depressive disorder
- Additional concerns: lack of support system and grief at loss of father.

## ⬛ SUGGESTED THERAPEUTIC INTERVENTIONS

Individual cognitive behavioral therapy (CBT) could be effective with Carla. CBT could help Carla with distorted thoughts—for example, thoughts that dwell on the negative ("I'm never going to fit in or feel better") or self-blame ("I wasn't a good daughter so I deserve pain or I deserve to be lonely"). CBT could be useful with unrealistic beliefs that Carla may be experiencing. Some examples of this may include labeling such as, "I'm stupid and not capable of taking care of myself" or overgeneralization "Nobody believes my pain, and everyone is against me."

CBT can assist with behaviors that prompt health anxiety. Health anxiety includes emotions and thoughts that all feed into anxiety about health. Going to the ED and being admitted may feed into the anxiety that something is terribly wrong or that one might be dying. Having medical staff continue to conduct tests may result in anxiety around "nobody knows what's wrong with me so they won't be able to help me feel better." Being afraid of the unknown or embarrassment around how you are being treated by medical staff (maybe feeling worried that the staff doesn't believe you or are speaking ill of you) may also feed into health anxiety.

In addition to therapy, Carla needs to work with a primary care physician who can be consistent, take her medical concerns seriously, and treat her as needed. It would also be important to have Carla participate in all decision-making for both her mental health and medical care. This will help her gain a sense of control.

Carla could benefit from psychoeducation to teach her that physical symptoms can be exacerbated by stress and how to reduce stress responses. Somatic symptom disorder can also co-occur with anxiety and depression; so, it would be important to screen for both of these.

## ▨ FOR YOUR CONSIDERATION

1. How would you have worked with this family in a culturally competent way to explain the relationship between physical symptoms and stress?
2. What additional therapeutic interventions would you consider using with Carla?
3. Are there any other symptoms or historical facts that you would want to know prior to making a diagnosis?

# CHAPTER TEN

# FEEDING AND EATING DISORDERS

*Feeding and eating disorders are characterized by eating behavior that results in health and/or psychosocial problems. This chapter includes two cases of diagnosed eating disorders—anorexia nervosa and bulimia nervosa. Anorexia nervosa is characterized by restrictive eating that leads to dangerously low body weight and disturbances in self-perceived shape or weight. Bulimia nervosa is a disorder that includes episodes of binge eating and compensatory behaviors (e.g., purging, exercising). Questions for consideration follow each case.*

## 10.1    *Case of Jamie*

### ▓ INTRODUCTION

Jamie is a 14-year-old female who is currently in counseling for assistance with restrictive eating disordered behaviors. She entered treatment with her current counselor almost 2 years ago upon discharge from an inpatient eating disorder treatment center. Jamie has received treatment in patient programs a total of four times, the first two times in a program affiliated with the local children's hospital, and the last two times at a hospital specializing in the treatment of eating disorders in children and adolescents. Jamie was first admitted to treatment when she was 10 years old, the second time was 7 months later at age 11, and the third time was 6 months later at age 12. The fourth time was approximately 1 year later when she was 13. At present, she has been out of inpatient treatment for almost 1 year.

    Although Jamie's illness first became severe enough for inpatient treatment when she was 10 years old, she has experienced difficulty eating since she was 10 months old. Jamie's mother attributes this in part to jaw size and bite problems, which are now being corrected with dental procedures including extraction of some adult teeth and orthodontia. She has also received speech therapy services throughout her earlier school years due primarily to pronunciation challenges and occasioned by the dental problems. At this time, Jamie is considerably more verbal and easier to understand that when first entering treatment with her current counselor.

Jamie's father and two older siblings have been diagnosed with higher functioning autism. During her last inpatient treatment, Jamie's assessment results indicated that she might also be mildly autistic in addition to having attention deficit hyperactivity disorder (ADHD) and dyspraxia. She is currently taking 80 mg of Strattera daily for the ADHD, which has resulted in better focus and grades at school, as demonstrated by the fact that she is currently on the honor roll in her first semester of high school. For the last several years, she has also been involved in ballet classes, a puppeteering group, and other extracurricular activities which have aided in the development of muscle coordination and social skills. She uses her Ventolin inhaler for asthma as needed.

In terms of Jamie's immediate family, her mother has been almost entirely responsible for Jamie's care. This is particularly true as Jamie's father is out of town for his employment approximately 50% of the time. This responsibility for Jamie, and the other family members, in conjunction with some medical problems has resulted in Jamie's mother becoming worn down physically and emotionally. As mentioned previously, Jamie's older brother and sister also struggle with mental health disorders. Her older sister frequently displays behavior that is very disruptive to the family. Jamie, her mother, and her brother have all reported that the family environment has improved significantly since the older sister moved out of state to live with relatives after graduating from high school earlier this year.

Recently, Jamie has again begun to restrict her intake of both food and fluids, resulting in the loss of approximately five pounds. Her expressed goal is to stop the eating disordered behaviors, regain the lost weight, and avoid going back to inpatient treatment. While she demonstrates more insight into her own thoughts and feelings, and her health situation, it will be necessary to continue close monitoring of Jamie's weight and orthostatic information (blood pressure and pulse rate) in the event that she may again need to be admitted to inpatient treatment.

## ■ DIAGNOSTIC IMPRESSIONS

Jamie continues to struggle with restrictive eating behaviors that seem to be attributable, at least in part, to physiological factors that surfaced when she was only 10 months old. The related symptoms were exacerbated to the point of inpatient admission and treatment at the ages of 10, 11, 12, and 13. Currently, she has been out of inpatient treatment longer than before, and seems to have more control over the eating disordered behaviors, as evidenced by her increased intake of food and fluids in response to concerning orthostatic and weight loss information obtained through her weekly check-in with her pediatrician.

It is important to note that there had been a consistently elevated stress level in Jamie's family environment due in large part to emotional outbursts by her older sister. Jamie's mother has also experienced some health challenges, including gastrointestinal problems, that have contributed to a higher level of stress at mealtimes. As mentioned earlier, the older sister moved out during the previous summer, which has resulted in a significantly lower stress level at home, particularly as Jamie had shared a bedroom with the older sister. Jamie's mother strategized with Jamie and Jamie's counselor to determine ways to reduce the stresses around mealtime due to her (the mother's) medical issues. Jamie and her mother report that these strategies have been effective in creating a more relaxed experience at meals. It is possible that this reduction of stress at home may make it more possible for Jamie to successfully reverse the recent downward trend in her eating behaviors and avoid another admission to inpatient treatment.

## ▩ DIAGNOSTIC CONCLUSIONS

- Anorexia nervosa, restricting type
- Attention deficit disorder, predominantly hyperactive/impulsive presentation
- Asthma
- Dyspraxia

## ▩ SUGGESTED THERAPEUTIC INTERVENTIONS

Thus far, Jamie has responded well to cognitive behavioral therapy (CBT)/rational emotive behavior therapy (REBT) techniques, including homework regarding eating behaviors and her related thought and emotional processes. Dialectical behavior therapy (DBT) self-management skills have also been a focus of treatment, particularly emotional regulation, along with some Acceptance and Commitment Therapy (ACT) values clarification work. Family therapy has also been conducted with various combinations of family members, and Jamie's mother typically participates in at least part of each session for the purpose of reporting her observations regarding food/fluid intake and weekly check-in information from Jamie's pediatrician.

## ▩ FOR YOUR CONSIDERATION

1. Considering the successful results of Jamie's inpatient treatment, what might be some other approaches or techniques from inpatient treatment that could also be utilized in outpatient treatment? For

example, might a group be helpful at some point? How might one be found?

2. While Jamie and her mother have been working with Jamie's counselor to shift responsibility for Jamie's eating behaviors to her from her mother, what would be reasonable goals regarding the complete transfer of accountability for Jamie's eating behaviors to Jamie?

# 10.2   *Case of Dominique*

## ■ INTRODUCTION

Dominique, or Nique as she prefers to be called, is a 19-year-old college freshman at a public Midwestern college. She presented to the college counseling center at the request of her resident assistant, Ebony. Nique's roommate went to Ebony to share her concern that Nique has been consuming a great deal of food in the dining hall or in their room and then purging. Nique denied that this is a problem and said that the "cafeteria food is making me sick." However, a few days later, Nique ate two boxes of cookies that her roommate had received in a care package from home. Her roommate was furious and confronted Nique; this violated their roommate agreement to "ask before using or eating something belonging to the other roommate." Ebony was brought in to mediate and suggested that if it is a problem, Nique ought to talk to someone in the college counseling center. Nique agreed and made an appointment.

## ■ FAMILY HISTORY

Nique was born to married parents and for the first 6 years of her life, she was the only child and doted on by both parents. Nique's mother, Amy, is a vice president at a pharmaceutic company. (Nique likes to joke that her mom "sells drugs" for a living.) Nique's father, Martin, is a self-employed electrician. Nique said those years were "glorious" and then "Shaun showed up and everything went to hell." Shaun is Nique's younger brother who was born when she was 6. As a baby, Shaun had colic and other allergies and needed a great deal of care. He began having seizures at age 2. When he was nearly 3, he began regressing in speech and would not make eye-contact. Shortly afterwards, he was diagnosed as being on the autism spectrum.

Nique's parents' marriage collapsed under the strain of constant interventions, specialists, in home services, and special diets. Martin moved out and began dating. Nique was heartbroken and felt replaced, especially as one of Martin's girlfriends had a daughter in Nique's dance class. Feeling rejected, Nique did not have much contact with him after that.

Amy redoubled her efforts to care for Shaun and Nique. She hired a nanny to help her with the kids while employing a stable of babysitters to transport Nique to school and extracurricular activities. Nique said that her mom is "amazing" for all that she has done for her and especially for Shaun. As Shaun has aged, he has been increasingly prone to aggression and has punched holes in the walls, thrown items such as phones and televisions, and has threatened to hit both Amy and Nique. Amy has resisted suggestions from family-based therapists and other clinicians to find a residential treatment facility for Shaun or even use a respite care service.

Nique was ambivalent about going away to college. She was not only reluctant to leave Amy with Shaun but also wanted to get away and make her own decisions. Nique felt like she walked on eggshells to keep Shaun happy and avoid outbursts. For example, he commandeered the television and if someone changed the channel, he would become enraged. Nique chose the college that she did because it was 2 hours away from home reasoning that it is close enough to go home if she wanted to but far enough it would not be on a regular basis.

## CURRENT FUNCTIONING

Nique made an appointment in the college counseling center. She said that she is there because her "resident assistant is making her do this." When if Nique thinks she might have a problem, she said that she wished people would leave her alone and that she is "fine and it isn't like I'm super skinny or anything." Upon further discussion, Nique disclosed that she had hooked up with a guy on her floor. She had feelings for him but then she found out that he was hooking up with another girl on campus. Nique did not have romantic relationships in high school as she feared bringing a guy to her home with Shaun there. She was confused as to why he chose the other girl when she "did everything that he wanted her to do." This made Nique feel empty and unwanted. It reminded her of the rejection she felt when she was younger and her father chose another woman and her child over her, Amy and Shaun, whom she blamed for his departure.

Nique felt that if she lost weight, she would attract guys. She began to vomit and exercise for 2 to 3 hours each day. However, the emptier she felt, the more she ate and the more she would vomit and/or exercise. She weighed herself constantly. Several weeks later, she began dating another guy and because she was fearful that he would end the relationship if she gained weight, she focused on meeting his needs sexually and began to vomit after nearly every meal.

Nique had always been a good student. Unfortunately, with her concentration on her new romantic relationship and her weight, her academic performance was subpar. She would attend class but not complete the assignments. Nique admitted that she feels out-of-control and does not know what to do. She is embarrassed to ask her mother for help because "she has enough on her plate between work and Shaun. She does not need to worry about me too."

## ■ DIAGNOSTIC IMPRESSIONS

Nique experiences recurrent episodes of binge eating, defined as eating in a discrete period of time an amount of food that is a lot larger than most people would eat under similar constraints. Additionally, there is a lack of control on overeating during these episodes where Nique cannot stop eating until she reaches a certain level of fullness. To compensate for overeating and to prevent weight gain, Nique vomits and excessively exercises.

Additionally, Nique has unresolved abandonment issues related to her father's departure from the family. Abandonment issues arise when an individual has a strong fear of losing someone that they care for and is a form of anxiety. For Nique, this began when she was a child and her experience of loss (e.g., her way of life, her father). Nique also harbors a great deal resentment toward her brother, Shaun. She acknowledges that his disability is certainly not his fault, she likes to imagine counterfactual situations such as if Shaun was not born or if Shaun was "typical."

## ■ DIAGNOSTIC CONCLUSIONS

- Bulimia nervosa
- Generalized anxiety disorder

## ■ SUGGESTED THERAPEUTIC INTERVENTIONS

To break the cycle of bingeing and purging and/or excessively exercising, Nique may be referred to a nutritional counselor so that she may learn to structure and pace meals, and to adjust daily calorie intake to the amount needed to maintain weight.

Cognitive behavioral therapy (CBT) is the most effective type of psychotherapy for adults with bulimia nervosa (Hail & Le Grange, 2018). This therapy helps patients identify and change distorted thoughts about themselves (e.g., I am unwanted) and food (e.g., food is bad) that underlie their compulsive behavior. It may also help Nique find better ways to cope with life stressors.

Although CBT can rapidly break the cycle of bingeing and purging, combining it with medication may help to support Nique in dealing with underlying psychological symptoms and avoid relapse. Thus, a referral to the campus psychiatrist may be needed.

## FOR YOUR CONSIDERATION

1. Nique's college has a counseling center, on campus psychiatrist, and resources for referrals. If she were attending college in a rural or underserved area, or at a college without clinicians on staff, how might Nique's disorder be treated?
2. Nique's counselor did not think that her eating disorder was severe enough to merit an inpatient or intensive outpatient level of care. Do you agree or disagree?
3. How do you think Nique's relationship with both her father and her brother have impacted her relationship toward men?

## REFERENCE

Hail, L., & Le Grange, D. (2018). Bulimia nervosa in adolescents: Prevalence and treatment challenges. *Adolescent Health, Medicine and Therapeutics, 9*, 11–16.

# CHAPTER ELEVEN

# ELIMINATION DISORDERS

*The elimination disorders in this chapter involve the inappropriate elimination of urine or feces and are the result of trauma in a midlife female and an adolescent male. This group of disorders includes enuresis, the repeated voiding of urine into inappropriate places, and encopresis, the repeated passage of feces into inappropriate places. Questions for consideration follow the case conceptualizations.*

## 11.1    *Case of Ruby*

### ▨ INTRODUCTION

Ruby is a 55-year-old female who recently purchased a home in a large city with her partner of 10 years. She works as a Case Manager in a group home for children and has been employed in the same field for over 20 years. Ruby has a bachelor's degree in social sciences and reported that last month she enrolled in her first graduate course online. She states that she does not have any biological children but enjoys spending time with her partner's older son who has two children of his own. Ruby states that she loves her partner but feels that her partner may not love her the same. She states that they currently sleep in different rooms, has been arguing more than usual, and reports that they do not go out much as Ruby fears that her inability to control her bladder is "embarrassing." Ruby states that her partner does not know the extent of her traumatic childhood and this may also be causing a strain on their relationship.

Ruby currently identifies as a lesbian female but was in a prior heterosexual relationship with her ex-husband for 5 years. Ruby states that the relationship was healthy in the beginning but 3 years into the relationship, her ex-husband became emotionally abusive, in which she decided to pack up her belongings and move in with a friend at work. Ruby states that she had two miscarriages earlier in the marriage and states that her ex-husband viewed her as being "less than a woman" when they found out she could likely not carry children. Ruby states that she made attempts to "save" her marriage but eventually filed for divorce after meeting her current partner at a church event.

Ruby states that she participated in therapy as a child and states that she was diagnosed with posttraumatic stress disorder (PTSD) and enuresis. When asked to describe current symptoms, Ruby states that she often has nightmares, difficulty getting out the bed, sleep issues, mood swings, crying spells, and continues to experience bedwetting, in which her doctor labeled as "nocturnal enuresis." She also states that she gets angry easily and is often triggered for "no reason at all." Ruby states that she does not have any ongoing medical conditions but has experienced night sweats in which her doctor suggested that this could be due to menopause.

## ■ FAMILY HISTORY

Ruby states that she is the oldest of six and reports that her younger sister died 2 years ago due to complicated diabetes. She reports that her parents did not cope well with the loss and states that her mother goes to the grave site every few months. Ruby states that her parents are no longer together and shared that they divorced when she was 12 due to domestic violence concerns. Ruby reports that her four brothers are all married; two live in the same city as she and the other two reside in another State. She reports that she was close to her younger sister but does not have a good relationship with her brothers because they disapprove of her current relationship. She made a point to mention that they grew up in a Christian church and "lesbian relationships" were always frowned upon.

Ruby's mother is a retired nurse and currently resides in senior living housing. She suffers from depression and never fully accepted the divorce. Ruby states that her mother blames herself for her marriage not working out and often makes statements to suggest that their father beat her because she provoked him. Ruby states that she does not have a good relationship with her mother because her mother knew that her father would "beat" her and states that her mother stood by and watched. Ruby also discloses that her father would beat her siblings as well which eventually resulted in them being removed from the home and placed in the care of child protective services for 2 years. Ruby states that they were eventually reunified with their mother once their father went to jail. Ruby states that her mother was required to attend family therapy and parenting classes prior to them being placed back in the home. Ruby states that her mother also blames her for the "family not working" because she was the first one to report the abuse to a teacher.

Ruby's father has since remarried and lives in a small apartment with his wife on the opposite side of town. He worked as an electrician but would often get fired from jobs due to alcohol abuse and domestic violence charges. Ruby states that her father spent his prime years in and out of jail for domestic violence and child abuse. Ruby states that her father would beat her and siblings with extension cords, made her eat dog food, pull their hair, and made them watch as he beat their mother. Ruby states that one day her father made her drink a pint of alcohol and could recall "throwing up." Ruby states that she has not talked to her father in 10 years but saw him at her sister's funeral.

Ruby states that it was difficult seeing the "abuser" at her sister's funeral. She states that she "lost it" and stood up in midst of the crowd and yelled obscene words at her father. She states that she did not get the response that she expected from her father and reports that he just stood there frail and in disbelief. Ruby states that she does not know what came over her but realizes now that it was not an appropriate place to "let out" her emotions. Ruby states that she feels bad that her partner and other family members had to see her act in that manner and wishes that she could take back what happened.

## ■ CURRENT FUNCTIONING

Ruby is a reliable and independent individual who has distanced herself from family due to past traumatic experiences and feelings of not being accepted due to current relationship. She feels as if her current partner is embarrassed of her inability to control her bladder and feels that this is causing a strain in their relationship. Ruby reports that her identity is based on a negative view of herself and she feels as if she would never live up to her partner's or family standards and because of this incongruence, she often experiences difficulty in her daily activities. Ruby enmeshes herself in work, recently enrolled in school, and participates in an exercise class in an attempt to keep herself busy. She views herself as a smart individual and is proud of her educational accomplishments.

Ruby admits to smoking at least five to eight cigarettes per week and states that she will often have two glasses of wine on occasion to suppress her emotions, relationship problems, and irregular sleep patterns. She makes statements such as, "I do not want to end up an alcoholic like my father, so I do not drink regularly." She is concerned that her partner of 10 years will also leave her if she found out that she was smoking and drinking in any amounts. Ruby states that her partner is not a fan of substance use, so she hides the smell by spraying perfume and washing the cigarette smoke from her clothes.

Ruby states that she cannot get over the trauma she experienced as a child and reports that the "scary dreams of the experience" is causing her to wake up at night. She states that most nights she wakes up in a bed full of urine, in which she immediately jumps up and changes the sheets. She states that she is embarrassed and feels that her pride would not permit her to wear an adult diaper. Ruby states that she must figure something out because her partner has decided to sleep in another part of their home. She reports that her partner is a big support but feels as if she is letting her down.

## ■ DIAGNOSTIC IMPRESSIONS

Ruby is a smart, personable, and caring individual who appears to have her finances in order. She presents with stable housing and has maintained a semi-healthy relationship for the past 10 years. Ruby has experienced a traumatic childhood which includes being physically and emotionally abused by her father and neglected by her mother. As a result of this trauma, she was diagnosed with PTSD and enuresis at an early age. She continues to experience distressing nightmares of the abuse, avoids being around her father, isolates from other family members, and has disturbed sleep which includes two to three nights of waking up from urinating on herself. In addition, she has also experienced emotionally abuse by her ex-husband.

Ruby currently does not feel loved in her current relationship. She self-medicates with alcohol and cigarettes on occasion in order to suppress her feelings and this is also an attempt to cope with sleep issues. She feels the need to hide her symptoms from her partner due to fear that her partner will leave her and is afraid that her partner will "judge" her if she knew the details of her traumatic childhood.

Ruby lacks the ability to utilize effective communication skills with the people she loves and uses alcohol and outside activities to cope with difficult emotions. Although Ruby participates in exercise activities and educational programs, she lacks a healthy list of coping strategies to deal with past traumatic events and general relationship problems.

## ■ DIAGNOSTIC CONCLUSIONS

- PTSD
- Enuresis not due to a substance or known physiological condition; nocturnal only (past and present)
- Other depressive episodes
- Relationship distress with spouse or intimate partner

## ■ SUGGESTED THERAPEUTIC INTERVENTIONS

Cognitive behavioral therapy—Ruby reveals a significant number of symptoms related to PTSD and could benefit from receiving trauma-specific interventions to facilitate the healing process (Monson & Shnaider, 2014; Morton et al., 2012).

This evidence-based therapeutic approach can be utilized to assist Ruby with techniques to reevaluate her thinking patterns and can assist in reconceptualizing her understanding of traumatic experiences. In addition, receiving psychoeducation and relaxation instruction can help to facilitate healthy coping strategies. It may also be beneficial for Ruby to discuss medication options with her primary care doctor in which taking desmopressin can assist in controlling enuresis (Osterberg et al., 2006).

Strategic family therapy—Ruby is isolating herself from family members and having difficulty communicating her feelings to current partner. Family therapy is a therapeutic approach that can assist Ruby and family members in problem-solving, communicating effectively, and acting toward change by incorporating therapeutic goals and techniques (Hillary & Chappie, 2014; Szapocznik & Hervis, 2020).

## ▓ FOR YOUR CONSIDERATION

1. How is enuresis related to PTSD?
2. What other therapeutic and treatment interventions can be utilized to assist Ruby in addressing childhood trauma and conflict with family members?
3. How can Ruby address her concerns regarding the problems that she is having with her partner of 10 years?
4. Is it appropriate for Ruby to hide her childhood trauma and use of substances from her partner?

## ▓ REFERENCES

Hillary, C., & Chappie, C. (2014). The evaluation and treatment of adult nocturnal enuresis. *Current Bladder Dysfunction Reports, 9*, 84–89.

Monson, C. M., & Shnaider, P. (2014). *Treating PTSD with cognitive-behavioral therapies: Interventions that work.* American Psychological Association.

Morton, L., Roach, L., & Reid, H. (2012). An evaluation of a cognitive behavioural therapy group for women with low self-esteem. *Behavioural and Cognitive Psychotherapy, 40*, 221–225.

Osterberg, O., Savic, R. M., Karlsson M., Simonsson, U. S. H., Nørgaard, J. P., Vande Walle, J., & Agersø, H. (2006). Pharmacokinetics of desmopressin administrated as an oral lyophilisate dosage form in children with primary nocturnal enuresis and healthy adults. *Journal of Clinical Pharmacology, 46*, 1204–1211.

Szapocznik, J., & Hervis, O. E. (2020). Applying brief strategic family therapy to different circumstances. In *Brief strategic family therapy* (pp. 157–172). American Psychological Association.

# 11.2    *Case of Jerrick*

## ▩ INTRODUCTION

Jerrick is a bright 14-year-old, African American male who currently resides in a therapeutic foster care home with one foster parent, a 55-year-old Hispanic woman with no other children living in the home. They reside near the urban environment where he was born. At birth, he tested positive for methamphetamine and experienced detox symptoms as well as low birth weight. His biological mother abandoned Jerrick at the hospital shortly after his birth and was not located until 3 years later, at which time she was incarcerated and consequently terminated her parental rights. She reported having no other biological children. No biological family members are involved in Jerrick's life.

## ▩ CURRENT FUNCTIONING

The teachers at his current school describe him as curious, insightful, and creative, and admit that they struggle to connect with him as he is often dismissive and condescending when they or other students disagree with his remarks in class that are often negative and provocative. He loves music, and often talks about the new bands he discovers while listening to music on his iPod, the only electronic device he is permitted to use. He often ignores social cues and rambles on about songs he likes and dislikes, long after his classmates have lost interest. He has trouble concentrating when he is asked to participate in discussions, he finds little interest in it, and despite a battery of assessments conducted by the school psychologist, Jerrick does not seem to have any learning disabilities and is an average student. He has not had any referrals for disciplinary issues at his school, is consistently on-time for class each morning, and has displayed appropriate behavior with his peers.

Jerrick reports not having any "real" friends at school and admits to being bullied by other kids because he is poor and lives with a foster parent because his mom is in prison. He stated he coped with the harassment by just ignoring them and then going home and writing songs about the ways in which he hoped they would die. His foster mother continues to work with him on finding other creative outlets for his anger and frustration with little success. She often confiscates his journal and shares her concerns with his case manager, but Jerrick reassures them both that he is not homicidal and is not a danger to himself or others.

Jerrick is in the process of getting to know a potential adoptive family through weekly visits and supervised outings. The potential adoptive parents, both in their mid-30s, Caucasian, middle-class, clinical social workers who work within the agency responsible for his care, are expressing concerns that Jerrick has had several episodes of encopresis during their visits. While embarrassing for Jerrick, these incidents are becoming increasingly problematic over the past 4 months. After a routine annual medical exam, his pediatrician concluded that there were no medical issues causing his encopresis, and stated he showed no signs of constipation. They hope that Jerrick will agree to engage in treatment (counseling and medical interventions) to help him address this problem. They reported that during a recent visit, Jerrick soiled his underwear when they were playing a board game and then denied doing so when they asked if he needed to use the restroom. During another visit, he soiled himself and then left his underwear in the restroom trash can which was discovered by the potential adoptive father shortly after. When questioned, Jerrick denied that the underwear was his and refused to talk about it. The potential foster parents do not have any children of their own and are committed to adopting an older child to complete their family. Jerrick expressed that he would like to get to know them before making any kind of commitment to living with them. His current case manager, with whom Jerrick stated he has a "pretty good" relationship, is concerned that his history of anger outburst and destruction of property, anxiety, depression, and most recently, his threatening songwriting and bouts with encopresis are impacting his ability connect with potential adoptive parents and possibly find his forever family. While she has only known him for 10 months, she seems committed to his care and often goes out of her way to celebrate Jerrick's accomplishments in school and his progress in his current therapeutic foster placement.

The potential adoptive parents also expressed concerns and suspect that Jerrick may have been sexually abused by a former foster father, but according to his case files, Jerrick has never disclosed as much to any of his case managers or former foster parents. They believe this to be true, based on several comments Jerrick has made about, "people using him," and "having to leave some foster homes because of things people did to him." They have tried to get him to open up about his journey in foster care, but he is reluctant to engage and often diverts the conversation away from his trauma story and on to the current video games he is allowed to play or recent TikTok videos he has watched with his foster mom. According to his case manager, Jerrick has been in seven different foster care homes throughout his life. The records show that he was removed from his initial placement, where he lived from birth to age 3, when his foster mother died unexpectantly of a heart attack. He then moved between a number of homes and was always re-fostered to another placement due to the parent(s) complaints about Jerrick not fitting into their current families due to his continued anger outbursts and/or physical violence toward other children in the home, or for destruction of other children's belongings. He had been removed from two other homes for neglect related to poor living conditions and lack of available food, both occurred prior to Jerrick being placed in therapeutic foster care. The case manager reports that he has had 12 different case managers during his time in the system and that his engagement in counseling services, while required, has been inconsistent until his last placement in the therapeutic foster care home, where he has been for the past 11 months. She reported that Jerrick seemed to be doing well in his current placement, but that he hopes to be placed with an adoptive family where he can live until he turns 18. His case manager is committed to helping him obtain the necessary treatment he needs while in therapeutic foster care in order for him to be successful within the potential adoptive parents' home and is seeking treatment options for Jerrick to aid in this process.

## ■ DIAGNOSTIC IMPRESSIONS

Jerrick seems to be struggling with his past and current living situations in relation to his mother's abandoning him at the hospital upon his birth. He may be finding solace knowing that she is in prison, serving a life sentence, and that she could not come get him, even if she wanted to. He has been hurt by those in charge of his care because of multiple placements within the foster care system where he may have experienced both physical and sexual abuse. Jerrick has not opened up about the abuse, but the statements he has made indicate that there is something he experienced in his childhood that has caused him deep pain/trauma. He is fearful of not being good enough for the potential adoptive parents to agree to keep him until he turns 18, and thus the onset of soiling and instances of encopresis have occurred most often when he is spending time with them. He is uncertain of his future and reports few friends, which contributes to his feelings of inadequacy, which he is expressing through threatening song lyrics. He seems depressed and anxious, especially at school where he does not seem to fit in or express a desire to engage. He may lack the knowledge of how to appropriately relieve his bowels daily, and no tracking of his eating habits or fiber intake has been documented. His caregivers have become concerned about his "accidents," which compounds his embarrassment and lack of self-esteem or self-efficacy to be a part of anyone's family. Jerrick lacks consistency and deep connections to others in his life and, while he has maintained his current placement for 11 months, he fears he will do something that will get him moved to yet another abusive home. This fear is brewing under the surface, contributing to his trauma response and his body is responding through soiling (some trace feces present in underwear) and encopresis (full release of the bowels into inappropriate places, such as his underwear).

## ▧ DIAGNOSTIC CONCLUSIONS

- Encopresis, without constipation and overflow incontinence
- Other specified depressive disorder (provisional)
- Child sexual abuse, suspected
- Upbringing away from parents

## ▧ SUGGESTED THERAPEUTIC INTERVENTIONS

This case presents a complex set of symptoms that warrant further consideration. To effectively address Jerrick's needs, a holistic approach is indicated (Geroski & Rodgers, 1998). Beginning with his medical issues, a referral to a gastroenterologist is indicated to rule out potential complications related to Jerrick's encopretic episodes such as, Hirschsprung's disease or other dysfunctions related to medical issues of the colon. It is possible that his behavioral issues, while seemingly under control at present, may be related to a constellation of behaviors related to psychogenetic megacolon concerns, where soiling and chronic constipation are just a part of a more interconnected medical/behavioral issue (Olaru et al., 2016; Kara & Yilmaz, 2018; Zhao et al., 2015; Gontard, 2013). It is also unclear if Jerrick was honest with his pediatrician regarding his bowel movement frequency and, until tracked, could be contributing to his elimination issues (Culbert & Banez, 2007; Gleason, 2019). Once other medical concerns are ruled-out, Jerrick would benefit from further evaluation for potential physical and/or sexual abuse that he may have suffered while in multiple foster care placements. Understanding the implications of the abuse might help his counselor, case manager, foster parent, and potential adoptive parents to support him as he works through the trauma and attempts to understand how his reactions to the trauma have impacted his ability to connect with others in his life.

The counselor might also consider using music as an intervention strategy for helping Jerrick process his current health issues and past trauma wounds, possibly connected to narrative therapy and his interest in writing song lyrics. Narrative therapy has been shown to be effective in treating encopresis in adolescent clients and within the context of family therapy (Fife & Hawkins, 2019). This might also help Jerrick feel more in control of his treatment plan, given that he would be the creator and writer of his own story, potentially empowering him to rewrite his current story or engage in writing a positive future narrative, filled with goals he created for himself.

Another consideration would be to encourage the use of behavior modification through a consistent reward system at home as he adjusts to keeping track of his daily elimination progress to establish scheduled, predictable bowel movements each morning, or as indicated by his doctor (Shepard et al., 2017). Possible rewards might include being able to purchase new music for his iPod each week as he shows improvement, leading up to a live concert with a trusted adult, should he maintain progress for 1 month or longer. No punishments would be used in conjunction with this process, as it is contraindicated with effective treatment for encopresis in adolescents (Fennig & Fennig, 1999).

Jerrick would also benefit from education around healthy eating and the importance of adequate nutrition to assist in his ability to eliminate in a healthy way. This could be accomplished by obtaining a referral to a registered dietitian whom he could work with to establish healthy eating patterns and learn more about the foods that will contribute to his overall mental and physical health. His foster mother and potential adoptive parents would benefit from psychoeducation around the stigma, anxiety, and depression associated with encopresis and how they might assist Jerrick as he struggles with the emotional impact of encopresis. Jerrick and his current parental team (current foster mom and potential adoptive parents) might also benefit from family counseling to assist with the impending transition, should they wish to continue to engage in the adoption process.

In addition to these strategies, Jerrick might benefit from a peer mentoring program or engagement in a school-sponsored club to increase his engagement and sense of belonging at school and to help him build relationships with his peers. There might also be benefits to Jerrick engaging in relaxation training, possibly incorporating music to entice him to practice deep breathing, meditation, and mindfulness in order to connect with and listen to his body as a means for relieving stress and enhancing overall mood and wellness.

## ■ FOR YOUR CONSIDERATION

1. What impact do you think the differences in ethnicity and race plays in Jerrick's increased anxiety as he considers the opportunity to finally be placed with a forever family?
2. What are the implications of Jerrick's mother's incarceration and his first foster mom's death on his mental health and ability to feel safe with other adults? What other relationships in Jerrick's life have impacted him, and in what ways?
3. How might the counselor provide support for Jerrick as he works through the physical/medical aspect of encopresis treatment?

## ■ REFERENCES

Culbert, T. P., & Banez, G. A. (2007). Integrative approach to childhood constipation and encopresis. *Pediatric Clinic of North America, 54*, 927–947.

Fennig, S., & Fennig, S. (1999). Management of encopresis in early adolescence in a medical-psychiatric unit. *General Hospital Psychiatry, 21*(5), 360–367.

Fife, S. T., & Hawkins, L. G. (2019). Doctor, Snitch, and Weasel: Narrative family therapy with a child suffering from encopresis and enuresis. *Clinical Case Studies, 18*(6), 452–467.

Geroski, A. M., & Rodgers, K. A. (1998). Collaborative assessment and treatment of children with enuresis and encopresis. *Professional School Counseling, 2*, 128–134.

Gleason, W. A. J. (2019). Soiling. In *Magill's medical guide* (Online ed.).

Gontard, A. (2013). The impact of DSM-5 and guidelines for assessment and treatment of elimination disorders. *European Child & Adolescent Psychiatry, 22*, 61–67.

Kara, T., & Yilmaz, S. (2018). Encopresis developing following exposure to bullying at school in a 14-year-old adolescent. *Asia-Pacific Psychiatry, 10*(3), 1.

Olaru, C., Diaconescu, S., Trandafir, L., Gimiga, N., Olaru, R. A., Stefanescu, G., Ciubotariu, G., Burlea, M., & Iorga, M. (2016). Chronic functional constipation and encopresis in children in relationship with the psychosocial environment. *Gastroenterology Research & Practice, 2016*, 7828576.

Shepard, J. A., Poler, J. E., & Grabman, J. H. (2017). Evidence-based psychosocial treatments for pediatric elimination disorders. *Journal of Clinical Child & Adolescent Psychology, 46*, 767–797.

Zhao, P. T., Velez, D., Faiena, I., Creenan, E., & Barone, J. G. (2015). Bullying has a potential role in pediatric lower urinary tract symptoms. *The Journal of Urology, 193*(5), 1743–1748.

# CHAPTER TWELVE

# SLEEP–WAKE DISORDERS

This chapter includes a case on narcolepsy as experienced by a college-aged female. Narcolepsy is a chronic neurological disorder that affects the brain's ability to control sleep–wake cycles. The client in this case felt rested after waking, but then feel very sleepy throughout much of the day.

Narcolepsy greatly affected the daily activities and may impact the future of the client who had hoped to be a typical college student. Questions for consideration follow the case study.

# 12.1     *Case of Caitlyn*

## ▨ INTRODUCTION

Caitlyn is a 19-year-old female who presented to the University Counseling Center (UCC) after multiple professors "flagged" her as a student of concern. Caitlyn had been sleeping during her classes or not attending classes at all. Caitlyn reports that she sleeps throughout the day and does not feel that she has any control over her need for sleep. She is worried that she will not be able to succeed academically and will be dismissed from the University as a result of her excessive sleepiness.

## ▨ FAMILY HISTORY

Caitlyn grew up in a rural Pennsylvania town and is the oldest of three siblings. She is the first in her extended family to attend college. Caitlyn reports that she has a "wonderful" relationship with her family, especially her mother, who is Caitlyn's "rock." Caitlyn's father died when she was 14 in a weather-related automobile accident. It was a snowy evening and a car was stopped by the side of the road. Her father, a mechanic, offered to assist a stranded motorist. As he walked back to his own vehicle to retrieve tools, another car spun out of control and struck her father directly. While the family mourned the seismic loss of her father, they took solace that he died in service to helping others.

Caitlyn was an excellent student in high school and earned a full scholarship to participate in a specialized teacher education program. She hopes to fulfill her father's legacy by working as a middle school teacher and giving back to her community. Her school community supported her after the loss of her father and her academics gave her renewed purpose.

There is no family history of anxiety, depression, or other mental health disorders. There is not a family history of substance abuse by Caitlyn's parents. However, Caitlyn's paternal grandmother abused alcohol for decades and died from complications of cirrhosis before she was born. Because of his mother's alcoholism, Caitlyn's father was anti-drinking and anti-drug. Her immediate family members did grieve the loss of her father. However, the grief response was uncomplicated, and the family leaned on each other for support.

## ▨ CURRENT FUNCTIONING

During her initial session, Caitlyn had a general appearance of being drowsy. She slumped in her seat and seemed distracted during the meeting, yawning and closing her eyes frequently. She reported that since the start of the semester, the amount that she sleeps each day has increased. When asked where she sleeps, Caitlyn reported "everywhere." To clarify, the counselor inquired specific locations and Caitlyn shared that she sleeps in class, in her room, in the lounge on her floor during meetings, and even at meals.

Caitlyn confided that her relationship with her roommate has deteriorated from the first few weeks of school. They hung out at first but no longer do so. Caitlyn is not sure what happened and does not remember having a disagreement with her roommate or anything that would indicate why her roommate does not speak to her. When asked to guess why her roommate no longer seeks her company, Caitlyn responded, "She is very looks-conscious, and I've gained a lot of weight." Caitlyn reported that she gained approximately 35 pounds in the past 3 months. She shared that she was "always curvy" but now is considered overweight.

At times, Caitlyn experiences sudden and uncontrollable muscle weakness whenever she experiences intense emotions such as sadness or finds something hilarious such as when her sister sends her funny memes and gifs. She explained that "out of the blue" she feels like she is very weak and that her legs would buckle beneath her. It is frightening to Caitlyn when this happens, and she is fearful that it will happen in public. Thus, she spends a lot of her time in bed in her dorm room.

Caitlyn is very concerned that she will lose her scholarship as a result of her sleepiness. She does not endorse alcohol or drug use and does not understand how she can be so sleepy when she gets so much sleep every day. She has tried caffeine pills and energy drinks and they do not seem to help. She wondered if there was a medication that she could take to stay awake. The UCC is attached to the University Health Center and the campus physician was asked consult on her case and discuss medical reasons for her excessive sleepiness.

## DIAGNOSTIC IMPRESSIONS

The campus physician facilitated a referral to neurology to rule out any brain abnormalities. So that Caitlyn would not sleep through her appointment time, the University Health Center arranged for her resident assistant to knock on her door repeatedly to wake her. The MRI of the brain, EEG, complete blood count, biochemistry tests (e.g., liver functioning), and hormonal tests were administered. All of the results were normal. A referral for endocrinology was also obtained to rule out diabetes or polycystic ovarian syndrome given the sudden weight gain and exhaustion. Caitlyn's excessive sleepiness is associated with significant weight gain prior to the onset of her symptoms. This weight gain might obscure the correct clinical diagnosis of narcolepsy in favor of other sleep disorders such as sleep apnea (Sullivan, 2010). However, endocrine-related conditions were also ruled out.

The University Health Center physician suspected Caitlyn might be experiencing narcolepsy. However, to assess hypocretin deficiency, a lumbar puncture must be made to draw out the cerebrum spinal fluid. Caitlyn refused to do this. Instead, Cailyn agreed to visit a sleep center to have a polysomnography. Polysomnography records brain waves, blood oxygenation, heart rate and breathing, muscle movement, and, importantly eye movements during sleep. Caitlyn entered rapid eye movement (REM) sleep within 15 minutes of falling asleep. This, as well as her other symptoms, is highly indicative of narcolepsy (Andlauer et al., 2013).

Caitlyn also experiences cataplexy. Cataplexy is a brain disorder that causes a sudden and temporary loss of muscle tone and control. The episodes or "cataplectic attacks" are triggered by strong or extreme emotions. Most people experience cataplexy do so as a result of having narcolepsy.

## DIAGNOSTIC CONCLUSION

- Narcolepsy with cataplexy but without hypocretin deficiency

## ▨ SUGGESTED THERAPEUTIC INTERVENTIONS

Psychopharmacology—Stimulant medication and antidepressants may help Caitlyn regulate her sleep cycle. The stimulant may help her to stay awake during the day whereas an antidepressant may help Caitlyn's cataplexy.

Ongoing counseling—Regular counseling appointments may help Caitlyn stay on track with her medications and encourage her to live a healthier lifestyle that includes a sleep schedule, nutritious meals, and exercise. An empathetic counseling relationship may also create a space for Caitlyn to talk about her relationships, self-image, and other struggles related to narcolepsy and other stressors.

## ▨ FOR YOUR CONSIDERATION

1. Narcolepsy is a debilitating disorder that leads to impairment of social and academic performance. It is a disorder that may be misunderstood by patients, parents, teachers, and healthcare professionals. When reading through Caitlyn's case, what else did you consider to be potential diagnoses? Depression? Drug use? Complicated bereavement? Posttraumatic stress? Why?

2. Caitlyn attends a university that has a counseling center, health center with physician access, psychology clinic, and offered referrals to specialists. What are the resources and supports for students at your college or university? How likely would a correct diagnosis be reached if this consultative team approach did not exist?

3. What do you suppose is the prognosis for Caitlyn?

## ▨ REFERENCES

Andlauer, O., Moore, H., Jouhier, L., Drake, C., Peppard, P. E., Han, F., Hong, S. C., Poli, F., Plazzi, G., O'Hara, R., Haffen, E., Roth, T., Young, T., & Mignot, E. (2013). Nocturnal rapid eye movement sleep latency for identifying patients with narcolepsy/hypocretin deficiency. *JAMA Neurology, 70*(7), 891–902.

Sullivan, S. (2010). Narcolepsy in adolescents. *Adolescent Medicine: State of the Art Reviews, 21*(3), 542–555.

# CHAPTER THIRTEEN

# SEXUAL DYSFUNCTIONS

*For a sexual problem to be considered a sexual dysfunction, the symptoms must be present for at least 6 months, cause significant distress, and cannot be caused exclusively by a nonsexual mental disorder (e.g., substance use, depression), significant relationship distress, medical illness, or medication. The three cases in this chapter represent various sexual dysfunctions, such as female sexual interest/arousal disorder and erectile dysfunction disorder, and their respective treatment. Questions for consideration follow each case.*

# 13.1    *Case of John*

## ▨ INTRODUCTION

John is a 58-year-old Caucasian male who initially presented to individual counseling in a private practice facility about 2 months ago because of feelings of depression. John reported that his work hours were recently cut, resulting in financial stressors. John has been with his current employer for many years and fears that due to his age and lack of additional workforce training, he would be unable to find a job. John reports health issues related to hypertension and obesity. He identifies binge eating as a coping skill, which has negatively affected his health. In a subsequent session, John was referred by the counselor for a medical evaluation and to be assessed for an antidepressant. His physician gave him an antidepressant, citalopram. John was told to continue psychotherapy and to follow-up with his physician in a month.

John returned to counseling and informed his counselor that he was prescribed an antidepressant. He is currently taking the antidepressant citalopram—a daily dose of 40 mg. He also reports that he is taking 80 mg valsartan for hypertension control. He has been taking his hypertension medication for the past 6 months. Both prescriptions are prescribed by his primary care physician (PCP). John complains that over the past 6 months, he has felt an overall lack of energy and pleasure. He reports that he feels his antidepressant has helped. Prior to the antidepressant, he was unable to get out of bed. John says that he continues to binge eat and eats whatever he can find. He indicated that this morning he ate an entire apple pie before coming to his appointment. In the past 6 weeks, he has gained 15 pounds. John already struggles with obesity—he is 5-foot-10 and weighs 262 pounds. John spoke in the session about how things have just "piled up." In a subsequent counseling session, the patient disclosed that he has been having some problems with his wife. He complains of marital stressors related to intimacy. He states that he is experiencing erectile dysfunction (ED) and that it seems to have gotten worse over the last several weeks. John indicates that he has not been in the mood to have sex and really has no desire for it. John states that this is causing marital discord between him and his wife. He denies that intimacy and sexual relations have been a problem in the past for his relationship. He does acknowledge some mild periods of "lack of interest" when he is having increased symptoms of depression. He states that what he is experiencing now is different from that and more significant. John reports significant distress related to this new symptom.

It was recommended that John return to his PCP for a follow-up appointment and to assess for potential side effects of his antidepressant medication. In addition, John expresses that he would consider bringing his wife to counseling for couple's sessions while he continues to focus on coping skills for his depression and current stressors.

## ▓ DIAGNOSTIC IMPRESSIONS

Substance/medication-induced sexual dysfunction is the term used to describe various sex-related impairments that result from the use/abuse of drugs, alcohol, or medications. The condition differs from the group of unique mental disorders known as sexual dysfunctions or known collectively as substance/medication-induced disorders (National Institutes of Health [NIH], n.d.). Doctors classify substance/medication-induced sexual dysfunction according to the specific impairment that occurs in any given case. Although many of the drugs that can trigger the disorder are illegal, an unusually wide range of legal drugs can also potentially trigger sexual problems, even when used according to standard prescription guidelines (NIH, n.d.).

One of the main features of substance/medication-induced sexual arousal that leads to clinical significance is when there is a development of interpersonal conflicts or difficulties that lead to distress (NIH, n.d.). In the case of John, he reports that his sexual dysfunction has caused a significant amount of marital discord. According to Tufan et al. (2013), multiple sexual adverse effects or in essence sexual dysfunction can be the cause of using psychotropic medication. Approximately 30% of sexual complaints are clinically significant, with the majority from antidepressants being related to orgasm or ejaculation. Issues with desire and erection are also reported, but with less frequency (APA, 2013). However, it is important to note that regardless of prescription medication, depression may be associated with sexual dysfunction as well. Depressive cognitions may interfere with sexual arousal (Tufan et al., 2013). Differentiating between underlying mental health issues and a substance/ medication-induced sexual dysfunction can be complicated. Balon and Segraves (2008) note how there has been an increase over the last two decades in sexual dysfunction associated with selective serotonin reuptake inhibitor (SSRI) antidepressants. In the case of John, he is taking the SSRI antidepressant citalopram. According to the American Psychiatric Association (APA, 2013), the prevalence of substance/medication-induced sexual dysfunction is unclear because of underreporting and variance depending on the substance causing the dysfunction. In regard to antidepressants, including SSRIs, approximately 25% to 80% of individuals report sexual side effects. Determining the cause and potential diagnosis is usually related to the relationship between symptoms and medication initiation or dissipation of symptoms with substance/ medication discontinuation.

Substance-induced sexual dysfunction is different from primary sexual dysfunction. The sexual dysfunction is occurring from prescription medications or substances taken and not related to any other condition (NIH, n.d.). It has also been suggested that likelihood of disturbance can increase with age. In this case, John reported no negative side effects related to his hypertension medication that he began 6 months ago. Sexual dysfunction can be due to John's prescription medication for depression because it is a side effect of SSRIs. Should there be evidence that the dysfunction persists after a change in medication, then it may be due to another cause and no longer a diagnosis of substance/medication-induced sexual dysfunction (NIH, n.d.).

## ■ DIAGNOSTIC CONCLUSIONS

- Citalopram-induced sexual dysfunction with onset after medication use, moderate
- Adjustment disorder with depressed mood
- Eating disorder—binge eating disorder
- Overweight, financial distress, marital discord

## ▨ SUGGESTED THERAPEUTIC INTERVENTIONS

In order to assess for sexual dysfunction and diagnosis, it is very important for the practitioner to adequately assess the underlying cause of the problem because treatment might be handled differently (Pesce et al., 2002).

Sexual functioning in general can often be impaired by depressive disorders owing to a loss of pleasure or interest. Therefore, an antidepressant medication can exacerbate the sexual dysfunction. This can lead to the client or patient discontinuing antidepressant treatment because a consequence of medication-induced sexual dysfunction is medication noncompliance (APA, 2013; Clayton et al., 2007). It is important to ask clients about their sexual function in an effort to identify sexual dysfunction early because this is a preventable and treatable side effect of antidepressants and other medications. Otherwise, this can compromise treatment (Werneke et al., 2006).

As commencement of medication-induced sexual dysfunction is often coupled with medication initiation, discontinuation, or dosage change, the treatment of the sexual dysfunction is often related to a change in dosage or discontinuation of medication (APA, 2013). It is important to work with the client and the physician to determine a timeline of symptoms. If the symptoms are a direct result of the medication, then they may be reduced or eliminated with a change in dose or discontinuation of the medication.

In some cases, sexual dysfunction can be easily treated through a number of different libido-boosting medications such as Viagra. This decision would be up to the medical provider because there may be danger in prescribing this medication in combination with other medications or medical issues. However, these types of medications do not address other potential mental health issues, relationship issues, or life stressors that might be affecting libido, desires, or feelings. In this case, the client may simply be experiencing the side effects of medication (NIH, n.d.). For this reason, it is again important for a counselor to work in conjunction with the medical provider to treat both the physical and mental contributions of symptoms.

To treat John appropriately, his doctor needs to do a complete physical examination and blood work, including testosterone hormone levels that affect one's sex drive (NIH, n.d.). This does not mean that lab tests or a physical examination will show the cause. It is also important to ask about John's cultural, religious, social, and ethnic background, as that too can influence sexual desires and expectations (NIH, n.d.).

John recently began psychotherapy for his depression. Addressing depression symptoms and life stressors may decrease or eliminate his symptoms of sexual dysfunction.

It can also be recommended that John and his wife seek marital counseling for further improvement in their interpersonal relationship. Sex therapy is often recommended for couples that are struggling with sexual issues or intimacy that is not related to organic causes. This may be a potential referral after medication concerns have been addressed/eliminated.

## ▦ FOR YOUR CONSIDERATION

1. What additional information do you need to know in order to feel confident you arrived at the correct diagnosis? What questions do you still have?
2. What specific questions might you ask the client in regard to sexual dysfunction?
3. How might your diagnosis change if the client reported a different timeline? For example, if the sexual dysfunction started prior to the antidepressant initiation? If the symptoms started 2 months after the antidepressant initiation?
4. When might sex therapy be an appropriate referral? Any thoughts about when it might be contraindicated?
5. How important is collateral information in this case? Would you like the client's wife to attend treatment?
6. What if the PCP does not agree with your diagnosis? How would you support your conclusions?

## ▦ REFERENCES

American Psychiatric Association. (2013). *Diagnostic and statistical manual of mental disorders* (5th ed.). American Psychiatric Publishing.

Balon, R., & Segraves, R. T. (2008). Survey of treatment practices for sexual dysfunction(s) associated with anti-depressants. *Journal of Sex & Marital Therapy, 34*(4), 353–365.

Clayton, A., Kornstein, S., Prakash, A., Mallinckrodt, C., & Wohlreich, M. (2007). Changes in sexual functioning associated with duloxetine, escitalopram, and placebo in the treatment of patients with major depressive disorder. *Journal of Sexual Medicine, 4*(4i), 917–929.

National Institutes of Health. (n.d.). *Erectile dysfunction.* MedlinePlus (U.S. National Library of Medicine). www.nlm.nih.gov/medlineplus/erectiledysfunction.html

Pesce, V., Seidman, S. N., & Roose, S. P. (2002). Depression, antidepressants and sexual functioning in men. *Sexual and Relationship Therapy, 17*, 281–287.

Tufan, A. E., Ozten, E., Isik, S., & Cerit, C. (2013). Discerning the effects of psychopathology and antidepressant treatment on sexual dsyfunction. *International Journal of Psychiatry in Clinical Practice, 17*(3), 223–226.

Werneke, U., Northey, S., & Bhugra, D. (2006). Antidepressants and sexual dysfunction. *Acta Psychiatrica Scandinavica, 114*(6), 384–397.

# 13.2   *Case of Luz*

## ▨ INTRODUCTION

Luz is a 43-year-old female born in Nicaragua who became an American citizen after studying physical therapy in the United States. She has been living in the United States for 26 years and is married to a U.S. Federal Marshall who is a 58-year-old Caucasian male. Her religious faith is Roman Catholic, and she explained that her faith is a strong component of her life. She came to counseling owing to sexual problems in her marriage and wants to be "happy with her husband again." Her husband, David, had a previous marriage from which he has two children who are now adults. David and Luz have one child together, a 10-year-old daughter named Elizabeth, who lives with them. During her pregnancy with Elizabeth, David's other children came to live with them, which caused some transitional stresses. Some of the challenges with the transition were the result of David's ex-wife making negative statements about Luz to the children who avoided her and rejected her attempts at developing a relationship. In addition, Luz had a very difficult and complicated pregnancy and childbirth.

Upon the delivery of Elizabeth, David took notice of Luz's struggles and informed her that he would not put her in such a predicament again. However, when Luz heard this, she interpreted the message as a negative statement. Thereafter, as she reflected on what David said, she thought to herself: "I'll make sure it never happens again." Since that moment of reflection, Luz and David have not had sexual intercourse or any other sexually oriented touching, though they are physically affectionate, with limitations, and do hold hands. They are respectful to each other, but whenever David tries to cuddle with her, Luz quickly turns away owing to fears that he may try to turn the cuddling into a sexual advance.

David joined Luz for a couples' session since the struggle presented as a systemic concern. David would like to retire and move to another state but is insistent on a full emotional, physical, and spiritual relationship together before he commits to them moving as a family. David has been patient for the past 10 years but is increasingly becoming frustrated with the lack of her willingness to engage in physical intimacy. Luz stated that she has a low libido, and after a physical exam from her gynecologist, there were no physical reasons for her libido to be low. The gynecologist ruled out early menopause or any other physical conditions that would contribute to a low libido and suggested counseling to explore any mental health barriers.

## ■ DIAGNOSTIC IMPRESSIONS

Simons and Carey (2001) conducted an extensive literature review of 10 years of data on the prevalence of sexual dysfunctions for both men and women. Two studies within their literature review are pertinent to the prevalence of female sexual arousal disorder for women in the United States. Laumann et al. (1999) reported a 1-year study of prevalence of female sexual arousal disorder that indicated 19% in a representative U.S. sample. However, Chandraiah et al. (1991) reported a lifetime prevalence of 21% in a primary care setting based on *DSM-III* (*Diagnostic and Statistical Manual of Mental Disorders, Third Edition*) criteria.

Female sexual dysfunction in general is a complex and little understood condition affecting women of all ages and ethnicities. According to Markovic (2010), several factors may influence sexual desire, including "life experiences, stresses and anxiety; body image; communication issues; economic situation; sexual education; belief system, sexual technique and habits; cultural expectations" (p. 260). Comorbidity may present as mood and/or anxiety disorders, panic attacks, depression, phobias, or bipolar disorder (Hurlbert et al., 2005).

Women with low sexual desire often have low self-image and mood instability (Basson et al., 2005). Specific knowledge of these factors is pertinent for the clinician in developing a treatment plan for the disorder, with a goal of improvement in the enjoyment of sexual activity by the client. As illustrated by the case of Luz, what may be often overlooked is the role that a closeted memory can play in inhibiting sexual enjoyment and thus precipitating individual stressors as well as marital discord.

During the diagnostic process, Luz admitted to never really having much interest in sex. She recalls as a young woman how her coworkers would discuss their sexual escapades and how she did not find such experiences interesting or exciting. Luz admitted to being willing to engage in sexual physical contact with David upon their marriage but explained that she wanted to be a mother, which was the motivating factor for her willingness to be sexual with David. Still, she never initiated physical intimacy. She denied ever having had any sexual fantasies regarding anybody, and unfortunately not even her husband. She does feel a little guilty that she has not desired her husband physically, although she does love him and adores him in many other ways. Luz explains that sexual intercourse was neither pleasant nor painful, but it was uncomfortable to some degree owing to feeling inadequate for not feeling pleasure. She also feels guilty for avoiding sexual contact with David because of the lack of pleasure and discomfort she felt during sex. Luz feels as though she cannot win because she feels guilty either way, but she worries more about David thinking he cannot satisfy her during intercourse and the potential resulting impact on his self-esteem. Therefore, she prefers to avoid sexual contact and work through the guilt by loving David in other ways (caretaker, homemaker, etc.), which she gladly takes on in addition to her work. Luz highlighted that she would love to be able to enjoy sex and for it to not be so unfulfilling and uncomfortable but does not know exactly how to make that happen. When questioned about her attempts to address the problem, she explains that she has avoided working on it with David because of her past experiences and inability to enjoy sex or feel aroused and the subsequent guilt she experienced when sex was over.

Luz completed the Female Sexual Distress Scale—Revised (FSDS-R) resulting with a total score of 27 (a score of 11 and above helps differentiate between female sexual dysfunction [FSD] and no FSD). In addition, exploring the diagnostic criteria for female sexual interest/arousal disorder provides a clear indication that Luz meets several of the criteria to include a lack of interest (or reduced interest) in sexual activities, lack of sexual thoughts and fantasies, lack of initiation in sexual activity, and being unreceptive to sexual advances from her husband (American Psychiatric Association [APA], 2013). However, in order to ensure an accurate diagnosis, a differential diagnostic process was applied.

Given the lack of sexual desire that can be present with other mental disorders, such as major depression, Luz was questioned regarding her overall mood presentation. She denied feeling sad or having other symptoms of depression such as fatigue, difficulty concentrating, or lack of interest in activities (APA, 2013) with the exception of feeling guilty about her lack of sexual involvement with her husband. She completed the *DSM-5* Emerging Measures Level 2—Adult form, for Depression (www.psychiatry.org/psychiatrists/practice/dsm/dsm-5/online-assessment-measures) with an overall score of 12, indicating no significant level of depression. The items that she endorsed as "sometimes" were associated with feeling sad and hopeless. When questioned about her answers, Luz explained that it usually occurred after David approached her for sexual intimacy and she would decline his advancement. She further clarified that such feelings were often associated with her guilt and feeling hopeless about the possibility of a sexually satisfying relationship for her marriage.

Luz was also questioned about possible avoidance associated with trauma reactions and Posttraumatic Stress Disorder (APA, 2013). However, Luz denied feeling as though her life or the life of the child was ever in real danger during the pregnancy or delivery. She said that she has not had any unpleasant dreams about the pregnancy or childbirth and that she is fine talking about the experience because it resulted with a very positive outcome—the birth of her child. Luz did not demonstrate any other symptoms associated with any other mental disorder. Luz does drink on occasions, but her drinking is so infrequent and without any related symptoms associated with any substance use disorders. In addition, since her doctor completed a panel of tests and a thorough examination regarding her physical health, medical conditions were also ruled out.

Given Luz's cultural background, the concept of *marianismo* was explored. Sanchez et al. (2016) defined *marianismo* as "a gender role construct that describes the expectations and norms for some Latina women (and girls) based on a collectivistic worldview in which interdependence and familial hierarchy are the cultural norm" (p. 396). The authors further explained that the potential negative component of *marianismo* "may reinforce sexual silence and the avoidance of communication about sexually intimate behaviors" (Sanchez et al., 2016, p. 397). Although the Sanchez et al. (2016) study was mainly focused on adolescent girls hypothesizing that such negative components would contribute to sexual engagement in order to reduce distress in romantic relationships, the concept of avoidance was specifically applied to Luz because she was not willing to engage in sexual intimacy with David beyond the birth of their first child together. Luz admitted to her strong religious beliefs as a factor when she was a younger girl but denied any contributions of *marianismo* factors to her lack of sexual interest or arousal.

## ▓ DIAGNOSTIC CONCLUSION

- Female sexual interest/arousal disorder, lifelong, generalized, moderate

## ▓ SUGGESTED THERAPEUTIC INTERVENTIONS

Treating female sexual interest/arousal disorder is complicated by the fact that there is rarely a single causative factor that can be traced as the reason for the problem, and this is exacerbated by the fact that there are limited psychotherapy treatment options. A review of published articles highlights the plethora of studies associated with addressing abnormal physiological findings. A review of the literature gleans some studies of recommended psychotherapy approaches with encouraging outcomes.

Treatment of clients who meet the *DSM-5* criteria for Female Sexual Interest/ Arousal Disorder requires an individualized approach that may include a combination of counseling, cognitive behavioral interventions, pharmacotherapy, and/or remedies for concomitant medical or psychiatric conditions (Graham, 2010). Pharmacological treatments such as hormone therapy may be options for treating physiological needs, imbalances, or other symptomatic complaints, and comprise one part of the overall treatment management of clients with female sexual disorders.

The family doctor will likely refer a client to a qualified specialist, who may be a sex therapist or a psychotherapist specializing in behavior modification or cognitive behavioral therapy (CBT). As the case of Luz represents, some clients state that their reason for seeking treatment is that if they could increase their own level of desire, it would be easier to deal with their partner's sexual demands. "The key for successful therapy evidently lies in identifying the 'motivations (reasons/incentives)' for being willing to attempt to become sexually aroused by their partners in order to experience responsive sexual desire and then enhancing those motivations" (Basson et al., 2005, as cited in Durr, 2009, p. 299).

Therapy may include education about how to optimize the body's sexual response, ways to enhance intimacy with their partner, and recommendations for reading materials or couples' exercises (Palacios et al., 2009). CBT and sensate focus techniques (progression from nonsexual contact up to sexual touching, similar to systematic desensitization but focused on resensitizing) are useful therapies (Basson et al., 2005). A mindfulness program designed by Brotto and Barker (2014) incorporates Buddhist principles to establish a connection between the mind and body. The program includes education in the basics of mindfulness meditation, practicing mindfulness for a period of time, along with the woman engaging in observation and examination of her body in nonsexual ways. In addition, engagement in reducing distracting thoughts, that is, judgments about their physical appearance, is another component of the program. The mindfulness program has been shown to be successful by women with various sexual disorders.

## ■ FOR YOUR CONSIDERATION

1. Would you consider Luz's condition a disorder? Do you believe that diagnoses like female sexual interest/arousal disorder should be included in the *DSM-5*?
2. What other diagnoses, if any, would you consider for Luz if she were from a different culture? Why?
3. If Luz were unresponsive to recommended treatment, would you change any aspect of her diagnosis? If so, what diagnoses come to mind?

## ■ REFERENCES

American Psychiatric Association. (2013). *Diagnostic and statistical manual of mental disorders* (5th ed.). American Psychiatric Publishing.

Basson, R., Brotto, L. A., Laan, E., Redmond, G., & Utian, W. H. (2005). Assessment and management of women's sexual dysfunctions: Problematic desire and arousal. *Journal of Sexual Medicine*, 2, 291–300.

Brotto, L. A., & Barker, M., (Eds.). (2014). *Mindfulness in sexual and relationship therapy*. Routledge.

Chandraiah, S., Levenson, J. L., & Collins, J. B. (1991). Sexual dysfunction, social maladjustment, and psychiatric disorders in women seeking treatment in a premenstrual syndrome clinic. *International Journal of Psychiatry in Medicine, 21*, 189–204.

Durr, E. (2009). Lack of 'responsive' sexual desire in women: Implications for clinical practice. *Sexual and Relationship Therapy, 24*(3–4), 292–306.

Graham, C. (2010). The *DSM* diagnostic criteria for female sexual arousal disorder. *Archives of Sexual Behavior, 39*(2), 240–255.

Hurlbert, D. F., Fertel, E. R., Singh, D., Fernandez, F., Menendez, D., & Salgado, C. (2005). The role of sexual functioning in the sexual desire adjustment and psychosocial adaptation of women with hypoactive sexual desire. *Canadian Journal of Human Sexuality, 14*(1–2), 15–30.

Laumann, E. O., Paik, A., & Rosen, R. C. (1999). Sexual dysfunction in the United States. *Journal of the American Medical Association, 281*, 537–544.

Markovic, D. (2010). Hypoactive sexual desire disorder: Can it be treated by drugs? *Sexual and Relationship Therapy, 25*(3), 259–263.

Palacios, S., Castano, R., & Grazziotin, A. (2009). Epidemiology of female sexual dysfunction. *Maturitas, 63*(2), 119–123.

Sanchez, D., Whittaker, T. A., Hamilton, E., & Zayas, L. H. (2016). Perceived discrimination and sexual precursor behaviors in Mexican American preadolescent girls: The role of psychological distress, sexual attitudes, and marianismo beliefs. *Cultural Diversity and Ethnic Minority Psychology, 22*(3), 395–407. https://doi.org/10.1037/cdp0000066

Simons, J., & Carey, M. P. (2001). Prevalence of sexual dysfunctions: Results from a decade of research. *Archives of Sexual Behavior, 30*(2), 177–219.

# 13.3    *Case of Jason*

## ▓ INTRODUCTION

Jason is a 23-year-old gay male who has recently graduated from college for sports management. While attending college, Jason found himself engaging in various sexual activities with a multitude of partners, claiming he was always safe, used protection, and got tested regularly for sexually transmitted diseases. Jason remarks that his sexual history was relatively normal until he met his now longtime boyfriend Mark. After having numerous sexual encounters with Mark, Jason started experiencing difficulty maintaining an erection during sexual acts with Mark, causing great strain on their relationship. Mark constantly remarks to Jason that he feels he "doesn't find him attractive anymore," whereas Jason continuously validates Mark's attractiveness to him.

    Jason has come to therapy hoping for a solution to his sexual dilemma as a recommendation from his PCP. Jason explains that his PCP had found no biological reason behind his ED and that he should seek counseling to see if any mental health strategies could be implemented to alleviate his issue. Jason explains that this issue has lasted for the past 9 months of his relationship with Mark, roughly starting 6 months after the beginning of their relationship. While going over their relationship, Jason explains that until this issue appeared, he and Mark were extremely happy and carefree. Both had gotten an apartment together and found great jobs out of school, and Mark had a great relationship with Jason's parents.

Jason explains that in the last month, his work schedule has caused his and Mark's relationship to be further strained, causing Jason to drop interest in his fantasy football league that he and Mark both ran with a mutual friend group. Jason explains that since his shift in work a month ago, he has felt even more sad and hopeless with his relationship with Mark, expressing how much he loves him, but that he does not feel he can fix the rift he feels in their relationship. Jason also remarks that he never feels "fully focused" at work and that he is never able to concentrate fully on his work like he had been able to in the past. Because of these stressors, Jason explains that he "lies awake at night, thinking about all of the aspects of his life that are going wrong" and that he has found he loses more and more sleep each night. During a session with both Jason and Mark, Mark commented "how much less energy and passion Jason seems to have lately" and that he seems to "not be able to make up his mind" when given choices.

After much questioning, Jason and Mark finally reveal more personal details about Mark and his sexual relationship, explaining that his ED happens no matter what kind of sexual act he and Mark are performing. Mark explains that the issue has caused strain on his relationship with Jason but that he is even more concerned with Jason's mental health as of late than the lack of sexual intimacy. Jason explains how he does not feel "like the man Mark needs" in his life because he is unable to pleasure him physically, mentally, and emotionally.

Jason explains that Mark is a very strong-willed individual and can be very blunt with criticism. Beyond this, Jason remarks that Mark is "nearly perfect for me. We always seem to be on the same page, and we both have goals and desire to achieve them together in life. Whenever I feel down, Mark is always there to try to support me and help me. The only thing about Mark I would like to change is how blunt he can be with his words." Jason explains that Mark can try to be dominating whenever Jason is working on a project or when they are partaking in sexual activities. Jason explains that within the last month, Mark has also made very blunt statements about his changes in mood and behavior, causing Jason to feel less open to explain to Mark his feelings of hopelessness and sadness for fear of criticism from Mark.

## ■ DIAGNOSTIC IMPRESSIONS

When it comes to a relationship and sexual encounters, there is a level of nervousness that is normal, and individuals may report that there may be difficulty coping with the anxiety and anticipation in order to enjoy the experience. As is the case with many ED cases, something is blocking a person's ability to enjoy and partake in the sexual experience, be it trauma, self-confidence issues, or something undetermined. With this disorder, the occurrence of distress and issue happens nearly always with the individual, and this disorder can come paired with other issues.

Jason experiences great difficulty with his ED, and as such it starts to take a toll on the rest of his life. As this issue lasts longer and longer, his relationship with Mark falls apart to an ever-increasing degree. Because of the stress associated with the ED, coupled with his work stress, he begins to develop symptoms of depression, further hurting his relationship and creating more concern for his mental well-being. Jason experiences feelings of sadness and hopelessness rather often with all of the stressors in his life. He also starts to lose interest in his favorite activities and feels a loss of energy and general sleep health. Finally, his depressive symptoms have caused him to have difficulty maintaining his concentration at work, further exacerbating his feelings of hopelessness.

## DIAGNOSTIC CONCLUSIONS

Individuals with ED disorder may find themselves with other comorbid conditions. For ED to be the true diagnosis, the individual must experience the issue more than 70% of the time during sexual interactions, for at least 6 months. This dysfunction must not be better explained by a mentally distressing event or from severe relationship distress. Also, for the dysfunction to be diagnosed, it must cause severe impairment in a client's life. Without these criteria being met, the dysfunction may stem from a lack of self-confidence, trauma, and abuse, or can be better explained by substance abuse.

Major depressive disorder involves meeting the criterion of at least five of nine different symptoms that can manifest in a client's life, and these five symptoms must also be seen within a 2-week period for the diagnosis to be made. With major depressive disorder, individuals must also not have any schizophrenic-related disorders that would better explain the symptoms or major depressive episode that the client may be experiencing.

Individuals with depression may lack the confidence to maintain an erection, while the lack of the ability to maintain an erection may cause more depressive feelings and ultimately be the true cause of the depressive episode.

- ED disorder
- Major depressive disorder, recurrent episode, moderate

## ■ SUGGESTED THERAPEUTIC INTERVENTIONS

Traditional counseling methods involving empathy and validation would be effective in pinpointing the direct cause of the ED. Jason most likely can pinpoint when the ED began, and with a strong rapport may be able to go into more detail around the mental processes that happen while performing sexual acts that cause the loss of his erection. Sex therapy may also be used to help address relationship issues that may be contributing to the dysfunction, noted heavily in the case study with Mark's blunt criticism.

CBT may be utilized to help dispel negative thinking, behavioral, and systematic patterns to help reduce the symptoms of the depression. The fact that both partners also are trying to help salvage the relationship means that validating the clients through their depressive thoughts may allow them to see the supports that they have more clearly, creating stronger support networks for the client to navigate when depressive episodes strike, or even before, to help the client remain above the depression.

With this kind of delicate case in which the information is personal and relatively secretive, a strong rapport is necessary for therapy to be most effective. Individuals do not always share their sexual experiences (especially embarrassing or troublesome ones) lightly, which requires the counselor to have a strong rapport with his or her client. Owing to the coexistence of the depression in this case, the counselor will have to go below the depressive emotions and behaviors to find the true source of the client's ED, another layer of difficulty posed in the treatment of the client.

## ■ FOR YOUR CONSIDERATION

1. Could Jason's ED stem from a previous, albeit minor, major depressive episode that went undetected? If so, how could this change the diagnosis at hand, and how would treatment need to change, if at all, to address this difference?
2. How well do you think Mark will react to the idea that his harsh criticism could be the cause of Jason's worsening condition?
3. Could the idea of commitment be causation for Jason's ED given his freer nature throughout college?
4. Would this idea be worth pointing out to the client, or would this cause more difficulties in the already strained relationship?
5. Is this case more of a relationship dysfunction or an individual dilemma? Would therapy be more productive with both Jason and Mark present in each therapy session, or in this case would individual therapy with Jason be most beneficial?

# CHAPTER FOURTEEN
## GENDER DYSPHORIA

*Gender dysphoria is the feeling of discomfort or distress that might occur in people whose gender identity differs from their sex assigned at birth or sex-related physical characteristics. The cases in this chapter include two cases of adolescent gender dysphoria. In the first case, the adolescent is considering future transition against the backdrop of family acceptance and cultural issues while the other adolescent highlighted in this chapter has transitioned and manages depression and a history of child abuse. Questions for consideration follow each case.*

# 14.1     *Case of Sujin*

### ▨ INTRODUCTION

Sujin is a 14-year-old female of Korean descent who lives with her parents in an upscale suburb of a large city in the United States. Sujin is a freshman at the local public high school and is enrolled in honors and advanced placement courses; her current grade point average is 4.3 on a weighted scale. Sujin enjoys her classes; she is also enrolled in the Junior Reserve Officers' Training Corps (JROTC) program at her high school. Sujin is the only child of her parents, who emigrated to the United States when she was a baby. Sujin was brought to counseling by her parents, who are concerned about her "acting like a boy."

According to her parents, Sujin has always been "a good girl" as demonstrated by her obedience to her parents and her academic achievement. Her father states that Sujin never seemed to like "girl things" but that he was not concerned about this when she was younger. However, now that she is a teenager his concern is growing. The father reports that Sujin refuses to wear dresses and has no female friends. She spends all of her free time with her male friends from JROTC, which her father finds socially unacceptable and borderline scandalous. He states that Sujin "thinks she's a boy" and asks the counselor to "make her into a girl." Sujin's mother adds that she is concerned for her daughter's happiness and thinks she may "just be rebelling."

When asked to respond to her parents' perspectives and share her own thoughts about current issues or challenges, Sujin does not speak and does not make eye contact with the counselor or with her parents. When asked what she wants from the counseling experience, Sujin simply shrugs her shoulders; her father answers for her with "she needs to learn to be a girl." The father continues by adding "She *must*. I will not have this in my house." He adds that he has been patient thus far but "this nonsense has to stop." After some convincing and a hard push back from the parents, Sujin is permitted to speak with the counselor alone.

In the absence of her parents, Sujin relaxes noticeably. She states that no one ever stands up to her father and thanks the counselor for the time alone. Sujin explains that she loves her parents very much, but they do not understand her. She has often lived in fear of her father, who is very traditional and very controlling. Sujin has tried to be an obedient daughter, but no longer feels she is being true to herself by doing so. She adds that while she has always felt very different from her peers and never quite fit in, she now feels more connection with the friends she has met in JROTC. She states that they accept her for who she is, and do not "make (her) fit into their mold" as her parents do. Sujin is finally "just one of the guys" which is all she has wanted to be. This has given her the confidence to be more assertive about her identity and individuality—though she acknowledges this has also caused tension and conflict with her parents.

Sujin has always felt more like a boy than a girl and believes this to be the root of the conflicts with her parents. She shares that her father punished her by grounding her for a month the last time she cut her hair, which she keeps very short in an almost military style. She also states that she has been binding her breasts since sixth grade but does so while she sleeps or after she leaves the house so her parents do not know. Sujin has also recently started menstruating, which she finds "disgusting" and wishes she could take pills to make it stop. When asked if she would surgically change her gender if she could, Sujin responds "Does it matter? My parents would disown me."

When asked again—in the absence of her parents—what she wants out of counseling, Sujin replies that she wants to figure out how to get through the next 4 years and to make her parents love her for who she is. Sujin shares that after graduation she intends to make a career for herself in the military; in fact, this career plan was the impetus for Sujin's joining JROTC. Her father was initially in support of her joining, believing it would "make her more disciplined." However, he now wants Sujin to quit as he believes JROTC is "destructive to her femininity." Sujin tears up as she shares this, adding that JROTC is the first time she has "had any real friends."

## FAMILY HISTORY

Sujin's parents emigrated to the United States along with several extended family members. The family members live within a short drive of each other and work together in Sujin's father's business. Sujin's mother is in her mid-50s and her father just turned 60. They tried for many years to have a child and consider Sujin to be their "miracle baby." Sujin was raised in a family environment heavily influenced by the collectivism of her heritage, though she describes herself as more individualist than collectivist. The extended family system spends the majority of their free time together, frequently sharing meals, holidays, and family events.

Sujin's family is Catholic and are conservative in their beliefs and traditions. The women in Sujin's family do not work outside the home and are generally not consulted in important decisions. The men in the family are responsible for financial stability while the women tend to the children and maintain the home. At family gatherings, there is a general separation between the men and women, with younger children being tended to exclusively by the women in the family. Older children and adolescents in the family also divide by gender, with the girls helping the mothers with cooking and childcare while the boys play soccer or video games. Sujin states that while she respects her parents and their beliefs, these traditions are not a fit for her and not what she wants for her own future.

## CURRENT FUNCTIONING

Sujin attends school consistently and performs well in her classes. She enjoys learning and being challenged by the academic opportunities at her school. In the past she had difficulty making friends and was often bullied in middle school. However, since joining JROTC, she has developed a support system of male peers. Sujin's parents are very strict and limit her freedom to maintain her own social life outside the home, which is a source of stress for her. This has been especially true recently, as her parents are uncomfortable with her primary peer group being strictly male. Sujin often finds herself at odds with her parents' rules and expectations, but she is unable to voice her opinions or desires as such is considered very disrespectful.

Sujin presents with an appearance more traditionally masculine and she verbalizes her dislike of feminine secondary traits and behaviors. She identifies more comfortably as a boy than a girl, but believes her parents would disown her if she ever considered surgically changing her gender. At this time, Sujin prefers the pronouns she/her, but acknowledges she doesn't know if they really fit. She wants to be loved and accepted by her family for who she is.

## ▪ DIAGNOSTIC IMPRESSIONS

Sujin's affinity for a masculine identity are fairly straightforward. She has always felt more like a boy than a girl, she actively attempts to more closely resemble a boy than a girl, and she wishes to be treated like a boy within her family and friend circles. Her identity and preferences in behaviors have caused challenges for her, both in her peer group (in the past) and in her family system. Specifically, her culture of origin and immediate family system impart a significant amount of pressure on her to be traditionally feminine. Thus, though Sujin seems comfortable with and sure of herself in many ways, she is experiencing significant distress from the lack of acceptance around her.

The cultural component in this case is strong. It is important to recognize and validate Sujin's culture of origin as well as her own more "Americanized" personal experience. Further, Sujin is at an important stage of development in which it is not uncommon to desire more individuality and recognition of personal differences. Sujin wants to be seen, understood, and accepted by her parents and extended family. Sujin's struggle with this element is arguably more of a challenge for her than navigating her gender-minority identity.

Another important and related consideration in this case is to recognize Sujin's gender dysphoria within the context of her life experience. Sujin has been raised with rigid constructs of gender and gender role, which conflict with her own gender identity experience. In the course of exploring this with Sujin, it will be important to clarify what gender identity means *to her*. Recognizing that part of her distress is rooted in the rigid traditions of her culture will be important to her healthy identity development in the short and long term. This can present a challenge for the counselor in that it must be done in a manner that honors Sujin's culture and family system while also acknowledges its limitations on Sujin.

Lastly, Sujin's age is a significant element in this case. She is on the front end of adolescence and has a lot of development yet ahead of her. Currently Sujin "feels more like a boy" though she continues to prefer she/her pronouns. It is unknown at this time whether this preference is reflective of her own identity or a manifestation of her cultural influences. As she develops cognitively and emotionally, Sujin will likely come to understand that gender exists on a continuum. She may find that she moves away from the restrictions of a binary gender construct and into a more individually defined, nonbinary gender identity. She could also find more comfort in embracing her masculine self fully and transition surgically sometime in the future. Unfortunately, either of these would likely be challenged by the traditional and restrictive views of her parents.

## DIAGNOSTIC CONCLUSIONS

- Gender dysphoria
- Parent–child relational problem

## SUGGESTED THERAPEUTIC INTERVENTIONS

Transgenerational Family Therapy: Considering Sujin's age as well as the significant influences of her family system on her presenting issues, family therapy is indicated. A transgenerational family approach (e.g., Bowenian, psychodynamic, or contextual) would be well suited for this case as it allows for significant attention to cultural and systemic influences across the system. Further, transgenerational family therapy provides empathy and validation for the individual's perspectives while also acknowledging and addressing the problematic dynamics across the family system.

Existential Individual Counseling: Sujin is facing developmental challenges in addition to her parent–child conflicts. As she continues to grow into her own identity, it would be helpful for her to explore her identity and its meaning. Though she has limitations to many of her choices due to her age, she may find solace in acceptance of her transient circumstances. In addition, existential counseling may help clarify Sujin's desires regarding her gender identity, including how she wishes to self-identify and whether she might desire to transition in the future.

## FOR YOUR CONSIDERATION

1. How does cultural context affect the diagnoses in this case?
2. Why is it so essential to include Sujin's parents in her treatment?
3. How would you respond to the parents' request to teach their daughter "to be a girl?"

# 14.2   *Case of Michael*

## INTRODUCTION

Michael is a 15-year-old Caucasian transgender male (female to male), who is seeking counseling to assist him in beginning testosterone hormone therapy. Michael reports knowing that he was male from the time he was 7 years old.

He describes always wanting to play with his older brother's toys and a refusal to dress in anything feminine. Michael prefers to dress in either androgynous or masculine clothing.

Michael reports that he informed his mother at the age of 7 that he was a boy and he wanted to be treated as such. He states that his mother dismissed what he said by "laughing it off" and informing him that this was "just a phase." She would often refer to Michael as being a "tom boy." From time to time, Michael's mother would insist that he wear a dress or other feminine clothing for church, school pictures, and family events. Michael reports feeling very upset when his mother would force him to wear "girl" clothes and stated that he felt like "he was dying inside." Michael states as he grew older, the battles between him and his mother over clothing became more intense. Michael's parents are divorced, and he rarely sees his father. During the times he is "forced" to visit with his father, he states that his father continually berates him for looking like a "Goddamn boy."

Michael reports when he began to go through puberty at the age of 12, he begged his mother to allow him to take hormone blockers. His mother denied his request, stating that it was too dangerous and that he would most likely grow out of his "obsession with being a boy." She would also cite financial problems as being a barrier for Michael receiving his desired medication. Michael reports experiencing extreme symptoms of depression when he began developing breasts. He states that he tried everything he could to keep them from growing and hide their appearance. Michael also reports feelings of hopelessness and having an increase in suicidal thoughts when he began to menstruate. He states that he felt alone, and he had no one to talk to about what he was experiencing. He also did not know what was going on with him, he just knew he was different from his peers and he did not feel like he fit in with anyone. He reports that at this time he began to emotionally distance himself from the few friends he had.

Michael discloses he first entered counseling at the age of 13 to deal with depression. He states at that time he was having frequent suicidal thoughts and a lack of desire to attend school. He also describes how he began to withdraw from his friends and spend most of his time at home in his room, often sleeping. Michael states his mother became very concerned about him after he told her he was having thoughts of ending his life. Her concern was amplified after finding a journal Michael had been keeping, in which he wrote that he hated himself and he wanted to die. Michael's mother confronted him about the writings, and he told her that the world would be better off without a "misfit" like him. It was at this time she sought professional help, even though the family was struggling financially.

Michael reports that his previous experience in counseling helped him deal with his depression and helped him discover what he was experiencing had a name; he was transgender. His mother also engaged in some of the counseling sessions with Michael and began to take what Michael was experiencing seriously. She bought him a binder for him to wear to hide his breasts. She also began to allow him to dress in the masculine clothing he picked out. However, his mother continued to deny him access to testosterone treatments because of the unknown potential side effects, and the cost associated with the testosterone. She also continued to call him by his birth name. Michael states his depression improved temporarily, but he continued to feel invalidated by his mother and returned to his feelings of hopelessness.

Michael reports 2 months ago he made a suicide attempt. Michael states that during his inpatient hospitalization, he worked up the nerve to tell his mother how much it hurts him when she invalidates his feelings and continues to call him by his "dead name." He told his mother that he just wants to be loved and accepted for who he is. Michael reveals that following this conversation, his mother sought out medical consultation to allow him to begin testosterone therapy and is assisting him with legally changing his name to Michael.

## ▨ FAMILY HISTORY

Michael is the youngest of two children. He and his older brother have always had a close relationship. Michael mentions that his older brother is the only person who has been supportive of him throughout his life. He describes growing up in a very unstable home. Michael's father is a police officer and his mother is an elementary school teacher. His parents married when they were in their early 20s, because his mother became pregnant with his older brother.

Michael remembers seeing and hearing his parents fight a lot when he was younger. The family struggled to make ends meet and put food on the table during the time Michael's father was training to become a police officer. Michael also recounts how his father would drink after coming home from the police academy and he would often become violent with his mother and the two children. Michael's older brother would often try to shield him from their father's wrath, which would result in his brother taking the brunt of the abuse.

The family members were active in the Latter-Day Saints (LDS) religion. Michael recounts how they had to keep up appearances of being a happy family every Sunday when they attended church. The church provided them with food and other assistance because of their financial difficulties, which Michael described as an embarrassment to his proud father. The pressure to appear as though all was well within the family was reinforced daily. Both Michael and his brother were threatened not to tell anyone what was really going on inside their house, or else there would be severe punishment. When attending church Michael was forced to wear dresses. He struggled with attending church because he felt judged by other church members for being different. Once at church, he would often try to hide and not participate in the meetings and children's activities. This would often result in his father becoming physically violent with him once they returned home because he was such an embarrassment to the family.

When Michael was 10 years old, his father came home from work in a drunken rage and proceeded to beat his mother. Michael and his brother ran to a neighbor's house to call 911. Because Michael's father was a policeman, he was not arrested. Instead, he was told to figure out a better way of handling his anger. Michael's parents were also referred to their religious leader, the Bishop of their church, for marital counseling. The Bishop was not a trained member of the clergy, as is the tradition in the LDS church. Therefore, the Bishop informed Michael's mother that she needed to learn how to be a better wife to her husband so he would not get so upset with her anymore. The next day, while her husband was at work, Michael's mother packed herself and the kids up and went to stay with a distant relative. During the separation, Michael's father sought visitation rights, which were granted to him. Michael's brother was able to avoid participating in many of the visits with his father because he was over the age of 14. However, Michael was forced to spend time with his father, although the visits were erratic.

After being separated from her husband for 2 years Michael's mother filed for divorce and worked two jobs to save up enough money to afford a rental home for her and her children. In addition, she worked to pay for a lawyer who would eventually help her gain full custody of her children. The family also never returned to church and did not seek further assistance from their church, even though they continued to struggle financially.

## ■ DIAGNOSTIC IMPRESSIONS

Michael's suicide attempt is the only way he believes he can highlight the depth of his pain and suffering for his mom. He is experiencing gender dysphoria in adolescents. The presence of gender dysphoria is evidenced by his reporting that he is a male in a female's body, the desire to be rid of his female characteristics, such as his breasts, menstruation, and his female name, and his strong desire to begin testosterone treatments to assist him in physically transitioning into a male. He is also experiencing distress in his social and familial relationships, along with his inability to perform in school. Michael identifies as a male and wants to be treated as a male.

He is also experiencing a major depressive disorder. This diagnosis is evidenced by his depressed mood for most of his days, social isolation, a lack of interest in regular activities, hypersomnia, and suicidal ideation with an attempt. Because Michael's depression is chronic, over a period of 2 years, I would diagnose him with persistent depressive disorder.

In addition, Michael has a parent–child relational problem with his father. Michael's relationship with his father causes him significant distress whenever he is required to interact with his father. Michael believes his father hates him and does not accept him for who he is. In the past, Michael's father has used intimidation to force him to dress like a girl and has threatened violence against Michael if he did not do what his father said while he was in his father's care.

Finally, Michael is dealing with a history of physical child abuse, perpetrated by his father. During his parent's marriage, Michael was regularly subjected to physical violence by his father. Following his parent's separation and divorce, Michael has not been physically abused by his father. However, there is still psychological intimidation and abuse present in their relationship.

## ▩ DIAGNOSTIC CONCLUSIONS

- Gender dysphoria in adolescents
- Persistent depressive disorder, early onset, with intermittent major depressive episodes, severe
- Parent–child relational problem
- Personal history (past history) of physical abuse in childhood

## ▩ SUGGESTED THERAPEUTIC INTERVENTIONS

First and foremost, clinicians working with transgender children and adolescents must educate themselves on transgender issues as a whole, along with the specific population of transgender youth. The transgender population has unique challenges and needs that must be understood and acknowledged in order for clinicians to be effective in working with these individuals. There are many books and articles that have been written on working with the transgender population, along with a wide variety of internet resources. It is imperative that clinicians are educated about transgender individuals, their challenges, and their needs, long before a transgender client enters their counseling room. One of the best resources for counselors is the American Counseling Association Competencies for Counseling with Transgender Clients (2010).

For working with Michael individually, I would recommend utilizing narrative therapy. Narrative therapy is a strength-based approach that views clients as being the experts of their own lives. According to Constantinides (2012), narrative therapy with transgender clients provides a nonpathologizing perspective and gives control to clients who have been historically marginalized. Narrative therapy can also assist clients in making meaning of their gender identity and can assist them in developing a story of how they would like to be seen in the world.

Family therapy is recommended for Michael and his mom, which would include a psychoeducational component for his mom. Family therapy would include exploring possible feelings Michael's mom might be experiencing after realizing that her child is transgender. According to Mallon and DeCrescenzo (2006), some of these feelings experienced by Michael's mom might include: "shock, denial, anger, grief, misplaced guilt, and shame." Michael's mom might also be worried about Michael's safety, health, future employment opportunities, and future romantic relationships. It will be important for Michael and his mother to discuss these emotions and concerns in a safe environment. Part of the psychoeducational piece would include presenting information to Michael's mom on the Family Acceptance Project developed by Dr. Caitlin Ryan. Ryan and Rees (2012) explored parental behaviors that can either hurt or enhance the lives of LGBTQ children. Their research notes that parental behavior toward their LGBTQ children can have a direct impact on their children's well-being including risk for physical and mental health problems. This research assists parents in understanding the behaviors that increase a child's risk of physical and mental health problems, and the behaviors that help promote physical and mental well-being in their child.

## ▨ FOR YOUR CONSIDERATION

1. What further information do you need to be confident that you arrived at the correct diagnosis?
2. What other interventions do think would be helpful for Michael and/or his mother?
3. What are some other resources you might use to educate yourself regarding working with transgender clients?
4. What are the effects of poverty and religion on transgender individuals and their mental health treatment options?

## ▨ REFERENCES

American Counseling Association. (2010). Competencies for counseling with transgender clients. *Journal of LGBT Issues in Counseling, 4*(3), 135–159.

Constantinides, D. M. (2012). Working with transgender clients: A person-centered and narrative therapy model. www.goodtherapy.org/therapy-for-transgender-web-conference.html

Mallon, G. P., & DeCrescenzo, T. (2006). Transgender children and youth: A child welfare practice perspective. *Child Welfare, 75*(2), 215–241.

Ryan, C., & Rees, R. A. (2012). *Supportive families, healthy children: Helping families with lesbian, gay, bisexual, and transgender children*. San Francisco State University.

# CHAPTER FIFTEEN

# DISRUPTIVE, IMPULSE-CONTROL, AND CONDUCT DISORDERS

*Disruptive, impulse-control, and conduct disorders include conditions involving problems in the self-control of emotions and behaviors. Unlike other cases in this book, the two cases highlighted in this chapter are unique in that these problems are manifested in behaviors that violate the rights of others such as aggression, and/or that bring the client into significant conflict with societal norms or law enforcement. Questions for consideration follow each case.*

## 15.1    *Case of Billy*

### ▧ INTRODUCTION

Billy is a 9-year-old Caucasian male who was brought to counseling by his mother, Tina. At the beginning of the session, Tina expressed concern regarding Billy's temper outburst and reluctance to follow rules. Tina mentioned that they moved to the area about 6 months ago owing to her husband's job relocating the family. They have adjusted well overall, but Billy has continued to be somewhat defiant and argumentative when redirected by his mother. Tina explained that her husband works a lot but that he is supportive of the consequences imposed by her when Billy does not listen. She also mentioned that Billy has been somewhat withdrawn and isolated since he started playing soccer with a local kids' team a month ago. Tina mentioned that the other children he was playing soccer with were not very nice and would pick on Billy. She worries that he is sad and is not sure how to help him.

During the interview, the counselor found out that Billy has been somewhat oppositional and defiant since the age of 3 years. He would argue with his parents, refuse to do what was asked of him, and then become really angry and throw things in his room. Billy blamed his parents for making him angry and for messing up his room. Although Billy does throw things in his room, he does not typically break things or damage his belongings or the house. Billy often also blamed his younger sister for annoying him. When Billy does become angry and explosive, it only lasts for up to 20 to 30 minutes and he usually calms down. He is not continuously upset, irritable, angry, or moody outside of the situations where he does not want to do what he is told. Interestingly, his mother indicated that Billy is an excellent student and behaves appropriately at school. Teachers praise Billy's behavioral compliance while in class. In addition, Tina stated that other parents also comment on Billy's behavior being so positive whenever he visits a friend or spends the night.

Billy took part in the interview without his mother present, which went well. He was respectful to the counselor and answered questions without hesitation. He willingly completed an age-appropriate depression scale (the Center for Epidemiological Studies Depression Scale for Children [CES-DC]) to explore the potential for depression given Tina's concerns about his mood. Tina completed the National Institute for Children's Health Quality (NICHQ) Vanderbilt Assessment Scale—Parent Informant to explore potential attention deficit hyperactivity disorder (ADHD) symptoms as well as some disruptive impulse-control and conduct disorders (i.e., oppositional defiant disorder [ODD] and conduct disorder). She also completed the *DSM-5 (Diagnostic and Statistical Manual of Mental Disorders: Fifth Edition)* Emerging Measures Level 2—Parent/Guardian of Child Age 6 to 17 scales for both depression and anxiety.

## ■ DIAGNOSTIC IMPRESSIONS

Considering the potential for different diagnoses or clinical struggles is important in the case of Billy. A thorough evaluation of depressive disorders, disruptive impulse-control, and conduct disorders is warranted given that irritable mood may be present instead of a sad or depressed mood for children and adolescents struggling with major depressive disorder (American Psychiatric Association [APA], 2013). Exploring disruptive mood dysregulation disorder is also important; however, Tina did clarify that Billy's mood is pleasant outside of the outbursts. Therefore, Criteria D for Disruptive Mood Dysregulation Disorder would not be met, and the diagnosis could be ruled out.

Tina mentioned that Billy's mood shifted to what she observes as sadness that started about a month ago when he started playing soccer. Exploring a major depressive episode would be important, and Billy's CES-DC score was elevated (score of 19 [a cutoff of 15 indicating depressive symptoms]) and the Level 2—Parent/Guardian of Child Age 6 to 17 scale for Depression also indicated a moderate level of depression (T-Score of 63.6). However, other than the sadness expressed by Billy's mother and Billy's own acknowledgment of feeling sad at times, Billy (and his mother) denied any complications with his eating, sleeping, energy level, lack of interest in activities, restlessness, or suicidal thoughts.

They did, however, admit to some concentration struggles and feeling "less than" others (i.e., low self-esteem) to some degree. Three symptoms of major depressive disorder are clearly identified in Billy's case—depressed or irritable mood, feeling more worthless than usual, and problems with concentration (APA, 2013, pp. 160–161). Still, the three symptoms are not enough to warrant a diagnosis of major depressive disorder, for which five or more symptoms are required. A diagnosis of adjustment disorder with depressed mood would be appropriate given the three symptoms of depression, the depressive symptoms being exhibited after the experiences with his soccer team within 1 month of joining, the assessment results of the CES-DC and Level 2-Depression—Parent/Guardian of Child Age 6 to 17 scale, and the distress caused by the symptoms to the individual and the family system.

Billy's other area of concern surrounds the anger outburst and oppositional and defiant behaviors. Disruptive mood dysregulation disorder has already been ruled out; however, other potential diagnoses need to be explored. An exploration of disruptive impulse-control and conduct disorders provides some avenues to consider, including (a) ODD, (b) conduct disorder, and (c) intermittent explosive disorder. The explanation of symptoms expressed by Tina and exhibited by Billy coincides with the diagnostic criteria for ODD. In order to be diagnosed with ODD, Billy must demonstrate at least four symptoms within the possible eight symptoms listed together with distress or impairment and the ruling out of other disorders (bipolar disorder, etc.; APA, 2013, p. 462).

The case study clearly presents that Billy loses his temper, gets easily annoyed, becomes angry, argues with his parents (authority figures), refuses to follow rules and directives, and blames others for his anger and misbehaviors, which are all associated with the symptoms of ODD (APA, 2013, p. 462). Tina's concern and her own distress regarding Billy and his outbursts are clear indication of significant distress. In addition, Tina's completion of the NICHQ Vanderbilt Assessment Scale—Parent Informant provided some psychometric support for ODD, with five of the eight symptoms endorsed as occurring "Often" or "Very Often" as well as a "problematic" rating on the Relationship with Parents performance subscale. The results of the NICHQ Vanderbilt Assessment Scale—Parent Informant also indicated four symptoms of inattention and five symptoms of hyperactivity/impulsivity as endorsed with an "Often" or "Very Often" frequency; however, Billy's school behavior is always appropriate, and his academic functioning is exceptional. Therefore, the behaviors endorsed by Tina for Billy's NICHQ Vanderbilt Assessment Scale—Parent Informant are more associated with his oppositional behaviors. The *DSM-5* (APA, 2013) cautions clinicians to be aware of this possibility in the differential diagnosis information for ADHD where it highlights how those diagnosed with ODD would refuse to follow the demands of authority figures but is separate from aversion to school work or other tasks demanding concentration and attention. Because Billy happily completes his homework and schoolwork while in class, he does not exhibit an aversion to work that requires mental effort. Because the symptoms of ODD are only present at home (one setting), the severity specifier would be mild. Counselors will still want to rule out any other potential diagnosis prior to solidifying the ODD diagnosis.

Intermittent explosive disorder should be explored because of the arguments and temper tantrums (APA, 2013, p. 466). The frequency of verbal aggression would meet criteria A.1. (APA, 2013, p. 466), but the differential diagnosis information associated with intermittent explosive disorder is not met due to the verbal arguments occurring only with his parents and not within a variety of settings. In addition, intermittent explosive disorder requires that the outbursts are not focused on getting something (criteria C; APA, 2013, p. 466), but Billy usually has his temper tantrums and outbursts when he does not want to do something and is trying to intimidate his mother into giving up and allowing him not to follow the directive. Lastly, conduct disorder is explored; however, the symptoms and criteria for conduct disorder are much more severe than what Billy is exhibiting. Therefore, conduct disorder can be easily ruled out.

## DIAGNOSTIC CONCLUSIONS

- ODD, mild
- Adjustment disorder with depressed mood

## SUGGESTED THERAPEUTIC INTERVENTIONS

Counselors are encouraged to consider the culture of the child and/or family system when working with individuals diagnosed with ODD. Cultural considerations will help clinicians better determine the most appropriate intervention. Some interventions that have proved to be beneficial in general include cognitive behavioral therapy (CBT) (Battagliese et al., 2015) and behavioral interventions via parent education and training (Kledzik et al., 2012).

CBT may be helpful in providing a combination of efforts focused on changing the thought processes of the client and/or the family system. Battagliese et al. (2015) conducted a meta-analysis of 21 studies that explored either a cognitive behavioral, cognitive, or behavioral intervention. The authors combined all three approaches and cohesively identified them as CBT. The CBT interventions within the 21 studies were specifically focused on externalizing behaviors that included ADHD, ODD, and conduct disorder. The meta-analysis included 10 factors such as ODD symptoms, parental stress, and aggressive behaviors

(Battagliese et al., 2015). Results of the meta-analysis did provide support for the use of CBT interventions for reduction of ODD symptoms based on parent report measures (Battagliese et al., 2015). However, CBT may be difficult to implement depending on the age of the client diagnosed with ODD and/or the client's openness to exploring his or her own role in the struggle. Therefore, behavioral interventions are also considered and often touted as the initial treatment approach when it comes to addressing ODD (Kledzik et al., 2012).

Some concepts presented by Kledzik et al. (2012) included how verbal praise and other forms of positive reinforcements tend to help parents and children change their negative interaction cycle to healthier dynamics (p. 559). Included in the behavioral interventions are parent trainings to help them better approach their child with rules and rewards. The authors recommended prioritizing behaviors (two or three) and to phrase the rules for behaviors in "do" versus "don't" terminology (Kledzik et al., 2012, p. 559). For example, instead of saying, "don't touch anything that doesn't belong to you," say, "only touch things that belong to you." Lastly, Kledzik et al. (2012) explained that regular information on psychopharmacological interventions for children solely diagnosed with ODD was not available but that those who have comorbid ADHD often do benefit from stimulant medication and/or atomoxetine for impulse control.

In Billy's case, his parents would be provided with behavior modification training focused on implementing rules with specific consequences. They would be encouraged to use choice terminology that would emphasize the personal responsibility of Billy in his experience of consequences (Dean, 2015). An example of choice terminology focused on emphasizing the positive reinforcement is "Billy, if you choose to put up your clean clothes within the next 10 minutes, you choose to watch television for an hour today." An example of how the choice terminology emphasizes the personal responsibility is "Billy, you did not choose to put up your clean clothes within the 10 minutes allotted; therefore, you chose to give up 15 minutes of your television time." Parents would be encouraged to fragment positive reinforcements and avoid all-or-nothing consequences to allow the child (Billy) to still see that he has something he can work toward if he would choose to follow the rules. Billy's parents would be provided with detailed guidelines; however, they would be encouraged to adjust the behavior modification plan to fit their family personality as well as the components that work best with Billy.

## ▪ FOR YOUR CONSIDERATION

Billy's parents would be asked to continue to monitor his symptoms of depression and ODD. Counselors can continue to explore whether depressive and/or ODD symptoms are still present through both clinical interviews and/or readministration of the assessment measures completed during the initial visit.

1. If Billy and his family were African American or Hispanic, would you have any diagnostic considerations based on possible cultural factors?
2. If Billy's depressive symptoms increased or grew more severe, would you change any of his diagnoses? If so, what disorder(s) come to mind?
3. If Billy's disruptive behaviors became more severe to include stealing and sneaking out at night, would you change or add any diagnoses? If so, what would you consider?

## ▨ REFERENCES

American Psychiatric Association. (2013). *Diagnostic and statistical manual of mental disorders* (5th ed.). American Psychiatric Publishing.

Battagliese, G., Caccetta, M., Luppino, O. I., Baglioni, C., Cardi, V., Mancini, F., & Buonanno, C. (2015). Cognitive-behavioral therapy for externalizing disorders. *Behavior Research and Therapy, 75*, 60–71.

Dean, C. J. (2015, February). *Addressing problematic behaviors in children: Integrating behavioral family therapy & choice theory.* Presented at the Louisiana Association for Marriage and Family Therapy Annual Conference, Baton Rouge, Louisiana.

Kledzik, A. M., Thorne, M. C., Prasad, V., Hayes, K. H., & Hines, L. (2012). Challenges in treating oppositional defiant disorder in a pediatric medical setting: A case study. *Journal of Pediatric Nursing, 27*, 557–562. https://doi.org/10.1016/j.pedn.2011.06.006

# 15.2    *Case of Antonio*

## ▨ INTRODUCTION

Antonio is 16 years old and has been referred to the Emotional Support (ES) Classroom at East High School. He previously attended a day program for adjudicated youth after an altercation with a police officer after he was caught shoplifting from a pharmacy. The East School District established the ES Classroom for district students who could appropriately be brought back from placement, saving the district money and giving students an opportunity to be a part of their community school. As part of his placement in the ES Class, Antonio's individualized educational plan (IEP) includes 90 minutes per week of mental health therapy, along with social skills training and case management services.

## FAMILY HISTORY

Antonio was adopted from foster care at age 2 along with his older brother, Carlos, who was age 4. Antonio and Carlos' mother had died from a drug overdose after their father was incarcerated for attempted murder in a gang-related shooting. There were no relatives able to care for the young boys, so they were place in foster care when Antonio was an infant and Carlos a toddler. The foster parents were thrilled to have the boys and petitioned the court to terminate their father's rights so they could adopt the boys.

When the boys were 8 and 10, their adoptive mother told them about their history and their parents. That was the first time Antonio realized that his "real father" was still alive. Antonio became obsessed with the idea of meeting him. He asked to write letters to him, and his parents agreed. Antonio started a pen-pal correspondence with his biological father.

Two years ago, Antonio and Carlos's father wrote a letter explaining that he was diagnosed with prostate cancer and he did not have long to live. He asked Antonio to visit him before he died. Unfortunately, by the time the letter reached him, and his mother inquired to figure out logistics for a potential visit, their biological father had died. After this, Antonio began to skip school on several occasions and would be out past his curfew. When he did attend school, he would bully or threaten other students. Carlos informed his parents that Antonio had recently joined a gang and he was concerned that Antonio was rumored to have vandalized the principal's home. Antonio's behaviors escalated after this and he became increasingly violent, contributing to the juvenile charge that led to his placement.

## CURRENT FUNCTIONING

Antonio had been a good student throughout his school years according to his academic records. His ES teacher finds him to vacillate between being uncommunicative and combative. Antonio bullies the other students in the classroom, pressuring them for their snacks or outright stealing, and the ES teacher is recommending that he be excluded from that class, as it disrupts the learning for the other students.

During the initial session, Antonio said that he did not like authority, and he wasn't crazy so therapy would not work. He refused to complete the assessments or engage in any activities. The clinician decided to build rapport with Antonio during subsequent sessions to develop trust so that he would feel comfortable enough to speak openly about what was going on with him, his history, and relationships. Antonio started to discuss his feelings toward his adoption, his biological father's death, and how being in a gang made him feel closer to his father whom he regrets not meeting.

Unfortunately, in March 2020, East High School, as other school districts, shut down due to the Covid-19 pandemic. Therapy services were offered via telehealth. The clinician set up an appointment time with Antonio, but he did not keep the appointment. Subsequent appointments were scheduled, and Antonio did not attend any of the appointments. The clinician called the home and Antonio's mother said, "He said he will see you in the Fall. He does not want to talk to a computer."

## ▨ DIAGNOSTIC IMPRESSIONS

Antonio has a pattern of aggressive behavior that is more severe than typical adolescent behavior. He has a history of physical violence, destruction of property, stealing, and threatening and bullying others. He also was involved in the juvenile justice system and is a member of a gang.

## ▨ DIAGNOSTIC CONCLUSION

- Conduct disorder

## ▨ SUGGESTED THERAPEUTIC INTERVENTIONS

CBT was introduced with Antonio after trust was established. It was explained to Antonio that CBT may help him understand his current difficulties and how it impacts his life. They discussed how situations influenced his thoughts and that negative thinking activates both physical and emotional responses, which influence his behaviors. He seemed interested in how these things are all connected and that he does not have to act on every emotion. It is recommended that CBT be reintroduced to Antonio when school resumes in the Fall.

## ▨ FOR YOUR CONSIDERATION

1. What are the issues around trust and boundaries when working with a client with conduct disorder?
2. Antonio needed a lot of time to develop trust with the clinician. Instead of completing assessments and activities, Antonio refused. How might you handle a client's refusal to your clinical suggestions?
3. When the schools shut down in March 2020 due to Covid-19 concerns, it became difficult to fulfill the terms of students' IEPs. Telehealth was an option for Antonio. Why do you think that he was reluctant to take advantage of it?

# CHAPTER SIXTEEN

# SUBSTANCE-RELATED AND ADDICTIVE DISORDERS

*The misuse and abuse of substances such as alcohol and drugs put people at risk for short-term and long-term harm. This chapter highlights the cases of four individuals and one family who have diagnosed substance-related disorders such as alcoholism or opioid addition. Questions for consideration follow each case.*

## 16.1    *Case of Rebekka*

### ▓ INTRODUCTION

Rebekka is a 27-year-old Hispanic female with a history of hospitalizations, both psychiatric and substance related. She was referred to substance use disorder (SUD) treatment after her most recent psychiatric hospitalization. Rebekka shares that she has been using alcohol and cannabis to manage social relationships as well as mood swings and boredom. She has a great deal of anxiety when she is around groups of people. She currently is not working; for the last 7 years she has worked as a certified nursing assistant. Though she is currently not in an intimate relationship, she has had boyfriends in the past. She has never been married and has no children. She lives with a roommate and has three people she considers as her close friends. She lives close to her family; she comes from a large family with five siblings where she is the youngest. Her drinking and cannabis use has impacted her mood swings which in turn have impacted her friendships, connections with family, and employment.

Rebckka experienced her first complex episode of mania when she was 23. During that episode, she had strong feelings of superiority, exaggerating her achievements, and believing herself to be one of the most intelligent people in the world. She quickly became quite angry when her delusions were challenged. Rebekka had used substances sporadically between the ages of 14 and 21; her use of alcohol and cannabis increased and became chronic when she turned 21. When she was evaluated at the psychiatric facility, the psychiatrist eventually stabilized her using lithium (bipolar medication) and risperidone (antipsychotic medication). Since that initial episode, Rebekka has had three additional hospitalizations because her impairments were significant. Each of those episodes leading to hospitalization included heavy drinking and pot smoking, and medication non-compliance. After each manic episode Rebekka experiences depression for several weeks, even when she is taking her medications. When Rebekka is stabilized on her medications, she is able to hold down a job and have a boyfriend. When she is sober and medication compliant, Rebekka is able to function well and does not present with any mental health or SUD concerns.

During her second and third hospitalizations, the psychiatrist recommended that Rebekka should seek treatment for her SUDs. He explained to her that the alcohol and cannabis use disorders were impacting her ability to remain mentally stable and functional; the substances were destabilizing her mental health disorder. The substances were contributing to her rapid cycling between mania and depression. Rebekka had never been in treatment for her SUDs nor has she participated in any recovery-oriented support group, like 12 step meetings. She was very reluctant to consider this recommendation, in part due to her anxiety with agoraphobia and in part due her belief that she can manage her disorders on her own.

## ■ FAMILY HISTORY

Members of the Hispanic/Latino community, here in the United States, come from over 20 different countries and account for a significant portion of the overall U.S. population. Immigration can have a lifelong, negative impact on an immigrant due to the many traumatic, multilayered experiences—with higher incidences of mood dysregulation and anxiety. There are so many challenges to be faced as an immigrant, including: differences in culture, language, and customs; racism, discrimination, and microaggressions; lack of employment opportunities; lack of legal protection; fears of deportation; and separation from relatives and family who remain in the country of origin. Acculturation is associated with SUDs among Hispanic individuals in the United States; substance use tends to increase with acculturation.

Her mother, who is Mexican, occasionally abuses pills and her father, who is Puerto Rican, consumes a six-pack of beer most nights. The absence of social and emotional support from friends and family have resulted in Rebekka relying solely on herself to manage her stress. She is experiencing fear and insecurity regarding her legal status in the United States. She is concerned about not having a job and being judged by her roommate who is Caucasian. In Rebekka's traditional family home, women are not allowed to drink or use marijuana socially, publicly, or casually. Drinking was reserved for special occasions and celebrations. Hispanic men in her family drink outside of the home with friends. Because she has a higher level of acculturation, Rebekka is drinking several times a week with friends and family. On the days when she is not socially drinking, Rebekka is drinking in isolation. On average, she might consume two or three drinks socially.

She is consuming six to seven drinks when alone. Rebekka regularly drinks in quantities that are dangerous physiologically, cognitively, and emotionally. She worries about being judged by her family, friends, and SUD counselor so she is minimizing the need for such interventions.

## ▓ CURRENT FUNCTIONING

Rebekka functions best when she is medication compliant for lithium and risperidone, and not consuming psychoactive substances like alcohol and marijuana. When she is sober and taking her medications, she is able to date, work, and complete all the tasks of daily living. When she is using, the negative consequences add up quickly. Alcohol causes her to experience her depression more deeply and her mania more expansively. Cannabis likely increased the number of depressed and manic episodes Rebekka was experiencing, putting her at risk for more rapid cycling. When Rebekka first presented for SUD counseling, she passed a mental status exam, demonstrated clear cognitions and emotions, and was engaged in the assessment and treatment process.

## ▓ DIAGNOSTIC IMPRESSIONS

Rebekka entered SUD treatment at the prompting of her psychiatrist. She is an adult child of a mother with a mild SUD and a father with a moderate to severe SUD. All of her siblings drink socially and in moderation. Her mother and grandmother both were diagnosed with generalized anxiety disorder and major depressive disorder when they were teens and young adults. Her mother periodically displays symptoms of mania. Rebekka completed high school, has worked on and off since she was 14, and has no prior history of counseling. While she has experimented with many substances while in high school, Rebekka ultimately landed on alcohol and marijuana as the two best substances to help her cope with her cycling of moods, social anxiety, and bouts of paranoia. These two substances are used frequently in Hispanic communities and are not implicitly frowned upon. Her use has increased in the last 3 years, as have the severity of her mental health concerns. Rebekka is a binge drinker (five or more drinks in one setting) and smokes marijuana several times a day. The longest that Rebekka has been sober, since the age of 14, has been 2 years. When asked what helped her maintain her sobriety, she says she was in an intimate relationship with a Hispanic male 2 years older than her who did not use any psychoactive substance including alcohol. She broke up with him because he was so boring. The break-up frustrated her parents because they want her to settle down and find a nice Hispanic man to love. She worries that a Hispanic partner would try to control her through male chauvinistic attitudes. She has no legal charges. She is unemployed when she drinks and smokes pot. She has engaged in several high-risk behaviors including unprotected sex and public intoxication. Rebekka does not have a history of sexual or physical trauma or abuse; Rebekka may be experiencing familial trauma related to immigration. She does not have any health conditions that need to be addressed at this time. She states that she has had a few blackouts when drinking and can get restless and fearful with heavy binging. Rebekka does not see a correlation between her manic and depressive cycling and her substance use. She feels very alive and energized in her manic phases and her sexual libido is stronger in those phases. She does not like that alcohol and marijuana seem to make her less sexually responsive.

Rebekka is experiencing symptoms that align with co-occurring bipolar I disorder, alcohol use disorder and cannabis use disorder. It would be necessary to rule out posttraumatic stress disorder (PTSD) and anxiety disorder. It would be important to complete a PTSD assessment, a cultural acculturation screen, and the Cultural Formulation Interview (CFI) from the *Diagnostic and Statistical Manual of Mental Disorders, 5th Edition* (*DSM-5*) cohort of tools.

## ■ DIAGNOSTIC CONCLUSIONS

The *DSM-5* Diagnoses for this case include:

- Alcohol Use Disorder (AUD), severe
- Cannabis Use Disorder, moderate
- Bipolar I Disorder, most recent episode depressed, severe

## ■ SUGGESTED THERAPEUTIC INTERVENTIONS

Individual Therapy—Rebekka might benefit from one or more of the following: cognitive behavioral therapy (CBT), acceptance and commitment therapy (ACT), emotionally focused therapy (EFT), dialectical behavior therapy (DBT), mindfulness-based CBT (MB-CBT), trauma-focused CBT (TF-CBT). Individual sessions would use Motivational Interviewing (MI) to learn what she is motivated to change and help her move along the change continuum. Individual therapy could help her look at her bipolar diagnosis and what she is struggling to accept there. The therapist would need to understand the family dynamics within Hispanic families as well as understand her concerns about her mental health and SUDs and how they are explained within her culture.

Group Therapy—Topics that Rebekka needs to work through include: relapse prevention; psychoeducation of psychoactive substances; healthy relationships;

conflict resolution; anxiety management—coping and grounding strategies; effective communication skills.

Equine-Assisted Psychotherapy—Rebekka would benefit from this evidence-based practice that has been shown to help with addictions, depression, anxiety, trauma, and eating disorders. This therapy would offer nonverbal opportunities for Rebekka to learn self-awareness, identify maladaptive behaviors and their consequences, recognize, negative feelings and face feelings, and cognitions that damage more than they heal.

Pharmacotherapy—Rebekka should schedule an evaluation with a psychiatrist to assess the appropriateness of using Naltrexone for the AUD, along with an anti-craving medication like topiramate or bupropion. She might be a candidate for BuSpar for her anxiety.

Peer Recovery Coach—Rebekka would benefit from having either one peer mentor or two peer mentors to walk alongside her for (a) the addiction recovery support and (b) bipolar life management support.

## ▦ FOR YOUR CONSIDERATION

1. How does the Hispanic culture (from Mexico) view alcohol use disorders and cannabis use disorders?
2. What treatment options for SUDs does the Hispanic culture support and which ones do they struggle with?
3. Is Rebekka a good candidate for Naltrexone or other medication? Why?
4. What cultural supports exist that would help Rebekka achieve and maintain sobriety?
5. In what areas of Rebekka's life does she need empowerment? Would a peer recovery mentor/coach be helpful to Rebekka? If yes, how could they help her?

# 16.2    *Case of the C Family*

## ▦ INTRODUCTION

The C Family consists of the following people: The biological father, Jeff, age 41, the stepmother, Dillon, age 38, and three children, Kayla (17), Samantha (15), and Jill (8). The family presents as a result of a referral from the School Counselor at

Samantha's school. Over the past several months, Samantha's behavior has become troubling. She is often defiant and aggressive toward her teachers and classmates. Kayla and Jill have not shown any similar behaviors in school or at home.

## ■ FAMILY HISTORY

Jeff is a widower, having lost his wife in an automobile accident a year ago. He is the biological father of Kayla, Samantha, and Jill. Jeff is self-employed as an electrical contractor. This is a business that he started on his own immediately after graduating from a local community college. The business is active and successful, having established a reputation as a solid company in the community for the past 21 years. The business has several dozen employees and is known for its civic engagement, often supporting local charities, school athletic programs, and other local causes.

Jeff and his previous wife had been married for 19 years when the auto accident happened. Jeff struggled quite a bit after the death of his wife. He questioned his abilities to raise three daughters and often felt the need to "find a wife" to take on that role. Earlier in his life, at age 35, he was arrested for Driving While Impaired. He attended a mandatory drug education and treatment program, yet he continued to drink. He attended Alcoholics Anonymous for 3 weeks but decided that he could handle sobriety on his own volition. Drinking alcohol seemed to steady his nerves and help him get through bouts of sadness.

Jeff and Dillon met at a school function 6 months ago, quickly fell in love, and got married after a 3-month relationship. Dillon has never been married but has been in several relationships in the past. She does not have any children and has tended to stay away from committed relationships, preferring to focus on her professional goals. She works from home as a consultant for a petroleum research firm. She has a Master's Degree in Earth Sciences from a prestigious university and is a recognized figure in her respective profession.

The female children—Kayla, Samantha, and Jill—have all been considered "good kids." Before the death of their biological mother, the family was very close. They attended church on a regular basis and attended community events together. The parents were involved in the school PTA and were very engaged in their daughter's lives. After the death of their mother, the girls went through what could be considered a "typical" grief process. They went through a period of sadness, anger, and doubt. They questioned their faith and stopped going to church for a while. They also experienced developmentally appropriate reactions to death and mortality. The three children still express grief in different ways. They often speak of their mother as if she were still there, express disbelief of the mother's death, have bouts of tearfulness, and all three children report seeing their deceased mother in their dreams.

## ■ CURRENT FUNCTIONING

The family presents as a result of a referral from Samantha's school counselor. The referral indicated that, over the past 2 months, Samantha has become increasingly defiant, angry, and aggressive toward teachers and classmates. She has also demonstrated a loss of interest in school and her grades have dropped. Samantha has been tardy for class on several occasions and she has neglected to submit homework quite frequently. The school counselor has been working with Samantha for approximately 4 weeks on study skills. The school counselor indicates the application of solution focused brief therapy with little or no improvement in behavior. However, Samantha does come to see the school counselor on a regular basis and feels comfortable talking about the things going on in her life.

The other children (Kayla and Jill) seem to be doing fine in school and elsewhere. Kayla has kept up her grades and Jill is also doing well in school. Both Kayla and Jill are participating in school athletic teams and both have received academic honors in school.

Jeff and Dillon both stay very busy with work and they maintain a considerable income. Jeff often comes in from work late and Dillon is often on the phone until late at night in her home office. The family is well-resourced in terms of food, housing, transportation, and medical care. Jeff has abandoned parenting responsibilities and has "assigned" Dillon to that role. Jeff and Dillon have not had sex in the past 30 days.

Kayla has taken over responsibility for preparing most of the meals, getting the other children ready for school, and other household responsibilities, such as grocery shopping and cleaning the house. Because her parents are not attentive to her actions, her boyfriend has been spending the night with her for that past 2 weeks.

Jeff's use of alcohol has increased over the past several months. He keeps alcohol in his work truck and often drinks between visits to job sites. He has kept this hidden from his family as much as possible, but the children and Dillon notice that he comes home inebriated. Dillon has spoken with Jeff about this, but the conversation often ends up in a shouting match. Jeff reports that he drinks at least six-pack of beer per day while on the road, but he claims that he does not drink at home. He is drinking more frequently than before, but the amount consumed seems to be the same. Dillon has forbidden the presence of alcohol in the home and Jeff seems to abide by that rule.

Dillon keeps to herself, locked away in her home office. She does not drink or use drugs, preferring to immerse herself in her work to keep herself distracted. She questions her decision to marry Jeff and regrets being forced into the role of raising someone else's children. She and Jeff never discussed parenting, household roles and responsibilities, finances, or anything else prior to getting married.

She describes meeting Jeff as a "whirlwind romance" that fulfilled many deep desires for her but wishes now that they had taken their time getting to know each other better prior to getting married.

At the intake/assessment session, all five family members arrive on time. All family members are well-dressed with good hygiene. The family seems a bit unsure of the process but are engaged in the process of informed consent and the seeking of "release of information" forms. Jeff and Dillon state that they want the situation to improve and seem to be genuinely concerned about the referral for Samantha's behavior. The family begins discussing a recent episode at home in which Samantha and Dillon got in an argument at dinner. In an effort to enhance the assessment process, the family is asked to engage in an enactment of the situation which lead to the argument. The counselor asks the family to recreate the situation, which presents an opportunity for both the family and the counselor to gain insight into the process surrounding communication and family dynamics.

As the family recreates the scenario, the family is gathered around the table in the clinician's room. The argument begins as the family is wrapping up dinner, and Dillon asks the children to clean up the table. Kayla and Jill respond with a polite, "Yes m'am." Samantha remains silent and does not move. Dillon once again asks Samantha to help clean up and Samantha replies, "No, you are not my mother and I am not doing anything for you." Dillon immediately responds, repeating Samantha's exact words in a mocking manner. Samantha bursts into tears in session and Dillon, tearfully, says to you, "This is what I have to put up with everyday. I am tired of all of this." Kayla and Jill sit in stunned silence, while Jeff picks up Samantha in his arms, hugs her tightly, and sits down on the floor with her in his arms.

## ▨ DIAGNOSTIC IMPRESSIONS

In the case of family counseling, we often have to engage in two different diagnostic processes. We must look at individual diagnostic concerns, and we must also engage in the process of systemic diagnosis.

Individually, there is a concern for at least two individuals: Jeff and Samantha. Jeff is demonstrating some concerning behaviors related to substance use. He is using alcohol more frequently than before, and the use continues despite warnings from Dillon about having alcohol in the house. He also mentions a craving for alcohol that intensifies when the stress at home or at work becomes overwhelming. There is also the concern about Jeff drinking while at work; he works as an electrical contractor and visits job sites regularly, which indicates alcohol use in situations that might impact his safety and the safety of those around him. His history of criminal charges and prior treatment history are complicating factors. We also see some lingering grief and bereavement issues.

Samantha has been demonstrating anger, defiance, and aggression for the past 2 months, which began almost immediately after the marriage of Jeff and Dillon. Additionally, we see a decline in academic performance. Several diagnostic considerations arise here. The clinician may jump to a conclusion of something like oppositional defiant disorder, attention deficit hyperactivity disorder, or conduct disorder. Given the situation—a recent, significant change in the family dynamic, and the possibility of lingering grief and bereavement, the clinician is urged to consider the context and its impact on any diagnostic impressions. A close look at adjustment disorders, PTSD, or a mood disorder is warranted. In this case, based upon the findings if the initial assessment, a diagnostic impression of adjustment disorder, with disturbance of conduct is suggested.

In either the case of Jeff or Samantha, further assessment may reveal the impact of trauma, complicated grief and bereavement, or any number of complicating factors. Systemically speaking, the clinician must assess the overall functionality of the family. A "family diagnosis" is less grounded in the *DSM* and more grounded in one's theoretical perspective. In any case, we see immediate dysfunction in several areas.

## COMMUNICATION

The family demonstrates ineffective communication patterns and processes, beginning with the lack of discussion around the new blended family system. It seems as if the family were "thrown together" without much planning and forethought. The parental role was "assigned" to Dillon and the children had little or no awareness of how quickly a new parental figure would arrive in the family. Jeff never told the children that he and Dillon were getting married, thus the children were thrust into the new family dynamic without warning. Currently, effective communication is nonexistent. Jeff works late every day and Dillon stays locked away in the home office until late in the day, which leaves the children to fend for themselves. Kayla has assumed many parental roles in the family at this point.

## PARENTAL HIERARCHY

This parental hierarchy in this family aids in the dysfunction and is complicated by the lack of effective communication. Jeff and Dillon rarely speak and are not connected physically or emotionally at this point. Kayla has become "parentified" and exercises a great deal of power in terms of the family's day to day survival, especially as it relates to caring for the children and managing other aspects of the house. There is little or no respect for Dillon's role as a parent/caregiver coming from Samantha, however Kayla and Jill seem to be on good terms with their step-mother. Furthermore, Jeff and Samantha are forming a coalition against Dillon.

## ■ DIAGNOSTIC CONCLUSIONS

- Jeff—alcohol use disorder—moderate
- Samantha—adjustment disorder with disturbance of conduct
- *DSM-5* systemic indicators
  - ○ Parent–child relational problem
  - ○ Relationship distress with spouse or intimate partner
  - ○ Uncomplicated bereavement

## ■ SUGGESTED THERAPEUTIC INTERVENTIONS

Family Counseling—This family will benefit from family counseling in many ways. Family counseling would provide growth opportunities for this family in many domains. For example, family counseling can address communication issues, enhance parenting skills, increase attachment, empower the parental hierarchy, and improve parental nurturing. Grief and bereavement may also be addressed in family counseling. Essentially, each of the diagnostic impressions above can be addressed through family counseling. There is also a case to be made for couples counseling with Jeff and Dillon. In couples counseling, the clinician may address issues related to intimacy, communication, role stress/strain, and power differentials.

Collaborative Care—As a family counselor, the clinician may make the decision to work with the family as a whole and with individual family members as needed. In either case, the clinician should consider referral for Jeff specifically for a substance use assessment and treatment, if needed. Jeff may also have other issues related to grief and bereavement that may be suited for individual counseling as well.

Samantha may benefit from individual counseling as well. It appears that she has a good relationship with the school counselor, and the clinician should continue supporting the work being done there. A referral to an individual counselor may also benefit her as it relates to any grief/bereavement, anger management, or coping skills.

Peer Support—The clinician may also consider the use of support groups for substance use for all members. Groups such as Alcoholics Anonymous and Al-Anon may be helpful. The clinician should also consider support groups for other issues such as grief, blending and blended families, and spiritual needs.

## FOR YOUR CONSIDERATION

1. As you reflect on this case, what role might trauma play here, if any? Jeff lost his wife and the children lost their mother in a tragic automobile accident and the family still experiences grief. Is trauma a complicating factor here?
2. What other diagnoses should we consider for Jeff? Is substance use a symptom or a cause in this case?
3. As a family counselor, you will have to address the larger family systems issues here. Where would you start? What would be the first thing you work on with all five members of the family present?
4. What other diagnoses should we consider for Samantha? Consider the impact of trauma, grief, and bereavement from the developmental perspective of a 15-year-old child in making further diagnostic impressions.
5. What is your prognosis for this family? In 6 months, where do you see this family in terms of healing, health, and functioning?

# 16.3    *Case of Carol*

## INTRODUCTION

Carol is a 36-year-old Caucasian female who is presenting to outpatient counseling after being referred by her probation officer. Carol is a legally involved client with an extensive criminal history involving solicitation, prostitution, public intoxication, and menacing. The referring officer believes Carol's legal issues are secondary to her alcohol use. Carol has made previous attempts to address her substance use through treatment episodes and community supports.

Carol grew up in rural Alabama and was raised primarily by her mother. Carol indicates that her father was never an active participant in her life and that her mother had a number of boyfriends. Carol recalls that for most of her adolescent and teenage years, her mother was a chronic alcoholic. She recalls numerous episodes of volatility in the household. Carol is the oldest of four siblings and is the only girl of the family. As the elder child, she felt she was parentified at a young age as she took on the role of caregiver to her younger brothers.

Carol recalls an ongoing physical relationship with one of her mother's boyfriends that began with touching when she was about 10 years old. Carol began experimenting with alcohol as early as age 11. Out of fear, Carol did not disclose the sexual assault to her mother until she was 13 years old, at which time the incidents had escalated from touching to sex. When this information was disclosed, she indicates that her mother was accusatory of her and blamed her for the acts. Carol continued to drink recreationally with friends until she dropped out of school at the age of 16. During this time, her mother was diagnosed with cirrhosis of the liver, and Carol had her first run-in with the law for underage drinking. She was kicked out of the house at this time.

With little to no resources, Carol began exchanging sex for money. In order to engage in this behavior, she would drink until the point of feeling numb. Having lost all communication and connection with her family, she continued in this pattern for many years. After garnering an extensive arrest history, Carol attempts to gain sobriety by engaging in treatment for the alcohol use. She recalls her first attempts at treatment beginning around the age of 24. She does not successfully complete any of the treatment episodes.

Currently, Carol lives in a hotel room, which she has used to engage in prostitution. She was recently physically assaulted and brutally raped during a sex encounter for money. She attempted to address the assault in the way that she knew how, drinking to excess. She reports decreased appetite and some concerns of sadness. Her most recent arrest involved public intoxication and solicitation of a law enforcement officer. Carol did not qualify for drug court, yet her probation officer feels that she might meet success with this treatment attempt. Carol indicates that she often drinks more than she intends, and efforts to decrease drinking have not been successful. Although she has a history of trauma and a current traumatic event, she does not connect her increased drinking with risk. She has few friends and minimal social support. She believes she is beginning to experience conditions similar to those experienced by her mother during her alcohol use.

## ▓ DIAGNOSTIC IMPRESSIONS

Carol is an adult child of an alcoholic. She has a long history of alcohol use beginning in early adolescence. Her use has increased throughout her lifetime and involved risky behavior to include solicitation, prostitution, public intoxication, and menacing. Her behaviors have resulted in criminal charges resulting in prosecution and probation. These behaviors have resulted in this referral to outpatient treatment. Periods of her life are marred by homelessness and current living instability. With continued use, she reports blackouts, restlessness, and nausea. Carol has previous unsuccessful treatment attempts.

She is a childhood survivor of sexual assault and was recently physically and sexually assaulted during a work (prostitution)-related episode. Carol has no history of counseling for her childhood abuse or the current assault. Since the incident, she has increased her alcohol use and is experiencing appetite loss, restlessness, and sadness. Although she does not see a correlation between this incident and her substance use, the issues are likely tied. Carol is experiencing some concurrent symptoms that align with alcohol use disorder and PTSD. When discussing her assault, her presentation is flat and characterized by little to no eye contact with periods that are difficult to hear her.

Although Carol does not present with significant medical concerns, it is important to rule out any medical concerns that would explain the blackouts, restlessness, appetite loss, and nausea. Equally important will be a general medical exam because no care was sought post physical and sexual assault. Carol has limited education, strained family relationships, and lacks a stable support system. To summarize, the following are Carol's presenting concerns:

- Tolerance to alcohol
- Increased alcohol use
- Blackouts
- Trouble sleeping, restlessness
- Appetite loss
- Sadness
- Engaging in behavior resulting in risk (excessive drinking, criminal activity)
- Intermittent nausea
- Lack of support

## ▥ DIAGNOSTIC CONCLUSIONS

- Alcohol use disorder, severe
- R/O PTSD
- R/O Unspecified depressive disorder
- R/O any medical conditions
- Additional concerns: strained family relationship, limited education, gainful employment, and lack of support system.

## ▥ SUGGESTED THERAPEUTIC INTERVENTION

A full assessment of readiness to change should be undertaken in order to identify the stage of change that Carol is in, so that a treatment plan can be developed accordingly. Based on previous unsuccessful treatment episodes, Carol would likely benefit from beginning treatment at the intensive outpatient level in accordance with the American Society of Addiction Medicine Patient Placement Criteria. Treatment episodes would involve group treatment at a frequency of three times per week and individual sessions weekly. Based on engagement, readiness, and motivation, introduction to community supports are likely—for example, celebrate recovery, alcoholics anonymous, and so on. As treatment progresses, Carol will be linked with a peer support specialist, who will further add to her support network.

Therapeutic efforts would involve CBT and MI. CBT will be utilized to help Carol learn about maladaptive behavior patterns. Efforts will be made to assist her in identifying her own behaviors along with positive and negative consequences for continued use. Attempts will be made to identify high-risk situations, environments, and triggers for use and developing coping strategies to address these situations along with cravings. Open-ended questions, reflective listening, expressing empathy, developing discrepancy, and rolling with resistance, which are essential to MI, can be utilized to help facilitate the therapeutic relationship and to aid in behavior change. The group therapy environment should allow Carol to normalize her childhood and current experiences while developing additional supports. As she makes treatment gains, the potential for supports can be expanded to a larger community network through Celebrate Recovery, Alcoholics Anonymous, and so on. To enhance potential for long-term sustained recovery, Carol will be matched with a peer support specialist who will help with transition posttreatment to aftercare. A minimum of three family sessions will be recommended to facilitate reconnection and integration to the family.

Should PTSD be determined, elements of CBT can be used to identify self-defeating thoughts and to develop counters to these thoughts. This will assist with minimizing and ultimately eliminating pervasive thoughts that do not support her sustained treatment and recovery. Combining these interventions with some aspects of systematic desensitization could help benefit any fears that may be associated with certain environments or situations related to the assault. Pervasive thoughts and fears could be a contributing factor in restlessness and addressing them could aid in remedying the sleep concern.

A referral for a general medical exam will be facilitated, and follow-up on the results of the exam will be of benefit. The exam can assist to rule out any medical explanation for physical symptoms. The exam can also address the physical and sexual trauma experienced to include testing for sexually transmitted infections and HIV.

A referral for general educational development (GED) testing will be provided to address educational limitations. A concurrent referral will be made for job skill training to assist in developing soft skills for marketable employment.

## ▓ FOR YOUR CONSIDERATION

1. Given the chronicity of the issues, which presenting issue would you address first and why?
2. What other theoretical orientations show promise to address the history of this client and the diagnostic impression?
3. What additional therapeutic interventions would you consider using with Carol?
4. With whom would you want to gain consent through releases of information to communicate with on her behalf and why?
5. What additional information do you need that might assist in making a diagnosis?
6. Are there other ASAM PPC-2r levels of care that you would consider for Carol?
7. What stage of change do you think Carol is in, and how would this affect your therapeutic interventions?

# 16.4    *Case of Lisa*

## ▓ INTRODUCTION

Lisa is a 36-year-old African American female who lives with her husband and three daughters from her previous marriage, age 14, 9, and 8. I opened the session asking Lisa to share her story beginning with what she believed to be her problem. She stated saw seeking help with relapse prevention planning and identifying triggers that initiate opioid use and dependency. Lisa reported completing outpatient treatment for opioid dependence about 8 months ago. She described being distressed about several life changes at the time. In 2009, Lisa remarried, moved to a new city, and became jobless because the 1-hour commute was too strenuous. Lisa reported she also had a tooth pulled and was prescribed Percocet for pain. She remembered the calmness and the numbing sensation that kept her from feeling. "I took the pills that were prescribed, and then I went and bought more. Later, when my husband and I had an issue, I took a pill so I could be nonchalant." Soon after, she faced an unexpected and unwanted pregnancy. "At first, I wasn't going to keep the baby because of complications with my last two children." She described undergoing a root canal and receiving Lortab for pain about a month before delivering her baby. She had taken a few pills, and a few weeks later, she has rushed to the clinic after concerns that her baby was not moving. Doctors discovered her baby had no heartbeat, and the urine drug screen showed Lisa had Lortab in her system. Lisa stated she took the pain meds during pregnancy, which increased her blood pressure, triggering eclampsia. "I almost lost my life, and my baby didn't make it." Lisa said she attended outpatient treatment for 3 months and learned how to face the pain of losing her baby instead of numbing her feelings. She reported being without physical or mental cravings for opioids and does not think she will be prescribed pain medication ever again.

Lisa reported feeling sad, lacking motivation, tired, fatigued, restless, wanting to be alone, and feeling alone. She stated she is not taking any birth control because she is weaning off Depo Provera shots. Lisa denies any real financial problems or legal. Issues. "I have to take care of a suspended license." Lisa has been an episodic marijuana smoker since age 18. Her current marijuana use involves one or two puffs three times a week for insomnia and stress. "Though most days I don't smoke till bedtime because I have insomnia, and it helps. Or if I'm stressed, I will."

According to Lisa, her opioid use was related to the medications she was taking. She could not take traditional forms of birth control because they contain estrogen, which drove her blood pressure out of whack. She suffered migraines and depression with other forms of birth control. The first opioid use started as a treatment plan from her neurologist to control her migraines. Lisa controlled her migraines with Tylenol since age nine and with Excedrin Migraine later when the Tylenol no longer worked. She took her first opioid pill when she was 27. Lortab 5 mg replaced the Excedrin Migraines when she became pregnant with her second child. "Before that, I never took anything." Lisa started taking Oxycodone sevens day following the birth of her third child at age 28. Lisa had eclampsia with her third child. She stated the stress of the eclampsia exasperated the migraines three to four times a week, and she was prescribed 350 mg of Oxycodone three times a day.

Lisa stated that she learned from previous treatments that some of her triggers to use derive from PTSD she experienced during her first marriage and other traumas. Lisa acknowledged she has been battling depression for a long time, intensified by preeclampsia and postpartum depression following each of her pregnancies. She is not sure if it was solely an environmental factored depression or if it was related to the birth control, she has taken over the years. She also used Implanon implants for 7 years, which caused depression and exasperated migraine headaches. She reported that her migraines only occurred once or twice a year until puberty, then cyclical around her menstrual cycle. Her last migraine was 1 month ago.

Lisa has a history of depression and anxiety symptoms. She noticed depression and sadness around the age of 14 when her parents divorced. "I was real snappy and angry." She described experiencing anxiety attacks and paralyzing social anxiety at the thought of doing something among people who were not close to her. "Like they were judging me." She recalled being at school during her first anxiety attack. She remembered her head pounding, chest tightening, and she could not breathe. "I was hyperventilating." Other anxiety and panic attacks followed. "That's what made me continue smoking weed." According to Lisa, she realized that she did not feel so anxious when she smoked marijuana. Lisa reported smoking about a blunt a day between the age of 18 and 21. She denied drinking alcohol.

When asked if she had ever been sexually abused or molested, Lisa said no. However, she disclosed that at age 15, her mom dated a man who would do inappropriate things around her. He would sit across from her in his underwear and fondle himself and expose himself to her. When she told her mother, she responded by telling him to put on clothes around her. When she was 17, he made her a hot toddy to tend a cold she had. She stated she was afraid he had put something in it and poured it out instead. She went to bed and he got into her bed with no clothes on. She got up and ran to a neighbor's house. Lisa stated that her mother's response was not what she expected because she did not leave him. She said that her relations with her mother changed drastically.

Her first attempt to address her depression was at the age of 21, when she was prescribed Paxil by her primary care physician (PCP) to treat postpartum depression. She switched to Lexapro because she did not like how Paxil made her feel and then stopped taking it after 6 months. Suicidal thoughts surfaced after she stopped taking Lexopril and following a series of significant losses. Lisa reported that her maternal grandmother died in August 2007, and her mother forced her to get an abortion in December 2007. "My mother drug me out of bed down to the abortion clinic." Her paternal grandfather died in April 2008. Lisa recalled feeling like she did not want to live. "I didn't have a plan, but I didn't care if I lived." She stated she changed her mind realizing that her 18-month-old child would be the one who found her, and she did not want that heaviness on her child for the rest of her life. "I thought that would be incredibly selfish." At that moment, Lisa said she realized that she was more than just sad; she was clinically depressed. "I was in such a dark place." Lisa did not receive counseling for depression or anxiety. Instead, she reported that she decided to channel her energy on something productive and enrolled in a program for LPN, graduating in December 2009. She married the father of her first child 2 days after graduation.

Lisa's first marriage lasted 7 years. She reported a relationship where her husband was manipulative. She described having a constant feeling of impending doom as if she were walking on eggshells, never knowing when things would implode. She reported working 12-hour shifts 5 days a week and working weekends trying to juggle the entire family's financial responsibility. She said she was stressed and experienced debilitating migraines trying to keep up with everything. She described it as a cycle that never ended, going from taking the pills to keep up to being physically sick if she missed a dose. The physical withdrawals lasted a couple of days to a few weeks, depending on how much she took. She reported insomnia, along with anxiety and physical withdrawal symptoms that lasted longer. Lisa stated she was unable to take the time to take off work to tend to herself and so she just tried to keep it going because everyone depended on her. After 2 years, she started working the day shift at a nursing agency due to her husband's infidelity. Lisa took a pay cut due to the shift differential and lost health benefits, which meant she could not afford to get her pills from the neurologist, but the physical dependency persisted. So, she bought pills from a paralyzed friend. "It was a difference between paying $4.00 a month for a bottle of pills and paying $20.00 a pill." Lisa described spacing doses and weaning herself down to a dosage that blocked withdrawals and helped her function. Lisa said she took Oxycodone to not cry in front of people and get the numbing sensation that calmed her. By now, they are $30.00 a pill.

In 2015, Lisa experienced significant deaths and losses within 5 months. She reported losing a cousin and an uncle. She also lost her best friend to suicide, but she believes someone killed her. The guy she bought pills from died from an overdose, and she lost another close friend to cancer. Besides that, her marriage was ending. She separated from her ex-husband when she found out that he got another woman pregnant. She stated she left him, took the clothes in the hamper and her children's clothes, and moved in with her mother. "My previous therapist said I suffered from PTSD because of all of the things that were happening back to back."

Her first outpatient treatment experience for opioid dependence occurred in 2018. From 2015 to 2018, Lisa said she did not want to feel anymore. "It was so difficult to start over sober; I just chose not to feel it." In 2018, she abused Percocet, entered outpatient treatment, and was given 40 mg of Methadone for 9 months. According to Lisa, she entered treatment because she realized that her children were getting older, and they could tell that she had an issue with drugs. She felt like she was failing them and did not want them to deal with having a parent with an addiction. "My children were a catalyst for making me want to get myself together."

## ■ FAMILY HISTORY

A family history of depression and alcoholism was revealed among her maternal grandmother. Her mother suffered from postpartum depression when her brother was born. "My dad was gone overseas and there were days when she would not even get up so, I stepped up as a 6-year-old to take care of him when she couldn't," Lisa reported that her paternal grandfather was depressed and addicted to Percocet. "When he didn't get it, he was mean." She reported her paternal grandmother suffered depression and domestic abuse for over 40 years. She said her father suffers from depression, anxiety, and insomnia. "I don't believe he has ever been happy." No history of treatment was reported for any family member.

More social history reveals Lisa and her second husband have been married for 14 months. Together with her three daughters from her previous marriage, her husband has three daughters, ages 21, 17, 8. Her relationship with her stepdaughters is good but distant among the three mothers. She reported a contentious relationship with her ex-husband. "My ex-husband is a stressor because he's an asshole I have to deal with until my girls are grown." She has a close relationship with her younger brother, who lives in California. She describes her parents as covert narcissists. Her mother lives close by, and her father lives in Minnesota. She wishes that her relationship with her parents was closer. Lisa completed 2 years of college and also obtained a license as a LPN. She worked for various contract nursing agencies until she remarried. Her last job was part-time at Walmart.

## ▨ DIAGNOSTIC IMPRESSIONS

Prior history of OUD and failed treatment outcomes will also be used to guide diagnosis and level of care. Lisa's history indicates a past trial of Methadone maintenance with a poor treatment response as well as outpatient psychotherapy with partial remission. While many patients do well with medication treatment for OUD, others engaged in abstinence-based recovery struggle to accept being dependent on another type of opioid. Lisa discontinue Methadone because she did not want to trade one drug for another one. Lisa meets *DSM-5* criteria for OUD, with early remission as a specifier. Given the duration of her most recent relapse and treatment experience 8 months ago, none of the criteria have been present for at least 3 months but for less than 12 months. While opiate withdrawal symptoms are uncommon more than 2 months after use, she is experiencing restlessness, feelings of depression and anxiety, insomnia that she attributes to birth control. Signs of anxiety might be secondary to withdrawal. At the somatic level Lisa is dealing with anxiety, insomnia, hot flashes, bleeding, weight loss, and headaches from the depo Provera birth control which was discontinued 3 weeks ago. She smokes marijuana at bedtime for insomnia or when she is stressed. She also takes labetalol 30 mg and hydrochlorothiazide 25 mg for hypertension.

Anxiety is also present, as evidenced by restlessness, agitation, irritability, and stress. Although her functioning has improved, and opioid use has temporarily been arrested and stabilized, there appear to be significant stressors that put her in risk of relapse. Lisa recently worked part-time at Walmart. She stopped working because she felt overwhelmed by working, attending school, and raising a family; "it was not easy to meet obligations." She currently attends college full-time for Logistic Transportation to support her husband who works as a truck driver. There is also a secondary depressive component seems embedded in a dependent personality. While she reports that her mother is supportive, her distrust makes this unreliable. She relies on her husband for emotional and financial support. She denies any current suicidal or homicidal ideation. She reports she feels peace for the first time due to her support system and plans for college.

She has had success with past treatment experiences, achieving partial remission and control of physical symptoms. Her help-seeking behavior indicates a desire to change, and some recognition of her problem. She meets the criteria for outpatient treatment, but it is not clear that she would accept or use more intensive resources since she has not been taking advantage of current opportunities and support resources (e.g., 12-step meetings, individual or psychosocial group counseling) to address cannabis use and mood swings. Nevertheless, if she were willing to use them, a brief period of aftercare treatment would help stabilize comorbid disorders. She could subsequently maintain her recovery at a lower level of care like Narcotics Anonymous (NA) meetings and possibly an NA sponsor.

Several risk factors that make Lisa more prone to relapse are visible. Besides her relapse history of multiple previous relapses, her longest period of sobriety is about 9 months. She stated that this admission is relapse related. Her relapse risk potential also shows limited insight about the relation between illness management (e.g., contraceptive planning and chronic pain) and OUD. Lisa stated that she is not taking any birth control to prevent a potential pregnancy. There is also inadequate coping skills to manage depression and anxiety symptoms to prevent relapse. The change in her employment situation may cause some moderate stress, and she currently has little support available in the community. Although she seeks help when distressed, her recovery skills are minimal due to limited involvement with professional sources of support. Also, her recovery environment has changed since previous treatment episodes, potentially taxing her current prevention strategies.

## ▓ DIAGNOSTIC CONCLUSIONS

- Opioid use disorder (OUD), early remission
- Cannabis disorder

- Generalized anxiety disorder
- Chronic migraine without aura
- Hypertension

## SUGGESTED THERAPEUTIC INTERVENTIONS

Whether active or in remission, OUD is a chronic condition that requires continuous care over episodic, acute-care treatment approaches (Chang & Compton, 2013). Proper treatment of Lisa's chronic pain and OUD requires an interdisciplinary and multi-model approach tailored to manage her pain and sustain recovery. Given Lisa's medical history of high blood pressure, preeclampsia during pregnancy, and migraine headaches, integrating appropriate treatment of comorbid depression, anxiety, sleep disturbance, migraines, and hypertension, including alternative birth control treatments, will be beneficial. Better pain management options to address migraine headaches and pain following elective surgery are also needed. Attempts to treat OUD without treating medical and psychosocial comorbidities are not likely to sustain recovery.

An interdisciplinary approach where all care providers communicate and work together to manage Lisa's OUD, medical, and psychosocial comorbidity can produce meaningful outcomes. Advanced planning for pain management following elective surgeries should focus on nonopioid medications whenever possible. A multi-model approach should integrate pharmacological and non-pharmacological therapies to manage Lisa's chronic migraine pain, insomnia, and psychosocial comorbidities. Medication-assisted treatment (MAT) that is less stigmatizing and tailored to Lisa's needs can help Lisa manage withdrawal. Nonpharmacological therapies like CBT, massage therapy, meditation, and yoga can help Lisa reduce pain and cannabis cravings, while addressing the depression and anxiety.

Long-term aftercare and relapse prevention treatment have been shown to reduce relapse the first year out of treatment (Menon & Kandasamy, 2018). Treatment should focus on stabilizing symptoms and optimal functioning. Aftercare programs should have a variety of activities to fit Lisa's personality. CBT-based psychotherapy can develop effective strategies to manage stress. Psychoeducation groups can teach Lisa about her treatment options for pain management, physical health management, and lifestyle changes, including nutrition and exercise. A relapse prevention plan should be developed to help Lisa reduce her risk for relapse and identify triggers to drug use. Community-based support services such as NA to address her cannabis use. The 12-step program and interpersonal relationships and support systems of NA can provide tools to help manage her life better and regulate emotion, coping processes.

## ■ FOR YOUR CONSIDERATION

1. OUD has been declared a public health emergency in the United States. What assessment instruments would you use to accurately screen, diagnose, and measure treatment outcomes for OUD?
2. Research indicates that best practices for the treatment for OUD include MAT, psychosocial treatment, and relapse prevention treatment. Differentiate between MAT, psychosocial treatment, and relapse prevention treatment for treating OUD.
3. Lisa's life has been dramatically affected by comorbid medical, mental health, and opioid use. What other treatment recommendations would you make for her?

## ■ REFERENCES

Chang, Y., & Compton, P. (2013). Management of chronic pain with chronic opioid therapy in patients with substance use disorders. *Addiction Science & Clinical Practice, 8*, 21. https://doi.org/10.1186/1940-0640-8-21

Menon, J., & Kandasamy, A. (2018). Relapse prevention. *Indian Journal of Psychiatry, 60*(Suppl 4), S473.

# 16.5    *Case of Sebastian*

## ■ INTRODUCTION

Sebastian is a 34-year-old Latinx male who is currently under court order for counseling. Sebastian was arrested 2 weeks ago following a routine traffic stop. The officer noted that Sebastian appeared impaired; he searched Sebastian's vehicle and found a container of unlabeled oxycodone. Sebastian first claimed that they were his prescription medication, but eventually admitted to purchasing them on the street. He spent 2 days in the city lockup before being arraigned. Because it was his first offense, the judge was lenient, only requiring Sebastian to pay a fine and to attend NA and individual counseling for a period of no less than 90 days. Sebastian shares this information in a somewhat mocking tone, adding that he "isn't some druggie" and denying that he needs treatment. Still, he accepts the terms as his employer insists on documentation of his compliance with the court order to keep his job.

Sebastian is currently on administrative leave from his job as a junior partner at a small law firm. He has had a very promising career thus far, specializing in corporate law. Sebastian is very physically active and competes in triathlons several times a year. About 5 months ago, Sebastian suffered a severe injury during one of his competitions; a fellow competitor ran him off the road during the cycling component of the race, causing Sebastian to crash his bike at a high speed. He suffered a dislocated shoulder, broken ankle, and broken arm. The break in his arm was complex and required surgery to correct. The rehabilitation following the accident was lengthy and painful, and Sebastian was prescribed Vicodin (hydrocodone) for the pain. After a few weeks, Sebastian found that the Vicodin was not working as well as it had been, so he increased his dosage. His doctor learned of this when Sebastian needed a refill sooner than expected and warned him of the risk of addiction. Because Sebastian was still in severe pain and struggling through his rehabilitation, the doctor switched his prescription to Oxycontin (oxycodone) with the rationalization that a different narcotic may give Sebastian more relief. The switch was successful for a while, but Sebastian eventually found himself needing more of the drug. Not only did his tolerance continue to increase just as it had with the hydrocodone, but he also liked the way he felt when he took the oxycodone. Sebastian again began increasing his dosage by his own accord and running out of his medication early.

At 2 months postaccident, Sebastian's physical therapy was winding down and his doctor would no longer refill his prescription. By that point, however, Sebastian had found other sources of the medication, including a questionable pain management center outside of town. For a small fee, the doctor at the center was willing to write additional prescriptions for Sebastian; all he had to do was visit once a month and state that he was still in great pain from his accident. This worked well for him for a while until the center was shut down. Again, Sebastian was left without a source for a drug he had now come to depend upon.

Sebastian confided in one of his colleagues that he really needed help with the ongoing pain from his accident but didn't know what to do. His colleague connected Sebastian with a friend who had access to prescription medications and could get him oxycodone. Sebastian began buying oxycodone from this contact and continued to use regularly. It was after one of those buys that he was stopped for speeding and the drugs found on him. As Sebastian relays this story, he states that he understands that he "probably should have stopped (the drug use) by now" but adds that he doesn't see the use as a "real problem." He notes that he performs well in his job as evidence that his substance use is not a significant issue. He also states that he likes the way he feels when he takes oxycodone, adding that when he takes oxycodone he's relaxed, happy, and feels almost no pain. Lastly, Sebastian admits to "quitting cold turkey" a few times over the past few months but couldn't stand how it felt to go through withdrawal so he kept using the drug. He does not recognize that withdrawal is a sign of addiction.

Sebastian is unmarried but has been living with his girlfriend since shortly after they met; they have been together for almost 8 years. Sebastian describes her as "too good for (him)" and states that he loves her very much. He also adds that she "was a saint" through the accident and recovery. He does admit, however, that recently they've been arguing more frequently and that she has been pushing him to stop using the oxycodone. Sebastian says that she's only worried about what the drugs are costing and denies that there is any other impact on his relationship.

## ▓ FAMILY HISTORY

Sebastian is the youngest of four brothers, all of them are very successful in their chosen fields. His oldest brother is a state senator, his second oldest brother is a neurosurgeon, and his third oldest brother is a partner in the same firm when Sebastian works. Sebastian wanted to be an actor when he was younger as he loved performing in school plays, but his parents would not allow it. His father, in particular, insisted the Sebastian must have "a career that makes money" and pushed him to excel in school. Academics did not come as easily to Sebastian as it had for his brothers, but eventually he found his way into law and followed the path of his older brother. Sebastian shares that he enjoys his job, but adds that he never really had a choice about his career; he often wonders about what might have been had he followed his dream.

Sebastian's parents were born and raised in Colombia and moved to the United States shortly after they were married. Sebastian's father—who is now retired—was a brilliant engineer who was recruited by a large defense contractor in the Unites States for his groundbreaking work with robotics. Though both of Sebastian's parents come from large, tight-knit families, the civil unrest and unsteady economy in their region, combined with a job offer too good to refuse, motivated them to leave their home country. Sebastian's parents lived in the United States for many years on his father's work visa, eventually becoming permanent residents. All of their children were born in the United States, and though his parents strongly embrace the culture of their new homeland, Sebastian notes that they "are *definitely* Colombian!" He explains that his parents have never forgotten their roots and have raised their boys to have strong ties to the Colombian culture.

Sebastian and his brothers were raised Roman Catholic, though they are somewhat less conservative than their parents are. Sebastian describes himself as "having strong faith" but not feeling the need to attend church on a regular basis. Sebastian believes strongly in God and finds his faith to be a source of strength.

Sebastian describes his childhood as full of love and laughter, and notes that his parents are very kind-hearted people. However, he also shares that his father tended to be very critical, particularly when it came to Sebastian. The oldest son was "clearly the favorite" and remains so to this day. Sebastian shares that a running joke in the family is that the other sons are actually invisible—his father is so proud of "his son the senator" that he barely acknowledges the achievements of the other sons, though they are impressively successful in their own right. Sebastian insists that he does not resent his father for this, saying "that's just how he is" and noting that "at least (he's) not the only one (his dad) ignores!"

Sebastian reports that other than feeling like he will never be good enough for his dad, he gets along well with him. He also shares that he is very close to his mother and talks to her a few times a week. Sebastian also considers his brothers his best friends and feels fortunate to have such a close family. Still, Sebastian also admits that he has not told any of his family about his oxycodone use "because it wasn't their business." The brother with whom he works found out about Sebastian's leave of absence at work through "the office gossip" but Sebastian has yet to discuss it with him at length. He knows that he cannot avoid that topic forever and will eventually have to discuss this with his family.

## ▓ CURRENT FUNCTIONING

Sebastian is in good health and is very fit. He lost some of his fitness during the rehabilitation after his accident but remains above average in this area. Sebastian reports that during his rehabilitation he gained a bit of weight initially, but that he was almost back to where he used to be. He adds that the oxycodone helped him get there, since it allowed him to tolerate discomfort in his workouts and push himself to recover faster. This perceived benefit is part of why Sebastian does not believe his oxycodone use is a "problem;" still, he is willing to consider that he might be better off without it.

Sebastian denies any other substance use, though he admits to having "an occasional drink." He notes that he makes sure not to mix alcohol and oxycodone, so his alcohol use is very minimal. Sebastian does not use nicotine in any form, though he does drink a lot of coffee—usually a full pot over the course of the day.

## ▓ DIAGNOSTIC IMPRESSIONS

Sebastian meets the criteria for OUD as evidenced by his taking larger amounts of oxycodone and for a longer period of time than was intended, increased tolerance, unsuccessful efforts to quit, and impairment in social functioning. Furthermore, his substance use is impacting his job and his personal life and has gotten him into legal trouble.

Sebastian is also struggling with some moderate self-esteem issues as he still feels like he is not good enough in his father's eyes. Sebastian may also have some unresolved identity issues to address as he has admittedly not followed his passion but has ended up on a path that was chosen for him. Though Sebastian's family can be seen as a source of stress in some ways, it is also a protective factor. Not only do the family members love each other very much, but also there does not appear to be any family history of substance abuse. These are helpful elements when someone is attempting recovery. Sebastian also has a strong faith which can provide a positive influence as someone with addiction attempts to change.

## ▨ DIAGNOSTIC CONCLUSION

- OUD

## ▨ SUGGESTED THERAPEUTIC INTERVENTIONS

Motivational Interviewing—MI would be a very good choice in this case. A key challenge right now is in Sebastian's engagement in the process of treatment and recognition that he actually has a problem. A principle element in MI is the resolution of ambivalence and the empowerment toward personal growth. Right now Sebastian minimizes and rationalizes his drug use, though he is sometimes able to admit that "perhaps" it should change. MI is very client-focused and would require Sebastian to develop his own treatment plan, thus giving him a sense of power and control in the process.

Psychodynamic Family Therapy—It is important to note that a case such as this would probably also benefit from some systems-focused interventions. However, given the current state of Sebastian's use and the likely resistance from his family-of-origin, this is not a requirement as of yet. Should Sebastian's use continue to worsen and more intense treatment be indicated, it would be wise to integrate psychodynamic family therapy with Sebastian's family and his girl-friend. This approach would focus on the dynamics across the system, patterns of interaction, and the role of the addiction within the system. This approach could also lend some additional insight into some of the weaker areas of Sebastian's identity and help him strengthen his self-constructs.

12-step Program—Sebastian is currently court-ordered to attend NA. Participation in 12-step programs does not always resonate with every individual in recovery, however for Sebastian it is likely to have a positive impact. Sebastian has a strong religious background, which aligns well with NA foundations. Furthermore, Sebastian is currently minimizing the significance of his drug use and is unable to clearly see how it has affected his life. Hearing the stories of others with similar addictions and sharing his own experiences may help him to see that he has more in common with them than he realizes. He will also gain the support of a group of individuals on a similar path who can empathize with where he is in his journey.

Medical referral—Because Sebastian has not been able to quit using on his own, referral to an outpatient methadone clinic may be appropriate. Methadone treatment provides an avenue for mitigating the adverse effects associated with abruptly stopping opioid use. Using methadone in the short term while he is detoxing from oxycodone will likely make the experience less difficult. It is recommended that methadone treatment be combined with is individual therapy and attendance at NA to maximize the chances of his success in treatment.

## ▓ FOR YOUR CONSIDERATION

1. What influence might Sebastian's family-of-origin have on his current addiction issue?
2. What is the significance of Sebastian's high caffeine use?
3. Why do you think Sebastian is resistant to accepting that he has an addiction?
4. Would a harm-reduction model be appropriate for Sebastian? Why or why not?
5. In what ways could you integrate cultural and spiritual elements into Sebastian's treatment?

# CHAPTER SEVENTEEN

# NEUROCOGNITIVE DISORDERS

*Neurocognitive disorders describe decreased mental function due to a medical disease other than a psychiatric illness. In this chapter, cases related to substance-induced major neurocognitive disorder and major neurocognitive disorder due to Alzheimer's disease are presented. Questions for consideration follow each case.*

# 17.1    *Case of Ms. Ruth*

## ▩ INTRODUCTION

Ms. Ruth is a 75-year-old African American woman residing in an upper middle-class suburb of a major metropolitan area. Walt, her husband of 57 years, died 10 months earlier from lung cancer. Ruth is close to her immediate relatives. She has two adult children that reside within a 30-mile radius of her home. Her five grandchildren, range in age from 15 to 5 years old. Her children and their families regularly visit and rotate staying the night with her. The bi-weekly rotation of her children and grandchildren spending the night with her began when Walt passed. Her children are committed to providing her with support and desire to be involved in all her decision-making processes.

For five years Ruth has participated in Silver Sneakers at the local community center. She meets with her female friends monthly to have a delicious meal, play cards, and laugh. Recently Ruth discontinued her involvement in Tai Chi (enrolled for 5 months). In addition to discontinuing her enrollment in Tai Chi, she does not attend church weekly like she has for past 38 years.

Recently Ruth, has become forgetful. Her daughter recently received a call from Ruth's hairstylist informing her she did not arrive for her bi-weekly appointment. Ruth's daughter called her mother and there was no response on her cell phone. She concluded work abruptly and drove to Ruth's home. When she arrived on her mother's street, she saw Ruth pulling her car into the driveway. The two got out of their vehicles and her daughter informed her of the concern she had about her well-being. Ruth stated she was driving, daydreaming, thinking of what she would have for dinner, and forgot she was going to the hairstylist. Ruth said when she realized she forgot her hair appointment, she decided to come home. She assured her daughter there was nothing to be concerned about and asked her to stop worrying; called her dramatic and informed her, if she did not stop questioning her about what occurred she would ask her to leave the property. Ruth's daughter conceded and went into the home with her mother. Upon entering the home, she noticed Ruth was not keeping her home as neat as she has in the past. She looked in her prescription medication pill box and noticed Ruth is not taking her medicine as prescribed. While her mother was napping in front of the television, she opened her mail. Ruth's water bill was marked, urgent. When her daughter opened the bill, she discovered her mother's delinquent payment and the learned her service was scheduled to be discontinued, if a payment is not received. Her daughter was perplexed. Her family decided to join her to stay overnight with Ruth. Ruth's daughter texted her brother but asked him not to come to the house because she did not want to argue with her mother. The siblings talked after Ruth went to sleep for the night; both are worried about their mom, have committed to praying, and are trusting God to learn the best course of action to support their mom.

Approximately, 1 month later, Ruth's second-oldest grandson was off from school and he decided to spend the day with Ruth working in the yard and helping her do chores around the home. In the morning, the two completed clearing her flower bed and garden. They discussed the vegetables she will plant, and they looked forward to seeing her prize-winning Peonies bloom in the summer. Ruth received numerous beautiful home awards that are bestowed upon the residents in her community for stellar landscapes. She was eager to make her home pleasing to the community again. After completing the yard work, they had lunch and her grandson went to take a shower, while Ruth cleaned the kitchen. After completing his shower, her grandson ran to the kitchen table to get his laptop and discovered two of the gas stove burners were on; while Ruth sat on the porch reading the newspaper. He quickly, turned the burners off and ran out to his grandmother to inquire if she was aware the burners were still on. She replied with a laugh, shared she forgot to turn them off, and told him not to worry. He quickly called his mother (Ruth's daughter) and informed her of what occurred. She told him thank you and assured him all will be well, and his uncle planned to stop by later that evening to check on her.

When Ruth's son visited, he found his mother was no longer using bath towels. She had numerous face clothes all over the bathroom. She shared she is now using a different one throughout the day to make sure she is not spreading germs. He also overheard her talking to someone. When he looked in the room, he saw her standing talking to a photo of his dad. Ruth noticed her son's gaze and said to him "I always talk to your dad so he can tell me what to do throughout the day." He decided to leave her alone because he felt this is a part of her grief process. He went into a guest room and was looking at her bookshelf to see what she was currently reading. Ruth loves visiting her local library after she attends her Silver Sneakers class on Thursdays. On top of several shelves he discovered plastic bags that contained soiled undergarments. He decided not to say anything to his mother, but he knew it was time for him and his sister to schedule a meeting with her primary care physician. Before leaving he saw a childhood friend who expressed how pleased he was to see him. The friend shared he planned to look for his information on social media because he is concerned about Ruth. The man began to inform Ruth's son about his concerns for his mom (i.e., forgetting his name, the date, etc.) and how he felt distressed when he saw her walking down the street at 11:30 p.m. last night. He expressed his gratitude for her recognizing who he was last night, and he was able to walk her to her home and get her securely in the home.

Ruth's medical history: Ruth's primary care physician prescribed a statin for her hypercholesterolemia and a beta-blocker for her hypertension. Five years ago, when Ruth's husband became ill, she was prescribed a selective serotonin reuptake inhibitor to assist with the management of her anxiety.

## ▓ FAMILY HISTORY

Ruth is currently the oldest living relative from in her family. She has lived longer than her parents and her siblings. Ruth's mother and brother died from lung cancer due to cigarette smoke. Her sister died from pancreatic cancer. Ruth has a family history of hypertension. There is no known family history of psychological disorders.

## ▓ DIAGNOSTIC IMPRESSIONS

Ruth had a recent, significant loss, the death of her husband after being married over 50 years. She is adjusting to life without her spouse. Emotional and mental distress maybe affecting her memory and ability to manage daily activities. It will be salient to consider underlying depression and grief that is interfering with concentration, memory, and focus. It is probable that she has had a low-lying depression and/or unresolved grief for many years with multiple deaths of family members over the years. Often the loss of life, depending on cultural aspects may affect how a person grieves. Some people believe that they see their lost loved ones and may often talk to them or simply process their feelings of sadness, anger, depression to a picture or inanimate object. Here inability to complete daily activities, forgetfulness, inconsistency with medication as well as her bills should be considered. Diagnoses considered includes adjustment disorder unspecified, bereavement, mild neurocognitive disorder (NCD) due to Alzheimer's disease with behavioral disturbances (mild difficulty with activities of daily living), major NCD due to Alzheimer's disease.

## ■ DIAGNOSTIC CONCLUSION

• Major NCD due to Alzheimer's disease

## ■ SUGGESTED THERAPEUTIC INTERVENTIONS

Behavioral/cognitive therapy—Assist Ruth with staying active with regular exercising, maintaining hygiene regimen, developing memory-enhancing activities/strategies, and help her come to an understanding and acceptance of her limitations. Include the utilization of cultural humility strategies to increase cultural awareness and provide support.

Reminiscence therapy—The benefits of reminiscence therapy will assist Ruth with processing of feelings of depression while coping with the effects of loss and aging. It would also allow for her to reestablish meaning while connecting to the past.

Case management (clinical team social worker or referral)—Identify dependable, support people who can provide supervision and assistance should the cognitive decline develop further. Referral for a social worker who will be able to identify community resources (i.e., daily adult care center; home safety resources; caregiver support group; residential resources outside of the home [i.e., Ruth to relocate with children, assisted living, etc.]).

Grief therapy—Arrange for Ruth to explore feelings of grief related to death of her husband with a grief support group or therapist that specializes in grief work.

Psychological testing—Arrange for Ruth to have psychological testing administered (i.e., General Practitioner Assessment of Cognition [GPCOG], Patient Health Questionnaire [PHQ-9], Beck Depression Inventory [BDI]) to determine nature and degree of cognitive deficit; as well as cognitive impairment.

Referral to neurology—Refer to neurologist or physician to further assess any organic deficit and determine possible causes. Be aware physician may schedule a MRI and/or CT.

## ■ FOR YOUR CONSIDERATION

1. What impact might Ruth's physical health concerns have on her on clinical presentation?
2. Ruth's husband recently died. How is this psychosocial stressor a variable when creating your diagnostic impression?
3. How will cultural considerations be included in the diagnostic and case conceptualize processes?
4. Ethically and legally what should you do to ensure you maintain confidentiality and client privilege when you communicate with Ruth's family?
5. How will you provide counseling services virtually and/or in person? What should be considered when deciding on how to provide counseling services?

*This case is in loving memory of Audrey M. Walton, our grace gift.*

# 17.2    *Case of Mike*

## ■ INTRODUCTION

Mike is a 43-year-old, single male. Having never been married, he lives with his mother and receives Social Security's Supplemental Security Income (SSI) benefits. He graduated from high school and has had a few odd jobs doing construction and yard work; however, he has not worked in 15 years. He reports he began drinking a couple of alcoholic beverages twice a week when he was 9 years old and began drinking heavily beginning at the age of 14. He states that he has not been sober for more than a couple of months at a time throughout his life, and these months of sobriety "have been few and far between."

## ■ CURRENT FUNCTIONING

Mike states he spends his days drinking and panhandling for money so that he can buy more alcohol. He states he wakes up during the night and has to drink to "stop the shakes" (i.e., delirium tremens). He admits that drinking consumes his life but states he "does not really see it as a big problem." He reports that his mother has been increasingly concerned about him.

Mike has been arrested 47 times so far this year for public drunkenness, which is a significant increase from his previous arrest record of once or twice per year for public drunkenness. When the police finally put him in jail, he could not understand why he was being incarcerated. The medical staff at the prison helped Mike detox from alcohol and helped him get stabilized on medication. He spent 4 months in jail; the prison staff reports that Mike had some trouble during his incarceration because he did not follow some of the basic rules, such as making his bed. They said it was almost as if he could not remember to do it, rather than him blatantly breaking the rules. They also reported that Mike fell down frequently. Overall, the prison staff described Mike as likeable, kind-hearted, and a "good" inmate.

Within 3 days of his release from jail, he was hospitalized in a psychiatric unit because he was experiencing difficulty with coordination (e.g., walking and getting in and out of a chair) and with memory (e.g., he got lost on the sidewalk in front of his home). Within a week after his release from the unit, he needed to be hospitalized again. Mike was linked with an outpatient treatment facility and was assigned a case manager. A few days after he was released from the hospital, he was arrested for public drunkenness. Fortunately, the police contacted Mike's new case manager and did not put him back in jail. He was placed in a lockdown long-term treatment facility for 6 months and was then transitioned into a group home.

Mike can no longer take care of himself independently. He needs to be reminded to shower and brush his teeth. He is confused about how to operate a washing machine. Although he is pleasant and has an overall good disposition, he has difficulty interacting with others. Mike forgets what is being discussed and begins to make up stories to try to stay in the conversation; unfortunately, the stories have little or nothing to do with the conversation. He rambles and ruminates about irrelevant things (e.g., having to repair the concrete foundation of a home that no longer exists). He demonstrates difficulty staying on task and needs frequent redirection during conversations. His abilities to function and comprehend information are impaired.

## ■ DIAGNOSTIC IMPRESSIONS

Mike meets criteria for a substance-induced major NCD, as evidenced by his inability to comprehend, hold, and recall new information. He is also easily distracted and has difficulty following conversations. He ruminates and has difficulty finding words to explain himself; he repeatedly talks about having to repair a concrete foundation and has difficulty finding the correct word to denote "house." Although once prompted he will complete simple tasks (e.g., showering), he requires frequent reminders and redirection. He is unable to take care of his finances. His judgment and decision-making are impaired. He does not seem to understand consequences, as evidenced by not understanding why he was being incarcerated; he would frequently ask prison staff and other inmates, "Why am I here? Why are you keeping me here? I want to go home." In addition, other residents at the group home have taken advantage of Mike's good nature; for example, at mealtimes, if they tell Mike they are hungry, he will give them his meal. Then later he will forget and tell the staff that he is hungry and missed the meal.

## ▓ DIAGNOSTIC CONCLUSIONS

- Severe alcohol-induced major NCD, amnestic-confabulatory type, persistent
- Alcohol use disorder, severe

## ▓ SUGGESTED THERAPEUTIC INTERVENTIONS

For clients who are diagnosed with an NCD, assisting them to develop coping skills for activities of daily living (ADLs) and independent ADLs (IADLs) is a key component in helping them live as independently as possible. For example, some clients do not want to ride the bus because they believe that they will get lost or that other passengers may bully them. In such a situation, counselors would help the client modify behavior—the client needs to ride the bus (their only form of transportation), so the counselor helps the client develop a plan to ride the bus (e.g., keep the bus schedule handy, write down specific bus numbers and routes, sit as close to the front as possible, limit conversation).

Mike seldom leaves the group home unattended. Nonetheless, Mike carries a laminated piece of paper in his pocket at all times with his full name, address, and the group home phone number written on it because this is beneficial in helping Mike (or others who are trying to help Mike) find his way back to the group home in case he wanders away. Placing reminder cards in several easily seen locations will help Mike complete tasks such as showering; establishing a routine will also help Mike remember daily tasks. Actively listening to Mike, being fully present, and providing unconditional positive regard is important. Also, focusing on positive things and Mike's qualities is beneficial. One of the most crucial aspects in counseling Mike is validating his feelings, helping him feel cared for, and helping him feel worthy as a person.

## ■ FOR YOUR CONSIDERATION

1. What are the environmental factors that can help people diagnosed with NCDs stay safe at home and in public?
2. Mike might be feeling lonely in the group home and might be missing his mother. What can mental health professionals do to help Mike with this transition? How could mental health professionals help Mike understand that he may not be able to return to live at his mother's house, especially in light of such a delicate topic?
3. How could mental health professionals help Mike understand that he needs to refrain from drinking?

# CHAPTER EIGHTEEN

# PERSONALITY DISORDERS

*Personality disorders are a type of mental disorder in which individuals have a rigid and unhealthy pattern of thinking, functioning, and behaving. The three individual case studies presented in the following chapter have trouble perceiving and relating to situations and people, causing significant problems in relationships, social activities, and the workplace.*

## 18.1   *Case of Nathan*

### ▓ INTRODUCTION

Nathan is a 39-year-old married man who lives in an exclusive gated community in an urban area with his 25-year-old wife, Jeanette and her 6-year-old daughter. Nathan has a master's degree in finance and has owned several businesses since his graduation from a private ivy league university. Nathan heads a nonprofit organization which mentors young men recently released from prison to better themselves by attending community college or enrolling in a trade school. Nathan solicited and received community support and was recently awarded a Citizen's Community Service Award from a local men's service organization. Several newspapers and local television programs featured Nathan and his efforts to rehabilitate these formally incarcerated young men. Jeanette says she admires Nathan for his endeavors to help others who may not have been as fortunate as he and especially respects his self-described rehabilitation with a "healed heart" following his missteps in business. They attend a local church as a family and the church has a parlor named for Nathan's grandfather. Jeanette's daughter loves to tell her friends, "We are famous."

Nathan began this latest entrepreneurial endeavor following his own brief incarceration for misuse of funds in a prior publishing business. Nathan explained that he was attempting to keep this publishing firm afloat and protect his investors after a disastrous gamble on a picturesque coffee table book highlighting a local university's historic football legacy. Nathan willingly testified to his misdoings after being confronted by his friends in the banking business, packed his bags, and headed to a federal prison in the neighboring state. His wife and college sweetheart swiftly filed for divorce and was awarded custody of their twin boys. Nathan served his time as a model inmate often spending time teaching writing to the inmates and was granted early release. He made amends to his former wife and visited his sons on holidays and weekends. Nathan met Jeanette at his son's baseball game where she was watching her nephew play on the opposing team. Jeannette was immediately infatuated with Nathan's good looks, charm, and wit. Not long after the initial meeting, they were married.

Recently Jeanette discovered that Nathan was having an affair with his business partner which resulted in a domestic dispute call to the police. Jeanette says she was devastated and now questions everything Nathan is doing. She fears he has deceived her throughout their 2-year marriage but feels trapped as she has only worked briefly as a paralegal prior to her first marriage. Jeanette's daughter was witness to the scene and is now having nightmares and cries when dropped off at her school. Her teacher reached out to Jeanette and recommended the family seek family therapy and counseling for Jeanette's daughter.

Nathan is adamant that the affair meant nothing to him and that he wants to do what is necessary to repair his marriage to Jeanette. However, prior to their first session, Nathan's business partner resigned from the company and sent a letter to Jeanette. In the letter, she apologized to Jeannette for her behavior but warned her that she does not know the "real" Nathan and suggested she ask him about his "massage therapy" sessions. Jeanette insisted that Nathan begin his own therapy and "be honest with me" before she would consider couples counseling.

## ■ FAMILY HISTORY

Nathan describes himself as a "super active" kid who was always into something. He was second of five children born to very affluent parents and grandparents. His grandfather often took Nathan to work with him and told Nathan he would one day be head of the company. His parents were loving but often traveled leaving the children in the care of his grandparents and their nanny. Nathan's mother was a socialite who enjoyed bridge and cocktail parties. She was a very intelligent woman who, when not traveling, was active in local community politics. She loved her children but delegated much of the daily care to the housekeeper and the nanny. Nathan remembered their housekeeper fondly and grieved when she died. Nathan's dad was an avid reader, but somewhat emotionally distant, and considered a failure in living up to the corporate standards of his father, Nathan's favorite grandfather. Their household was full of activity with five children and their friends, but it often seemed chaotic and disorganized.

Nathan was often bored with children his age and preferred to talking to adults who found him entertaining, bright, and charming. In elementary school, he was often in trouble for disrupting the class with antics which entertained the other students and frustrated the teachers. By early high school, Nathan had been elected class officer each year followed closely by suspensions for removing the flag and substituting women's underwear for the flag, painting his girlfriend's name on the baseball field before the regional tournament, hosting parties with underage drinking when his parents were out of town, and skipping school to hang out with the college students on the beach. Once he was picked up by the police after taking his neighbor's car without their permission and driving without a license. His parents gave his behavior little attention and often thought his actions humorous. He was sent for a summer to a military school after his principal threatened to suspend him for the first term of his senior year. Despite his lack of attention to his academic demands, he managed to graduate salutatorian of his class.

After high school, Nathan attended a private ivy league university where he was elected president of his fraternity. He majored in finance, but his love was journalism. He became the editor of the school paper and soon was publishing a local magazine. He was popular with the girls but preferred to solicit sexual favors from local women who did not demand a committed relationship. Nathan enjoyed his secret life and kept these escapades from his friends. Soon after college he married his college sweetheart, a union blessed by his grandfather who shared business associations with her family. Upon graduation he began buying publications and created a publishing firm and was highlighted as the young entrepreneur of the publishing world. Several years and after the birth of their twin boys, Nathan found himself in financial trouble. He began kiting checks from one of his publications to the other until he was discovered and sentenced to prison. His family forgave him, wrote to him, but visited infrequently during his time in prison.

## DIAGNOSTIC IMPRESSIONS

Nathan demonstrates a lifelong pattern of irresponsible and at times criminal behavior. Nathan has an insatiable appetite for attention and the need to feel special. Due to his intellectual ability and his wit and charm, Nathan was able to avoid serious repercussions until his incarceration. However, even then, he set himself above the inmates by taking on the role of teacher and model inmate. Following his release, he again set himself as the standard bearer who now intends to "save" the other inmates by creating a nonprofit company which also gives him community respect and admiration. One must look beyond the surface to question if Nathan's motive is altruistic or another exploitive strategy to put himself in the spotlight.

Nathan clearly lacks empathy for his wife or his business partner as he engages in a continued pattern of sexual behavior without regard for his wife or affair partner. The "massage parlor" message sent to his wife by his affair partner indicates a continued pattern of high-risk sexual behavior. This pattern of irresponsible behavior, lying, and failure to conform to social norms is pervasive throughout his life and represents a repetitive pattern in which others are harmed both emotionally and financially.

One area for consideration is the culture in which these behaviors occurs. American society has an embedded bias in favor of the "rugged individual" who is allowed to break the rules in achieving success. As long as one is not caught, many "arrestable" and "nonarrestable" but irresponsible behaviors will be accepted in affluent social society. Bankruptcy, unethical business practices, tax evasion are all part of the corporate milieu. In this case, Nathan crossed the line of acceptability and was caught, but was accepted back into his social world after his incarnation and even given service awards and recognition despite being a felon. One must look at issue of social and economic justice as we are asked to "label" our clients with a mental illness diagnosis. Mental health professionals must be sensitive to the cultural and societal influence which impact our work.

## ■ DIAGNOSTIC CONCLUSIONS

- Antisocial personality disorder
- Narcissistic personality disorder

## ■ SUGGESTED THERAPEUTIC INTERVENTIONS

Traditional empathic counseling strategies are ineffective with this population. The counselor must have a working knowledge of the thought processes of these clients and be prepared for the lying, secretiveness, and lack of empathy for others. The sociopath will use his charm to "seduce" the counselor into colluding with them, if not careful. The counselor must find an often-uncomfortable space of both liking the client and not believing the client at the same time.

These clients are very insecure at the core but hide the insecurity behind a wall of grandiosity and entitlement. A pattern of anti-dependence appears to develop early when emotional investment by caregivers in the early stages of the child's life are lacking or unavailable. These children learn to depend on their own guises for survival. Much like wounded animals, they retreat and lash out or discount those who attempt to help them. As adults, they do not adhere to traditional interdependent relationships, preferring to operate from their own set of standards behind a veil of entitlement. Their relationships, which may seem genuine at first, more likely add value to the status of the client and can be quickly abandoned when they no longer reflect the desired image. Thus, any empathic therapeutic connection is very slow to develop and most likely the client will drop out of therapy unless there is outside pressure (pending legal action, divorce, etc.) to attend counseling. The counselor must accept this possibility and work toward creating some transparency in Nathan's thought processes without early confrontation which will cause the client to shut down. As the counselor finds the space to confront the many "cons" and irrational thinking with empathy, the client may begin to be curious enough to engage with the counselor in some self-discovery. The promising outcome is that these irresponsible behaviors tend to decrease with age and some forms of empathy may begin to emerge.

## ▓ FOR YOUR CONSIDERATION

1.  Do you find yourself curious or even fascinated at Nathan's ability to charm, lie, and cheat his way through the world with minimal repercussions, even after an incarceration?
2.  What might happen to Nathan if this ability to be "special" fails? Could this be a suicidal risk for him?
3.  How will Nathan "con" you in counseling? These clients are masters at reading others and telling others what they want to hear to get their way. What is it that Nathan *really* wants from counseling? Start here.

# 18.2    *Case of Rhonda*

## ▓ INTRODUCTION

Rhonda is a 28-year-old woman who has been referred to your agency by a local probation officer. Rhonda reported that she has "fired" three counselors in the past and most recently was "kicked out" by her counselor at a local community agency. Rhonda stated that the reason she "fired" her previous counselors is that they were "clueless and didn't get me." She states that she thinks her most recent counselor "kicked me out because I threatened to kick his ass if he didn't back off." You note that she is smiling as she reports the threat she made to the previous counselor. She then lets you know that she is currently on probation for substance use and her "anger issues."

Rhonda states that she is looking for a counselor who can "handle my past and actually knows how to help me get over it." Rhonda then proceeds to tell you she had 19 surgeries before the age of 10 to resolve a genetic heart defect. She reports that she continues to be under the care of a cardiologist because her heart condition will continue to be an issue throughout her life. Rhonda reports experiencing significant anxiety whenever she drives by a hospital or has to go into a hospital to visit friends.

## ▧ FAMILY HISTORY

During the first 10 years of Rhonda's life, she was sexually abused by a neighbor. Rhonda reports that she was also sexually abused by her sister during the same period and continuing until her sister moved away to college. Rhonda was 16 years old when the sexual abuse from her sister stopped. Rhonda disclosed to her mother the abuse she experienced from the neighbor and her sister shortly after the neighbor was charged for sexually abusing another child in the neighborhood. Rhonda's mother stated that she did not believe Rhonda's sister had abused Rhonda because "I'm a good mom and I would know if anything like that was happening under my roof." However, her mom did believe Rhonda's disclosure of sexual abuse by the neighbor, but felt that there was no need to report Rhonda's abuse when the neighbor, who had already being charged for abusing a different child in the neighborhood, would be going to jail in any case. Rhonda states that her relationship with her mother has been "hot and cold" ever since Rhonda disclosed the abuse.

She also reports that she is unsure whether her father is aware of the abuse she endured from the neighbor and her sister; Rhonda never disclosed this information to him directly, but she suspects that her mother would have told him. The family never discussed Rhonda's disclosure of sexual abuse, and Rhonda doesn't know whether anyone ever confronted her older sister about the abuse. To date, Rhonda has never talked with her sister about it, and avoids most family gatherings that she expects her sister will attend. Rhonda states that she regularly gets high if she finds herself at family gatherings that her sister is attending.

Rhonda reports that she continues to have flashbacks of different episodes of abuse. She identifies her heart surgery scars as a trigger. She states that when her scars are touched by anyone, including herself, she gets flashbacks of the sexual abuse by her neighbor because his large hands would brush over her scars when he was fondling her breasts. She also identifies the smell of a particular lotion to be a trigger of the abuse she endured from her sister. She states that she is still unable to tolerate the smell and texture of any lotion and has never bought a bottle of lotion as an adult.

## ■ CURRENT FUNCTIONING

Rhonda is currently unemployed but is looking for a job. She reports that she has a difficult time maintaining employment because she moves around a lot. When asked what causes her to move around a lot, she reports that she has had a few relationships (six in the last year) that did not work out well and that she was living with each of them at the time of the breakups. Rhonda states that she is currently "trying on" being a lesbian because she believes that "women are more understanding than men, so maybe a woman would *get* me better and not leave me." Rhonda reports that she struggles to manage her money or maintain any relationship, stating that "most people in my life end up leaving me."

When asked what she has been working on with previous counselors, Rhonda states that she has been working on different coping skills. In the past, Rhonda would burn herself or get high when her trauma was triggered. She states that she now tries to engage in deep breathing and relaxation techniques, but "they aren't as effective as burning myself." Rhonda does report a history of suicidal ideation and identifies that she typically will feel suicidal when her romantic relationships are ended by the other person. Although Rhonda reports a history of suicidal ideation, she reports no attempts to take her life.

Rhonda is attending counseling as compliance with probation. She is currently working on her substance abuse issues with another counseling agency. Rhonda is coming to your agency with the hopes to work on her past sexual trauma. She states that she believes sexual trauma is the root of her anger, relationship problems, and substance abuse issues. She believes that if you can just "make the bad stuff in my past go away" she will be able to get off probation and stay out of trouble.

## ■ DIAGNOSTIC IMPRESSIONS

Rhonda clearly is a complex individual who has experienced a variety of trauma throughout her life. Rhonda's disclosure of sexual abuse for the first 16 years of life is a significant trauma. She also has experienced trauma from the significant medical interventions to treat her genetic heart defect. Rhonda reports experiencing flashbacks and triggers of both the sexual abuse and her medical treatments, which has created discomfort and anxiety for her. She avoids known triggers like the hospital and lotion when possible and struggles with disparaging thoughts about herself. Rhonda has been very transparent about her anger and struggle with managing her anger appropriately. Based on these symptoms, a diagnosis of posttraumatic stress disorder (PTSD) would be appropriate.

The diagnosis of PTSD is just one piece of the puzzle. Rhonda's symptoms are also indicative of a personality disorder, specifically borderline personality disorder (BPD). Rhonda's pattern of relational strain with a number of significant relationships is one component to attend to when looking at diagnosing her. Some other symptoms addressed by Rhonda in support of a diagnosis of BPD are her impulsive behaviors of substance abuse, self-harming, and report of suicidal ideation. She struggles with her identity as she is currently "trying on being a lesbian" and struggles to manage her emotions effectively.

It should be noted that Rhonda has financial distress because she struggles to maintain a job and moves frequently as a result of her relationship decisions. Relationship issues are a component of the BPD, so you may choose to note the strained interpersonal relationships. Because she is currently on probation, it would be wise to note the legal issues as well.

Considering Rhonda's disclosures about her issues with substance use, it would be important for a clinician to evaluate them and assess their depth. Rhonda stated that the substance use is part of the reason she is currently on probation and that she is already receiving treatment. Because Rhonda disclosed being in treatment for the substance use already, it is imperative that the clinician secure a release of information form from Rhonda so that the clinician can coordinate care with the substance abuse counselor.

## ■ DIAGNOSTIC CONCLUSIONS

- PTSD
- BPD
- Child sexual abuse, initial encounter
- Sibling relational problem
- Problems related to other legal circumstances
- Personal history of self-harm
- R/O Substance abuse (not enough information given at this point)

## ■ SUGGESTED THERAPEUTIC INTERVENTIONS

Rhonda expressed a true desire for a counseling relationship that will promote feelings of safety, understanding, and acceptance. Counselors providing mental health counseling services for clients of sexual abuse benefit clients by attending training and education on treatment options for counseling the sexual abuse experiences and developmental factors affecting mental, emotional, and cognitive functioning. Given Rhonda's traumatic abuse history, challenged coping skills, suicidal tendency, and feelings of being overwhelmed by the demands in her life, she needs a theory that attends to her past and present unstable emotional and interpersonal challenges and a counselor who is prepared for the predictable turbulent counselor–client relationship. Rhonda may greatly benefit from dialectical behavior therapy (DBT) because this theory was developed by Marsha Linehan to treat individuals who have been diagnosed with BPD and those who had chronic suicide attempts through a therapeutic counseling relationship that fosters self-respect, collaboration, and acceptance (Linehan, 1993a). DBT would provide Rhonda with a team-based approach to treat her symptoms of BPD, emotional regulation challenges, and trauma. DBT is structured to provide four treatment components: skills training for emotional regulation, individual outpatient psychotherapy, telephone consultation or coaching, and peer consultation and supervision for the counselors (Decker & Naugle, 2008). The individual outpatient psychotherapy focuses on factors specific to the client. Rhonda will need a specific treatment for her childhood sexual abuse, need for validation and acceptance, self-harm tendencies, and suicidal ideation (Linehan, 1993b). The skills training component to this treatment approach requires group counseling for Rhonda to address four sets of skills: interpersonal relationships and communication effectiveness, emotional distress tolerance, emotional regulation, and mindfulness (Decker & Naugle, 2008).

DBT offers two stages of treatment to balance Rhonda's emotional reactions and responses. In stage I, Rhonda will participate in treatment that directly works to support acquisition of behavioral and coping skills while addressing and eliminating life-threatening behaviors that reduce the effectiveness of treatment (Decker & Naugle, 2008). As Rhonda develops a balanced response to life stressors and gains the coping skills needed to sustain healthy responses, she will begin exposure treatment. Stage II supports Rhonda's exploration of exposure to the abuse and trauma. This stage will not be experienced until effective coping skills are in place to assist Rhonda in coping with the consequences of being exposed to traumatic life events such as her medical condition, childhood sexual abuse, and family secrets about Rhonda's victimization by her sister. The following treatment considerations are stage I counseling activities:

## HOLIDAY DISTRESS TOLERANCE SKILLS

Rhonda expressed that being in situations with others that remind her of past trauma and any contact with her sister induces emotional, mental, and physical distress. A distressful experience for Rhonda may be the holidays, where she needs to acquire useful techniques to accept and tolerate these painful events with family and friends. In counseling, Rhonda will be taught crisis-survival skills when the pain cannot be avoided but needs to be tolerated with mindful actions rather than impulsive and destructive harm (Decker & Naugle, 2008). For an event at which

Rhonda might be faced with meeting family and friends that create distressing memories, she will be given a smooth rock that offers soothing emotions when touched and stroked. On the rock, Rhonda will write positive coping skills or positive reminders to support her through these stressful situations. This rock will be kept in her pant pocket to be touched and held when Rhonda mindfully assesses her current emotions to exceed her capacity to self-soothe mentally. Touching the rock will help Rhonda stay grounded in the moment and physical space so that she can assertively communicate her personal needs.

## PERSONAL TIMELINE: MY LIFE AS I KNOW IT

Treatment integrating counseling activities to foster exploration of life events may *enhance* Rhonda's comfort and reduce reactive impulses of deliberate harmful behaviors. One treatment activity may be creating a timeline of her life events. Rhonda will be asked to place a line horizontally across the middle of a large sheet of paper. The life-span outline will capture her memory of past events and present emotions. Rhonda will be asked to write and/or draw out symbols to represent experiences she wishes not to share but to represent on the timeline.

Life-span outline: Use symbols to represent experiences you wish not to share. Bottom of line indicates typical experiences across your life span. Top of line indicates surprises and unexpected changes, whether positive or challenging. List your future expected achievements, accomplishments, events, and traditional life-span developments.

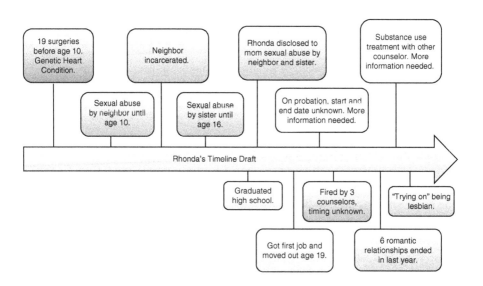

Exploring with Rhonda:

- Discuss her emotions and experiences when creating the timeline.
- Explore her coping strategies from one traumatic event to the next.
- Process how she has survived and her personal strengths for surviving.
- Review how she works to mindfully change her relationship choices to enhance her well-being.
- Process what she wishes to work on as treatment progresses.

## FOR YOUR CONSIDERATION

1. Knowing that Rhonda has threatened her previous counselor, how would you address this and ensure your own personal safety?
2. Rhonda has discussed her mother's response to Rhonda's disclosure. Based on the mother's response, what might be going on for the mother? How might a more empathetic perspective of the mother help you work with Rhonda and heal past attachment injuries?
3. Rhonda is clearly a complicated case. On the basis of the multiple layers, which issue would you choose to address first during your sessions with Rhonda? Why?
4. If you took the past sexual abuse component away from this case and focused only on the surgical trauma, would your diagnosis of this client change? If so, what would the new diagnosis be? Would your treatment strategy change? If so, how?
5. Based on your current state laws and professional ethical code, what are you legally obligated to do in terms of reporting the past child sexual abuse? What are you ethically obligated to do in terms of reporting the past child abuse?

## REFERENCES

Decker, S. E., & Naugle, A. E. (2008). DBT for sexual abuse survivors: Current status and future directions. *Journal of Behavior Analysis of Offender and Victim Treatment and Prevention, 1*(4), 53–68.

Linehan, M. M. (1993a). *Cognitive-behavioral treatment of borderline personality disorder.* Guilford Press.

Linehan, M. M. (1993b). *Skills training manual for treating borderline personality disorder.* Guilford Press.

# 18.3  *Case of Jack*

## ■ INTRODUCTION

Jack is a 45-year-old, married father of two grown-up children and two stepchildren. Jack is a real estate entrepreneur who is co-owner of a real estate brokerage firm. Jack is married to his second wife, Suzanne, who is a respected professor at a major university in their community. Suzanne discovered Jack was having an affair when she logged on to his computer while hers was being repaired. A week after discovering the affair, the bank notified Suzanne of a large overdraft on their joint investment account. Until the discovery of the affair, Suzanne thought they had "the perfect marriage."

Jack indicates he had come to counseling to "save my marriage." He reports Suzanne is devastated and is seeking individual counseling to cope with the betrayal. Jack says he has not been able to sleep since Suzanne found out about the affair and swears that woman "meant nothing to me. It was just a time when I was so distracted about the biggest deal I have ever worked, and she was, frankly, flirting with me for quite a while. She is new in the business and asked for my advice. One thing led to another—that stuff happens—but I don't want to end our marriage."

When asked about the overdraft, Jack says he was just a little short of funding, and it is no big deal. He insists he will pay it back. "That is just part of this business." Jack reports he is a successful real estate broker who has been ranked in the top 10 producers in his community for the past 5 years. He prides himself on being one of the best in his business and hopes his adult son will join the firm. "You gotta be willing to take risks. Not everyone is willing to do what it takes, and that's why I've been tops in this business. When this deal closes, I'll be number 1 and be honored at our yearly banquet."

His business partner is a woman who, as Jack reports, "was at first a real friend and we did all our deals together, but she began to question me on how I put our deals together, and now we rarely speak to each other." He hopes she will leave the firm but sees no room for negotiation at this time. "I just close my door and don't speak to her unless it is absolutely necessary. She'll be sorry when she falls flat on her face without me helping her create the deals."

Jack reported he has always had a tremendous amount of energy. "As a kid I was always in some sort of trouble for having too much fun." Jack reports he was arrested at the age of 15 for underage drinking and racing his four-wheeler along a creek in a residential neighborhood. He reportedly did community service, and the incident was erased from his record when he turned 18 years old. "I was bored in high school and by my senior year, I was skipping as often as I could. I never got caught and the teachers would get furious because I still made good grades on my tests. I think I was more intelligent than most of them and they knew it. We used to go to Mr. Ted's grocery and steal a couple of beers and head to the pool. He never figured us out, but when I was old enough to buy beer legally, I would stop by and buy beer or get some milk. I figured that made us even."

Jack currently plays competitive tennis and lifts weights at a local gym. He reports drinking occasionally but alleges no drug use. He does receive testosterone injections "to keep my energy up." Jack concluded by stating, "I'll do whatever you tell me to do. I don't want another divorce."

After obtaining permission to speak to Jack's wife, Suzanne, she revealed that she often worried about Jack's financial dealings and knew he often "rolled the dice" but was confident he would never put their personal finances at risk. Now she is not so sure. She says she was attracted to Jack for his personality. "He was always the life of the party and never met a stranger. He was ambitious and knew how to get things done. I knew he would be a success. I never dreamed he would cheat on me." She further revealed Jack had a previous bankruptcy and reorganization of his company, which resulted in a long-term lawsuit with his former partner. She added, "He's not like that at home. He always remembers my birthday and our anniversary and buys me wonderful gifts. Last year he gave me and my daughters a trip to Las Vegas. He was always so generous with them—they adore him." Suzanne shared that Jack is not close to his youngest son because he sided with his mother in their divorce. His first wife is reportedly still bitter about Jack leaving the family.

## ▨ DIAGNOSTIC IMPRESSIONS

There is often a fine line between irresponsibility and criminal activity. Most of us have participated in some illegal behavior at one time or another, but with little harm to others and few consequences. Who has not gone above the posted speed limit or cruised through a stop sign when no cars were in sight? However, one can begin to place patterns of behavior on a spectrum of irresponsibility. Some behaviors are irresponsible and out of the cultural norms but are not criminal and thus are *nonarrestable*. Further across the spectrum are the *arrestable* behaviors ranging from white-collar crime to violent acts of aggression.

Jack, like most psychopaths, has a long history of irresponsible and sometimes criminal behavior, which pervades his life and has caused distress to those around him. Jack clearly demonstrates this pattern of irresponsibility, beginning in his adolescent years with high-risk behaviors, and a disregard for rules and regulations. Yet he prides himself on being a good person in spite of his questionable business practices and his recently revealed infidelity. He has a history of conflicted relationships and is quick to blame others for the conflict. Jack appears to be concerned about his image in maintaining the marriage with little empathy for Suzanne's distress. Jack relishes the adoration of his stepdaughters and emphasizes his success by buying expensive gifts and trips, although he rarely spends time with any of his family.

## ▓ DIAGNOSTIC CONCLUSIONS

Although the person with an antisocial personality disorder may have many of the features of a narcissistic personality disorder, the distinguishing features for a diagnosis of antisocial personality disorder are irritability or aggressiveness, deceitfulness, lying, and irresponsible or unlawful behavior throughout his or her history. Another distinction may be made between a person who is educated with a viable career and who takes calculated risks, and another who is disenfranchised, lacks opportunity and education, and commits impulsive criminal acts out of rage toward an oppressive environment. Although neither is excused from responsibility, there is an environmental factor to be acknowledged with the latter.

The *Diagnostic and Statistical Manual of Mental Disorders, 5th Edition (DSM-5)* diagnosis may be the same for each, but the treatment options are markedly different. One client will likely obtain legal counsel and be seen in a private practice or chic counseling setting, whereas the latter will find themselves using whatever mental health and legal services are available in the criminal justice system. Jack's *DSM-5* diagnosis is:

- Antisocial personality disorder
- Other problems related to employment

## ▓ SUGGESTED THERAPEUTIC INTERVENTIONS

Traditional empathic counseling strategies are ineffective with this population. The counselor must have a working knowledge of the thought processes of the psychopath for any chance of creating an opportunity for change. The thinking is continuous, and fantasies of power and control are pervasive. Jack likely has many more irresponsible behaviors, which he does not intend to reveal. He probably does not want a divorce, either because he does not want to share his wealth, or he wants to maintain his image. The psychopath keeps attachments as long as the relationship is to his or her advantage (including with the counselor).

The counselor must investigate the underlying reason for counseling through deductive reasoning. One should assume Jack's goal is not to change but to pacify others for some hidden agenda. The only time that change is possible is when the psychopath is vulnerable. This opportunity may come for Jack if further business failures, legal implications, or loss of his wealth and/or image is at risk.

Underlying the grandiosity is extreme fear, which is kept at bay at all costs. There appears to be such an inner void that some have termed the dreaded state a *zero* state. However, the counseling strategy should be primarily focused on Jack's thinking and the ultimate responsibility for his behavior. The goal is to create transparency into Jack's thought processes. As the consequences of the irresponsible behavior are pointed out to the client, a typical response is "Everyone does it." The counselor must find a balance between confronting each "con" and remaining nonjudgmental. The first "con" in Jack's presentation is "Tell me what to do."

## ▪ FOR YOUR CONSIDERATION

1. Could Jack become suicidal when and if he becomes vulnerable to his inner fears? Would hospitalization be beneficial?
2. Would having access to significant others in Jack's life be beneficial to know the extent of Jack's irresponsibility? How might this affect the counseling?
3. How will Jack con you? After all, counselors are good at establishing trust through rapport, aren't we? Good counseling is all about the therapeutic relationship. Or is it?

# CHAPTER NINETEEN

# PARAPHILIC DISORDERS

*A paraphilic disorder exists when recurrent, intense sexually arousing fantasies, urges, or behaviors cause distress and/or impairment to the individual. In some individuals with paraphilic disorder, their sexual satisfaction has entailed personal harm or the risk of harm to others. The cases in this chapter represent studies of sexual sadism and voyeuristic disorder and how each of the men diagnosed with these conditions respond to court-appointed therapy. Questions for consideration follow each case.*

## 19.1    *Case of George*

### ■ INTRODUCTION

George is a 32-year-old Caucasian male who presents at a counseling agency as a condition of court-appointed treatment. During a recent sexual encounter, George demanded that his girlfriend allow him to strangle her until he reached orgasm. When his girlfriend refused, George punched her. As a result, George was ordered by the court to attend 10 sessions of therapy.

When the therapist asks about the assault, George dismisses the assault by stating that she "overexaggerated" the assault and states that his now ex-girlfriend is an "attention-seeking slut." George also states that she is not nearly pretty enough or wealthy enough to accompany him to all the prestigious events that he is "continuously" invited to. He states that he is glad she is gone and knows that there will be many more women "lining up" for a chance to date him.

George alludes to a history of violent sexual encounters. He states that he finds it nearly impossible to achieve sexual arousal without spanking, paddling, or verbally and/or physically degrading his partner. George indicates that he has always engaged in what he refers to as "physical sex" but admits that he has become increasingly violent in the past years. He states that he is now at the point where he must strangle or suffocate his partner in order to achieve orgasm.

## ▓ FAMILY HISTORY

George is the only child of a very wealthy upper-class family. He states that he never had a close relationship with his parents because they were very involved in themselves and did not have enough time to focus on him, despite his many accomplishments. George says that he only sees his parents during holidays, but he states that he is not upset by his lack of relationship with his parents because he enjoys his trust fund much more than he ever enjoyed their company.

## ▓ CURRENT FUNCTIONING

During the interview, George appears to be arrogant and aloof. He seems irritated and inconvenienced at the prospect of having to attend 10 sessions of therapy. He states that he is much too busy and way too important to devote his time to therapy. He further complains about having to wait 5 minutes before being seen, stating that "he does not wait for anyone." When he notices the therapist's degree hanging on the wall, he scoffs that "anyone can get a degree from a state school." He insists on mentioning that he graduated from an Ivy-League school. George goes as far as to ask that he be transferred to a therapist with a degree from a better school because he does not want to waste his time talking to someone who graduated from such a pitiful institution.

George is currently unemployed. He was discharged from his most recent position as a pharmaceutical sales representative after he failed to make his sales quota several months in a row. George states that he believes that he was fired because his boss was threatened by and jealous of his superior intellect and natural-born talent as a salesman. George is unconcerned about being unemployed because he believes that he will be offered a prestigious position soon, despite the fact that he does not have any résumés out to potential employers, due to his "natural-born ability as a salesperson."

Several times during the interview, George brags about his fancy car, his designer clothes, and his expensive jewelry. He seems preoccupied by material possessions and seems to equate his possessions with power. He states that he has "no use" for people who do not spend money on clothes and cars.

George seems to display little empathy when talking about a friend who recently separated from his wife; George expressed irritation at his friend's late-night phone calls. He stated that his friend should get over the "cow" and stop wasting his time. When asked if he had any feelings of sympathy for his friend, George responded incredulously "Sympathy for him?! He's the one inconveniencing me and he's trying to drag me down with him! He should have sympathy for me!"

George indicates that people have "always been jealous of me" and states that he did not have many friends in high school because everyone envied him.

George says that he does not care about having close friends because he has yet to find anyone on "his level." He also states he has been criticized for being too shallow and lacking empathy.

## ▓ DIAGNOSTIC IMPRESSIONS

George was court-ordered for treatment following an assault of his girlfriend who refused to engage in a violent sexual act. The aggressive acts were perpetrated against a nonconsenting adult. He meets criteria for sexual sadism, a paraphilic disorder characterized by sexual arousal from psychological and physical suffering of a nonconsenting adult (American Psychiatric Association [APA], 2013). However, in this case, his sexual sadism is comorbid with a personality disorder.

It is likely that narcissistic personality disorder (NPD) is intensifying George's sexual sadism. Like many people with NPD, he displays a pervasive pattern of grandiosity, need for admiration, and lack of empathy. This pattern is evident in George's grandiose sense of self-importance and entitlement, perceived sense of success and beauty, elated social status, need for excessive admiration, exploitation of others, lack of empathy, and arrogance (APA, 2013).

## ▓ DIAGNOSTIC CONCLUSIONS

- Sexual sadism
- NPD
- Problems related to occupational system (unemployment)
- Problems with primary support group (lack of close relationship with parents)
- Problems with social support (lack of close friendships, recent breakup)
- Problems with legal environment (court-ordered therapy due to assault)

## ▓ SUGGESTED THERAPEUTIC INTERVENTIONS

George, like others diagnosed with sexual sadism, may not present for counseling until they are encouraged to do so by an unwilling participant or sexual partner or a court order. Little is known about the prevalence of sexual sadism in the general or clinical population; however, most individuals treated in forensic populations are male (APA, 2013). The Severe Sexual Sadism Scale (SSSS) is a useful screening device for forensic populations and may assist with the identification of the disorder. The SSSS consists of 11 items answered yes or no. The item responses are used to code behavioral indicators of sexual offenders who demonstrate symptoms of sexual sadism (Mokross et al., 2012).

Prognosis and participation in treatment may be dependent on client motivation (i.e., clients experiencing symptoms as problematic and desiring change may be more motivated). The treatment success of paraphilic disorders depends on the duration, frequency, and severity of the symptoms. Cognitive behavioral therapy (CBT) is recommended to decrease sexual urges, teach coping skills, identify triggers, and redirect inappropriate behaviors to more socially acceptable behaviors (APA, 2013).

A single treatment strategy has not been proven superior or reliable with clients with NPD. To date, none have been empirically tested for evidence of efficacy (Ronningstam, 2011). Despite limited treatment data, a strong therapeutic alliance is positively correlated with successful treatment of individuals diagnosed with a personality disorder. The alliance can be strengthened with the NPD population through the identification of specific treatment goals and target behaviors that are agreed on by both the client and clinician. Given the focus on specific behaviors and concrete goals, CBT is recommended for use with personality disorders including NPD. The focus is placed on educating the client about problem behaviors, validating the client, and identifying target behaviors that are problematic. CBT strategies can also be used to identify and replace cognitive distortions and thinking that perpetuate the primary diagnostic features of NPD—grandiosity, need for admiration, and lack of empathy (Ronningstam, 2014).

## FOR YOUR CONSIDERATION

1. How might your diagnosis change if George was having sexual fantasies about a minor?
2. What information do you feel you still need to know in order to feel confident that you arrived at the correct diagnosis?
3. How might your diagnosis change if George's symptoms and behaviors were limited to consensual sadomasochistic role-play?
4. How is George's diagnosis of NPD intensifying his diagnosis of sexual sadism?

## REFERENCES

American Psychiatric Association. (2013). *Diagnostic and statistical manual of mental disorders* (5th ed.). American Psychiatric Publishing.
Mokross, A., Schilling, F., Eher, R., & Nitschke, J. (2012). The severe sexual sadism scale: Cross-validation and scale properties. *Psychological Assessment, 24,* 764–769.

Ronningstam, E. (2011). Narcissistic personality disorder. *Personality and Mental Health, 5,* 222–227.
Ronningstam, E. F. (2014). Narcissistic personality disorder. In G. O. Gabbard (Ed.), *Gabbard's treatments of psychiatric disorders* (5th ed., pp. 1073–1086). American Psychiatric Publishing.

# 19.2    Case of Bryant

## ▓ INTRODUCTION

Bryant, a 20-year-old male, college student, sought treatment for his voyeuristic urges after he was caught by his roommate "peering" across the quad at the girls' dormitory with binoculars. The roommate threatened to report him, and Bryant is concerned that he will lose his college scholarship and be expelled from the university.

Bryant articulated that he has no problems attracting sexual partners and has an active sex life. He reports that he hooks up, on average, one or two times per week. However, these sexual relationships do not provide Bryant with the level of pleasure that he gains from his voyeuristic endeavors. He reports that he began voyeurism in junior high school when he had a new neighbor move in and he could see her bedroom from his bedroom window. The neighbor, a young woman, did not shut her blinds, and Bryant viewed this as an invitation to watch her change clothing, apply beauty products, and have sex.

With the binoculars and, at times, night-vision goggles, Bryant admitted peering into the windows of the dormitories on campus, local apartments, and sorority houses to watch females undressing or having sex. When Bryant finds a suitable target, he masturbates to orgasm either while he watches or shortly thereafter. Bryant has not pursued sexual relationships with the women he observes and denies that this is his goal. He denies any plans, impulses, or fantasies to engage in rape. Bryant endorses pleasure from the voyeuristic act, and the threat of being caught makes it "hotter" for him.

On several occasions, Bryant was nearly caught by a bystander or one of his targets. He was shocked that his roommate caught him in the act and blames his target for "taking so long" as the reason for his roommate walking in on him. Bryant feels neither guilty nor ashamed about his voyeuristic tendencies and says that he is not harming anyone. However, given the current legal landscape toward sexual offenders, Bryant is motivated to seek help to change his sexual behavior.

## ▓ DIAGNOSTIC IMPRESSIONS

Bryant's desire to watch others in sexual situations is common; there is an entire industry—pornography—built around the idea that people like to watch others having sex. Voyeurism usually begins during adolescence or early adulthood. In

Bryant's case, his voyeurism is pathological, and he spends a considerable amount of time seeking out viewing opportunities to the exclusion of other important responsibilities and relationships. It seems that Bryant's voyeurism developed accidentally and now seems to be a method of achieving orgasm.

Voyeuristic disorder is a *paraphilic disorder*—disorders that cause distress or impairment to the individual or entail a risk of personal harm. In the *Diagnostic and Statistical Manual of Mental Disorders* (5th ed.; *DSM-5;* American Psychiatric Association, 2013) it is said that up to 12% of males and 4% of females may meet clinical criteria for voyeuristic disorder; most do not seek medical evaluation and treatment unless compelled.

## DIAGNOSTIC CONCLUSIONS

- Voyeuristic disorder
- Potential problems with university authorities, legal system; tension in living situation

## SUGGESTED THERAPEUTIC INTERVENTIONS

Psychopharmacology may be used to diminish Bryant's unusual sexual urges, in addition to behavioral therapy to encourage those with impulse control difficulties to control their urge to watch nonconsenting targets. Lastly, social skills training may be helpful to Bryant to acquire more acceptable and harmless ways of sexual gratification.

## FOR YOUR CONSIDERATION

1. Would you consider an individual like Bryant to be a sexual predator? Why or why not?
2. Is pornography simply a legalized version of voyeurism? Why or why not?

## REFERENCE

American Psychiatric Association. (2013). *Diagnostic and statistical manual of mental disorders* (5th ed.). American Psychiatric Publishing.

# CHAPTER TWENTY

## CULTURAL CONSIDERATIONS IN TREATMENT

*Race, ethnicity, and culture influence client identity and life circumstances. Other factors, such as gender and gender identity, sexual orientation, age, socioeconomic status, religion, and ability may also play into the context of a client's mental health or personal issues. The four cases in this chapter feature cultural aspects that have a significant role in the treatment and conceptualization by their clinicians. Culturally competent clinicians practice cultural humility and understand that clients' backgrounds influence the ways in which they view the world and that the clinician's role must change to accommodate these perspectives.*

## 20.1    *Case of Linda*

### ▓ INTRODUCTION

Linda is a 15-year-old female from Mexico who moved to a Midwest suburban town 5 years ago, with her parents, a fraternal twin sister, and 16-year-old brother. Her father started a family-owned business with his brother, which was the cause for her family to be relocated. Linda stated her aunt and uncle were more proficient with the English language, and her parents did not speak English before the move. Linda shared she had learned some English before her family moved but started in the program at school for English language learners. During her first year in the United States, when she started Middle School, she stated it was "an awful year." She stated her favorite aunt, with whom she was very close, died in a car accident that year. Linda was there when her parents were informed of the accident. Since her siblings were not at home, Linda stated she helped interpret the details of the tragic news the police officer was reporting. She was also with her parents when they saw what was left of the car. She said she associated the move with so many "terrible" experiences because she had so many challenges with language, with academics, and making friends. Due to her struggles that year, she had missed a lot of school, which resulted in failing grades. At that time, it was recommended that she should repeat sixth grade. She stated this was very stressful, as she had always been in the same grade with her sister up until that time. In seventh grade, she attended school regularly, and shared that she now has an individualized educational plan (IEP) as she was evaluated by the school psychologist and was identified with having a specified learning disability in both reading and math. When asked, she clarified that the assessment tool was in English, but she had a Spanish translator to help her understand the questions.

Currently, Linda is 5 months into her first year of high school and stated "it has been really scary" beginning high school by herself and without her sister (as her twin sister is already in the sophomore class). She stated the high school is too big and she has concerns with some of the course requirements while giving oral presentations. Linda stated she has no interest in participating in any of the high school activities or sports. She further shared she is "embarrassed" when students in her sister's class see her, as she stated she worries what they think of her for "flunking" the sixth grade. She stated she does not want to go to school and would rather "go (to school) online."

## ■ FAMILY HISTORY

Linda stated she remembers her mother cried a lot when they lived in Mexico but is not sure what had "made her" so unhappy. When asked about her mother now, she stated, her mother is often occupied and busy with completing daily tasks. Even though she doesn't think her mother is "less sad," she does not see her crying as she did before. Linda's mother has always stayed home to raise her and her siblings. Since the death of her aunt, Linda's cousins often come to her house as her uncle works long hours with Linda's dad. Linda's mother takes care of her female cousin, who is in third grade, as well as her male cousin who is the same age as Linda's brother, 16.

Linda stated her mother is often busy with her cousins, especially her third grade cousin. Linda noted her mother does not spend as much time with Linda as she did before. Linda shared that she is often worried about her mother dying (like her aunt.) She further stated her mother does not talk about her aunt much at all.

Linda stated her father had always worked long hours and continues to do so. Often her brother and male cousin are working with her dad, and she stated she feels he (Dad) values them because they are male and help out at the family business. When he comes home, she stated he is often edgy and seems upset. Linda stated he does not talk much to her as most of his communication is with her mother or brother.

Linda shared she had always gravitated toward her aunt, as everyone always gave her twin sister the attention. Linda described her fraternal twin sister as "the pretty one" who was smart, fit, and outgoing. But Linda's aunt had always made Linda feel special and would ask her about her life and include her in various activities. Linda stated she really misses her aunt and their relationship.

## ■ CURRENT FUNCTIONING

Linda has recently received disciplinary action from the school, as she stated she "got in trouble" for stealing another student's ear buds from their gym locker. Linda had been caught skipping classes and now has stealing on her disciplinary record. Therefore, she stated her parents think "there is something wrong" with her and have brought her into counseling to be "fixed."

Linda shared that last week was the fifth year anniversary of "losing her aunt," and she has been experiencing nightmares of "her aunt's death." As noted earlier, Linda was with her parents when they were notified of her aunt's death, and she also saw what was left of the car and heard the descriptions of the accident. She shared she often worries about her mother and is afraid something bad will happen to her. Linda stated she often feels irritated and only gets along with her brother when she needs a ride from him to get somewhere. Linda shared he (her brother) often has friends over, who she says she "cannot stand" because they give her a hard time about her weight or say sexually suggestive things to her which makes her feel uncomfortable. His friends are often hanging out at her house with her cousin as well. When she sees her brothers' friends at school, they try talking to her, and she stated she tries to avoid them as much as possible. Linda confessed that one of her brother's friends told her if she gave him a pair of ear buds, he would leave her alone. However, she stated she gave him the ear buds (that she had taken from another student) and now she is in trouble (with both the school and her parents) and he still "isn't leaving (her) alone."

She stated when she needs to do her homework, she often falls asleep, and cannot concentrate to do her homework. Linda reported that her mother often goes to help her dad after school and takes her younger cousin to the family business. Linda stated she feels her mother "cares more" about her cousin than she does of Linda. Linda shared that sometimes she skips class and sits in the bathroom crying, because she is so worried something bad will happen to her mother when she is not there.

Linda stated she feels worried, scared, isolated, abandoned, often cries herself to sleep, and wants her life to "go back to the way it was" when she lived in Mexico. She shared she really doesn't want to go to school and there is too much homework. Linda reported that she would rather just work for her dad than finish school.

When asked about what she does like in her life right now, she stated she loves her dog, who is her closest companion. She has made some friends in her current class but noted that she still "feels stupid." She stated the students she feels comfortable around "get into trouble a lot" with the school and party on the weekends—when asked, she said she has never attended any of these parties but considers participating in the future. When asked how she gets along with her sister, she stated they "are fine together," but now that they are in different grades, her sister takes harder classes, has more friends, she participates in many clubs and sports; therefore, they spend limited time together. Linda stated that her sister's friends are nice to her, and many remember her from sixth grade, but she still feels uncomfortable and worries about how they view her.

When asked what she currently does to help herself feel better at difficult times, Linda reported that she typically isolates herself and cries. She stated that when she was in Mexico and before her aunt's death, she used to like to go for walks and spend time with her friends when she was upset. She stated that since she grew up with her friends in Mexico, they had more in common, could talk about anything, and they didn't judge one another. Linda stated she misses her friends and looks forward to going back to visit them. Linda shared she does not currently have friends she is as close with or whom she can trust. Instead, she reported she often sleeps, not only because she is tired, but she stated she gets overwhelmed with all of her feelings. She reported using food as a coping skill in order to stay awake while doing homework and occasionally to feel better. Linda mentioned not being able to walk in her neighborhood due to it being an "unsafe" area. She stated that going to a gym or community recreation center for exercise would be a challenge because she would not have a ride to the gym, as her parents are working, and her siblings either stay after school for their extra-curricular activities (her sister) or go to the family business to help her family (her brother). Linda's coping mechanisms are eating, sleeping, and avoidance.

## ▨ DIAGNOSTIC IMPRESSIONS

Linda presents with a typical build, even though she calls herself "overweight." On the surface, Linda seems very conversational and polite. She desires someone to listen and validate her concerns. Linda tends to get very emotional and raises her voice when expressing her frustrations with her family and when addressing miscommunications experienced at school. The death of her aunt seems to have impacted her life substantially years ago as well as currently. Some examples of the current impact of her aunt's death include anxiety and fears about her family as well as having negative residual effects on her school experiences—including attendance, academics, and interpersonal relationships. Her tendency to use food as a coping mechanism may lead to greater concerns she has with her weight, further affecting her negative self-image.

With her family having so many different schedules and priorities, it will be challenging to help Linda without gaining familial support. As earlier stated, her father interacts with her minimally, while her mother's focus is on her younger cousin. As Linda reported having immigrated to the United States from Mexico, further exploration into Linda's culture and family dynamics will be important. Linda's parents may be focusing more on the grief implications of her cousins and may not realize how much Linda is still affected by her aunt's death, as her siblings seem to be functioning well in their lives. Linda has symptoms of generalized anxiety disorder persistent, complex bereavement disorder, as well as posttraumatic stress disorder (PTSD).

## ▓ DIAGNOSTIC CONCLUSIONS

- Generalized anxiety disorder
- PTSD
- Specified learning disability (per patient self-report)
- Persistent complex bereavement disorder

## ▓ SUGGESTED THERAPEUTIC INTERVENTIONS

Cognitive Behavioral Therapy—Since Linda demonstrates symptoms of generalized anxiety disorder, it would be helpful to focus on replacing negative thought patterns with positive cognitions along with implementing new behaviors (Powers & Kalodner, 2016). Learning new coping skills could be helpful to improve Linda's quality of life with her interpersonal relationships as well as her school functioning. Working with Linda to focus on what she has control over may be an important step in the healing process.

Person Centered Therapy—Foundational to fostering a supportive relationship, active listening along with empathy help to nurture a trusting relationship, which would encourage Linda to express her feelings openly (Hazler, 2016). This approach would be beneficial in offering support to Linda as she processes her feelings related to grief. As previously noted, having someone to listen to her seems to be valuable and therapeutic to Linda.

Eye Movement Desensitization and Reprocessing (EMDR)—EMDR has also shown positive effects when working with clients who have experienced past trauma and are currently experiencing PTSD or trauma symptoms (Lewey et al., 2018), depression (Gauhar, 2016), anxiety (Farima et al., 2015), persistent complex bereavement disorder (Lenferink et al., 2020), and more. Linda describes her aunt's death as a traumatic experience with some trauma symptoms such as nightmares, intrusive thoughts, and emotional distress. Linda also experiences symptoms of generalized anxiety such as excessive worry, fatigue, and irritability. Based on Linda's presenting concerns and symptoms, EMDR would be beneficial in assisting Linda in resolving her trauma symptoms connected to her aunt's death as well as addressing her current anxiety symptoms.

## ■ FOR YOUR CONSIDERATION

1. Linda's life prior to moving to the United States seems to have been positive (as reported by Linda). Initially, considerations could have been included for an adjustment disorder. However, with Linda experiencing her aunt's death, concerns for her bereavement should not be overlooked. How has Linda processed her aunt's death? What other treatment options or recommendations would you include for Linda?
2. How is anxiety related to grief?
3. Linda's family moved together, and from what has been reported, seemed to have had a close relationship prior to the move; what dynamics have changed due to the move and as a result of her Aunt's death?
4. How might Linda's culture play a role in her treatment of anxiety and bereavement in counseling?
5. How might language be a factor in the counseling process and therapeutic relationship with Linda?
6. Given that Linda was assessed for a learning disability at the school using a translator, what concerns might you have about the validity of her results?

## ■ REFERENCES

Farima, R., Dowlatabadi, S., & Behzadi, S. (2015). The effectiveness of eye movement desensitization and reprocessing (EMDR) in reducing pathological worry in patients with generalized anxiety disorder: A preliminary study. *Archives of Psychiatry and Psychotherapy, 17*(1), 33–43. https://doi.org/10.12740/APP/39259

Gauhar, Y. W. M. (2016). The efficacy of EMDR in the treatment of depression. *Journal of EMDR Practice and Research, 10*(2), 59–69. https://doi.org/10.1891/1933-3196.10.2.59

Hazler, R. (2016). Person-centered theory. In D. Capuzzi & M. D. Stauffer (Eds.), *Counseling and psychotherapy: Theories and interventions* (6th ed., pp. 169–194). American Counseling Association.

Lenferink, L. I. M., de Keijser, J., Smid, G. E., & Boelen, P. A. (2020). Cognitive therapy and EMDR for reducing psychopathology in bereaved people after the MH17 plane crash: Findings from a randomized controlled trial. *Traumatology, 26*(4), 427–437. https://doi.org/10.1037/trm0000253

Lewey, J. H., Smith, C. L., Burcham, B., Saunders, N. L., Elfallal, D., & O'Toole, S. K. (2018). Comparing the effectiveness of EMDR and TF-CBT for children and adolescents: A meta-analysis. *Journal of Child & Adolescent Trauma, 11*(4), 457–472. https://doi.org/10.1007/s40653-018-0212-1

Powers, Y.O., & Kalodner, C. R. (2016). Cognitive-behavior theories. In D. Capuzzi & M. D. Stauffer (Eds.), *Counseling and psychotherapy: Theories and interventions* (6th ed., pp. 227–252). American Counseling Association.

# 20.2   *Case of Samuel*

## ■ INTRODUCTION

Samuel is a 19-year-old African American, single male who was admitted to an inpatient substance use disorder (SUD) treatment program after he tried to kill himself during an alcohol-induced blackout. He was physically and sexually assaulted at age 15 and did not tell anyone but his best friend. He did not tell his family for fear that they would judge him negatively for not preventing or fighting off the assault. He has been binge-drinking since age 11 (five or more drinks in one setting) and now regularly (3–5 times per week) swallows a variety of pills (opioids and benzodiazepines) without any concern about what he is ingesting. He has a history of depression and anxiety. He has put out cigarettes on his arm, in order to feel pain.

Samuel dropped out of high school but did earn his GED. He works at night as a server at a local restaurant and tries to pick up day jobs on construction sites. He loves working with his hands and he wants work that physically exhausts him so he can fall asleep. When he is not working, he is at home playing video games and drinking alcohol. He has tried crack cocaine in the past but does not like how quickly the high dissipates. He likes pills, which he buys on the streets, because they numb him enough that he does not hear the voices in his head. Ever since the assault, he has heard the voices of the perpetrators. Periodically, he will have a flashback, especially when he is in an area where there are a lot of shadows.

Samuel states that he has never been arrested and charged for a crime; he has been detained by the police 12 times so far in the last 2 years for being in the wrong place at the wrong time. He has no legal record. He is in "decent health"—he likes to push his body by running early in the morning before going to work. When he runs, he can tune everything out and clear his head for the day.

He has never been picked up for public intoxication. His mother worries about him a lot; she senses he is carrying a dark secret but has been unable to get him to tell her what happened. Samuel's parents have been divorced for 10 years and his mother remarried 6 years ago. He likes his stepfather better than he likes his father. His father makes a point to connect with Samuel a couple of times a year and sees no need for additional interaction. Samuel has two sisters and one brother. His brother is 2 years older than him and his sisters are younger than him. His brother distributes marijuana and other street drugs; regularly Samuel gets a stash of pills and a couple of joints from him.

## ■ FAMILY HISTORY

Samuel's mother, father, and stepfather are African American. They were born and raised in a very poor section of Alabama. They have struggled to make ends meet and work long hours to put food on the table. Samuel's mother does not have a substance use history though she did have postpartum depression after delivering Samuel. She genuinely worries and cares about him. She left her husband and later remarried because her husband started hanging out with the wrong crowd, using crack cocaine a lot, and not meeting his employment or familial obligations. Her second husband is good to her and does not have a substance use history. However, he is very opinionated about how Black men are to handle themselves in the world. Samuel's stepfather used to be a boxer and was always encouraging Samuel to stand up for himself and fight when necessary. His stepfather also taught him that you had to be careful about how you handle yourself around the "White folk" and around the police—because assumptions are made long before the truth is discovered. Being poor and Black, Samuel learned early on that alcohol is a substance that is acceptable to drink. He also learned that crack and marijuana were accepted as well. His family and community did not agree with the use of pills; Samuel like pills because no one could tell he was on them. He also knew if he took enough pills he would go to sleep and never wake up. Some days that seemed like a viable option to stop the voices and flashbacks. His stepfather had no use for social services or counselors. He felt they meddled where they did not belong, judged without knowing the facts, broke up families just to be spiteful, and hated Blacks because they talked different. According to the stepfather, a person quit a substance cold turkey if they had a problem with it. Culturally, secrets stay at home or in the "hood." Strangers are not welcome to know secrets as they cannot be trusted to handle them wisely. This policy, of keeping at home what happens at home, was a cultural coping strategy for many of the societal injustices but it was also a way to preserve cultural traditions without outside interference. For example, assaults were dealt with in the family. If a member was assaulted, you talked to specific uncles about the mess to determine the best way to handle the situation.

## ■ CURRENT FUNCTIONING

Samuel functions well when he is working. He is taking care of his needs for nutrition, exercise, and sleep; however, sleep can often be elusive. He passes a mental status exam without any difficulty. The amount of alcohol that he is consuming has caused blackouts, some shakes, and gastrointestinal pain. He is able to track the interview well and asked questions when he did not understand a question or concept. He had a hard time relaxing during the interview. He states he has many experiences of feeling hypervigilant. He has two friends he has known for over a decade. He does confide in them and ask for their help when he needs it. The relationships are mutually respectful. He recognizes that his alcohol use and the hangovers are getting out of control. He has had recent suicidal ideation (twice in last month); thoughts of suicide appear when he is having flashbacks or hearing the voices. He acknowledges that he did attempt to commit suicide in the last week. He says his soul is tired and wants rest.

## ■ DIAGNOSTIC IMPRESSIONS

Samuel is an African American male who looms big in physical presence and is very tender-hearted and gentle in nature. He is cautious about the words in articulating his answers for each assessment question. He cares deeply for his mother and does not want to embarrass or shame her by his behavior. Samuel is spiritual and likes going to church with his mother when he can. He tries to not get too much of his stepfather's attention as he can talk too much about subjects Samuel is not interested in. He gets very quiet and anxious when describing the events of the assault. When asked about his anxiety, he states that he always feels a low level of anxiety and depression. Alcohol and pills are "his savior" as they help him function without thinking. Thinking is something he tries to avoid at all costs.

Samuel meets the criteria for an alcohol use disorder, severe and an opioid use disorder, moderate. He uses marijuana sporadically, so his use of cannabis does not meet the criteria for a cannabis use disorder. Samuel meets Criterion A for PTSD, as evidenced by actual sexual violence perpetrated against him. He meets Criterion B for PTSD, as evidenced by persistent reexperiencing of the trauma through upsetting memories (the voices) and flashbacks. He states that he does have nightmares on those occasions he falls asleep sober. Samuel meets

Criterion C for PTSD, as evidenced by his avoidance of trauma-related thoughts, feelings, and reminders using alcohol and opioids. For Criterion D (where he needs to have at least two negative cognitions or moods), Samuel has negative affect, feels isolated, has difficulty experiencing positive affect without substances, and blames himself for the trauma he experienced. For Criterion E, Samuel engages in risky behaviors, is hypervigilant, has episodes of irritability, has difficulty sleeping without substances, and is easily startled. All of the symptoms that Samuel is experiencing have been ongoing for the last 4 years, are causing him distress and functional impairment, and are not due to his substance use. He does not meet the criteria for dissociative or delayed specifications.

Samuel recognizes that he needs help. He states that he has no healthy coping strategies. His judgment about his own safety and ability to keep himself safe are skewed. The negative effects of alcohol are beginning to impair his ability to work, which is very concerning to him. He is highly motivated to get the help he needs to achieve sobriety and deal with his PTSD; he feels that "this is his last hope of finding peace this side of the grave." Samuel states that he wants to work with an African American male counselor as his first choice or African American female counselor as his second choice. He does not feel that a Caucasian counselor would understand him or his cultural background.

## ■ DIAGNOSTIC CONCLUSIONS

- Severe alcohol use disorder
- Moderate opioid use disorder
- Moderate benzodiazepine use disorder
- PTSD
- Child sexual abuse, initial encounter
- R/O Major depressive disorder
- R/O Generalized anxiety disorder

## ■ SUGGESTED THERAPEUTIC INTERVENTIONS

Case Management—Samuel might benefit from working with a social worker to determine what community resources are available to him so he can build a healthy support system. The social worker could help him find a group he could attend of Black males who have experienced sexual assault. The case manager could help Samuel find a peer mentor who could walk through the journey of doing counseling around PTSD, so Samuel is not alone and has a place to vent and process. Samuel needs a full physical with blood work to make sure that his hormones and biochemistry are in normal range. A sleep specialist may be able to help him develop effective personalized sleep hygiene. It would be good to find a 12 Step Meeting (AA and OA) for young Black adults, or a Black sponsor who could work with him until he is ready to join a 12 Step group. A social worker could determine what life skills Samuel needs to learn in order to achieve a greater sense of adulthood and independence.

Individual Counseling—Samuel needs to think of himself as a collaborative member of his care team. With his therapist, Samuel could create a safety plan that he would implement any time he felt danger and distress or suicidal ideation and start a log to help him identify his PTSD symptoms so that he can recognize them more easily. Samuel would benefit from experiential therapies (e.g., art therapy, play therapy, equine or feline therapy, wilderness therapy), acceptance and commitment therapy, mindfulness-based cognitive behavioral therapy (MB-CBT), and dialectical behavior therapy (DBT). Individual therapy would be a good place for him to develop an emotional language and explore his feelings of guilt, shame, and vulnerability. Therapy could challenge his brain to do the hard work to reinitiate and complete the developmental task of neural pruning. Samuel would benefit from understanding how drugs and alcohol interfere with his brain's ability to develop and mature.

EMDR—Samuel would benefit from reprocessing the sexual assault. EMDR would be a safe, evidence-based tool that could help his brain open up the internal loops and voices it is currently stuck in.

Pharmacotherapy—Samuel would need to be evaluated by a psychiatrist to determine if he would be an appropriate candidate for a medication like naltrexone to help him stop drinking. He might be a candidate for Suboxone, to address his opioid use disorder. Medications for anxiety and/or cravings may be helpful.

Peer Recovery Coach—Samuel might benefit from having a Peer Recovery Coach to help him maintain abstinence while working on his trauma. The Peer Recovery Coach would be a great person to help him learn new skills and find appropriate resources for sober living activities, and so on. The Recovery Coach would be able to share his journey with Samuel when Samuel is feeling overly discouraged, by normalizing what Samuel is experiencing.

## ■ FOR YOUR CONSIDERATION

1. How would you, as the counselor, establish rapport and connection with Samuel?
2. What concerns do you have about his suicidal ideation? How would you address his suicidal ideation?
3. In what ways are the tasks of case management different than the tasks of counseling?

4. What does Samuel need to understand about the short-term and long-term effects of drugs and alcohol on his brain?
5. How does the Black culture view substance use and dependence? What treatments have been shown to be effective in helping a client of color address their substance use?

# 20.3 *Case of Amy*

## ■ INTRODUCTION

Amy is a 42-year-old cisgender, heterosexual Filipino Caucasian woman who has been married to David for 17 years. David is a 46-year-old cisgender, heterosexual Caucasian man. Amy and David have two teenage children, Cooper and Ethan. The family lives in an upper middle-class neighborhood in a suburb of a metropolitan city. Amy was a stay-at-home parent for a few years when Cooper and Ethan were young but has been back to work full-time for over 10 years at a local accounting office. Amy grew up nearby and was raised primarily by her mother. Amy's parents have stayed married, but Amy's father was not very active in the family when Amy was a child.

Amy seeks counseling due to stress within her marriage. Amy shares, "David and I haven't been happy for a while now." When Amy first met David, she was attracted to his adventurous, outgoing personality. Amy was shy and withdrawn, and David helped her step outside of her shell. They were married within a year and soon Cooper was born. As soon as Cooper was born, Amy shares, "Life changed. I gained so much weight with that pregnancy! I never looked the same." Amy quit her job as Cooper was a difficult baby who did not sleep on his own, cried nonstop, and had a highly reactive temperament. Amy was exhausted and David began working longer hours and was home less often. Amy shares that she soon became pregnant with Ethan and felt as though she was raising two young children on her own as David began taking long work trips. She recalls being very lonely during this time in their life.

## ■ FAMILY HISTORY

After several counseling sessions, Amy opens up about childhood sexual trauma. She shares that her grandfather was often in their home to "help out" since her father was often gone. She didn't know that he was touching her inappropriately until she was around 7 years old when her younger sister told her this was happening to her as well. Amy felt the need to protect her younger sister and told her mother that their grandfather was touching them under their nightgowns in the middle of the night. Her mother yelled at Amy and her sister and told them not to lie. Amy recalls being mortified and never said anything again. Her grandfather never touched her again and she and her younger sister have not discussed the molestation since they were children. Discussing this in counseling was the first time she has brought this up since she was a child, never having discussed this with David, her mother, or her sister. Amy shares that she does not think of the molestation very often and doesn't think it impacts her current life.

Amy and her sister are 3 years apart. While they are very different, Amy always felt protective of her younger sister. She would like to talk about the molestation with her sister and see if her sister has ever recovered. During counseling, Amy realizes this has impacted more than she previously recognized. She experienced intense anger toward her mother's reaction of dismissing her experience and feelings. Amy began wondering her mother's own experiences and if she had been sexually abused as well.

As a mother to two teenage children, Amy has not discussed topics about sex with Cooper and Ethan. She said, "They have taken sex ed in school plus there is so much information on Internet. It would just make us all uncomfortable." David has also not discussed sex with their children. Amy's discomfort with her past and current experiences of sexual functioning appear to be impacting her comfortability to discuss sex with her children.

## ▓ CURRENT FUNCTIONING

As a full-time accountant, mother, and wife, Amy is very busy. She states, "The last 15 years have flown by." Amy spends the weekdays at work and cooking in the evenings for her family. The weekends are often spent at different activities that her children are involved in or completing household chores or duties. Amy does not have time for self-care as she always puts her family before her. Amy shares that due to this, she has not exercised in years and does not feel comfortable in her body due to weight gain. She and David are rarely physically or emotionally connected. Amy reports that she feels lonely, tired, and numb.

David joined Amy for a couple's session to discuss the couple's lack of connection with one another. David is frustrated with the lack of sexual intimacy, stating, "It has been years since we have had sex." Amy recently walked into David's at-home office to him masturbating to pornography. She was shocked and felt even less attractive after seeing the women on the computer screen. Amy stated that has had a very low libido ever since Cooper was born but did not realize that David felt as though they were not having "enough" sex. Amy has not initiated sex in several years and has never had any type of sexual fantasies.

David complained that he has tried to initiate sex, but Amy avoids sexual encounters by using work, house chores, or the children to avoid any type of sexual activity. In counseling, Amy presented with feelings of shame and guilt, stating, "I want to be intimate with you like we used to be, David, but I just can't seem to. I am just unable to get aroused and it's the last thing I want to do." Amy is certain that there is a hormonal imbalance or a biological cause of her inability to become aroused. She feels like a failure for not being able to sexually satisfy David and experiences further guilt based on her "failure" to have rewarding and satisfying sexual encounters like they used to.

## ■ DIAGNOSTIC IMPRESSIONS

Childhood sexual trauma can impact survivors' mental, physical, and emotional health long after the initial trauma (Narang et al., 2019). Amy experiences low libido, low self-esteem, and exhaustion, which she attributes to being a full-time working mother. Over 20% of female mental health clients have survived childhood sexual trauma (Cort et al., 2012). Survivors of childhood sexual trauma who do not undergo adequate mental health treatment after the traumatic incident(s) often experience symptoms of PTSD later in life (Miffitt, 2014).

Amy shared she always wear pajama pants to bed because it helps her feel safe, but she did not recognize that this was connected to the sexual trauma as a child. Amy's experience of sexual trauma from her grandfather has led to occasional distressful dreams and trigger reactions, which she was previously unaware of. In the beginning of their relationship and marriage, Amy and David would be intimate and sexual in different settings and not often in the bedroom. Amy wonders if she feels triggered in their bedroom.

Additionally, sexual desire varies among cultures. Research shows women of East Asian descent often have lower rates of sexual desire (Yules et al., 2010). Amy identifies as American with a Filipino mother and Caucasian father. Amy was raised in an environment where sexual desire was not discussed and there was more conservativism related to sex, which is typical in families of East Asian culture (Yules et al., 2010). This lack of open discussion is highlighted when considering the immediate refusal to acknowledge the sexual trauma Amy and her sister experienced from their grandfather.

Finally, Amy blames herself for her lack of sexual desire. She is certain there is something physically or biologically "wrong" with her that is impacting her ability to engage in sexual activity with David. She has not considered the lack of emotional connection with David, the stress in her daily life, and her negative body image as impacting her sexual desire.

## DIAGNOSTIC CONCLUSIONS

Based on the earlier impressions, this counselor's diagnostic conclusions are as follows:

- Female sexual interest/arousal disorder, acquired, generalized, moderate
- PTSD

## SUGGESTED THERAPEUTIC INTERVENTIONS

Amy has a few different concerns, including difficulties with becoming sexually aroused, the sexual trauma she experienced as a child, being stressed as a full-time mother with two children, and feeling unattractive in a culture which has a narrow lens of what is considered beautiful. Using an eclectic approach can help address these various concerns. Seeking extra training to become competent and knowledgeable may also be necessary.

As Amy is having physical symptoms, a referral to her gynecologist or primary doctor can help eliminate whether her challenges with becoming sexually aroused are due to a medical condition. Some medical conditions, such as neurological, cardiovascular, or endocrine conditions, can interfere with nerve signals and/or blood flow which impacts the body's ability to become aroused (Katz, 2007). A visit to her gynecologist or primary doctor can decide whether or not there are any medical conditions impacting Amy's sexual arousal.

Once a medical assessment is complete and decided there are no medical conditions impacting Amy's sexual arousal, a competent counselor (or, if needed, a certified sex therapist) may help provide Amy with education on sexual desire and interest. The counselor can provide information on how sexual desire is based on drive, motivation, and responsiveness, or arousal, to sexual stimuli (Bitzer et al., 2013). Additionally, suggesting a good quality lubricant as well as incorporating sex toys, such as vibrators, can help enhance arousal.

Amy and David may also benefit from couple's counseling to focus on their communication and emotional connection. Amy expressed surprise that David was unhappy with their sex life which shows a lack of healthy communication about their needs and desires. Couple's counseling may help Amy and David focus on relaxation techniques, creating a schedule for sexual activity, and to take time to explore each other's sexual desires. Kleinplatz and Menard's model of sexuality includes six building blocks of pleasure, including "being fully present, authenticity, intense emotional connection, sexual and erotic intimacy, communication, and transcendence" (Buehler, 2017, p. 41). These building blocks may provide a framework for Amy and David to become more connected communicatively to build a healthy understanding of each other sexually.

As Amy has experienced previous trauma, another suggestion is to consider trauma-focused cognitive behavioral therapy (TF-CBT). TF-CBT is utilized most often in treating those who have survived childhood sexual trauma (Narang et al., 2019). TF-CBT would provide a framework for Amy to process her childhood trauma in a safe space.

Sensate focus activities were originally designed for sex therapy and focus on connecting either couples or individuals with their own body. William Masters and Virginia Johnson established sensate focus as various activities for clients to practice outside of the counseling session. Sensate focus includes caressing your partner while fully clothed to help learn what one likes and, later on, building up to nude sensational touching (Buehler, 2017).

Additionally, seeking holistic counseling techniques may be beneficial. For example, dance and movement therapy can be utilized in the treatment of survivors of childhood sexual trauma (Ho, 2015). By utilizing the body to effect change and healing, clients learn to reestablish healthy relationships with their bodies. This leads to increased self-esteem, reduced anxiety, and creating healthy intrapersonal and interpersonal relationships (Ho, 2015). In addition to dance and movement therapy, trauma-focused yoga can help process childhood sexual trauma with clients (Clark et al., 2014). Trauma-focused yoga has been utilized to decrease symptoms of anxiety, depression, and stress (Clark et al., 2014).

Providing Amy a nonjudgmental space where she can process her sexual desire safely and comfortably is key. Mindfulness and grounding techniques can assist Amy with becoming centered and aware of her desires. This can help Amy with increasing her self-image, reducing her stress, processing her childhood trauma, and connecting with David.

## ▨ FOR YOUR CONSIDERATION

1. How comfortable are you with discussing Amy's sexual desire in a counseling session? How might you increase your confidence with discussing sexual desire with clients?
2. How does society's perception of "healthy sexuality" impact diagnosing clients with sexual dysfunction? How might Amy's cultural identity impact diagnosing her with a sexual dysfunction?

## ▦ REFERENCES

Bitzer, J., Girladi, A., & Pfaus, J. (2013). Sexual desire and hypoactive sexual desire disorder in women. Introduction and overview. Standard operating procedure (SOP Part 1). *The Journal of Sexual Medicine, 10*(1), 36–49. https://doi.org/10.1111/j.1743-6109.2012.02818.x

Buehler, S. (2017). *What every mental health professional needs to know about sex* (2nd ed.). Springer Publishing Company.

Clark, C., Lewis-Dmello, A., Anders, D., Parsons, A., Nguyen-Feng, V., Henn, L., & Emerson, D. (2014). Trauma-sensitive yoga as an adjunct mental health treatment in group therapy for survivors of domestic violence: A feasibility study. *Complementary Therapies in Clinical Practice, 20*(3), 152–158. https://doi.org/10.1016/j.ctcp.2014.04.003

Cort, N., Gamble, S., Smith, P., Chaudron, L., Lu, N., He, H., & Talbot, N. (2012). Predictors of treatment outcomes among depressed women with childhood sexual abuse histories. *Depression & Anxiety (1091–4269), 29*(6), 479–486. https://doi.org/10.1002/da.21942

Ho, R. (2015). A place and space to survive: A dance/movement therapy program for childhood sexual abuse survivors. *Arts in Psychotherapy, 46*, 9–16. https://doi.org/10.1016/j.aip.2015.09.004

Katz, A. (2007). *Sex when you're sick: Reclaiming sexual health after illness or injury*. Praeger.

Miffitt, L. (2014). State of the science: Group therapy interventions for sexually abused children. *Archives of Psychiatric Nursing, 28*(3), 174–179. https://doi.org/10.1016/j.apnu.2013.09.004

Narang, J., Schwannauer, M., Quayle, E., & Chouliara, Z. (2019). Therapeutic interventions with child and adolescent survivors of sexual abuse: A critical narrative review. *Children and Youth Services Review, 107*, 1. https://doi.org/10.1016/j.childyouth.2019.104559

Yules, M., Woo, J. S., & Brotto, L. A. (2010). Sexual arousal in East Asian and Euro-Canadian women: A psychophysiological study. *The Journal of Sexual Medicine, 7*(9), 3066–3079. https://doi.org/10.1111/j.1743-6109.2010.01916.x

# 20.4    *Case of Ismat*

## ▦ INTRODUCTION

Ismat is a 20-year-old queer hijabi Muslim of color who identifies as nonbinary and prefers to be addressed with the gender-neutral pronouns they/their/them. Ismat presents themself as an Arab-American person of Muslim faith who values both of their cultural heritages and seeks to incorporate them into their identity. Ismat is an independent and accomplished undergraduate student pursuing a degree in literature and gender studies. They live in their own apartment and work part-time to support themself through college. Ismat volunteers at a local lesbian, gay, bisexual, transgender, queer, questioning and other gender and sexualities (LGBTQ+) Muslim Youth organization and soup kitchen. They have a passion for advocacy and community service. Ismat aspires to continue graduate studies and become a university professor. Ismat was referred to the university counseling center by one of the youth leaders at the LGBTQ+ center to whom they have confided their struggles with returning home. They are seeking counseling to help them manage their recent anxiety attacks brought about by an upcoming visit to their parents' home.

## ■ FAMILY HISTORY

Ismat was born and raised in the United States. They are the youngest and fourth child of an educated and wealthy family of Middle Eastern immigrants. Ismat's father is an engineer and Ismat's mother is a housewife and community service leader at their local mosque. Ismat's describes their father as an educated man with a strong character and the main provider of their family throughout the years, someone who they really admire. Ismat expresses a strong bond with their mother and compassion with her struggles with depression that started soon after the family lost their third child to a severe illness. Ismat was born 6 years after this child's death and welcomed as a miracle and gift from Allah. Ismat describes their relationship to their older siblings as distant and problematic because of sibling rivalry and the significant age differences between them and their older siblings which often made them feel like an only child. Ismat reports their siblings have always viewed them as the "miracle child" of the household always favored by their parents. Other than their close bond to their mother, Ismat is good friends with other youth leaders at the LGBTQ+ Muslim Youth center they volunteer in. Ismat is currently in a romantic asexual partnership with a 25-year-old queer European American female and graduate student who they met at college.

Ismat was assigned female at birth and raised as a girl by their parents. They report experiencing a healthy typical childhood. Ismat describes themself as an active, energetic child who often enjoyed engaging in rough play with boys their age. They noticed their interests as a child varied from playing dolls and dress up to playing with their deceased brother's cars and trucks. Ismat warmly recalls locking themself in their room to try out their brothers' clothes and play with their toys in secret. Trying on their brother's stuff would make them very happy. They grew to despise wearing dresses, hijabs, and playing with dolls because it felt like that was the only thing they could do without getting in trouble. However, Ismat reports exhibiting gender conforming behaviors as a child because they did not want to make mom sad or anger dad.

As Ismat entered adolescence, they remember experiencing a lot of anxiety over the changes occurring in their body. Ismat became anxious about their developing breasts, how big they would grow, and started dressing in baggier clothes to hide them. Peers started teasing them because of their odd way of dressing.

The hijab that they hated to wear because it represented their femaleness became a tool to help cover their growing breasts. They recall experiencing an increasing sense of worry and anxiety about going out in public which led to withdrawing from friends and family. They no longer felt comfortable being out in the world and remembers experiencing high levels of anxiety when going out in public dressed as a woman. Isolation led to feelings of depression and suicidal thoughts which Ismat would not even dare to speak of. Grades and academic performance began to plummet and Ismat was referred to a counselor. In counseling they considered the cause of their anxiety and depression which to them at the moment looked a lot like an "identity crisis." Ismat also started exploring their gender identity in counseling but they quickly "put on the breaks" because they could not even bear the thought of their parents finding out. Feelings of anxiety and discomfort related to their assumed female gender persisted and Ismat took on writing as a way of coping. They internally resolved they were a "butch" which was confirmed by their growing attraction to women. Ismat continued counseling to treat their anxiety and focused on graduating high school and entering college.

## CURRENT FUNCTIONING

Ismat is currently enrolled in their second year of college. They are pursuing a major in literature and recently added a minor in gender studies. They continue to write now more creatively than before and are learning about alternative gender expressions. Ever since leaving the household for school they have experienced freedom to explore their inner self. Ismat has become involved with the local LGBTQ+ Muslim Youth organization which has helped them better understand themself, integrate their gender and religious identities, and also help other youth in similar circumstances. Ismat expresses themself as a nonbinary queer hijabi-wearing Muslim. They greatly fear all they have built for themself will be shattered upon returning home to visit their mother and father who are not aware of their newfound identity. Ismat feels like they are living in an alternate reality which is bound to their college environment and is not their true reality which lies at home with their family and the female they perceived them to be. This upcoming visit has caused an increased sense of distress and anxiety that triggers Ismat's past gender identity struggles. They feel restless, angry, irritable, express difficulty concentrating on school finals, and are not sleeping well. They despise their body for looking so feminine and in a burst of anger attempted to self-mutilate their breasts. Ismat has also become distant from their romantic partner which they feel exacerbates their crisis. They recently experienced a panic attack while at the LGBTQ+ center which prompted a leader to refer them to the college's counseling center.

## ■ DIAGNOSTIC IMPRESSIONS

Ismat exhibits clinically significant distress that has begun to impair their academic, romantic, and social functioning. They exhibit a marked incongruence between their expressed gender and the gender they were assigned at birth which is still recognized by their parents and family. Ismat expresses a strong desire to be recognized as a nonbinary individual and has transitioned to nonbinary on their college campus which better reflects their gender identity. Their current living environment at college is supportive of their gender and gives them the satisfaction of being treated in congruence with their gender identity. Ismat also exhibits great levels of anxiety due to an upcoming visit to their parents as expressed by their restlessness, irritability, difficulty concentrating, and sleep disturbances. Their anxiety symptoms are not out of proportion to the potential impact of this anticipated event. Associated nonsuicidal self-injurious behaviors have been reported.

## ■ DIAGNOSTIC CONCLUSION

- Gender dysphoria in adolescents and adults

## ■ SUGGESTED THERAPEUTIC INTERVENTIONS

Ismat's concerns about returning home to their parents have triggered a series of anxious reactions that have caused significant distress in their day-to-day functioning, academic performance, and relationships. According to Sennott and Smith (2011), transgender and gender nonconforming individuals feel more comfortable in queer-friendly spaces. Traveling or visiting parents can sometimes be very disconcerting, anxiety provoking, and raise concerns about their safety (Sennott & Smith, 2011). Gender nonconforming and transgender individuals may feel a need to dress or behave differently when traveling or visiting parents and family to protect themselves from discrimination, violence, and trauma (Sennott & Smith, 2011). Living in a cisgender society, gender nonconforming, and transgender individuals are often stigmatized, ostracized, and pathologized by the medical and mental health communities (Sennott & Smith, 2011; Sue & Sue, 2012).

Coming out is an ongoing lifelong process of self-acceptance and assessing who to trust and disclose one's identities to (Chaney et al., 2011). This process can significantly impact an individual's happiness, self-esteem, and overall satisfaction with life (Chaney et al., 2011). While there is an agreement that coming out can increase a person's happiness and satisfaction with life, feelings of distress are heightened during the early stages of the process and can become increasingly complex for those experiencing multiple minority memberships such as Ismat (Chaney et al., 2011; Sue & Sue, 2013).

Understanding the context in which Ismat's distress has developed, their multiple intersecting identities, and the barriers they face when wanting to fully express and disclose their gender identity, this counselor believes Ismat could benefit from a multicultural transfeminist therapeutic approach (TTA) that recognizes and affirms their multiple identities, promotes allyship, and advocates for social justice.

Multicultural Therapy—Sue and Torino (2005) defined multicultural therapy as a process that defines goals and interventions in congruence with clients' life experiences and cultural values; recognizes clients' individual, group, and universal dimensions; advocates for the use of culturally sensitive strategies; and balances individualism and collectivism in the process of assessing, diagnosing, and supporting clients. There a variety of resources available to guide therapists' work with culturally diverse clients. Some of these resources include the Multicultural and Social Justice Counseling Competencies (MSJCC); The Association for Lesbian, Gay, Bisexual, and Transgender Issues in Counseling (ALGBTIC) Competencies for Counseling with Transgender Clients; the ADDRESSING and RESPECTFUL models, and the Cultural Formulation Interview (CFI) (ALGBTIC, 2009; D'Andrea & Daniels, 2001; Ratts et al., 2015).

The MSJCC offer a framework to guide counseling professionals' implementation of theories and interventions so they respond to culturally diverse clients' needs and consider both clients' and therapists' multiple intersecting identities (Ratts et al., 2015). The MSJCC emphasize counselors' self-awareness, promote understanding of client's worldviews, consider the influence privilege and marginalization have on the counseling relationship, and encourage advocacy efforts (Ratts et al., 2015). The ALGBTIC (2009) Competencies for Counseling with Transgender Clients offer a wellness, resilience, and strength-based approach for working with transgender clients. These competencies incorporate principles from multicultural, social justice, and feminist theoretical backgrounds to affirm clients' identities and promote advocacy (Goodman et al., 2004; Sue & Sue, 2013; Worell & Remer, 2002). The ADDRESSING (Hays, 2008) and RESPECTFUL (D'Andrea & Daniels, 2001) models serve as framework to better identify and understand clients' diverse intersecting identities. Finally, the CFI is an interviewing tool included in the *Diagnostic and Statistical Manual of Mental Health Disorders, 5th Edition* (*DSM-5*) for the purpose of helping therapists assess the impact of culture on individuals' clinical presentation.

TTA—Sennott's (2011) TTA is an alternative conceptualization of feminist therapy that incorporates gender-aware and gender affirming therapy into feminist thought along with social justice and allyship principles. The TTA is a nonpathologizing approach that defies society's sex (male/female) and gender (women/man) binary constructs and highlights the oppression associated with being assigned female at birth (Lev & Sennott, 2012; Sennott, 2011). Transfeminist therapists understand that individuals construct their own gender identities based on what feels comfortable and authentic to them irrespective of society's binary assumptions of sex and gender. Transfeminist therapists combine an awareness of individuals' assigned sex, gender identity, gender expression, and sexual orientation to all their other intersecting marginalized and privileged identities which may include but are not limited to race, ethnicity, nationality, socioeconomic status, size, age, religion, and level of ability. The goal of the TTA is to support gender nonconforming and transgender individuals, as well as their families and partners and to shed light on the inequities and oppression individuals face solely because of their membership to this community.

Some of the resources available to therapists wanting to incorporate TTA to advance clients' goals include the Transfeminist Qualitative Assessment Tool (TQAT) and the Allyship Practice Model (APM) (Sennott, 2011; Sennott & Smith, 2011). The TQAT is designed to facilitate client's and their family's exploration of past, present, and future narratives, constructs, behaviors, and feelings toward gender and gender nonconforming individuals (Sennott, 2011; Sennott & Smith, 2011). The APM serves as a guide for incorporating TTA into therapeutic work with transgender and gender nonconforming individuals and their families (Sennott, 2011; Sennott & Smith, 2011).

While there are other effective and evidence-based approaches for supporting clients diagnosed with gender dysphoria, this counselor believes that a multicultural TTA will help advance Ismat's goals in therapy by honoring and affirming their intersecting identities and supporting them through their coming out process. This approach will also help solidify the counseling relationship by exercising the counselor's cultural competence and allyship which are essential components of effective therapy and support of transgender and gender nonconforming individuals. A list of additional resources for supporting transgender, gender nonconforming, nonbinary, and LGBTQ+ Muslim individuals has been included at the end of this case.

## ▒ FOR YOUR CONSIDERATION

1. What biases do you perceive in yourself that could interfere with your work with transgender, gender nonconforming, and culturally diverse clients? How could you develop competence in these areas?

2. How do you think society's rigid gender binary and transphobic sentiments influence our current understanding and classification of gender dysphoria as a mental disorder?
3. How could a client's religion and spiritual practices be incorporated as a source of support in cases like these?
4. What other diagnoses would you consider? Why?

## ▓ REFERENCES

Association of Lesbian, Gay, Bisexual, and Transgender Issues in Counseling. (2009). *Competencies for counseling with transgender clients*. Author. https://www.counseling.org/Resources/Competencies/ALGBTIC_Competencies.pdf

Chaney, M. P., Fillmore, J. M., & Goodrick, K. M. (2011). No more sitting on the sidelines. *Counseling Today*, 34–37.

D'Andrea, M., & Daniels, J. (2001). RESPECTFUL counseling: An integrative model for counselors. In D. Pope-Davis & H. Coleman (Eds.), *The interface of class, culture, and gender in counseling* (pp. 417–466). Sage.

Goodman, L. A., Liang, B., Helms, J. E., Latta, R. E., Sparks, E., & Weintraub, S. R. (2004). Training counseling psychologists as social change agents: Feminist and multicultural principles in action. *The Counseling Psychologist*, 32, 793–837. https://doi.org/10.1177/0011000004268802

Lev, A. I., & Sennott, S. (2012). Understanding gender nonconformity and transgender identity: A sex-positive approach. In P. J. Kleinplatz (Ed.), *New directions in sex therapy: Innovations and alternatives* (2nd ed., pp. 3210–3336). Routledge/Taylor & Francis Group.

Ratts, M. J., Singh, A. A., Nassar-McMillan, S., Butler, S. K., & McCullough, J. R. (2015). *Multicultural and social justice counseling competencies*. http://www.counseling.org/docs/default-source/competencies/multicultural-and-social-justice-counseling-competencies.pdf?sfvrsn=20

Sennott, S. L. (2011). Gender disorder as gender oppression: A transfeminist approach to rethinking the pathologization of gender non-conformity. *Women & Therapy*, 34(1–2), 93–113. https://doi.org/10.1080/02703149.2010.532683

Sennott, S., & Smith, T. (2011). Translating the sex and gender continuums in mental health: A transfeminist approach to client and clinician fears. *Journal of Gay & Lesbian Mental Health*, 15(2), 218–234. https://doi.org/10.1080/19359705.2011.553779

Sue, D. W., & Sue, D. (2012). *Counseling the culturally diverse: Theory and practice* (6th ed.). Wiley.

Sue, D. W., & Torino, G. C. (2005). Racial cultural competence: Awareness, knowledge, and skills. In R.T. Carter (Ed.), *Handbook of multicultural psychology and counseling* (pp. 3–18). Wiley.

Worell, J., & Remer. P. (2002). *Feminist perspectives in therapy: Empowering diverse women*. Wiley.

## ▓ ADDITIONAL RESOURCES

Brooks, K. D. (2014). Telling the stories of gay, lesbian, and transgender Muslims. *Sex Roles: A Journal of Research*, 71(9–10), 351–353. https://doi.org/10.1007/s11199-014-0420-6

Muslim for Progressive Values. (2019). *LGBTQI resources*. https://www.mpvusa.org/lgbtqi-resources

Muslim Youth Leadership Council. (2020). *I'm Muslim and I might not be straight*. https://advocatesforyouth.org/wp-content/uploads/2018/11/Im-Muslim-I-Might-Not-Be-Straight.pdf

Saeed, A., Mughal, U., & Farooq, S. (2018). It's complicated: Sociocultural factors and the disclosure decision of transgender individuals in Pakistan. *Journal of Homosexuality*, *65*(8), 1051–1070. https://doi.org/10.1080/00918369.2017.1368766

Siraj al-Haqq Kugle, S. (2010). *Homosexuality in Islam: Critical reflection on gay, lesbian and transgender Muslims*. One World Publications.

Siraj al-Haqq Kugle, S. (2014). *Living out Islam: Voices of gay, lesbian, and transgender Muslims*. New York University Press.

Translate Gender Inc. (2020). *(Re)writing access for trans, non-binary and gender nonconforming people in relationship, family and community*. https://www.translategender.org/

# CHAPTER TWENTY ONE

# FINAL REVIEW: YOUR SKILLS IN PRACTICE

*This chapter features five cases from across the* Diagnostic and Statistical Manual of Mental Disorders, 5th Edition (DSM-5) *and may be used as a final review. There is diversity in clientele, diagnosis, and treatment modality and may help students demonstrate their skills in diagnosis and treatment of mental health disorders.*

## 21.1    *Case of Jocelyn*

### ▨ INTRODUCTION

Jocelyn is a 9-year-old African American female who lives with her mother in a studio apartment in a small town. Jocelyn is in the second grade. Jocelyn was held back in Kindergarten due to homelessness and moving around while her mother was looking for a job. Once Jocelyn's home life was stabilized, she was able to academically catch up to her peers and she does not currently have any remedial school issues. She is actually excelling at her studies right now.

Jocelyn spent the past 2 years being cared for by her grandmother while her mother worked 12 hour shifts as a waitress at a truck stop. She would spend at least 5 days a week with her grandmother. Jocelyn and her grandmother were incredibly close, more so like mother and daughter. Jocelyn preferred to be with her grandmother over her own mother. On Jocelyn's mother's days off, Jocelyn would make up excuses to be able to go over and see "GiGi" (her grandmother).

Jocelyn's father lives over 600 miles away. She only sees her father on holidays and extended vacations. Although they talk on the phone, internet, and social media, she does not consider them to be very close. Jocelyn's father is remarried now and Jocelyn feels that her father chooses his new wife and kids over her. She tends to be pleasantly distant when speaking with his new wife and kids. Jocelyn is not looking for any relationship with him or "his new family."

GiGi had been secretly ill for the past 6 months and did not tell anyone that her breast cancer had returned. GiGi passed away in her sleep, while Jocelyn was on a trip with her mother to a water park. This event was overwhelming for Jocelyn as GiGi was her "favorite person in the universe" and at times her only friend. She was also fearful that there would be no one to watch her while her mother worked.

Jocelyn is now experiencing some mental health concerns since the passing of her grandmother. Her mother is reporting that Jocelyn is very sad in her heart. Jocelyn's mother states that she often catches Jocelyn looking off with tears in her eyes. She thinks that her daughter is thinking about GiGi, but when she asks her, her daughter does not want to talk about it. Jocelyn is having trouble falling asleep. Every night, Jocelyn and her grandmother would make a large bowl of popcorn and share it as they watched their favorite shows together before bed. Jocelyn is also not eating as much as she would normally. When Jocelyn's mother asks her to eat now, she tells her mother that she "cannot cook as well as GiGi."

The intense interactions between Jocelyn and her mother are further dividing their relationship. Jocelyn's mother is grieving the loss of her own mother, while attempting to keep her daughter and herself afloat. Jocelyn's mother has no idea what she will do with Jocelyn while she is working. She is considering sending her to her dad's house to live until she can become more stable.

## FAMILY HISTORY

Jocelyn's parents met in high school and dated for 3 years. At the end of their senior year, Jocelyn's mother became pregnant with her. Jocelyn's mother decided to drop out of school, because she did not want anyone to know that she was pregnant. She decided that she would take her GED. After she passed her GED, Jocelyn's father surprised her with an engagement ring. He wanted to "do the right thing" by marrying Jocelyn's mother who was now carrying his baby.

Jocelyn's parents moved away from their hometown due to her father finding a very good job in the auto industry. At night, he took college classes and was able to complete his bachelor's degree. Although Jocelyn's mother wanted to go to college, she was tasked with the care of Jocelyn. Jocelyn's mother's dreams of being a nurse would have to wait until Jocelyn was in school full-time.

Jocelyn's parents split up when Jocelyn was 5 years old. Jocelyn's father was having an affair with a coworker. Jocelyn's mother found out about the affair and she was unwilling to work on the relationship. She reports that his actions told her all that she needed to know about him. Jocelyn's mother quickly left the marital home but did not have a plan or too much money to make a new life.

Jocelyn always felt like her father dismantled the family unit and everything was "all about him." Even at 5-years-old, she felt that it was his fault that she had to leave her friends, school, and everything that she ever knew because of him. Instead of verbalizing her dismay with her father, she emotionally cut him off.

Although the court documents later outlined the need for visitation, she in no way wanted to have anything to do with him. Jocelyn's mother also did not accept child support. She did this on the premise that she could move away with Jocelyn and he would have to accept a limited visitation schedule.

Jocelyn and her mother bounced around from homeless shelter to friends' couches and basements for much of her kindergarten year. It was during this time that Jocelyn's grandmother asked Jocelyn's mother to come back to her hometown. GiGi stated that she would help Jocelyn's mother to get on her feet, get an apartment, and help with the care of Jocelyn, so she could find a good job.

## ▓ CURRENT FUNCTIONING

Jocelyn has been self-isolating and sad since the passing of her grandmother. Jocelyn completely avoids talking about her death. Jocelyn's mother has found Jocelyn in tears and staring off into space as if she is thinking deeply about something. Her mother assumes that she is having thoughts about GiGi, but Jocelyn shuts down any show of emotion immediately and goes into another room.

Jocelyn is not close with her mother or her father. Jocelyn still blames her father for breaking up the family unit. Jocelyn has been avoiding his calls and text messages. She also has not scheduled anytime to see him over the internet and continues to avoid him on social media. Jocelyn has created a "burner" account to freely surf social media without having to talk about her loss or talk about how she is doing with anyone.

Jocelyn has been doing exceptionally well in school. Jocelyn sees her education as a way out of the life that her mother has created for the both of them. Jocelyn has concerns that she will end up homeless again. This makes her fear that she will fall behind in school and be held back again if they continue to move.

Jocelyn does not speak of a social circle and she states that she does not make friends easily. She does not have a support system and she is not involved in any extracurricular activities. This gives Jocelyn a lot of time to think about her loss. Although she may like to engage in these activities, her mother does not have any extra money to spend and she would often not have any transportation to these events.

## ▓ DIAGNOSTIC IMPRESSIONS

Jocelyn is having a hard time coping with the death of her grandmother. Jocelyn was extremely close to GiGi. Jocelyn does not have close relationships with either biological parent. She blamed her father for the breakup of her family. She is also upset with her mother that she is unable to care for the two of them without the help of others. Jocelyn has closed herself off emotionally to her parents and she does not have any friends.

Jocelyn is experiencing sadness often since the passing of her grandmother. She is tearful at times when she is thinking about GiGi. However, she does not want to talk about it with anyone. Jocelyn is experiencing issues with sleep. She and her grandmother had a nightly routine before bed and all she can do at night is think about how that is no longer happening. Jocelyn is also concerned that she will soon be homeless or moving from shelter to couch to basement due to her mother's inability to make enough money.

Jocelyn has also lost most of her appetite. Meals were a special time for Jocelyn and GiGi. GiGi was beginning to teach Jocelyn how to cook and she was sharing family recipes with her. GiGi was a much better cook than her own mother. Jocelyn attempts to make her mother feel bad by pointing that out to her mother when she tries to make her eat something.

## ■ DIAGNOSTIC CONCLUSIONS

- Uncomplicated bereavement
- Parent–child relational problem
- Unspecified housing or economic problem

## ■ SUGGESTED THERAPEUTIC INTERVENTION

Grief Therapy and/or Grief Group for Kids—Jocelyn was extremely close to her grandmother. She does not have a huge connection to either parent. Jocelyn may want to process her feelings alone. She may also find it comforting to be involved in a grief group for children. It can be powerful for kids to see that they are not alone as they begin to build connections and a social support system with other children. Children need to be able to accept the reality of the loss (i.e., this person is not coming back). They need to work through the pain of losing their loved one. They need to adjust to their new normal without this person being physically present. They need to find ways to keep their connection to the loved one while moving forward with their life.

Adjuncts to Treatment—Children often love to make art. Drawing can be incorporated into sessions. Children can draw their favorite memories and special occasions involving their loved one. Children also enjoy looking at photographs. They can bring pictures of their loved one to session and make a scrapbook while processing the loss. Some children may even want to write a short story or make a book about their loved one.

## ▓ FOR YOUR CONSIDERATION

1. How can we be sure that this is a normal reaction to the death of a loved one and not a bio/chemical imbalance?
2. What is the typical timeframe for grief? How does culture impact this timeframe?
3. Do all people go through the stages of grief? If so, does it look different for children? How so?

# 21.2 *Case of Brigid*

## ▓ INTRODUCTION

Brigid is a 42-year-old twice divorced Irish/Italian American, currently a single mother living with her four children in a home that she is purchasing in a small city in Middle America. She has four male children, ages 18, 16, 12, and 4. She has a bachelor's degree and a master's degree, in differing fields and has worked in her current position for the last 10 years. This is the longest job she has held in her life; her previous employment has been between 2 and 4 years at a time in multiple fields. She has been working since she was 14 years old. She tends to get bored doing the same thing over and over again and craves work that is challenging and varied. She enjoys her current position because as she says, "When you work with the public, you can never be bored." She is a consultant in a law firm assisting with cases that are going through family court.

Brigid is heterosexual and is currently "too busy" to think of another relationship. She was married to her first husband for 10 years when she had her three oldest children. That marriage ended when "the love just seemed to disappear" from the relationship. Her second marriage occurred 4 years later, which was when she had her youngest child. After 2 years of marriage, the relationship ended when her oldest son told her that her new husband was seen making out with the babysitter in the car in front of the house. She confirmed that was the case and kicked him out of the house that night. Since she owned the home, she was able to stay in her own home, remodeling her bedroom, and adding additional rooms and bathrooms for the boys.

Brigid stated that she had been diagnosed with anxiety in her childhood by her pediatrician. She explained she experienced anxiety in fifth grade when she would randomly break out in hives on her legs, have to go home, and take the Benedryl prescribed by her doctor to relieve the hives, which would put her to sleep. Those symptoms began when her family moved from one state to another and she was attending a new school. The symptoms abated about halfway through her sixth grade and did not return during her childhood. She also stated that she had difficulty focusing on tasks in front of her but found that by having the television on while she was doing her homework, her mind would not wander, and the background noise helped her focus. She stated she did not have a "real" first date until she was a senior in high school. She described the boy she dated as very kind and sweet, which made her feel uncomfortable. She felt that she was attracted to "bad boys" and in fact, said she wanted to be in that crowd of friends although she had a very isolated time in school. However, she was an intelligent child with good grades, and other than wanting to cheat off her test papers, that crowd was not very inclusive of her in their group. Having moved in fifth grade and then again after 10th grade, she stated she was "invisible" in school where most of the friendship groups were already formed by the time she started attending new schools. She continued to exhibit symptoms of anxiety, nervousness, and would become very frightened at times throughout her school years, though did not take medications as she had in fifth grade.

## ■ FAMILY HISTORY

Brigid stated that her mother had a history of multiple traumas in her life and in her relationships. Her mother was married three times, the first time to a man who had raped her on in an alley when she was 15 years old and was then forced to marry him. She was severely physically and sexually abused by him during their tumultuous marriage. She had five pregnancies, and three live births, who are the older half-siblings of Brigid's. She ultimately divorced her first husband after he put their oldest child's head through a wall.

She was a single mother to two boys and one girl when she met Brigid's biological father. He had a band that played in the hotel where she was a waitress. He was smooth and kind and she had the sense he would protect her and her children. About 3 years after her divorce, she married him, he adopted the other three children, and about a year after their wedding, Brigid was born. By that time, her mother had become fearful of her husband, who was accused of child molestation, forgery, and was dishonorably discharged from the Air Force. They traveled to his city of birth where his parents resided, yet he continued to forge checks by stealing his family's and friend's checkbooks. When she was ready to leave him, he kidnapped her oldest son from school, called her, and threatened to cut off various parts of his body, such as fingers and toes, if she did not return to him. The Federal Bureau of Investigations (FBI) was called and she was advised to agree to meet him and walk to where he was with her two children walking beside and Brigid in the baby carriage. The FBI apprehended him as he came out of the house to meet her, and fortunately, he had not cut anything off the child. He was arrested, convicted, and sent to prison. She divorced him while he was in prison and set out on the run to get away from him. There was a permanent restraining order issued for her and each child so that he could not contact them. He had had the habit of sneaking up on her during their time together and she spent most of her life as a jumpy, suspicious, frightened woman with four children. Brigid did not remember her father as they were divorced before she was a year old. She felt abandoned by him and longed to be a "Daddy's girl." She did not see him again until she was 21 years old, married, and found him. She looked up to her oldest brother as a father figure; he was 10 when he was given that role by her.

She was told of the kidnapping event as she became independent and played outside without supervision so that she would not allow strange men to approach her. She had a resulting fear of being kidnapped throughout her life. She felt safest in her house, and in fact, safest in her closet behind the clothing where she would stay and read. Her siblings would sometimes fight when her mother was gone, so she found this safe place to hide. If they caught a glimpse of her, their wrath would be turned on her instead of them fighting each other. They lived in poverty, though in a neighborhood where everyone looked after everyone else. She was hungry, alone, and vulnerable, especially when the older kids were at school. She had those in the neighborhood who she would stay with during the day, and some that she felt very attached to. She was especially fond of "Peanut" as she called him because that's what he called her, and she called his wife "Teacher" for she taught her the preschool letters and numbers. They had a son who was special needs and older. She never knew what happened, but all of the sudden, she wasn't allowed to go to their house anymore and she once again lost the father figure she had adopted in her heart.

Her mother remarried again to a man who was an alcoholic bachelor who was clueless about how to interact with children, and suddenly had four children ranging in age from 5 to 15. She described that he generally "locked himself in his office with his vodka and would come out for dinner." She did not feel that he could be her Daddy, though she tried to call him that and even attempted to sit on his lap, but he was so uncomfortable that his muscles became rigid, and at 5 years old, she knew it would not work. She called him by his first name, which all the children did, and turned again to her big brother.

Brigid reported that she felt that she was carrying her mother's pain through much of her childhood. She described that her mother had a terrible ice-skating accident that resulted in a badly broken ankle. Shortly after that, Brigid fell out of her favorite tree and broke her arm, which her mother called a "sympathy break." Brigid would defend her mother to her older half-sister, begging her to stop being so hard on her mother as mom had a "tough time" through her life. Brigid was one who would withdraw when things got tense, and commented that when her mother and stepfather would go out, she would "run away to the bush at the end of the driveway" and hide, often falling asleep there until the adults came home, because of the fear of the two middle half siblings' fighting. By then, her big brother no longer lived with him, having moved out on his own in a different state.

When she was a college student, Brigid's lifelong fear of being kidnapped materialized. The kidnapper was not her father, but a stranger who abducted her by jumping into her car as she was dozing in the passenger seat while the driver was paying for the gas he had just pumped. A traumatic car chase was the result with police pursuit, roadblocks, and so on, until the kidnapper clipped a curb and the car spun out of control and hit a wall backwards at about 80 miles per hour. The police were immediately on scene, the kidnapper was arrested, and she was transported to safety. She thought she was going to die and had, indeed, accepted her pending death. She was sexually dysfunctional following that incident, which eventually led to the ending of her marriage.

As an adult, Brigid had a spontaneous memory about being sexually abused at the age of 3. She called her mother and told her about her crazy experience. Her mother was quiet. Brigid was very cautious, holding her breath. Her mother replied, "The doctors said you would never remember that." Further, her mother found the letter she had written to her mother describing what had happened to Brigid, and her older sister, and that her future stepfather, who was not yet married to her mother, had intervened to get the "man upstairs" evicted. Brigid struggled with that knowledge, receiving therapy for some time as she also remembered other times of being "bothered" during her childhood and adolescence. She began getting additional memories and at times, felt like she was a small child. She would sometimes awaken and find her herself sucking her thumb with her finger curled over her nose, as she did when she was a child.

She dabbled in some drugs and alcohol, but easily stopped using anything, feeling like the risk was not worth the high. She smoked cigarettes and drank quite a bit of caffeine to help her focus on the work she needed to do.

## ■ CURRENT FUNCTIONING

Brigid is an emotional eater and therefore significantly overweight. She recognizes her addiction to food, will do very well for quite a while and lose weight, but when she hits a certain weight, or becomes too tired or stressed, she feels compelled to eat junk, especially potato chips or other salty snacks. She will eat a whole bag of chips in one sitting, and in fact, anything she opens to eat, she will tend to devour until it is gone. Food and caffeine seem to be her "drugs of choice."

She has a well-paying job now, and usually does, but continues to live paycheck to paycheck as she also tends to spend what is left over after she has paid the bills and provided for her family. She will see something she wants online and order it, resulting in tension as the bills come through the checking account and she is never sure whether she will "make it" to the next payday without being overdrawn. The tension is something she does not like but finds it difficult to resist.

Brigid is intelligent and accomplished. She has very broad experiences in multiple fields of employment. The diversity of her experience is often what helps her get various jobs, yet she also maintains continuity by having skills that translate to strengths in many fields. She is affable and friendly at work but tends to need to be alone to recharge after she gets home, so she has trained her children that mom needs a "time out" for about 20 minutes after she gets home and then can prepare and serve dinner. She has been taking a prescribed anti-depressant for approximately 10 years; about 2 years ago, she tried to titrate off the medication, but found herself "standing in doorways just crying and crying" so she remains on the medication.

She has complaints of difficulty falling and staying asleep and complains of nightmares that awaken her in a state of extreme fear and panic. Just 2 years ago, as she changed jobs, she began having panic attacks for the first time in her life that she can remember, which include racing heart and pulse, shaking that she cannot control throughout her body, shortness of breath, uncontrollable crying, and a strong need to get away by herself.

## DIAGNOSTIC IMPRESSIONS

Brigid has had a history of multiple traumas occurring from the age of 3 on, and possibly earlier, though she has no memory of times prior to 3 years old. She commented that she cannot remember third or fourth grade but does remember kindergarten through second grade quite well. She has had a long-term depression that is treated with medication. Her history of sexual abuse, violence, poverty, a difficult relationship with her mother, and a biological father who spent his life in prison with multiple offenses reoccurring after any discharges, has affected her life, particularly in her relationships. She feels inadequate no matter how much she accomplishes, though she appears to be a successful professional.

While she no longer uses substances, including tobacco, she tends to drink one to two pots of coffee per day, beginning in the early morning. She tends to awaken before 6 a.m. and is going at high speed until 11 or 12 at night.

Brigid has never been able to manage her stress well, resulting in multiple physical and emotional behaviors that continue to be self-harming. She is not sure how to manage her life differently, and despite her fairly positive outlook in life, lacks self-esteem and self-efficacy. She does not like being overweight but continues to binge eat for one day to a week at a time, being unable to have self-control. She has no self-care strategies and lacks her positive coping skills.

## ▨ DIAGNOSTIC CONCLUSIONS

- Posttraumatic stress disorder (PTSD)
- Persistent depressive disorder (Dysthymia)
- Binge-eating disorder
- Personal history of child sexual assault
- Personal history of abuse from siblings

## ▨ SUGGESTED THERAPEUTIC INTERVENTIONS

Trauma-Focused Cognitive Behavioral Therapy (TF-CBT)—TF-CBT helps to normalize the traumatic exposure so that the Brigid can understand that she is not alone in having traumatic experiences. Because Brigid had a lifelong fear of being kidnapped, when it happened, there was some relief that the waiting was over, but there was also the trauma of the event itself to manage. Her understanding on more about how experiencing trauma works through some psychoeducation about how it can affect brain and body functioning, as well as the reassurance that she did what she had to do to survive the circumstances, should help her with a better understanding of the effects of trauma. Looking at patterns of the past and making connections with her behaviors may help her learn better choices to make and the positive power of self-care.

Eye Movement Desensitization and Reprocessing (EMDR)—This program may help her to better understand the multiple traumas in her past. Furthermore, it may also help with her anxiety, depression, and panic disorders so that she can become more stable in many ways. The multiple symptoms may be rooted in her complex trauma.

Panic-Focused Cognitive Behavior Therapy (PF-CBT)—This type of therapy may also assist in treating her panic attacks. While they may be symptomatic of the larger picture, she may benefit from successfully halting further panic attacks by gaining the skills here to apply to other areas of her life, which may support her feeling of self-efficacy and accomplishing a goal.

Overeaters Anonymous (OA)—Brigid expressed interest in getting her eating under control so OA may be an option for her that can not only provide some support and education to her but also help her dive into the reasons behind her eating, finding other methods to self-soothing that don't include food rewards. There is a group in her area that meets weekly.

## ■ FOR YOUR CONSIDERATION

1. Brigid appears to have had multiple traumas throughout her life, suggesting complex Trauma as a foundation for the other concerns. What other diagnoses may be present with her and which would be the first focus for treatment?
2. What specifiers would you include with your diagnoses?
3. Understanding more about Brigid and her history, how do you think her past is affecting her relationships now? Why?
4. How do her panic attacks, depression, and self-destructive behaviors keep her from enjoying life?

# 21.3    *Case of Cate*

## ■ INTRODUCTION

Cate is a 33-year-old divorced female who lives in her own apartment in a mid-size city with her 16-year-old daughter, 4-year-old daughter, and 18-week-old daughter. Cate has a master's degree in her field and has worked for the same company since her internship in graduate school 9 years ago and has received regular promotions and management opportunities. Cate states that she enjoys her current job and likes her coworkers, but she has recently changed supervisors, from a female that she had since her start date to a male from a different location within the company. She states that her new supervisor "hates her" because he knew that her former supervisor recommended her for the position. She fears termination because of this. Cate states that she did not apply for the position because she was newly pregnant but did not announce it yet to the company and thought that it would "look bad" if she took the job and then went on maternity leave.

Cate is heterosexual and is not involved in a current romantic relationship. She was married for 10 years and divorced last year, although she had been separated from her husband for the past 4 years. Her younger two children are fathered by her ex-boyfriend, the person she cheated on her husband with; however, she had recently broken up with him due to repeated physical and emotional abuse. The last time she saw her ex-boyfriend, he had thrown her into a wall while she was pregnant and her daughters were watching. The 16-year-old called the police, and charges were pressed against the ex-boyfriend.

Cate states that she has been having mental health symptoms for several years. She states that she had been diagnosed with anxiety and fears being alone. When asked to describe her symptoms, she states that they began when she was an adolescent and includes difficulty concentrating, impulsivity, and strained relationships. She falls in and out of romantic relationships easily, and most of those relationships are turbulent. Her most secure relationship was with her husband, but she could not take the "dullness of marriage" and had multiple affairs. The last affair leading to a pregnancy led her husband to separate. She noted that he wanted to try marriage counseling and pretend the baby was his, but she "couldn't live a lie."

Cate noted that her mother has a history of depression and her father has PTSD as a result of his combat experience in the Vietnam War. Cate said that her older sister probably has obsessive compulsive disorder, and when pressed about her sister's symptoms, Cate said that her older sister must have things "just so" and likes to control the situation. Cate denies suicidal ideation, homicidal ideation, and audio or visual hallucinations and can contract for safety.

Cate's father served two tours in the Army in Vietnam. During the second tour, he was ambushed by the Vietcong while on a patrol and severely injured his back and arm. He was rehabilitated but often had flashbacks of the ambush and a "friendly fire" air raid resulting from misinterpreted coordinates. Cate said that as children, she and her sister Brynn would be awakened by their father pulling them out of bed and screaming "Air Raid!" at them and instructing them to hide under the bed. Once, when Cate was about 8 years old and her sister was 10, Brynn tried to get him to snap out of it and their father punched her so hard that she was knocked unconscious. Cate tried to run to get their mother but she was tackled to the ground by her father and asked, "Do you want to get yourself killed?" Cate said her father kept her pinned down, half under the bed, half out, for the rest of the night. She said that she must have fallen asleep or passed out because she does not remember what had happened. In the morning, she awoke to the sound of Brynn crying in the kitchen as their mother put an ice pack on Brynn's face. Their mother insisted that Brynn "fell" and made the girls promise to tell everyone that story if asked. They were told that if they deviated from the "Brynn fell" script, they would be taken away and would live somewhere else.

Cate said that was not the first or most traumatic incident caused by her father's PTSD. Her most traumatic memory was when she was 5 years old. Cate said that her father was giving her a bath and they were laughing and singing the "Rubber Ducky" song from Sesame Street. She said that she took her duck and dropped it in the water with a lot of force, causing a large splash. Her father went silent, and she said that his "eyes went dead." The next thing she knew, her head was held underwater and he was whispering intently, "Hide, hide! They are coming!" She said that she remembers struggling to get air and that she could not slip from his grasp. She remembers how desperate she felt but said that there was a release and then she passed out. Cate found out later that Brynn walked by when she heard the splashing and started screaming for their mother. Her mother said that she came into the bathroom and flicked the lights on and off. Somehow that flicking, according to Cate's mother, brought him back. He got up and walked out of the bathroom and never gave the girls a bath again.

Cate does not give her children baths. She showers with them when they are babies or toddlers, and when married, she had her ex-husband bathe the children. One of the chores of her oldest daughter is to bathe her sisters. Cate is not afraid that she will hold them under the water, but she fears what would happen if they drowned. She does not want them to feel the panic that she felt that day.

Cate has used marijuana since she was 12 years old, except when she was pregnant or nursing. She said that she has some friends who like to smoke, and she often smokes a joint or two with her friends and purchases it directly from her friends, but it has at times progressed to the point where she will actually go and seek out marijuana from a dealer.

Cate uses substances, particularly marijuana, to numb herself so that she does not feel intense emotions and anxiety. They were her "coping mechanism that always seems to work"—at least for a short period of time. She reports that she often feels anxious, like she "needs to jump out of" her skin, and that marijuana mellows her out and enables her to "be a chill mom." However, Cate is concerned that her company will drug-test employees now that they are contracting with other firms to provide services on a consultation basis.

In addition, Cate is financially reckless. During her graduate school years, she took out the maximum amount of student loans, even though she had a full tuition scholarship and a husband who supported her financially. She does not recall what she purchased with that money, but she gave some of it away to her various lovers or has purchased marijuana. When she and her husband separated, she found herself in a mountain of debt, and "her credit is shot," despite making nearly six figures per year. She often "forgets" to pay her bills and has had her electricity shut off multiple times. Her mother recently made her a budget and has her bills being paid through automatic deductions so that this does not happen again.

Cate is intelligent and, professionally she is quite successful. Her mother is her biggest support and helps Cate whenever she can. Cate reports that she can always count on Brynn when she needs something, but they are not very close. Cate reports that her children are well adjusted. Her ex-husband serves as a father figure for her two older children and often takes all of them out to dinner, ice-skating, or other events. She reports that their relationship is actually quite good, and he is now her "best friend."

## ▓ DIAGNOSTIC IMPRESSIONS

Cate demonstrates the residual effects of childhood trauma on a person's life. On the surface, Cate is an attractive, educated, professional mother who seems to have her life in order. However, the trauma that she experienced as a result of having a father who was also traumatized has stayed with her, manifesting in various problems with substances and sexual and financial impulsivity and damaging relationships.

Cate self-medicates through cannabis use. She surrounds herself with people so that she can readily smoke when she feels the need and will put herself in potentially dangerous situations if she needs marijuana. Unfortunately, her use of cannabis may lead to employment woes if her company decides to drug-test.

Cate lacks positive coping skills, and to date, substance use and romantic relationships are her way of coping. It will be a challenge to teach her new coping skills and have her master their application. Cate has many symptoms of borderline personality disorder.

## ▓ DIAGNOSTIC CONCLUSIONS

- Cannabis use disorder, moderate
- Multiple criterions of borderline personality disorder
- R/O borderline personality disorder (BPD)
- Personal history (past history) of spouse or partner violence, physical
- Other personal history of psychological trauma

## ▓ SUGGESTED THERAPEUTIC INTERVENTIONS

Dialectical Behavior Therapy—Cate displays many symptoms of borderline personality disorder. Given that dialectical behavioral therapy is the only evidence-based treatment for borderline personality disorder, this therapeutic approach should be used so that Cate may learn distress tolerance skills and how to regulate her emotions without cannabis. These skills may prove helpful to managing Cate's symptoms.

Narcotics Anonymous (NA)—Cate might find it beneficial to attend NA groups so that she can work through her need to use cannabis as a way to self-medicate and cope with stressors. Having others who are in recovery and using NA as a support system may assist Cate in developing new, healthy relationships.

## ▓ FOR YOUR CONSIDERATION

1. Cate's early childhood traumas have greatly affected her life and still do to this day. What other treatment recommendations would you make for Cate?
2. How are features of borderline personality disorder related to trauma and addiction?
3. Given what Cate and Brynn have been through together, why do you think they are not close even though Brynn is always there if Cate needs her?

# 21.4   *Case of Alec*

## ▓ INTRODUCTION

Alec is a 19-year-old Caucasian male referred from his primary care physician for anxiety. Alec recently returned home after his first year of college. He reported that he did well academically but had issues with his roommate in his freshman year over a girl whom they both liked. He said that his roommate and several of his roommate's friends "jumped" him one evening. The attack resulted in Alec receiving 12 stitches on his forehead. University officials moved Alec to a new room. However, his former roommate was not suspended or expelled. His former roommate and his friends insisted that Alec started the fight. This seemed to shock Alec because he had expected to have a similar experience to that in high school where he was well-liked, played on the hockey team, and was the homecoming king. Alec will be transferring to another school for his sophomore year.

## ▥ FAMILY HISTORY

Alec had been in therapy before, when he was 12 years old, to manage his anxiety as he switched from a parochial to a public school. He and his mother (who was present for the initial session) said that after a few months of therapy and getting used to the new school, Alec did remarkably well. His former therapist used cognitive behavioral strategies to help Alec work through his anxiety, and Alec reports that he still uses these strategies today.

Alec's early development was typical, and his mother reports that he has always been a healthy kid. His parents are married and informed Alec that they will divorce within the year. Alec said that his parents have been living separate lives under the same roof (e.g., different bedrooms, separate vacations) for years now, and he is upset that they refuse to continue to live in this way. He seems devastated by the idea that his parents will divorce. Alec also has a younger brother, 11 years old, on the autism spectrum, and he worries what this will mean for his brother and his care.

## ▥ CURRENT FUNCTIONING

Alec shared that he had been having frequent panic attacks where he feels like he cannot breathe, feels nauseous and/or dizzy, and has chest pain and heart palpitations. He had been to the local ED twice and insisted that he was having a heart attack. The ED sent Alec back to his primary care physician and then received a referral for therapy to work on his anxiety therapeutically. His primary care physician prescribed a trial of Xanax, which his mother administers when needed.

Alec works at a local trampoline park, where he has worked since his sophomore year of high school. Alec has many friends who work there too, and when Alec has a panic attack or severe anxiety, they often cover for him. Alec has recently feared driving because of the panic attacks and has been relying on his mother, father, and friends to drive him to work, therapy, and other places. He wants to quit working, but he is afraid to do so because he needs the money to pay for books and other incidentals in college. He feels that he needs to do this, particularly if his parents decide to divorce.

Alec recently started dating a girl who he had liked since high school. He was supposed to take her out and had planned an elaborate date. He never made it to the place that they were supposed to meet because he experienced a panic attack. When he called her later, she refused to speak to him. Since then, Alec has made repeated efforts to "win her back," but he has been unsuccessful.

## ▓ DIAGNOSTIC IMPRESSIONS

Alec experienced a difficult first year in college and lived in fear of his room-mate and others who physically assaulted him. His parents are also discussing the possibility of divorce, which will strain family finances and perhaps change his relationships with his parents. It seems that Alec, given his first-year experience, is fearful of his return to college at the end of the summer. He also seems embarrassed that he cannot stop the panic attacks and presents as angry with himself that he has to go through such lengths to control his mind.

## ▓ DIAGNOSTIC CONCLUSIONS

- Panic disorder
- Disruption of family by separation or divorce

## ▓ TREATMENT INTERVENTIONS

Psychopharmacology—Continue with medication management as prescribed with frequent monitoring from physician.

Individual Therapy—Regular counseling sessions to help Alec monitor his symptoms and encourage him to develop coping skills to manage his anxiety.

Family therapy—Alec is struggling with his parents' impending divorce and what it means for their family. Working through his concerns with his family may be helpful to Alec and improve his symptoms.

## ▓ UPDATE

Approximately 3 weeks into therapy, Alec mentioned that he has frequent neck pain. At this point, Alec had quit his job at the trampoline park because he felt guilty that his coworkers were doing his job, and Alec was getting "paid to panic in the employee lounge." When asked if he slept in an odd position as explanation of his neck pain, Alec said that he did a flip at the trampoline park when he first arrived home after freshman year. He said that he smacked his neck and head off the bar that supports the trampoline. Alec saw "stars" and then walked it off. It was recommended that Alec have an evaluation for head and neck injury. Alec was eventually diagnosed with a concussion.

## ■ REVISED DIAGNOSTIC CONCLUSIONS

Postconcussion Syndrome is a complex disorder in which various symptoms last for weeks and sometimes months after the injury that caused the concussion. It is not uncommon that brain injury results in headaches, dizziness, and other symptoms that mimic anxiety and panic disorders. As the brain recovers, symptoms subside. In Alec's case, they were nearly gone by the time he left to begin his sophomore year at a new university.

## ■ FOR YOUR CONSIDERATION

1. Part of the intake questionnaire asked if there had ever been any head or neck injuries. Alec reported that he had stitches after a fight during his freshman year of college, but no other injuries. How else would you find out about any potential head or medical injuries that may contribute to a client's current psychiatric symptoms?
2. Alec was relieved when he found out he "just" had a concussion. Why do you think that is? How does the differentiation of the body versus the mind contribute to stigma about mental health disorders?
3. Now that he has been diagnosed with a concussion, Alec and his parents think that discontinuation of therapy is best. Would you recommend that? Why or why not?

# 21.5   *Case of Akito*

## ■ INTRODUCTION

Akito is a 24-year-old Asian American male who lives in the basement of his parent's home. Akito's 7-year-old brother and 5-year-old sister live upstairs with his parents. Akito's parents are first-generation immigrants who came to America to achieve a better life for their children. Akito has been living in the basement, since dropping out of college due to concerns that his professors were "poisoning" his mind. Akito told his parents that he knew that each time that he attended classes, they were "downloading" information into his brain to make him obey their commands.

Akito's parents tried to work on Akito's issues without getting mental health treatment. His family believed that if they admitted that he needed mental help, it would bring shame upon their family. Although his family was trying very hard to assimilate to their new homeland, seeking mental health treatment was thought of as a western phenomenon for weak people. His parents had extremely high expectations for Akito. The very meaning of his name is "bright person." Akito's parents wanted him to take over the family's business upon completion of college. Akito's issues were very hard for his parents to not only manage daily, but also for them to find peace.

Akito is heterosexual and has not had a girlfriend, since the decline of his mental condition. Akito had a girlfriend all through high school, but as his behaviors became more and more "odd," his girlfriend decided to the leave the relationship. Akito was enraged that "the people" got to his girlfriend and turned her against him. Akito believed that there was a group of people who were trying to gaslight him. He knew that they were doing everything that they could do to make him appear "crazy." Akito trusted no one and in return, he was unable to find anyone willing to deal with his erratic behaviors.

Akito has had some mental health concerns since his teenage years. It was at this time that Akito started smoking marijuana. It was very hard to ascertain at the time if the psychotic symptoms that he was experiencing were due to a mental health condition or if they were due to his substance abuse. It was starting to become clear that even when he was not smoking marijuana, he was still having issues with hearing and seeing things that were not there. Akito also became more and more fearful that someone was trying to ruin his life.

## FAMILY HISTORY

Akito comes from a very hard-working first-generation Asian-American family. They own three restaurants within a 100-mile radius. Akito's parents came to America with approximately $500 and the clothes on their back. Akito's mother was pregnant with him when they traveled to their new home. It is quite impressive to see what they have built in their 24 years in the United States.

Akito's father is stern and has never told Akito that he loves him. Akito also does not remember his father ever hugging him, since he was a very young child. Akito's mother is far more affectionate and is deeply worried for her son. She is afraid that if he cannot "get himself together" he will never be able to live on his own. Akito's father and mother easily work 12-hour days 7 days a week. Even his younger siblings help with the business. They roll silverware and help stock items in the restaurant.

Akito's parents decided to not have children for many years after Akito was born. They wanted to ensure that their business was thriving before they added more mouths to feed. Akito was 17 when his first sibling was born. He was essentially raised as an only child. Akito states that "the people" told him that his parents wanted to have more children, because Akito was such a disappointment to his parents.

Akito reported that he was experiencing what his uncle Cai went through right before he jumped off of a building. Akito states that Cai was having a lot of trouble in his life because "the people" were telling him to hurt himself. Akito reports that he is terrified that the "the people" will switch from trying to make him appear crazy and start telling him to hurt himself. Akito knows that his parents do not want him to seek mental help, but Akito is in fear for his life. Akito does not know if he can trust a counselor, but he is willing to try anything at this point.

## ▨ CURRENT FUNCTIONING

Akito has been smoking marijuana since he was 15 years old. He reports that he started smoking to "calm" his brain. Akito could not stop himself from randomly seeing "the people" spying on him or finding them hiding in Akito's car or closet. Akito did not tell his parents about seeing or hearing things that were not there. "The people" told him that it would only confirm his parent's thoughts that he is worthless and crazy. Instead, Akito's parents find him decompensating and they report that he looks "unsettled" and "unwell."

Akito reports that he has trouble telling dreams from reality. There are times when he believes that the people on television are speaking directly to him. He is fearful most days and finds it hard to leave the house. When he does leave the house, his mother goes with him. She makes sure that he is able to get to his destination and back safely without getting into any trouble. In the past, Akito has brought unwanted attention to himself through his actions.

Akito is dependent on his parents for survival. Akito has not been able to work in the restaurants since he ran out into the dining room yelling, "don't eat the food! Do not eat the food! It is poison. The people are trying to poison us all!" Akito's parents have been paying for his basic needs and they have asked him to stay in the basement and have limited interactions with his siblings. Akito's siblings are afraid of Akito when he starts behaving strangely. They scream and cry when his behaviors become erratic.

Akito has a high IQ. Akito's parents had high expectations for him. Both Akito and his family grieve the loss of his potential self. They also are devastated by his lack of social connections. Akito does not have friends and he has not had a romantic relationship with anyone since high school. He and his parents no longer dream of a wedding or children for Akito.

## ▓ DIAGNOSTIC IMPRESSIONS

Akito exhibits psychotic behaviors. This is complicated by his family's belief that not following the social order within their culture is a serious issue. They are well aware of the public's fear of the serious and persistently mentally ill. In their culture, they believe that it is important to control mental illness before treatment is necessary. They have been unable to "control" their son's behaviors. Akito and his family (especially his father) have significant conflict. This has led to decreased cohesion and more isolation for Akito. Although Akito's father sees Akito's behaviors as shameful. Akito's mother recognizes the stigma of mental illness and how her son is being discriminated against due to issues beyond his control.

Akito has self-medicated with marijuana, since age 15, Akito no longer has his own income and therefore cannot afford to buy marijuana. Akito has not smoked marijuana in 6-months, since he lost his job. This could possibly lead to a more accurate diagnosis of his mental health concerns.

## ▓ DIAGNOSTIC CONCLUSIONS

- Schizophrenia
- Parent–child relational problem
- Cannabis use disorder in early remission

## ▓ SUGGESTED THERAPEUTIC INTERVENTION

Medication Management—Akito displays many symptoms of schizophrenia. For most clients with schizophrenia, it is difficult to utilize any psychotherapeutic interventions without first utilizing antipsychotic medication. Clients who stop using their medications are at an increased risk of relapsing. These incidents can be so intense that they require hospitalization to stabilize the client. If medications do not appear to work, electroconvulsive therapy may be an option.

Psychotherapy –A counselor can help educate Akito on the importance of medication compliance during therapy. This is imperative as the most effective treatment for schizophrenia includes medication and therapy. The main goal of the psychotherapeutic treatment option for schizophrenia is decreasing symptoms, preventing relapses, and increasing daily functioning so the client can be integrated successfully back into society.

Family Support—In addition to medication compliance and psychotherapy, Akito will benefit from family support. Family support has been shown to keep clients with schizophrenia out of the hospital and improves their overall social functioning. Akito's family can learn how to monitor both positive and negative symptoms. They can report any findings to Akito's counselor and psychiatrist.

## ▥ FOR YOUR CONSIDERATION

1. Cai and Akito's mental health concerns appear to be similar in nature? How can we predict if Akito is at risk of hurting himself?
2. We know that Akito's family (primarily his father) is not on board for Akito receiving treatment. Should we involve the family? Why or why not?
3. It can be hard for clients with schizophrenia to be medication compliant. What can we do as counselors to help ensure that they follow this treatment recommendation?

# INDEX

CPSIA information can be obtained
at www.ICGtesting.com
Printed in the USA
BVHW052146200123
656791BV00014B/301